387

AIRLINE MARKETING AND MANAC

D1650386

Loughborough College

LC048214

Airline Marketing and Management

Sixth Edition

STEPHEN SHAW

ASHGATE

© Stephen Shaw 2007

All rights reserved. No part of this publication may be reproduced, stored in a retrieval system, or transmitted in any form or by any means, electronic, mechanical, photocopying, recording or otherwise without the prior permission of the publisher.

Stephen Shaw has asserted his right under the Copyright, Designs and Patents Act, 1988, to be identified as the author of this work.

Published by
Ashgate Publishing Limited
Wey Court East
Union Road
Farnham
Surrey, GU9 7PT
England

Ashgate Publishing Company
Suite 420
101 Cherry Street
Burlington, VT 05401-4405
USA

Ashgate website: http://www.ashgate.com

British Library Cataloguing in Publication Data
Shaw, Stephen, 1950-
    Airline marketing and management. - 6th ed.
    1. Airlines - Management 2. Airlines - Marketing
    I. Title
    387.7'4'0688

Library of Congress Cataloging-in-Publication Data
Shaw, Stephen, 1950-
    Airline marketing and management / by Stephen Shaw.
        p. cm.
    Includes index.
    ISBN: 978-0-7546-4819-2 (Hbk)
    ISBN: 978-0-7546-4820-8 (Pbk)
    1. Aeronautics, Commercial--Marketing. 2. Airlines--Marketing. I. Title.

    HE9781.S35 2007
    387.7'40688--dc22

                                                                                    2007002941

ISBN: 978-0-7546-4819-2 (Hbk)
ISBN: 978-0-7546-4820-8 (Pbk)

Reprinted 2009

Loughborough
COLLEGE est 1909

Mixed Sources
Product group from well-managed forests and other controlled sources
www.fsc.org Cert no. SA-COC-1565
© 1996 Forest Stewardship Council
FSC

Printed and bound in Great Britain
by MPG Books Group, UK

Contents

Introduction   xii

1   The Fundamentals   1

1:1 What is Marketing?   1
1:1:1 Definition   1
1:1:2 The "Marketing Mix"   2
1:1:3 Stages in the Application of Marketing Principles to   3
Airline Management

Successful Airlines   5

2   The Market for Air Transport Services   6

2:1 What Business are we in?   6

2:2 Who is the "Customer"?   8
2:2:1 Definitions   8
2:2:2 "Apparent" and "True" Needs   11
2:2:3 Industrial Buying Behaviour   12
2:2:4 The "Customer" in the Business Air Travel Market   15
2:2:5 The "Customer" in the Leisure Air Travel Market   18
2:2:6 The "Customer" in the Air Freight Market   20

2:3 Market Segmentation – Air Passenger Market   22
2:3:1 The Concept   22
2:3:2 Segmentation Variables in the Air Passenger Market   24
2:3:3 Customer Requirements – Business Travel Market   27
2:3:4 The Business Travel Market – Demographics and   34
Psychographics

2:3:5 *The Leisure Segment of Demand*   37

2:4 Segmentation of the Air Freight Market   40
    2:4:1 *Differences between the Air Passenger and*   40
       Air Freight Markets
    2:4:2 *Segmentation Variables – Air Freight Market*   42

Successful Airlines   48

3   **The Marketing Environment**   49

3:1 The Theoretical Basis – PESTE Analysis   49

3:2 PESTE Analysis – Political Factors   50
    3:2:1 *Terrorism Fears/Political Instability*   50
    3:2:2 *Deregulation and "Open Skies"*   51
    3:2:3 *Marketing Policies for a Deregulated Environment*   56
    3:2:4 *Privatisation*   58
    3:2:5 *"State Aid"*   60
    3:2:6 *Airport Slot Allocation*   61

3:3 PESTE Analysis - Economic Factors   64
    3:3:1 *Economic Growth and the Trade Cycle*   64

3:4 PESTE Analysis – Social Factors   66
    3:4:1 *The Ageing Population*   66
    3:4:2 *Changing Family Structures*   67
    3:4:3 *Changing Tastes and Fashions in Holidays*   67
    3:4:4 *The Uncertain, Deregulated Labour Market*   68
    3:4:5 *The Female Business Traveller*   69

3:5 PESTE Analysis – Technological Factors   70
    3:5:1 *Video-conferencing*   70
    3:5:2 *The Internet*   71
    3:5:3 *Surface Transport Investment*   72

3:6 PESTE Analysis – Environmental Factors   73
    3:6:1 *Climate Change and Global Warming*   73

3:6:2 Shortages of Infrastructure Capacity   74
3:6:3 "Tourism Saturation"   75

Successful Airlines   75

4   Airline Business and Marketing Strategies   76

4:1 Porter's "Five Forces" and their Application to the Airline
     Industry   76
     4:1:1 Rivalry amongst Existing Firms   76
     4:1:2 Substitution   77
     4:1:3 New Entry   78
     4:1:4 Power of Customers   81
     4:1:5 Power of Suppliers   84
     4:1:6 "Disintermediation"   86

4:2 Strategic Families   87
     4:2:1 Cost Leadership, Differentiation and Focus –
     *   The Principles*   87
     4:2:2 Cost Leadership in the Airline Industry: Background   90
     4:2:3 Fundamentals of the Business Model   92
     4:2:4 Cost Leader Airlines: Current Issues   100
     4:2:5 Cost Leader Airlines: The Future   102
     4:2:6 "Differentiation" in the Airline Industry   105
     4:2:7 Airline Alliances   110

4:3 "Differentiation" Airlines – The Future   117
     4:3:1 The Concept of the "Legacy Airline"   117
     4:3:2 "Legacy Airlines" – Strategic Options   122

4:4 "Focus" Strategies   129
     4:4:1 Types of Focussing in the Airline Industry   129
     4:4:2 "Value-Added" Focussing   129
     4:4:3 "Low Cost" Focussing   133
     4:4:4 "Lost-in-the-Middle"   135

4:5 Airline Business and Marketing Strategies –
Common Mistakes   135
   4:5:1 Objectives   136
   4:5:2 Diversification vs Specialisation   137
   4:5:3 Pace of Expansion   138
   4:5:4 Competitive Response   139
   4:5:5 "Control"   140
   4:5:6 Over-optimism/Fall Back Position   140

Successful Airlines   141

5   Product Analysis in Airline Marketing   142

5:1 What is the "Product"?   142

5:2 The Theory of Product Analysis and its Application to the
Airline Industry   142
   5:2:1 The Product Life Cycle   142
   5:2:2 Product Life Cycles in the Aviation Industry   148
   5:2:3 Managing a Product Portfolio – the "Boston Box"   151
   5:2:4 Balancing Risk and Opportunity – the Ansoff Matrix   156

5:3 Fleet and Schedules-Related Product Features   158
   5:3:1 Cabin Configuration and Classes of Service   158
   5:3:2 Network, Frequencies and Timings   161
   5:3:3 Punctuality   166

5:4 Customer Service-Related Product Features   168
   5:4:1 Point-of-Sale Service   168
   5:4:2 Reservations and Overbooking   169
   5:4:3 Airport Service   172
   5:4:4 In-Flight Service   173

5:5 Controlling Product Quality   174

5:6 The Air Freight Product   176
   5:6:1 Air Freight Capacity   176

Successful Airlines   180

6   Pricing and Revenue Management   182

6:1 Building Blocks in Airline Pricing Policy   183
     6:1:1 Pricing – A Part of the Marketing Mix   183
     6:1:2 Deregulation   183
     6:1:3 Dissemination of Fares Information   184
     6:1:4 Revenue Management Systems   184

6:2 "Uniform" and "Differential" Pricing   186
     6:2:1 The Principles   186
     6:2:2 Management of Discount Fares   194
     6:2:3 Pricing Response and Pricing Initiatives   198

6:3 The Structure of Air Freight Pricing   202

Successful Airlines ……   205

7   Distributing the Product   206

7:1 Distribution Channel Strategies   206
     7:1:1 Types of Distribution Channel   206
     7:1:2 The Concept of "Super Profits"   208

7:2 The Travel Agency Distribution System   211
     7:2:1 Advantages and Disadvantages   211
     7:2:2 Today's Distribution Channels   214
     7:2:3 The Future of Distribution   215

7:3 Global Distribution Systems (GDSs)   217
     7:3:1 History and Background   217
     7:3:2 Current Issues   220

7:4 Distribution Channels in the Air Freight Market   223

Successful Airlines ……   225

8   Brands Management in Airline Marketing   226

8:1 "Brands" and "Commodities"   226
    8:1:1 What is a "Brand"?   226
    8:1:2 Why Brands?   229

8:2 Brand-Building in the Airline Industry   231
    8:2:1 Foundations for Brand-Building   231
    8:2:2 Positioning Brands   232
    8:2:3 The Brand-Building Process   235

8:3 Brand Strategies   236

Successful Airlines ……   240

9   Relationship Marketing   241

9:1 Fundamentals of Relationship Marketing   241
    9:1:1 Some Definitions   241
    9:1:2 Building Advocate Relationships   243

9:2 Components of a Relationship Marketing Strategy   244
    9:2:1 The Management of Quality   245
    9:2:2 Customer Relations   246
    9:2:3 Marketing Communication   248
    9:2:4 Loyalty Schemes   248

9:3 Frequent Flyer Programmes   248
    9:3:1 History and Current Status   248
    9:3:2 FFPs – Programme Member Requirements   250
    9:3:3 FFPs – Airline Requirements   251
    9:3:4 The Future   253

Successful Airlines ……   256

10   Airline Selling, Advertising and Promotional Policies   257

10:1 The Anatomy of a Sale   257
   10:1:1 The AIDA Model and the SPIN Cycle   257

10:2 Sales Planning   259
   10:2:1 The Sales Budget   259
   10:2:2 The "Communications Mix"   263

10:3 Marketing Communication Techniques   263
   10:3:1 Sponsorship Policy   263
   10:3:2 Database Marketing   265
   10:3:3 Media Relations   273
   10:3:4 The Field Sales Team   274

10:4 Airline Advertising   279
   10:4:1 The Functions of Advertising   279
   10:4:2 Advertising Decisions   280
   10:4:3 What are the Features of "Good"   286
      Airline Advertising?

10:5 Selling in the Air Freight Market   287
   10:5:1 The Sales Task in the Air Freight Market   287
   10:5:2 Marketing Communication Methods   289

Successful Airlines   290

11   The Future of Airline Marketing   291

Glossary of Aviation Terms   295

Glossary of Marketing Terms   307

Index   317

Introduction

The life of the full time lecturer and writer is not generally seen as a very stressful one, with few worries and anxieties. However, one possible worry is that I will sit down to prepare a new edition of 'Airline Marketing and Management' and suddenly find that the airline industry has solved all its marketing problems and that there is therefore very little to discuss. Fortunately, for me at any rate, such a situation most certainly does not prevail at the present time. Whilst the industry has generally recovered from the very dark days during which the Fifth edition was written, many of the old problems remain, and new ones – notably the way in which the aviation industry has moved up the international agenda because of its role in global warming and climate change – have arisen. Preparing the new edition has therefore been as interesting and enjoyable as always – I am very fortunate that sales of the book have continued to be strong and that the opportunity to write the Sixth Edition has therefore become available.

Thanks are due to my good friends at Ashgate Publishing, Adrian Shanks and Guy Loft, for our continuing pleasant professional association and to our many students and friends in the aviation industry on whose ideas the book is unashamedly based. My wife Gill has – as always – masterminded the production of the text for the book and I continue to be greatly in her debt for all the love and encouragement she has provided.

Chinnor, Oxon, England
Email: ssassoc@dsl.pipex.com

1   The Fundamentals

1:1 What is Marketing?

1:1:1   Definition

There is a popular misconception when the term "marketing" is defined – that it is not a very edifying activity. According to its critics, the marketing concept is about producing things that people don't really need and then tricking customers into buying them through deceitful advertising. Such views will be totally rejected in this book. Marketing describes a complete philosophy for running a business, based on the meeting of well-researched, well-understood and genuine customer requirements.[1]

We will use the following definition of the subject:

> Marketing is the management process responsible for identifying, anticipating and satisfying customer requirements profitably.

This definition, used by the UK Chartered Institute of Marketing, provides a valuable initial framework for the study of the subject. In particular, its use of the word "anticipating" emphasises the fact that marketing is a dynamic discipline, where customer requirements are in a constant state of evolution and change. This is especially the case in the airline industry, where successful airlines are likely to be those which anticipate change and are ready for it when it occurs. Unsuccessful carriers tend to be those which wait for change to happen and then try to catch up with it. This is a theme which will recur frequently in the book, and one which is well-illustrated by the difficulties which many so-called' Legacy' airlines have had in recent years in responding to the challenges which the rapid growth of Low Cost Carriers have brought to them.

Though the definition is useful, it is not sufficient to fully describe all

---

[1] A selection of recommended recently published textbooks on marketing is as follows: R.Brenna, P. Baines, P.Garneau: 'Contemporary Strategic Marketing' McMillan 2003 K.Moore, N.Pareek: 'Marketing – the Basics' Routledge 2006.   I.Doole, R.Lowe: 'International Marketing Strategy' Thomson 2004 P. Kotler, G Armstrong: 'Principles of Marketing' Pearson 10th Edition 2002. D Jobber, 'Principles and Practice of Marketing': Mcgraw-Hill 2001. J.Growcutt, P.Forsyth, P Leadley: ' Marketing' Kogan Page 2004.

the facets of marketing, nor to give a framework for this book. We need to break it down further.

A common initial way of doing so is to distinguish between "Consumer" and "Industrial" marketing. Consumer Marketing is marketing activity targeted at the individual or the family. Industrial Marketing is the term used to describe business-to-business or firm-to-firm marketing.

There are many differences between the two. One of the most important is that in Consumer Marketing, identifying the "Customer" for a particular product is usually quite straightforward. Market research studies could, for example, easily identify the demographic characteristics of the individuals who bought chocolate bars or ice-creams. With admittedly more difficulty, it would also be possible to carry out the attitude studies which would highlight the factors taken into account by these people in choosing between the different products on offer.

Industrial Marketing gives no such straightforward opportunities. When firms need to make purchasing decisions for major capital items, they will normally do so using a complex decision-making process. As we shall see in section 2:2:3, this process will often involve large numbers of people, each of whom will be working, at least partly, to their own agenda. Understanding of this process is one of the central skills required in Industrial Marketing and considerable space will be given to it in this book.

Airline marketing provides a particularly fascinating illustration of the application of marketing principles because it includes examples of both Industrial and Consumer Marketing. Marketing to the business air traveller, and of air freight services, both illustrate well the concept of Industrial Marketing. Leisure air travel marketing, on the other hand, if carried out correctly, increasingly exhibits the principles of Consumer Marketing.

1:1:2 The "Marketing Mix"

Though the distinction between "Industrial" and "Consumer" marketing is a useful one, it does not describe any of the activities which must be undertaken in order to apply marketing principles to business. The concept which does do so is known as the "Marketing Mix".

It is useful to describe marketing activity as encompassing the following "4Ps":

Product
Price
Promotion
Place

The word "Place" is somewhat confusing. In our study of airline marketing we shall take this word to describe the distribution channels employed by airlines.

The "4Ps" model tells us that the application of marketing principles will require decisions to be made about the Products which will be offered and the Prices which will be charged for them. Firms must also decide on the methods of marketing communication they will employ in order to persuade people to buy, and the distribution channels which will be used to provide the link between the customer and the product.

The concept is also valuable for another reason. It emphasises that marketing decisions cannot be made in isolation. Instead, all decisions are linked, with the ability to make tradeoffs between them in order to optimise the overall result for the firm an absolutely crucial skill.

Such tradeoffs are at their most obvious in the relationship between Product and Price. Clearly, no firm should invest money in product enhancement unless it expects to obtain a return in the form of a higher selling price or an improved share of better yielding markets. They are though, equally significant in other areas. For example, in making decisions about their distribution channels, firms must often decide whether or not they are to be a wholesaler or a retailer. As we shall see in the airline industry, so-called charter carriers have traditionally sold mostly in a wholesale basis (indeed, in some cases, notably so in Europe, they were restricted to such a role by government regulation). They produced plane-loads of capacity in response to orders placed with them by Tour Operators. The Tour Operators in turn combined the aircraft seats with hotel or other accommodation to make up packaged holidays. In such a situation, the airline was merely the supplier of capacity. The Tour Operator took responsibility for reservations and retail selling. The airline's promotional spending needed only to encompass the costs of a field sales force which carried out sales negotiations.

In strong contrast, airlines focussing on the business travel market have tended to adopt a retailing philosophy. This has required them to keep in contact with travel agents, and to maintain a high promotional profile through such activities as media advertising, database marketing and the maintenance of an attractive Frequent Flyer Programme (see Section 9:3). All these tasks are costly ones, and need to be traded off against the undoubted advantages in terms of market control which retailing can bring.

1:1:3 Stages in the Application of Marketing Principles to Airline Management

The "4Ps" model is a powerful one, and describes much of what an airline must do if it is to apply the principles of marketing in order to achieve business success. It does not, though, give a complete description. In this book, it will be suggested that the application of marketing should consist of seven interlinked stages:

1. The Customer
The cornerstone of successful marketing activity is that firms should obtain full knowledge of their current and potential customers. This knowledge needs to encompass information about market size, demographics, customer requirements and attitudes. There also needs to be an ability to forecast the future size of the market, and any possible future changes in customer needs. The processes whereby airlines seek this information will be those of market research and market analysis

2. The Marketing Environment
The nature of sound marketing policies will clearly vary according to the constraints and opportunities provided by the external environment.

In analysing a firm's marketing environment it is usual to use the model known as PESTE analysis. This model categorises the factors in the marketing environment under the five headings of Political, Economic, Social, Technological and Environmental. The analyst's task is to isolate those factors in the external environment which will have a significant impact on the formulation of sound marketing policies and to assess their implications. In this book, such an exercise will be carried out for the airline industry in Chapter Three.

3. Strategy Formulation
Clearly, it will not be possible to define marketing policies without the marketing input being a crucial one in the definition of a firm's overall strategic direction. This strategic direction must identify the firm's goals and objectives, the markets in which it will participate and the methods it will employ to ensure successful exploitation of market potential.

4. Product Design and Development

5. Pricing and Revenue Management

6. Distribution Channel Selection and Control
Once an overall strategy has been selected, the next three stages should follow on logically. As we shall discuss in Chapter Four, today's aviation industry offers airlines many possible routes to success (and, interestingly, many different ways in which they can fail). What matters is that a clear

strategy is selected and pursued steadily over the long-term. Each possible strategic option will result in a requirement for a linked set of Product, Pricing and Distribution decisions. These subjects will be examined in Chapters Five, Six and Seven.

7. Selling, Advertising and Promotional Policies

A common mistake is to assume that the words "Marketing" and "Selling" are synonymous. They are not. The term "Marketing", as we have seen, describes a total philosophy for running an entire business. "Selling" is the concluding stage of a correctly-applied Marketing process, whereby customers are persuaded to buy the firm's products.

"Marketing" ought to make "Selling" easier. It is likely to be a great deal easier to sell something to someone which is available in response to a well-researched and well-understood customer need. Indeed, one of the traditional faults of industry in the past has been a so-called Production Orientation whereby firms made what they liked making, or found it easiest to make, and then tried to persuade reluctant customers through high-pressure selling to buy these less-than-ideal products. It should not be thought, though, that "Marketing" will make the skills of Selling obsolete. In today's competitive markets, customers will usually have plenty of choice open to them. Persuading them to exercise this choice in a particular way will require the use of professional skills of a high order. We will be discussing these skills in the context of the airline industry in Chapters Eight, Nine and Ten.

This chapter should give the reader a feel for the power and the complexity of the discipline of Marketing and its importance to airlines today. We will now begin our detailed study with the question of the Market for Air Transport Services.

SUCCESSFUL AIRLINES ......

✈   Are those that accept that the principles of Marketing provide a framework for all they do, and set out to apply these principles as widely and as rigorously as possible.

2 The Market for Air Transport Services

An airline which is to apply the principles of Marketing successfully needs a thorough knowledge of current and potential markets for its services. This knowledge should encompass an understanding of the businesses in which they participate, and of the market research techniques they must apply in order to gain the knowledge they need about the marketplace. They must be able to identify "Customers" and distinguish them from "Consumers". They must segment their markets and identify the requirements of Customers in each of the segments. Finally, and most importantly, they must examine their markets in a dynamic rather than a static sense and anticipate future changes in customer needs.

2:1 What Business are we in?

To begin this work, any airline first has to answer the question as to which market or markets are to be studied. To do so, it must answer the fundamental question about the business or businesses in which it participates.

In doing so, there are two possibilities. The first, and obvious way is to define business participation in terms of what the firm does. Thus it would be easy for an airline to say that it was a player in the aviation business.

There is a significant problem in doing so. It will result in a serious underestimation of both the extent and the nature of the competition that the airline faces. As a consequence, defining business participation in this way is often characterised by the term 'Marketing Myopia'. A far better way is to look at the question from the point-of-view of the needs that the firm is aiming to satisfy and the competition that it faces. A large combination airline will be working in at least the following areas:

1. Transportation
There is a clear economic, and, often, social need for transport. Those with this need will look for it to be satisfied in an optimum way. Whether use is made of air transport or a surface transport mode in order to do so will be less important to them. There are now many short-haul routes where

surface transport can provide a level of service in terms of comfort and door-to-door journey times which is as good or better than that available from airlines. In the future, this form of competition is likely to become more marked still, given the ambitious investment plans now in place in many countries for the improvement of surface, especially rail, transport.

2. Communication

Airlines have always assisted people to communicate, as travel allows opportunities for face-to-face meetings. It should not be assumed any longer, though, that travel is essential for such meetings to take place. The world is undergoing a revolution based on video-conferencing, conference-calling and email. The future will see video-conferencing becoming even cheaper, of better quality (with the spread of Broadband networks), and more widely available. More companies are now investing in video-conferencing suites for their staff. Also, increasing numbers of personal computers are being sold with in-built web cameras, allowing video-conferencing to come to the desk top. These are all indicators of the substantial amount of competition that airlines are already facing from the telecommunications industry. The degree of this competition will increase further in the future, especially during recessionary times when many firms are under acute pressure to save money. Its possible impact on the airline industry is further discussed in Section 3:5:1.

3. Leisure

Airlines today are increasingly involved in the intensely competitive leisure industry. Customers have to decide how they will use both their disposable income and disposable time. Disposable income can be used to purchase holidays. It can, though, also be used to buy a wide range of other consumer items. Disposable leisure time can be used for the taking of air-based holidays. Equally, it can be used for other leisure activities. It certainly will be if travelling by air becomes a tiresome experience through flight delays and more and more chaotic airport handling brought about by increasing congestion and growing security requirements.

4. Logistics

In the air freight industry, it is rarely possible for airlines to sell successfully against surface transport operators on the basis of price. Surface transport rates are almost always cheaper than those charged by the airlines. Commonly, surface rates are only a fraction of the air-based equivalent. As we shall see in Section 2:4:2, airlines are only able to succeed if they propose to the shipper a logistics concept based on fast transport, low inventories and limited investment in field warehousing.

They therefore compete in a Logistics business, with their rivals being the surface transport firms offering a different Logistics philosophy, as well as other airlines bidding for a share of the available air freight market.

5. Information

As a more minor, but still interesting issue, on the cargo side of their business, airlines certainly compete in businesses associated with the movement of information. For example, until the mid-1980s, many airlines had lucrative markets composed of moving urgent documents. Since then, this market has been progressively challenged by the electronic transmission of documents initially through fax machines and, more recently, E-mail.

Another example of competition for the airlines from electronic data transmission is in the field of newspaper publishing. Until recently, many airlines had profitable markets in the transport of newspapers. Newspapers were a classic air freight commodity in the sense that an out-of-date paper had no value and therefore speed was of the essence in getting them to their market quickly. The problem for airlines now is that newspaper publishers have realised that there are two ways of ensuring that this happens. They can, at great cost, ship printed newspapers. The alternative is to transmit the data contained in the newspaper very cheaply to satellite printing stations. The papers can then be printed near to where they will be sold and distributed by truck, at a far lower total cost.

6. Selling Services

Running a successful airline requires numerous skills to be developed, and many carriers have an important revenue source from selling these skills to others who need them. Traditional skills which are sold are those associated with aircraft engineering, airport ground handling and data processing and management.

As an overall summary, airlines participate in many businesses and must take a broad view when answering the question "What Business are we in?" If they do, they will be better placed to correctly identify their customers – the subject of the next section – and to take proper account of the extensive, and increasing, amounts of competition that they face.

2:2 Who is the "Customer"?

2:2:1 Definitions

We now turn to the task of addressing one of the most fundamental and commonest mistakes made in airline marketing – failure to make a proper distinction between the "Consumer" and the "Customer".

To begin with definitions, "Consumers" are those people who actually travel. They are therefore easy to identify and analyse. They make their existence clear by reporting for flights and their requirements and preferences can be analysed using questionnaires. They are therefore usually given a great deal of attention by those responsible for Marketing in the airline business. Unfortunately, they may not be decision-makers about the things that matter. In Marketing, such decision-makers are defined as "Customers".

There are at least four customer decisions which must be analysed:

1. Will a trip be made at all?
For many firms today, the cost of travel is a major item of corporate expense. In a recessionary period, firms will attempt to reduce expenditure in order to minimise the effect of recession on corporate profitability or, in extreme cases, to stave off bankruptcy. In such a situation, executives might present a case to their boss that a business trip should be undertaken, only to find that the necessary expenditure is not sanctioned. Instead, they are told to use, say, the phone, email or video-conferencing as a way of conducting the business in question. In such a situation the true "Customer" for the airlines might be the firm's CEO or VP-Finance.

2. What mode of transport will be selected?
As was mentioned in the last section, it is likely that the future will see a significant increase in the amount of competition that airlines face from surface transport operators, especially railways. On short-haul routes, railways are capable of giving superior door-to-door journey times and, arguably, a better quality of service than airlines. Carriers will face a significant challenge for the business travel market, and may well have to target those who formulate corporate travel policies in order to minimise the adverse effect on their traffic.

For leisure travellers, the impact of surface transport competition is likely to be greater still. Besides competition on service quality, surface operators will be able to challenge airlines on price, with both train and bus services likely to become increasingly significant. The "Customer" in such a situation might be the family member who has most influence in travel decisions.

3. For air trips, what class of service will be purchased?
With many airlines, passengers have a choice of flying First Class (at least

on long-haul routes), Business Class and Economy or Coach Class.[2] In the business travel market, the person who travels will have little or no say in the decision as to which class will be purchased. Almost all firms have a Corporate Travel Policy whereby very senior executives are allowed to travel First Class, those of middle rank in Business Class (at least on long-haul routes), whilst junior employees have to be satisfied with Economy Class. Interestingly, during recessionary periods, almost all firms have a downgrading policy in order to save money with, in particular, much First Class and Business Class travel being eliminated.

In order to maximise the amount of high yielding traffic available to them, carriers will have to target those who make decisions about Corporate Travel policies. They will, in particular, have to persuade these people that the benefits of buying travel in the premium cabins of the aircraft – for example, that these cabins allow better opportunities for sleep or work – outweigh the very substantially higher prices that are charged for access to them.

4. Which airline will be selected?

If it has been agreed that a particular journey will be made by air, the question of the choice of airline is clearly a crucial one. In the past, many business travellers did have the choice to make this decision themselves. It has been a major trend of the last ten years that this has become so in fewer and fewer cases. As we shall see in Section 2:2:4, during this time more and more companies have centralised travel purchasing in order to gain access to corporate discounts from airlines. Such policies narrowed the choice which the individual traveller could exercise, even if they were not restricted to using a single airline.

In leisure air travel, as will be discussed in Section 2.2.5, the market is still often a wholesale one. Many airlines still mainly confine themselves to selling blocks of seats to Tour Operators and Consolidators. The individuals who travel will therefore have very little say in the airlines that they fly with.

Given the importance of these four decisions, there is a crucial need to take account of them properly if effective marketing policies are to be established. In particular, the mistake of assuming that the "Customer" is the same person who boards the aircraft must be avoided.

---

[2] Though in recent years the number of airlines offering a First Class cabin has declined sharply, whilst others – notably Virgin Atlantic – have offered a 'Premium Economy' between Business and Economy Class

2:2:2 "Apparent" and "True" Needs

In analysing customer decision-making, all firms need to understand the factors that their customers take into account in making up their minds. In order to do so, the obvious method is to ask them to describe the factors in a properly constructed and administered market research survey.[3]

The problem for the analyst is that what people say may not be the truth. Rather, it may perhaps reflect what they regard as an acceptable answer, rather than an accurate description of the factors they really take into account. This difference between the claim and the truth is known in Marketing as the difference between "Apparent" and "True" needs.

To illustrate the point, a corporate business traveller asked to describe the factors that they take into account in choosing their airline might give a series of respectable answers, all reflecting the service features that permitted them to use their time as effectively as possible in their employer's interest. If they did, issues such as flight frequency (to allow for travel flexibility), punctuality and a roomy cabin (to permit working during flight) might figure prominently. The truth might be rather different. Today, many business travellers base their choice-of-airline decisions on their wish to support an airline on as many occasions as possible because this will maximise the personal benefits available to them (bought using their employer's money) through that airline's Frequent Flyer Programme. These benefits will of course, feed the True Need of greed.

As another example, almost all airlines attempting to exploit the business travel market find that, in order to do so, they must pander to the pride and ego of those who fly. Such features as separate reservations phone lines, a separate check-in desk (ideally with a piece of red carpet in front of it) and separate cabins on board the aircraft do, admittedly, sometimes have a practical purpose, of allowing the business traveller access to useful benefits. However, of equal, or probably greater, importance is that they massage the travellers' ego.

"True Needs" in marketing can cover other aspects as well. Some customers might, for example, be lazy and prefer to keep purchasing from an existing supplier rather than make the effort to change even if such a change might result in better value-for-money. Others might be risk-averse, preferring to stay with a tried-and-tested solution rather than an

---

[3] For a survey of current market research techniques, see V Kumar, D A Aakar, G S Day, Essentials of Market Research, John Wiley 1999. A Proctor, Essentials of Marketing Research, Prentice Hall 2003.

alternative which might be better but which also might go disastrously wrong.

"True Needs" are at the heart of successful marketing. In many ways they reflect the weaknesses of the human personality. They are also relatively constant in their importance through time. No-one who is concerned to make a success of an airline's marketing activities should make the mistake of assuming that a declared customer requirement is actually a true description of what is motivating purchasing decisions.

2:2:3 Industrial Buying Behaviour

As was noted in Section 1:1:1, a major difference between "Consumer" and "Industrial" Marketing concerns the question of the ways in which decisions are made. In Consumer Marketing it is usually possible with confidence to target the individual or the family. In contrast, in Industrial Marketing, purchasing decisions will often be made in a complex way with different corporate executives interacting in different ways through a so-called Decision-Making Unit or DMU.

Because of its importance, there is now a substantial literature dealing with the workings of Decision-Making Units, and the ways in which those who wish to sell to the firm should approach the different DMU participants. This literature suggests that these participants should be divided into five categories, each of which will be working to their own agenda in terms of both "Apparent" and "True" needs.

These categories are as follows:

1. Deciders

These are the people who will make the final purchasing decision. They will, no doubt, have an Apparent Need of making the decision which will be in the best interest of the firm that employs them. There may, though, also be a hidden agenda. For example some Deciders may be looking for personal inducements through bribes or offers of corporate entertainment. Others, perhaps fearful of losing their job, may be looking for a safe, risk-free solution.

2. Gatekeepers

"Gatekeepers" are defined as those who control the flow of information into the Decision-Making Unit. Gatekeeping may take on a number of forms. The Decider's secretary or Personal Assistant will be taking on a Gatekeeping role if they opt to protect their boss from timewasting visits by what they believe will be unwelcome sales people. They will do so by declining to offer appointments to these sales executives when they phone.

Another form of Gatekeeping occurs when someone attempts to keep people away from the DMU who might show up their previous decision-making as having been mistaken. Once a decision has been made, there are almost always people with a vested interest in ensuring that it remains unchallenged. They will try to isolate people who might be able to prove that the firm would have done better to buy from another supplier.

Anyone involved in Industrial Marketing will have to deal with Gatekeeping issues from time-to-time. There is a variety of methods open to them in doing so. They may try, for example, to by-pass the Gatekeeper. If the problem is a secretary who is refusing to offer an appointment, they could time their next phone call to ensure that it was after business hours when the secretary might have gone home but their boss is still in the office. If the boss answers the phone, an opportunity will present itself to attempt to persuade them that an appointment should be given. (If such attempts are successful, of course, they will invite a backlash from the secretary the next morning when they look at the diary. This may in turn result in them attempting to discredit the salesperson in the eyes of their boss).

A second method of addressing Gatekeeping problems will be through intimidation. Here, the sales person makes it clear to the Gatekeeper that they will offer a deal which will result in substantial benefits to the firm in question. These benefits cannot be given, though, if they have no opportunity to talk to the relevant decision-maker. It will reflect poorly against the Gatekeeper's judgement that their attitude is threatening to deny these benefits to the firm. It could even cause their job security to be brought into question if their attitude becomes more widely known – as the salesperson will ensure that it does unless they change their mind about their refusal to offer an appointment.

Whilst it may sometimes be necessary to use by-passing or intimidating tactics, they should be avoided if at all possible. The making of enemies seldom achieves the desired objective, in Industrial Marketing or anywhere else. By far the best tactic is to aim to convert the Gatekeeper so that they adopt an attitude of support rather than hostility. If the Gatekeeping problem is that of a secretary refusing to give an appointment then the offer of appropriate corporate entertainment may be sufficient. If the Gatekeeper is someone attempting to ensure that a previous decision they have made cannot be challenged, it is far better to address directly the root cause of the problem – the fact that they feel vulnerable and are worried about their status and job security. Reassurance that they will have an important future role to play if the decision is changed will be a way of calming these fears.

3. Users

Users are defined as those people who will actually use the product or service once it has been purchased. Because of this, they tend to be very concerned about the quality and utility of the product, and less worried about the cost of obtaining it.

In the next section, we shall be applying this model of Industrial Buying Behaviour to the situation where a firm is seeking to sign a corporate deal with airlines, whereby carriers will offer discounts in return for loyalty. In such a situation, the "Users" will be the business travellers who actually fly. They will lobby the "Decider" (commonly an executive with a job title such as Corporate Travel Manager) to deal only with airlines that offer extravagant service standards, a strong product reputation and an attractive Frequent Flyer Programme and with a prestigious brand position, even if these airlines do not offer such a good deal financially.

4. Buyers

Buyers are those who negotiate the final deal with the different suppliers. In a large firm, there will probably be a separate Purchasing function. In a small company, negotiations with suppliers may be the responsibility of the Finance Department.

In terms of true needs, those carrying out purchasing negotiations will certainly wish to protect their job security. They will probably conclude that the best way of doing so will be to demonstrate that their interventions save the company substantial amounts of money. To take account of this, salespeople will probably have to reserve the final concession that they are empowered to make until the last stages of a negotiation when the Purchasing Department is involved.

As a further aspect of saving money, those from the Purchasing Department are unlikely to share the enthusiasm of Users for extravagant product standards. They will probably favour more utilitarian solutions. For example, in the case of corporate dealing for business travel, those from the Purchasing function may well prefer deals with those so-called "Cost Leader"[4] airlines which are able to deliver the product basics of safety, frequency and punctuality, but which do not offer the frills of luxurious seating and high levels of provision of food, drink and in-flight entertainment. The fares on offer from such airlines will probably be cheaper. Such fares will also address the natural prejudice of people who probably do not fly a great deal on business themselves and may regard those who do as a pampered and privileged minority.

---

[4] See section 4:2:1.

5. Influencers

Influencers are those people who do not use a product, or become involved in detailed negotiations with suppliers, but who do influence the final outcome of the buying process.

Influencers can come from both outside and inside a firm. An example of an outside Influencer might be the Decider's partner, who had enjoyed some particularly pleasant corporate entertainment offered by one supplier involved in bidding for a piece of business. They then encourage their partner to continue to deal with this firm in order that further opportunities to accept hospitality might arise. A further example would be a government minister or civil servant urging the firm to take account of the national interest in making its purchasing decisions by considering such issues as employment and the Balance of Payments.

Internal Influencers might exist as a result of internal corporate battles. For example, one unscrupulous executive might be trying to discredit another . They might well argue that the firm should change its source of supply for a product or service if this would help to embarrass the person who had selected the original supplier.

2:2:4   The "Customer" in the Business Air Travel Market

It is hoped that enough has now been said to show that correctly identifying and targeting "Customers" rather than mere "Consumers" is a cornerstone of successful marketing in the airline industry. This leads to the question of the identity of different customers and their "True Needs" which should be taken into account in order to ensure accurate targeting.

We have already seen that, in the business travel market, there will still be occasions when the person who travels has an absolute right to select the mode of transport they will use and, if it is to be an air-based journey, the airline with which they will fly. For example, someone running their own small business will presumably have this right, whilst even in large corporations there are still cases where companies leave these choices to individuals. We shall be further considering the question of the requirements of these people in Section 2:3:3.

Even where someone is able to claim that they have the right to choose the airline they fly with themselves, it may not actually be the case that they exercise this choice. For example, a busy business executive might trust their secretary to select airlines, and make the necessary bookings. There can be no doubt that executive secretaries make up an important group of "Customers" in the business air travel market.

In making a choice-of-airline decision, a secretary will presumably not select an airline which they know their boss hates. They will also take account of requirements such as preferred departure airport, flight timings etc. However, from the point-of-view of Airline Marketing, there will presumably be occasions where two or more airlines both have a sound reputation, and offer an equivalent product in terms of timings. Here, the secretary will be able to exercise choice. As with all marketing decisions, they will have a set of True Needs which must be understood. For example, they will have understandable preference for the easy solution. It is unlikely that they will be prepared to wait for twenty minutes for an airline reservations department to answer the phone, when they know from experience that its rival will always respond instantly, or attempt to navigate a confusing website if other sites are easier to use. They will also get to know which airline is pleasant to deal with in terms of a warm and caring attitude from its customer contact staff.

Secretaries will also often have a True Need of greed, in that they may well prefer to deal with airlines that offer them an incentive. Thus many airlines have clubs for executive secretaries which provides a database to allow them to target secretaries with offers of corporate entertainment and discounted travel in return for loyalty.

Another example of a possible Customer in the business travel market is the travel agent. A business traveller may have the right to choose the airline they fly with themselves, but may leave the choice to their travel agent on the grounds that, perhaps, they are too busy to worry or that they regard the travel agent as an expert whose advice they should accept.

The role of the travel agent is still a controversial one in Airline Marketing and there will be repeated references to it throughout the book. It is easy to isolate the proportion of bookings which come through agents today. In some markets, still something over 70% of the bookings that traditional airlines receive come through agents, though the proportion is now generally declining. In terms of the subject of this section of the book, though, this does not mean that the travel agent is necessarily a "Customer" for them on such a high proportion of occasions. If someone specifies to the agent that one particular airline is the only one that is acceptable to them, the agent does not make a choice as a Customer, they merely take an order. The agent is a Customer, though, in any situation where, as described above, the person who travels leaves the choice-of-airline decision to them.

In terms of True Needs, senior agency managers will be motivated by greed, in that they will be predisposed to recommend the airline offering the highest rates of commission and certainly those which still pay commissions rather than those which do not. They do not have complete freedom to merely consider commissions, though, because if they recommend airlines that the person who travels finds unacceptable they run the risk that they will lose the account to a rival, and presumably more trustworthy, agency. There are, though, now a good number of respectable airlines where a recommendation for one giving better commissions would not arouse suspicion.

In the world of travel agency operations, airlines also have to take account of another set of customers. These are the travel clerks who actually make bookings and issue tickets. Generally, senior agency managers do not carry out this work. Equally, they rarely pass on to their staff the financial benefits of additional commission payments. In many countries, travel agency staff are poorly rewarded financially. Because of this, travel agency clerks often have true needs similar to those noted above for executive secretaries. They will prefer airlines that are easy and convenient to contact. They will also welcome the offer of incentives – particularly free travel opportunities on so-called educational or familiarisation visits arranged by airlines.

The final example of a "Customer" in the business air travel market has already been referred to in the last section. This is where a firm appoints someone to be responsible for corporate dealing with carriers. Under such an arrangement, freedom-of-action will be denied to the executives who actually fly. Instead, they will be required to choose from one or a small number of airlines. In turn carriers will be approached to offer substantial discounts in order to be one of the favoured airlines. In a large organisation, the management of business travel might be given to one executive with a job title such as Corporate Travel Manager. In a smaller one, it might be a task carried out by a senior manager from the Finance or Purchasing department.

As we have discussed, the growth of corporate dealing has been one of the major trends in business air travel marketing in recent years. In particular, recessionary conditions from 2001 until 2003 saw severe pressure being placed on travel budgets in many markets, and corporate dealing being recognised as a valuable way of reducing costs. The possible renewal of such conditions in 2007 will again bring pressure on travel budgets.

Today, the question of correctly identifying and targeting "Customers" in the business air travel market is a vital one for airlines, and one that is causing increasing controversy. The problem is that it is very difficult to be certain exactly who is making the relevant decision. The normal expedient adopted by many airlines of simply asking the person who flies the question as to who was responsible for their choice-of-airline decision is unlikely to yield much enlightenment, striking as is does at the heart of questions about corporate status and privilege.

Because of this difficulty, many airlines today follow the policy of giving incentives to everyone, whether or not the person in question is actually able to influence the amount of business obtained. Thus, today almost all airlines offer individual travellers incentives through a Frequent Flyer Programme. They may also give the firms that these people work for substantial corporate discounts. Finally, the travel agents that these firms use are still sometimes rewarded by the offer of override commissions, though the extent of this practice has declined in recent years.

The results of such profligacy was that selling costs were for a long period the fastest rising cost of doing business for many traditional airlines. Indeed, the escalation of such costs stood in sharp contrast to carriers' success in reducing many other costs. It will be a major challenge in the future to better identify "Customers" and to ensure that promotional spending is more effectively targeted. This is especially so because failure to do so is a mistake most of the newer "Cost Leader" airlines have avoided.

2:2:5 The "Customer" in the Leisure Air Travel Market

Identifying the "Customer" is just as difficult, and just as important, in the leisure air travel market.

As was mentioned in Section 2:1, when airlines are bidding for business from the holiday or vacation traveller, they are competing for the person's disposable time and disposable income. They must also ensure that, if it is decided to spend time and money on a holiday, an air-based vacation will be selected. The airline must then ensure that the holiday is taken at a destination which it serves, and that people travel to the destination on its flights, rather than on those of a rival carrier.

In analysing this complex set of decisions, it should first of all be born in mind that a great deal of holiday travel is undertaken in family groups. The question of how travel decisions are made within the family is thus a crucial one which should, for example, decide the creative content of advertising and promotional work, and the media buying decisions which are made.

Within the family, children can have an important influence on travel buying decisions made by their parents. For very young children, parents may deliberately choose an airline where they believe that facilities available for the care of babies are good. For older children, such factors as the availability of video games in an airline's in-flight entertainment system might be significant. For older children too, the choice of vacation destination may be made by their parents, but parents will take into account their children's preferences. This is something which is has been recognised in the creative strategies adopted by a number of vacation destinations, such as Disney resorts, in their advertising. Much of this appears to be designed to exploit so-called 'Pester Power'.

It is also a crucial issue as to whether or not men or women have a greater influence on holiday decision-making. Here, cultural influences assume great importance. Some societies are traditionally matriarchal, where women are dominant in family life. Others are patriarchal, where men dominate. In the UK, it is recognised that women are extremely influential in holiday planning, and the creative strategies adopted by airlines and tour operators have increasingly reflected this.

With other possible "Customers" in the leisure air travel market, it must be recognised that the travel agent is important, being in fact more so than is the case for business travel. In the leisure market, the question of the destination for a vacation is a significant one, where people will often accept the advice of their travel agent. Of course, with business air travel the destination will have been decided prior to contact with the agent.

Another difference between business and leisure travel market is that, as will be discussed in Section 2:3:4, the business travel market is a concentrated one. It consists of a relatively small number of people who each travel a great deal. Indeed, the average number of air trips made per year by a business traveller averages more than ten in many markets. The leisure market, on the other hand, has fewer frequent travellers. Some leisure travellers are making their only trip of a lifetime. Many more take only one air trip a year, for their annual holiday. Given, therefore, that they are relatively inexperienced, they may have to turn to someone for advice on such aspects as the making of bookings, visa applications etc. The natural place for them to look is to their travel agent. The result is that it is possible to argue about the importance of the travel agent as a "Customer" for airlines in the business travel market. No such argument should occur with leisure travel. Travel agents are still important, and airlines must cultivate their loyalty if they are to obtain a proper share of this market. They will do so through the traditional so-called offline agents, but will increasingly have to sell over the Internet to the rapidly developing on-line travel agency industry (See Section 7:2).

A further feature of the leisure market as far as airlines are concerned is that, as was noted in Section 1:1:2, it is often still a wholesale market. Despite the use of on-line booking leading to an increasing presence in retailing, many airlines still wholesale blocks of seats to organisations known generically as Tour Operators (or Travel Organisers) and "Consolidators".

The difference between a Tour Operator and a Consolidator is becoming more and more difficult to define, given that many firms now combine both functions. In principle, though, the difference is that the

Tour Operators are aiming to be value-adders, in the sense that they take airline seats, accommodation, surface transfers and add-ons such as tours, sports opportunities etc to make up packaged holidays. A "Consolidator" is simply a dealer in discounted air tickets.   More popularly known as "Bucket Shops", Consolidators provide an outlet whereby airlines can wholesale blocks of seats for a very low cost-of-sale. The problem, of course, is that because of the Consolidators' bargaining power, prices and yields can be extremely low.

In targeting the leisure air traveller, airlines must regard the senior managers and product managers of major Tour Operators as very important customers. They will have no hope of success in this market unless they can persuade Tour Operators to feature the destinations they serve in their brochures, and on their websites, and, when they do, to buy their seats to serve these destinations from the airline in question.

With the role of the Consolidator, airlines have difficult decisions to make, decisions which are further discussed in Section 7:1:1. Reliance on them as a significant channel of distribution, will result in a straightforward selling task, in that an airline will be able to act purely as a wholesaler. There is a grave risk though, of the carrier losing control of its distribution channels, with potentially disastrous financial consequences. If, though, a decision is made to make significant use of the Consolidator channel, then the owners of the major consolidators must be regarded as highly significant "Customers".

2:2:6 The "Customer" in the Air Freight Market

The focus of this book is mainly on the passenger side of the airline business. A full study of the application of marketing principles to the air freight business is available elsewhere.[5] It is nonetheless important that everyone who works for an airline should have an understanding of the air freight business, because the nature of the airline industry is such that frequent liaison will be necessary between passenger and freight departments. Air freight also gives another excellent illustration of the ways in which the application of marketing principles can make the difference between success and failure. No apology is therefore made for the inclusion of coverage of the air freight industry in this book.

In looking at the question of the "Customer" in the air freight market, it should first of all be born in mind that there are marked differences

---

[5] See "Effective Air Freight Marketing" by Stephen Shaw, Pitman Books, 1993. A new edition is in preparation and will be published in the autumn of 2007.

between the passenger and freight businesses. These are discussed further in Section 2:4:1.

In air freight, marketing intermediaries known as Air Freight Forwarders are extremely important to most airlines. Few carriers have a significant commitment to retail marketing. Instead, more than 90% of their traffic is typically provided by forwarders. There is every possible reason to regard the forwarder as a significant customer, more important still than the travel agent on the passenger side of the business. There seems to be a much greater degree of willingness on the part of freight customers to allow forwarders to make routeing and carrier selection decisions than is the case with travel agents. Also, a considerable proportion of air freight traffic is sent under the 'Consolidation' principle. Here, a forwarder will gather together a large number of small packages from individual shippers and present them to the airline as one large consignment. In return, the airline charges a much lower rate per kilo, and the forwarder passes on some of this saving to the shippers who generate the small consignments.

By definition, when shippers allow their consignments to be sent as part of a Consolidation, they are accepting that they will have no right to decide the airline that will be used to carry them. Instead, the decision as to which carrier will be given the traffic will be made by the senior management of the air freight forwarder, and all airlines must regard such managers as 'Customers'.

In the individual shipment, non-consolidated market, airlines will have another set of customers – the clerks who work for freight forwarding companies. A great deal of air freight moves at night, and is dealt with by an army of shift-working clerks. Also, as we shall see in Section 2:4:2, a considerable proportion of air freight moves as emergency shipments with no prior notice of the need to move goods being possible. In such a situation, routeing and carrier selection decisions will be made by clerks, late at night, when the senior managers of a forwarder are at home in bed. Airlines therefore have the task of building and maintaining a relationship with forwarder clerks as a significant customer group.

As has been noted above, many airlines only attempt to market their air freight services through air freight forwarders. For those that try and do more than this, a very much broader base of 'Customers' appears.

It should first of all be born in mind that in air freight there is a true 'retail' market of non-expert users. For example, a secretary may find that their boss tells them to send a small, urgent package of papers or samples. It is a major success of the so-called 'Integrators' (to be further discussed in Section 4:4:2) that they have been able to simplify their processes to such an extent, and to design and administer a retail marketing organisation, so that their services are easily accessible to all customers.

Away from the small shipment market, a limited number of airlines have taken this retail marketing philosophy in another direction, in that they have chosen to deal with the firms who produce freight, rather than merely rely on traffic offered to them by air freight forwarders. To say that such policies have proved controversial would be an understatement. The subject is covered fully in Section 2:4:2. For the moment, though, it is important to note that such a strategy requires a completely different view to be taken regarding the identity of the 'Customer'.

In bidding for business from the true originators of traffic, airlines will be facing two different situations. Firstly, they will have to attempt to obtain a good share of existing air freight flows. In order to do so, they will normally contact the Shipping Manager or some similarly-titled executive. Whether the correct person to approach is with the exporting firm or with the firm carrying out the importing activity will depend on the terms of trade under which a consignment is moving. Secondly, any cargo-orientated airline will also need to develop new air freight traffic by arguing that firms should use air freight in order to exploit new marketing opportunities, or to improve on the efficiency of existing logistics systems based on surface transport.

The exact arguments which should be used to do so are complex ones and are again covered in Section 2:4:2. For the moment, though, it should be noted that air freight can only be justified as part of a logistics philosophy in which higher transport expenses are traded off against cost savings and marketing benefits achieved elsewhere. In most firms, Shipping Managers are comparatively junior executives who do not have the authority to make these tradeoffs as they have no say over issues such as inventory and warehousing policy. In order to achieve a favourable outcome, airline salespeople will often need to target their message at a much higher level in the management hierarchy. In some firms, the Managing Director or President will be the right person to approach. In others, which take an integrated view of the management of the logistics function, there may be an Executive Vice-President or Board Director in place whose responsibilities include all the sub-functions of Logistics. If there is, this person should clearly be targeted in a sales campaign.

2:3 Market Segmentation – Air Passenger Market

2:3:1 The Concept

In Section 1:1, it was stated that the objective of a firm's marketing policies should be to meet the needs of its Customers, at a profit. We now have to deal with the problem that in one very real sense, this ideal objective is often unobtainable.

It is a truism to say that all Customers are different. If an airline was to carry out market research into the requirements of its Customers, the outcome would not be a uniform set of results. Rather, there would be a spectrum of needs, and it would be quite impossible for the carrier to meet all these needs exactly whilst at the same time retaining sound production economics.

The problem is a common one in all areas of Marketing. For example, a car company might set out with the reasonable-sounding objective of giving all its customers exactly the colour of car that they would like. This would mean, though, producing some cars in wildly eccentric colours in order to satisfy the most unusual requests, with the result of very high production costs. Instead, car manufacturers usually produce cars in, say, eight or ten different colours. This gives them the benefit of much lower costs, but they have to accept that they will not be able to fully satisfy the requirements of all of their customers. Those with outlandish tastes will only be able to choose from cars which in no way give them the colour they are looking for. Even more conservative customers may find that a particular shade is too light or too dark.

The process of trading off customer requirements against production economics occurs in almost all industries – notably so amongst airlines. It is called 'Market Segmentation', and leads to the following definition of a 'Market Segment':

> A market segment is a group of Customers who have sufficient in common that they form a viable basis for a product/price/promotion combination.

There are two possible mistakes which can be made when segmenting a market – those of under-segmentation and over-segmentation.

Under-segmentation occurs when Customers are grouped into segments which are too large, and where there is actually a high degree of difference in the requirements of those included in the segment. A finer segmentation might allow at least some of these differences to be incorporated in product, price and promotion policies without an undue cost penalty being incurred. Over-segmentation is the situation where too many segments are isolated, with the result that they give insufficient indicators with regard to policy development.

The correct segmentation does, of course, depend on the question of the use that will be made of it. With product planning, almost all airlines are handicapped by the fact that only two or three classes of service currently exist on board aircraft.[6] Therefore, a broad segmentation must be used for product planning purposes. In contrast, if the objective is to provide the basis for a Database Marketing campaign, a much finer segmentation can and should be employed.

2:3:2 Segmentation Variables in the Air Passenger Market

Segmentation of the air passenger market has traditionally been based on the use of three variables: the purpose of the passenger's journey, the length of their journey and their country or culture of origin. Each of these variable remains important in Airline Marketing today, and we will examine them in turn.

1. Journey Purpose
Journey purpose has always been the fundamental segmentation variable in the air passenger market, with the essential division being between business and leisure travel.

In using such a division, it should not be assumed that all air trips can be placed in one of these two categories. Some are completely outside them. For example, many airlines have significant markets which consist of pilgrims visiting Islam's holiest places in Saudi Arabia. Such trips cannot be viewed as either business or leisure – they constitute an entirely separate market segment. Or again, airlines often find that they derive business from the medical market where someone who falls ill finds that the treatment they need is not available locally. They therefore travel by air to a destination where medical facilities are better. Again, the medical market should be viewed as a separate market segment.

Despite the clear existence of exceptions, the distinction between business and leisure remains a valuable one in Airline Marketing and there is no doubt that a usefully high proportion of trips can placed in one of these two categories.

In looking at the Journey Purpose variable, worthwhile sub-segments can be isolated, in both the business and leisure categories.

In business travel, a useful distinction is between Corporate and Independent business travellers. Corporate travellers are those who travel for a company, and who are able to put the price of their ticket and other business travel costs onto an expense account. They may adopt a more cavalier approach to the costs of the services they buy, placing importance

---

[6] Though some airlines, notably British Airways and Eva Airways, currently use four classes.

instead on high product standards. Independent business travellers, on the other hand, are those who are self-employed or who work for small companies. These people feel to a much greater degree that the price of an air ticket is coming out of their own pocket. As we shall see in Section 2:3:3, some of their requirements are identical to those of the Corporate traveller. They do, for example, still regard a high frequency of flights and good punctuality as essentials. They are, however, often prepared to make sacrifices in terms of product frills – for example, by travelling in the rear cabin on board the aircraft rather than choosing costly First or Business Class products, or by using one of the so-called "Cost Leader" airlines. There are now many signs that the size of the Independent sub-segment of business travel demand is increasing relative to the size of the Corporate sub-segment. We shall look at the factors which explain this trend, and at its possible significance, in Section 3:4:4.

In the leisure segment of demand, again, two sub-segments can be isolated – those of Holiday and Visiting-Friends-and-Relatives (VFR) travel. When someone is travelling by air on holiday, they still have to pay for their meals and accommodation at their destination. This restricts the size of the market to those who have relatively high disposable incomes. With VFR travel, on the other hand, meals and accommodation are normally provided free-of-charge. This allows airlines to develop new markets amongst people with lower disposable incomes, especially in situations where recent population migrations have left strong residual ethnic links between two communities.

2. Length of Journey

There are fundamental differences between the requirements of a short-haul traveller compared with someone who is flying a long-haul route. As we shall discuss further in the next section, on short-haul routes, the airport experience is an especially important one, whilst in-flight aspects such as seating comfort or food assume rather less significance. On long-haul routes, on the other hand, the in-flight experience is very important indeed in ensuring customer satisfaction.

An interesting debate is where the cut-off point between short-haul and long-haul services comes. No-one would presumably dispute that a flight of, say, forty-five minutes' duration should be regarded as short-haul and one of ten hours as long-haul. The difficult area is that of flights of, say, three or four hours. Here, for reasons of operational convenience most airlines continue to provide their short-haul product, despite the fact that passenger expectation is often for something substantially better. In particular, passengers will almost certainly respond unfavourably to being offered service in a single aisle aircraft with six abreast seating and a narrow seat pitch.

3. *Country/Culture of Origin of the Traveller*

In the airline industry in recent years there has been considerable discussion of the concept of 'global brands' and the possibility of truly global branding becoming a feature of Marketing in the aviation business. At the same time, with many airlines grouping together in large alliances, attention has been has been focussed on the supposed need for seamless service concepts whereby wherever anyone flies, anywhere in the world, on the traffic system of the alliance, they should receive a comparable product.

Unfortunately, global branding and seamless service concepts in aviation come into conflict with the marked differences in customer requirements which occur between different cultures. For example, most people in north-west Europe or North America, would recognise a stereotype of the 'Business Traveller' as being someone who is middle-aged, and soberly dressed, carrying only a small amount of baggage. In contrast, in many third-world countries, 'Business Travel' takes on a quite different meaning. It largely consists of traders who fly to a destination where consumer goods are available cheaply. These goods are then purchased and flown to the developing country where they are in short supply and can therefore be sold at a premium. In strong contrast to the product standards that might be expected by a European business traveller, in many developing countries such standards are irrelevant. Instead, overwhelmingly the most important customer requirement is that the airline should offer a high free baggage allowance.

Even within the confines of market segments derived from developed countries, significant market-by-market differences in customer requirements occur. For example, different races often vary significantly in terms of height and weight, with people from many Far Eastern cultures often smaller on average than their European or North American counterparts. They may therefore regard seating comfort as being a rather lower priority. Or again, questions of appropriate food-and-drink to be offered will vary from market-to-market. A suitable 'breakfast' in France will be a different meal from what would be acceptable in the U.K.

All-in-all, the question of culture or country of origin of the person who is travelling must be seen as a highly significant segmentation variable in aviation marketing.

2:3:3 Customer Requirements – Business Travel Market

Given the segmentation of the air passenger market that we have been describing, it is useful to return to the definition of 'Marketing' given in Section 1:1. There it was stated that "Marketing is the management process responsible for identifying anticipating and satisfying customer requirements profitably". From this definition, it might be thought that our task is now a straightforward one. Having identified the main variables used to segment the market, we should now move on to discuss the requirements of customers in each of the main market segments. Unfortunately, there is a significant complication. Despite our definition of marketing encompassing the concept of satisfying customer needs it is rarely possible to immediately satisfy all possible customer requirements. The reason is that to do so would require a degree of spending that would prove uneconomic. Instead, airlines have to prioritise needs so that what they are able to invest is focussed on their customers' most important requirements, on which their choice-of-airline decisions are most likely to depend. Customer Needs, therefore do not just have to be identified, they have to be prioritised as well.

If this is the case, it raises the question of how both the identification and prioritisation can take place. There are, of course, standard techniques of market research and analysis that airlines can use. Many carriers, for example, carry out in-flight surveys of their passengers. Often, such surveys include questions which ask passengers to list the factors they take into account in choosing their airlines. Unfortunately, in-flight surveys only allow carriers to sample the opinions of people who are flying with them already. They are potentially even more interested in the views of people who are at the moment choosing to fly with their competitors.

To remedy this problem, it is possible to engage firms of market research consultants and instruct them to carry out a survey of the whole of a market, rather than just amongst the airline's own customers. These surveys may be carried out by mail or email, by telephone or through individual or group interviews. Interview-based research at least should have the benefit of a better structure and more reliable answers, though at the penalty of a substantially increased cost. Even with such research, though, there are risks. In particular, respondents may give answers that they feel the questioner wants to hear, or which match up to their own, not necessarily accurate, view of their own importance. As was mentioned in the last section, these latter issues often arise especially over questions as to who is responsible for the person's choice-of-airline decisions. There is a natural wish to give the impression that they are important enough to make this decision themselves, even if they are in practice bound by a company travel policy that allows them little or no flexibility.

An alternative way of understanding customer needs is increasingly open to airlines as the forces of deregulation and liberalisation advance in the industry. It is one thing to ask people what their requirements are. It is often a more convincing policy to observe what they actually do when they are presented with a choice. Such situations often occur when new competitors arrive in a market, offering radically different service concepts from the incumbent carriers that they are challenging. If these new competitors immediately achieve a substantial market share, it allows the analyst an opportunity to change and adjust views about the nature of market requirements.

As an example of this, as we will discuss in Section 4:2:1, in many markets one of the major trends of recent years has been the rapid rise of airlines offering very low fares, and asking passengers to make carefully calculated sacrifices regarding frills in the product to obtain them. In the USA, by far the most successful of these carriers has been Southwest Airlines. Recent estimates have suggested that upwards of 25% of US air travellers are now choosing one of the no-frills airlines, and that a significant proportion of these people are business travellers rather than the back-packers one might have expected to make such a choice. In turn, this has led to a reappraisal of the priorities of customers, especially in those markets with only a short flight time of an hour or less. Similar rethinking has been required in Europe as a result of the substantial growth achieved by, amongst others, Ryanair and Easyjet.

Having made these qualifications, it is now necessary to set out some opinions as to the nature of customer needs, starting with the business travel market. We shall divide our discussion between the Corporate and Independent sub-segments of business travel demand, and between short and long-haul routes. In turn, we shall begin with what the available evidence[7] suggests are the high priority issues.

1. Frequency and Timings

In short-haul markets, frequency and timings are all important for the business traveller. Most business people find that their lives are extremely busy, and that their plans often change at short notice. If they do, an airline offering them a high frequency will have crucial advantage. Frequency will ensure that business travellers can fly out for a meeting shortly before it is due to begin and return to their offices or homes very soon after it has

---

[7] See for example the Corporate Travel Survey carried out annually by IATA, the airlines' trade association, and the OAG Business Travel Lifestyle Survey. Again, this is an annual publication.

been completed. Because this is so, on almost all routes there will be a very strong correlation between the share of the frequency that an airline holds, and the share of the market it will obtain. Indeed, there is some evidence to suggest that this is an S-shaped relationship where the airline which dominates its competitors in terms of frequency will obtain an even higher share of the market than its frequency share would indicate.

Alongside the question of flight frequency, the timing of flights will also be a vital consideration. A high frequency of flights will be of no value if all the flights are concentrated at the weekend or during middle-of-the-day periods. It is essential that there should be extensive opportunities on short-haul routes for business travellers to make day-return trips. Flights will therefore need to be concentrated in the early morning and evening periods.

2. Punctuality

Punctuality of flights is of obvious, crucial, importance to the business traveller, with flight delays meaning inconvenience, missed appointments and, perhaps, the loss of customers. No airline can hope to obtain a large share of the available business travel market if it is saddled with the handicap of a poor punctuality reputation.

3. Airport Location and Access

On short-haul routes, passengers will prefer service from a local, easily accessible airport, rather than from a more distant hub. This rule may apply even if the service from the local airport is with a "No Frills" airline.

4. Seat Accessibility/Ticket Flexibility

"Seat Accessibility" is a piece of aviation jargon which refers to the probability of a passenger being able to book a seat on a flight shortly before it is due to depart. It is an important product need for the business traveller. Some business travel is undertaken in response to a sudden crisis, which requires someone to travel on a "next flight out" basis. In other situations, a flight may be booked well in advance, but at the last minute a change of plan means that the booking must be cancelled and a new one made on an earlier or later flight. This requires that the ticket held by the passenger should be a flexible one, and that seats should be available near to flight departure time on the alternative service. Clearly, an airline can be giving a very high frequency on a route, but this frequency will be of no value to the business traveller if all the flights are fully booked days or weeks in advance.

A further aspect of ticket flexibility is that many business travellers expect the right to no-show for a flight, and then to be re-booked on a later one, without any penalty being charged. Of course, because of this, airlines have difficult decisions to make about the extent to which they will overbook flights to take account of the likely extent of no-shows, an issue which is further covered in Section 5:4:2.

5. Frequent Flyer Benefits

Today, almost all airline operate their own Frequent Flyer Programme, or are partners in another carrier's programme. This whole, controversial, subject is dealt with in Section 9:3. In that Section, we shall be probing the question of the degree to which FFP benefits build market loyalty. It will be argued there that these benefits can be important in doing so, but that on short-haul routes their impact should not be exaggerated. For a short journey, the number of mileage points on offer will be quite small. It is true that the passenger will often happily take these by choosing the airline whose Frequent Flyer Programme they are currently supporting. However, what is uncertain is the extent to which they will actually change their behaviour and accept a less convenient option in terms of flight frequency, flight timings and departure airport in order to do so. The evidence is that on short-haul routes flights are chosen on the basis of an appropriate departure timing and the availability of a seat. If this is the case, then the offer of Frequent Flyer miles simply acts as a welcome bonus.

6. Airport Service

On a short flight, time spent at the airports at each end of the route may exceed the flight time. It is therefore not surprising that airport service should be a significant factor in choice-of-airline decisions. Business travellers will demand the opportunity to check in very late for a flight, by using a separate check-in desk to guard against the possibility of being delayed by a long line of less time-sensitive travellers. An online check-in facility may be even better. Today, they will expect expedited security and passport checks, and that a lounge should be available in which they can relax prior to a flight and make any last-minute phone calls or send emails. Finally, they will expect a premium baggage service. For many, this will mean that they do not check in baggage at all, but instead are able to carry their baggage on board with them. This requires airlines to provide large overhead baggage bins on their aircraft. When a larger amount of baggage is being carried and business travellers have to check it in, they expect an opportunity to retrieve bags very quickly at the destination airport.

Airport service provides a good illustration of the differences between 'Apparent' and 'True' needs discussed in Section 2:2:2. In all the factors mentioned above, the business traveller could make a good case for the service feature being as essential component of a product which will meet their air travel needs. For example, a late check-in will have a value in allowing them to maximise the time they spend in their office before leaving for an air trip. However, at the same time, the separate check-in desk also panders to True Needs associated with pride and ego and the need for a recognition of status, something of great significance in terms of effective marketing to the business traveller.

7. In-Flight Service

On short-haul routes, the fact that flight times are short means that in-flight service often assumes a lower priority than frequency, punctuality and airport service in choice-of-airline decisions. Nonetheless, it can still be extremely important. As we shall see in Section 5:3:2, in competitive markets airlines usually have little choice but to match the frequency of their rivals and to closely mimic their flight timings. Also, it is sometimes difficult to achieve a Sustainable Competitive Advantage through airport service, at least in the large number of countries where airport terminal facilities are provided on a common user basis by airport operators. Because of these factors, the in-flight experience may be a crucial one for choice-of-airline decisions, even on routes where flight times are only three-quarters-of-an-hour or so.

In terms of the factors which will be taken into account in evaluating the in-flight experience, seating comfort in terms of seat pitch and seat width will be significant. Also, a separate Business Class cabin may be appreciated. This will satisfy a need for a working environment away from crying children etc., where important documents, say, can be read before a business meeting. It does, though, once again pander to the True Need for the recognition of status.

A final requirement in terms of in-flight service will be meals and drinks appropriate to the time of day. Here, it seems that breakfast, and an evening meal on after-business returning flights are especially welcome.

Having set down some of the fundamental requirements of the Corporate business traveller on short-haul, point-to-point journeys, we can now use this basic model to probe customer requirements in related, but significantly different, situations.

Here, a first interesting case is to examine the requirements of the Independent rather than the Corporate, business traveller. We saw in the last section that the Independent sub-segment of demand is growing relative to the Corporate one. With Independent business travellers, the fundamental needs remain exactly the same in terms of frequency, timings, safety, punctuality, seat accessibility and ticket flexibility. Price, though, assumes a greater significance than in the Corporate market. As we discussed, Independent business travellers feel that the ticket cost is coming out of their own pocket in the way that the Corporate traveller does not, with only the fact that the ticket cost is tax-deductible lessening its impact. The Independent traveller will therefore trade off cheaper ticket prices against product frills such as standards of seating comfort, free drinks, and in-flight meals. Interestingly, the willingness to do this makes the Independent business travellers' set of requirements one which can be well-satisfied by the "Cost Leader" airlines we shall be describing in Sections 4:2:1 and 4:2:2.

A further difference between Corporate and Independent travellers comes in their attitude to Frequent Flyer points. For the Corporate traveller, Frequent Flyer benefits are usually no more than an attractive perk of the job, providing opportunities for enjoyable free leisure flights. For the Independent traveller, on the other hand, free flights are much more commonly used for business travel purposes and provide a welcome opportunity to reduce expenditure on air tickets. One would therefore expect a greater focus still on obtaining mileage points.

A next important area where the requirements of the business traveller can differ is between the short-haul flights we have been considering and long-haul journeys. On long hauls, flight frequency and flight timings remain significant, but they take on a rather different meaning. On many long-haul routes, an adequate frequency is that an airline should give a daily flight. On denser routes, double daily flights may be appropriate, especially if they allow the airline to satisfy the need for both morning and evening arrivals at the destination. In few cases, though, will there be the need for the six or eight flights a day which may be required to provide adequate customer choice and to discourage entry by competitors on short routes.

On long-haul routes today, a significant consideration alongside frequency is often that there should be direct, non-stop flights available. As aircraft manufacturers have innovated with aircraft having longer and longer ranges, so it has become possible to fly a greater and greater number of the world's air routes on a non-stop basis. As airlines have, in turn, exploited this opportunity by introducing non-stop services, so passenger expectations have changed. Today, it is difficult or impossible for an airline operating a stopping service to compete for high-yielding traffic with one which flies a route non-stop.

As aircraft ranges have increased in recent years, so it has also been possible for aircraft manufacturers to introduce cost-effective, smaller long-haul aircraft. Planes such as the Boeing 777-300ER, 777-200LR, and Airbus A330 and A340 all come into this category, as will the B787 and Airbus A350 when they are introduced. Such aircraft allow direct, non-stop services to be introduced on a secondary city to secondary city basis.

These services are removing from passengers the need to connect to hubs and are proving very attractive.

Another important difference between short and long-haul markets is in the attitudes to Frequent Flyer points. On a long-haul route, substantial numbers of points are at stake. Indeed, for many programmes, taking a long-haul flight with a particular airline, at least in First or Business Class, earns sufficient mileage for a short-haul flight on that airline's network to be taken free-of-charge. Because of this, there is a greater likelihood of a passenger on long-haul choosing the airlines whose FFP they are supporting, even if this means travelling earlier or later than they would ideally like.

As one would expect, there are differences in the attitudes towards airport and in-flight service on long-haul routes compared with short-haul. Seating comfort on board, a separate cabin to allow for sleep and work, meal quality and in-flight entertainment all figure prominently in the business traveller's-long haul expectations. An especially telling point may be the attitude of different airlines' customer contact staff. On a long-haul flight, passengers will be exposed to uncaring attitudes for many hours, with the likelihood of lasting damage being done to the airline's reputation.

Airport service may, correspondingly, be of rather less importance. Long-haul passenger tend to check in earlier than those on short trips, presumably because, with lower frequencies, the penalty of missing a flight will be greater. The offer of a very late check-in time may therefore be less important. In contrast, though, lounge facilities will be of greater significance.

With the questions of seat accessibility and ticket flexibility, these are of lower importance on long-haul routes. A long-haul trip will often require at least three days out of someone's diary. Finding such a gap will normally take a great deal more pre-planning in comparison with a short-haul flight which can be carried out on a day-return basis. Therefore, the last-minute availability of a seat is of less importance on a long haul flight.

A last, interesting way in which the requirements of the business air traveller can be viewed concerns the needs of the connecting traveller. Some airlines make the mistake of assuming that everyone who flies on their short flights is a short-haul traveller. This is not so. Many of these passengers – upwards of 50% or more on very short routes – are connecting at hubs onto long-haul flights. They are therefore a long-haul passenger, on a short part of a long and tiring journey.

The requirements of the connecting passenger are, as one would expect, a mixture of those which prevail in the short-haul and long-haul point-to-point markets. The question of flight timings is an especially interesting one in this situation. The connecting passenger requires a high frequency of flights in exactly the same way as the point-to-point market does. The optimum flight timings, though, may be quite different. The point-to-point market has a requirement which peaks early and late in the business day. The connecting market, on the other hand, requires a spread of flights throughout the day, because long-haul flights depart from a hub at different times.

Punctuality assumes even greater importance for the connecting passenger. A delay of, say, an hour will certainly annoy the point-to-point traveller. It may not, though, destroy their entire itinerary. A delay of an hour, though, to a connecting passenger's flight into a hub may result in the long-haul flight being missed. This, in turn, may cause an actual delay of a day or more, on routes which are only served at a comparatively low frequency.

A further difficulty with the connecting passenger concerns the question of cabin comfort. It was argued earlier in this section that for the point-to-point short-haul traveller, cabin comfort was a relatively low priority, given that the person concerned will only be exposed to poor standards of comfort for a relatively short time. For connecting passengers, on the other hand, cabin comfort assumes great importance. This will be especially so on return flights when they may have spent many hours in a long-haul business class with very comfortable seating only to be faced, when exhausted, with completing their journey in a very cramped environment which airlines are basing on the needs of the point-to-point passenger.

Enough has been said in this section to demonstrate that, for all airlines, the business traveller is a demanding customer. There is no easy or cheap way of meeting the business traveller's needs, with carriers heavily dependent on the better yields obtainable from the business travel market to cover what will, inevitably, be higher production costs. Crucially, at the time of writing many airlines are still finding these better yields to be insufficient to ensure reasonable profitability.

2:3:4 *The Business Travel Market – Demographics and Psychographics*

In market segmentation exercises, the word "Demographics" is used to describe the physical and tangible characteristics of the members of the segment. "Psychographics" is the term used to describe the intangible attitudes, preferences and, perhaps, prejudices of the members of the segment.

In terms of the Demographics of the business travel market, the traditional stereotype of the business traveller of being male and middle-aged still largely holds true. In Europe for example, still over 80% of business travellers are men, whilst the average age of those who travel on business is in the early forties. In some markets, this situation is unlikely to change radically. In Japan, for example, the part played by women in business is still a limited one, whilst the "jobs for life" principle still followed by many Japanese firms means that people continue to be business travellers up to the official age of retirement. In Europe and North America, though, radical change is beginning to occur. Women are becoming much more important in business travel, with forecasts suggesting that by the year 2010 perhaps 25-30% of all business travel will be undertaken by women. At the same time, many firms are attempting to down-size and to reduce their labour costs. The expedient to do so is often to insist on early retirement. Where this is done, the age profile of the firm's employees will fall, with a corresponding effect on the average age of those who fly on business. The possible impact of these changes in the age and gender structure of the business travel market will be further discussed in Section 3:4.

Another important Demographic feature of the business travel market is that it is undertaken by relatively wealthy individuals, drawn from that small – often very small – proportion of a country's population where average income levels are high. The significance of this is that such people are fortunate to enjoy a lifestyle of comfort and affluence. They naturally expect the airline that they choose to reflect this.

A final, vital, Demographic characteristic of business travel is that it is a highly concentrated market. As has been previously mentioned, in all countries, it is undertaken by only a small number of individuals, each of whom on average travels a great deal. In the UK, the average number of air trips made per year by a member of the business travel community is more than ten.

A number of consequences stem from this high trip frequency. Business travellers become experts, familiar with the standards offered by different airlines, and able – and willing – to make comparisons between them. They also become extremely attractive to airlines, because the carrier which can establish and maintain their loyalty over a lifetime of business travel (which may extend for twenty years or more) will gain a large amount of revenue as a result. Finally, the fact that these so-called Lifetime Values are so high justifies substantial investment in the establishment and maintenance of databases, and in a Relationship Marketing strategy designed to encourage and reward loyalty. This, of course, leads us into the subject of Frequent Flyer Programmes which is fully covered in Section 9:3.

In terms of the Psychographics of business travellers, two characteristics stand out. Business travellers tend to have strong opinions, and are often prepared to communicate these opinions loudly and frequently, especially when they wish to complain about a particular airline. Carriers should not be surprised by this. Over a long period of time, almost all airlines have tried to encourage people to fly with them using advertising approaches which make unqualified promises of service excellence. If they do this, they should not be disappointed if people complain when the promises that have been made to them are not fulfilled.

A further important feature of the business traveller is that attitudes vary through time, with a pronounced Life Cycle effect often discernible. The young executive who is first promoted to a job which will require extensive international air travel will probably regard such travel as exciting, and will do all they can to ensure that as many trips as possible are undertaken. After a few years, though, attitudes can change dramatically. The person concerned realises that travel is not all it is made out to be, often consisting of long, tedious and boring journeys, repeated doses of jet lag, interrupted weekends, and often acute difficulties in maintaining social and personal relationships. From then onwards, instead of trying to find reasons why trips should take place, efforts may be focussed on avoiding at least some of these journeys. Of course, it is at this stage of the Life Cycle that the possibility of using video conferencing and other forms of electronic communication to replace air travel will be at its most appealing.

As an overall summary of the characteristics of the business travel market it is true to say that many airlines have regarded the business traveller as being at the core of their marketing efforts. This is not surprising, bearing in mind the fact that yields per passenger-kilometre have generally been much higher than those obtainable from the leisure segment. It would be a mistake, though, to assume that high yield is the same thing as a high profit contribution. It is true that typically airlines obtain a high proportion of their revenue from business travellers. However, such travellers also account for a high proportion of airlines' costs. Besides the intrinsically high costs of meeting the product needs described in Section 2:3:3, in recent years the business travel market has become a bloodbath of costly competition. There have been successive rounds of innovation which have raised the product specification offered to the business traveller to higher and higher levels, without, sometimes, corresponding opportunities to raise fares in order to maintain profits. This phenomenon will be further investigated in Section 5:2:1, which deals with the theory of the Product Life Cycle.

At the same time as the costs of meeting needs and competing effectively in the business travel market have risen, so the proportion of air trips made up by business travel has progressively fallen due to the rapid growth of the leisure segment of demand. As has already been noted, though demand forecasting in air transport remains extremely difficult, all forecasters agree that this is a trend which will continue, with, if anything, the relative growth rates of business and leisure travel diverging even further as business growth slows and that of leisure accelerates. If this is the case it will lend further weight to the vital conclusion that today no airline is likely to be successful if it ignores the leisure segment. As we shall see in the next section, ensuring profitable exploitation of leisure demand is equally challenging, but the nature of the challenge is different from that in business travel due to the strong contrasts in the characteristics of business and leisure demand.

2:3:5 The Leisure Segment of Demand

The differences between business and leisure air travel begin with the Demographics of leisure travel. Unlike the domination by men of business travel, leisure travel consists of an approximate balance between males and females. Indeed, with leisure travel by older people – say, those over 65 – in many markets female travellers dominate because of their longer life expectancy.

In terms of age profiles, the situation is also very different. Business travel tends to be concentrated in the middle-aged 35-55 age group. Leisure travel, on the other hand, encompasses all ages. Children are important in leisure travel, whilst young adults, benefiting from reasonable incomes and few commitments, usually have an especially high propensity to fly. A period of lower disposable income then often follows, due to the costs associated with family life. Once children have left home, though, disposable income often rises and may remain at high levels until quite late in life if pension arrangements are good enough.

Average personal incomes in leisure travel are often in strong contrast to those in the business travel market. The days when air travel was only enjoyed by wealthy members of a so-called "jet-set" are long gone. Today, rising disposable incomes and even more the falls in the real cost of air travel which have taken place have broadened the base of the leisure market enormously, taking it well beyond the relative few who make up the segment of business travel demand.

Besides differences in demographic characteristics, there are also substantial contrasts in leisure customer requirements.

In leisure air travel, the dominant requirement is for a cheap air fare, for obvious, but vitally important, reasons. Unlike in at least the Corporate sub-segment of business travel demand, people are spending their own money, not their company's. Their spending is not tax deductible in the way that benefits someone who is an Independent business air traveller.

Often, too, leisure air travel is undertaken in a family group. If it is, the amount of cash payable will be multiplied several times over, making access to a low fare an even more important requirement. Finally, in the leisure market airlines suffer through being at the back of the queue in terms of people being willing to spend more. When a family travels on holiday a choice often has to be made between spending on a luxurious but expensive flight, or on a good quality hotel and meals in decent restaurants at the destination. Not surprisingly, the focus of spending tends to be on the destination, because people will only be on the aircraft for a few hours whereas they will be at their holiday destination for perhaps two weeks.

The overall effect of these factors tending towards price sensitivity is a clear one: the leisure air travel market is and always will be low-yielding. Revenue earned per passenger-kilometre is usually low, whilst decisive marketing advantage will always accrue to an airline able, through low costs, to charge and sustain fares lower than those of its rivals.

Despite the fact that yields tend to be low, it should not be assumed – as is often done – that involvement in the leisure market will necessarily result in airlines losing money. The leisure market has a number of characteristics which allow efficient airlines to meet their customers' requirements much more cheaply than is possible in the business travel market, in ways which may allow the leisure market to be a substantial, and welcome, source of profits.

Foremost amongst these characteristics is the fact that leisure travellers do not generally require frequent, on-demand service. This allows airlines to use relatively large aircraft to serve the leisure market, and gain the benefits of the lower seat-kilometre costs available from such aircraft. They can also operate at very high load factors – often in excess of 90% - because no last minute availability of a seat needs to be offered. This will minimise the difference between available and revenue seat-kilometre costs.

A further benefit of serving the leisure market is that its peaking patterns and timing needs are generally quite different from those which characterise business travel. It is true that leisure demand often shows pronounced seasonal peaking which increases the cost of serving it because of the need to provide costly peak-time resources which are poorly utilized at off-peak periods. This, though, is offset by the fact that flights for the leisure traveller can be spread throughout the day and, often, the night as well because there is none of the marked peaking of demand during the early morning and after-business evening hours which characterises the business market, at least on short-haul routes. The result is that airlines serving leisure routes can achieve very high annual aircraft utilizations. The so-called charter airlines in Europe have often been able to achieve utilizations of 4,000 – 4,200 hours per year, in contrast to scheduled carriers carrying large numbers of business travellers which only usually reach 2,500 – 2,700 hours. Therefore their fixed costs of aircraft ownership or lease rentals are spread much more widely, with a correspondingly beneficial effect on unit costs.

A final, interesting, point of debate concerns the willingness of leisure passengers to sacrifice product features which, though desirable, can be traded off against the availability of cheaper fares. Some product features leisure travellers will clearly not sacrifice, safety being the clearest example. It is also clear that reasonable standards of punctuality performance are essential, at least if people are to make repeat flights with a particular airline. Amongst the product areas where people will, apparently, accept sacrifices are seating comfort, airport service and catering.

With seating comfort, many carriers serving the leisure market find that their passengers will accept lower standards in both seat pitch and seat width. This allows many more seats to be placed in a given aircraft type. For example, in an Airbus A330-200 series aircraft, a typical scheduled service seating configuration would be to equip the aircraft with 8-abreast seating at a 32 or 33 inch seat pitch. This allows just over 250 seats to be placed in the aircraft. A charter airline, on the other hand will use 9-abreast seating at a 28 or 29 inch seat pitch. This increases the number of seats to over 340, reducing seat-kilometre costs by more than 20%. (Concern over Deep Vein Thrombosis may reduce the ability of these airlines to use very low seat pitches in the future).

In the area of airport standards, leisure passengers will often accept longer minimum check-in times. This allows carriers to process a flight using a smaller number of check-in desks.

With in-flight service of meals and drinks, a considerable number of "no frills" airlines now offer no complementary meal or drinks service at all. Many others give a free meal – sometimes of a lower, cheaper, standard than that obtainable on a scheduled flight, but charge for drinks, at least for alcoholic ones. This provides a useful cost saving, and also turns drinks service into a revenue, rather than a cost item.

Overall, the leisure segment of demand now constitutes the dominant one in the air transport industry today and we shall make further reference to it throughout the book.

2:4 Segmentation of the Air Freight Market

For many years, air freight was the "poor relation" of the passenger business. Freight income made up only a small proportion of airline revenues, and it was consequently starved of both resources and management attention. It was often seen as no more than a by-product operation, to fill belly-hold space in passenger aircraft that would be available anyway.

Such attitudes are no longer acceptable. Some airlines are now able to specialise in carrying nothing but air freight, and to be highly profitable in doing so. For many others, freight now accounts for a highly significant and increasing proportion of profits. With the exception of 2001 – a poor year for air freight – average annual growth rates in the air freight business have exceeded those in the passenger markets by two or three percentage points, for many years. This is a trend which is likely to continue, making freight's contribution through time greater still.

At the same time as freight revenues have increased, competition in the air freight market has grown steadily, and it is becoming less and less likely that airlines treating freight purely as a by-product will be successful. Professional marketing is therefore a prime requirement and it is essential that we should give proper attention to the marketing of air freight, beginning with the question of the segmentation of the air freight market.

2:4:1 *Differences between the Air Passenger and Air Freight Markets*

In order to do so it is first of all necessary to examine the principal differences between the air passenger and air freight markets. It is true to say that only the fact that aircraft are used to carry the demand coming forward links these two markets. In all other respects they are totally different.

A first area of contrast is that air freight travels only one way on a route. It is true that some passengers are emigrating. They therefore settle in the country they are flying to and do not return. A small number are unfortunate enough to die at their destination. However, almost all passengers who fly out on a route will also return on it. Therefore over a year most passenger markets end up approximately directionally balanced, even though there may be directional problems associated with particular seasonal traffic flows. On the freight side, a directional balance will be no more than a happy co-incidence. Directional imbalances will be most marked on routes to and from countries which are mainly primary producers. These countries, especially if they are relatively wealthy, such as Australia, may import many items which are suitable air freight commodities. However, a lower proportion of their exports will come into this category, consisting as they do largely of primary products. It is certainly possible to correct such a situation in the long-term by offering attractive low prices, in the weaker direction. Poor yields are, though, then being substituted for low load factors.

A further problem in air freight marketing is that freight is extremely heterogeneous. Passengers are homogenous in the sense that they each occupy a seat. Freight, on the other hand, varies in every possible way. Consignment sizes vary from small packages and letters weighing less than a kilo up to consignments of 30,000 kilos or more. Consignment density and "stowability" will also vary. Some commodity types – books are a good example – are both dense and easy to stow. Others – for example bicycles – are of low density and have poor stowing characteristics. Unless airlines keep a very close check on their pricing policies, carrying such commodities can easily become unprofitable.

A final area of variation is in the handling and stowage conditions that different commodities require. For example, some are fragile and need especially careful handling. Others are of high value, such as banknotes. Therefore, special security arrangements will be needed. A further, and increasingly common requirement is for the refrigeration of physically perishable goods.

The most important difference between the air passenger and air freight businesses concerns the nature of the competition that airlines face in these different markets.

On the passenger side, airlines are very fortunate that, on long-haul routes, almost all passengers who travel do so using air transport. With air freight, the situation is very different. Air transport faces intense competition from surface on all routes. This competition is especially difficult to meet because it is based on low prices. It is true that in some cases air and surface rates are comparable due to the different charging methods that are adopted with respect to consignment density. Such situations are, though, rare. In almost all situations, air freight will be significantly more expensive than the surface transport alternative, if analysis is confined merely to a comparison of freight rates. These differentials can be extremely large, often reaching the level where air freight is ten times more expensive than surface transport.

The competitive situation makes the marketing of air freight an especial challenge. Airlines have to find and demonstrate arguments to justify the use of an apparently much more expensive mode of transport. These arguments form the basis for the segmentation of the air freight market.

2:4:2 Segmentation Variables – Air Freight Market

Market segmentation is as important in the air freight market as it is on the passenger side of the business. Only if markets are properly segmented can airlines find a basis for their product, price and promotional policies.

Using the criterion of the reasons why air freight rather than cheaper surface transport should be employed, a clear first segment of air freight demand is that consisting of Emergency traffic. Emergency situations occur when goods have to be moved by the fastest possible mode of transport, with the costs of achieving a fast transit a secondary consideration. In turn, Emergency situations may be divided into two types. An Operating Emergency occurs when a firm has to rectify an operational problem. For example, an oil company may find that one of its rigs has to cease production because of a breakdown. Every hour of lost production time will then have a substantial cost associated with it – a cost which can be minimised if air freight is used to ship the spare parts which are needed to enable production to resume. Another example of this type of emergency is an ironic one. Deep-sea shipping companies are air freight's biggest competitor on long-haul routes, yet these companies are major users of air freight. When a ship has to remain in port because spare parts are needed before a fault can be repaired, the shipping line operating it would be very foolish if it did not use air freight to move these parts. If it did not do so, the ship in question would be stranded in port for a much longer period than is necessary.

The second type of emergency situation is termed the Marketing Emergency. Such a situation occurs when a supplier is in danger of missing a deadline or one of its customers has expressed dissatisfaction with service levels. Then, again, air freight is the obvious choice, though the justification will be based on the maintenance of customer loyalty rather than cost reduction.

In terms of customer requirements, the Emergency segment has clear customer needs which airlines must satisfy if they are to compete in the market.

A first need is for the fastest possible door-to-door transit time. In order to be able to offer this to the shipper, an airline has first-of-all to give a high frequency of flights. Emergency situations do not give advanced notice of when they will occur. Therefore, a carriers with a high frequency will give the shipper the best likelihood that a flight will be available within a short time after the need to ship the goods has arisen.

Frequency, though important, will not be enough on its own. It must be accompanied by a capacity management policy ensuring that space will be available to shippers who need to book Emergency consignments shortly before a flight is due to depart. It is of no value to an Emergency shipper if an airline has a high flight frequency, but all its cargo space is fully booked days or weeks before flights are due to leave. Of course, once a booking has been offered it is important that freight should be flown on the flight on which it is booked and that it should benefit from safe and reliable ground handling.

A very important customer requirement in the Emergency traffic segment is that the selected airline should have the ability to track shipments at all times and be able to communicate accurate and timely information about the status of a consignment. It will also be important to provide a door-to-door collection and delivery service, so that the shipper feels that once a booking has been made, their troubles are over with someone taking responsibility for the entire transit.

The Emergency traffic segment presents airlines with both problems and opportunities. As will be discussed further in Section 5:6, meeting the needs of customers in this market presents a very demanding and costly task. It does, though, often provide them with very high yields, a factor which makes it an area where airlines compete intensively.

The Emergency segment of demand has always been, and remains, highly important to an airline's air freight business. It would be an unambitious airline, though, which sought to do no more than exploit the Emergency market. This would confine air freight to a comparatively small role in the international logistics industry. To avoid this, it has been necessary to develop arguments as to why air freight should be the preferred option for the Routine as well as the Emergency shipper.

An area where it has been possible to do this constitutes the second major segment of air freight demand. It concerns traffic which is Routine-Perishable in nature – Routine as opposed to Emergency, and Perishable because the goods in question only remain saleable for a limited period of time.

Perishability in international logistics occurs for two reasons in particular. Physical Perishability describes situations where goods physically deteriorate. Cut flowers and soft fruits are good examples of this. With them, the argument for using air freight is clear. Producers of, say, cut flowers can always attempt to sell them in local markets close to where they have been grown. If they do so, prices will be low due to market saturation. A more profitable option might be to send the flowers to distant markets where they will have scarcity value. Then, though, air freight will have to be used in order to ensure that the goods reach the market in a saleable condition.

Economic Perishability is the second type. It occurs not when goods are prone to deteriorate physically, but when the Life Cycle within which they remain saleable is a short one. Newspapers have been such a commodity. Other examples include fashion clothing, children's toys, and pop music CDs. These goods can be sold in large quantities and at good prices if they reach the market when demand for them is still rising rapidly. Air freight often provides the only realistic way of ensuring that this happens, at least in long-haul markets.

In terms of customer requirements, the Routine Perishable market differs in some respects from the Emergency segment. At least for Physically Perishable goods, it may be possible to forecast further ahead when the need for shipment will occur. This is because many commodities which come into this category have a pronounced seasonal pattern to their production. In turn, though, this gives problems to airlines attempting to exploit the market. Flows of Emergency shipments occur throughout the year, even though it will not be possible to forecast exactly when a particular emergency will occur. Perishable traffic, on the other hand, may only be offered seasonally. Airlines may therefore have surplus capacity at the off-season.

A further problem of Perishable traffic is that it tends to result in routes having marked directional imbalances. As we have already noted, this is because an area noted for production of perishable foodstuffs may not be one which attracts significant in-bound flows of commodities suitable for air freighting.

Besides the problems associated with capacity being available at the right time and place, Perishable freight often needs special handling. It may be fragile in nature, or need refrigeration, both of which force up airlines' handling costs. It will certainly require airlines to achieve high standards of regularity and punctuality, and to ensure that freight should always be carried on the flight on which it is booked. There also needs to be a comprehensive monitoring and control service in place, to make sure that if a mistake is made it is discovered in time for it to be rectified.

The question of the importance of price to the Routine Perishable shipper is an interesting one. High service quality will clearly be necessary if goods are to reach the market in time and in the right condition. Airlines may thus reasonably hope that customers will be prepared to pay more if this is the only way to obtain the required service, and that the market will be a relatively high yielding one. In practice, this may be true, but only in the short term. The economics of exporting Perishable goods by air are based on the premium price being obtained in the distant market being sufficient to cover the extra costs of air freight while still leaving a profit. The more air freight rates rise, the more such profits are threatened, leading to the possibility that the trade may have to be abandoned. Therefore, the lack of price-sensitivity in the Routine Perishable market should not be exaggerated.

Both the Emergency and the Routine Perishable markets are important in the modern air freight industry. Despite this, though, by far the greater part of the goods which move in international logistics cannot be placed in either of these categories. They must therefore be described as being Routine and Non-perishable. The air freight industry must be able to demonstrate the value of its services for shippers of this type of freight. If it cannot do so, then the industry will never achieve its full potential.

The industry's problem in developing this market is that shippers of Routine, Non-perishable freight usually have an alternative. They can use a surface transport instead of air freight and they will normally pay a substantially lower freight rate if they do. The task of air freight marketing is to demonstrate that if air freight is used rather than apparently-cheaper surface transport, significant advantages will accrue, advantages which will often be sufficient to outweigh the freight rate differential. Isolating these advantages and communicating them effectively has proved to be a major challenge. The customer must be persuaded to compare all the costs associated with using surface transport with the benefits of employing air freight.

In three relevant areas, a direct comparison will be possible:

1. Packaging costs will generally be lower when air freight is employed. Air freight often allows less packaging to be used, due to its more favourable environment for carriage. Because of this, costs will be reduced both because of the lower cost of packaging materials, and because this cheaper packaging will result in a saving on freight costs due to each consignment having a lighter weight.

2. Insurance costs will usually show a substantial saving in favour of air freight – again, a reflection of air transport's superior environment for carriage, and the shorter times for which goods are at risk.

3. Air freight should bring important cash flow advantages. Most international trade is carried out on a credit basis. The consignor usually allows the consignee a period of time before they have to pay for goods that they have received. The credit period does not begin when the goods are dispatched but rather when the consignee takes delivery of them. If surface transport is used, the transit time on a long-haul route may be several weeks. During this time, the consignor will be incurring interest charges, because they will have invested money in producing the goods but will not

have been paid for them. If, on the other hand, they dispatch the goods by air freight they should be received by the consignor in a matter of two or three days. If they are, cash flow will be several weeks faster and interest payments will be correspondingly reduced.

Defining the remaining advantages of air freight over slower surface transport is more difficult, because they depend on a comparison of different Logistics philosophies.

If a manufacturing company wishes to minimise its transport costs it will, of course, use surface transport modes. Surface transport will therefore be used to bring raw materials to its production points and then to move finished products to customers. Though low transport costs will be the result of such a policy, significant adverse consequences will also ensue. With regard to the supply of raw materials and components to production points, it will be necessary to hold large stocks. This is because surface transport cannot generally provide the high frequency of deliveries which air freight can, and which allow supply to take place under so-called "Just-in-Time" (JIT) principles. With surface transport usage, stocks of components must be held in sufficient quantities to allow production to continue in the intervals between deliveries.

With delivery of finished products to customers, again the use of surface transport will require extra stock to be held. For many products, demand will rise from time-to-time, in a way which cannot be precisely forecast. For example, demand for some products is weather-related, so precise demand forecasts cannot be prepared for them more than a few days in advance. If demand for a particular product does rise, it is extremely important that firms should be able to keep their wholesalers and retailers supplied with stock to sell. If they fail to do so, they risk losing the loyalty of these marketing intermediaries.

Ensuring continuity of supply given random and unforecastable fluctuations in demand requires companies to hold substantial amounts of so-called "Safety Stock". In order to distribute such stock, again surface transport can be used, and direct transport costs will be minimised as a result. However, many other logistics costs will be increased substantially.

To illustrate this point, let us take the case of a European firm exporting electrical consumer goods to a distant market such as Australia. If surface transport is used by the exporting company, it will be necessary to invest in substantial local warehousing. This is because, with surface transport transit times of perhaps six to eight weeks, customers will not be prepared to wait for goods to be dispatched and sent once an order has been placed. Instead, they will expect their goods to be available within a few days of ordering them. In the case of the Australian market, full coverage will probably require a warehouse in the East – perhaps in Sydney – and one in Western Australia.

The consequences of the need to invest in local warehousing will be substantial and costly. As stated earlier, stock will have to be held which is not only sufficient to cover day-to-day demand. There must also be considerable Safety Stock to prevent the collapse of service levels should a random and unpredictable increase in demand occur. This will mean investment in warehousing to hold the stock, and also in the capital costs of stockholding. For some items, there may be a risk too of deterioration or obsolescence, with falling demand meaning that the value of the stock falls while it is held.

Besides the cost of local warehousing, the need to invest in such warehousing results in a significant loss of marketing flexibility because it makes entering a new market a very slow process. Before the firm can begin selling in the new market, it will need to obtain warehousing capacity and ship out substantial quantities of stock so that adequate service levels can be offered to early customers. This will take time. As a result, when selling does finally begin, the market conditions which prompted the decision to enter may have changed. The initiative may then fail, with the result that the stock has to be withdrawn – a costly process in itself – and the new warehouses sold off.

The use of air freight avoids all of these problems. Instead of large amounts of field stockholding being necessary, local stocks can be reduced or eliminated. Most stock – especially Safety Stock – can be held at one central location – in the case we are looking at, in Europe. This means that aggregate amounts of Safety Stock can be reduced, because it becomes a reasonable proposition that demand fluctuations in the different market that the firm serves will to some extent to cancel one another out.

If local stockholding can be reduced or eliminated, marketing flexibility will also be greatly increased. Markets can be entered quickly when demand is strong. Should demand falter at a later stage, withdrawal from the market will be equally easy. Therefore, the company concerned can market its product on a world-wide basis, focusing attention always only on those countries where demand for the product is buoyant.

Though there can be no doubt about the power of the arguments relating to the use of air freight for Routine Non-perishable Traffic, it is important that those concerned with the marketing of air freight should also understand the limitations of the concept.

Foremost amongst these is that the air freight solution can be portrayed as a high risk one. It is based on firms keeping field inventories to a minimum, and supplying customers from central stockholding points after orders have been placed. If something happens to prevent the warehouses at these central points from working effectively – a strike, for example – or if there are delays in transport from them due to such factors as industrial action or bad weather, service to customers will be immediately and seriously affected. Such problems are, of course, avoided to a degree if local inventories are held. It is therefore important that any logistics system based on low inventories and fast transportation should be a reliable one.

With the question of the use of air freight to minimize packaging and insurance costs, this argument only has weight if there are large differences between the so-called Environment for Carriage available from surface and from air transport. These differences are steadily being reduced through time as surface operators adopt the principles of containerisation and roll-on/roll-off. These allow goods to be sealed and protected from the beginning of a journey to its end, with a much reduced risk of damage.

Overall, this chapter should have made clear that a sound understanding of the marketplace is an absolutely essential building-block in the successful application of marketing principles to the airline industry. Without this building-block in place, all other aspects of marketing become pointless. It is therefore impossible to exaggerate its importance.

SUCCESSFUL AIRLINES ......

✈   Are those which take a broad view of the markets in which they participate, avoiding the mistake of "Marketing Myopia".

✈   Acknowledge the distinction between "Consumers" and "Customers", and concentrate their marketing efforts on "Customers".

✈   Segment their markets properly, avoiding the mistakes of both over and under-segmentation, and build a sound understanding of the needs of their customers in each of the major market segments.

3   The Marketing Environment

Chapter Two has established that an airline's marketing policies must clearly reflect the structure of its market. This Chapter deals with the other, crucial foundation: the Marketing Environment, or the background against which marketing strategies are developed.

The Chapter has three aims. Firstly, to look at the theoretical basis for the study of the Marketing Environment, applicable to any industry. Secondly, to analyse those factors from this environment which need to be considered by airlines. Thirdly, to discuss the specific impact which each of these issues should have on properly thought-out marketing policies.

3:1 The Theoretical Basis – PESTE Analysis

The literature on marketing provides one, particularly useful, model for the study of a firm's Marketing Environment. This model proposes that the relevant factors should be divided into the categories of *P*olitical, *E*conomic, *S*ocial, *T*echnological and *E*nvironmental.[8]

It should, of course, be born in mind that the categories are not mutually exclusive, and that it might be appropriate to discuss a particular issue under more than one heading. However, the model is still a powerful one, especially in the airline industry. Airlines cannot develop sound marketing policies independently of a range of political decisions. The industry has always been, and remains, intensely political. The fortunes of the world economy will also have a substantial impact, with marketing policies needing to ensure that favourable economic circumstances are exploited, and unfavourable ones countered. Social issues such as those relating to demographic trends will also be significant, especially at the present time. Technology provides both exciting opportunities and difficult challenges today, whilst problems associated with the environment may threaten the whole future of the industry.

---

[8] Sometimes, legal issues are added, to make the acronym PESTEL. In the aviation industry, most quasi-legal issues are better dealt with under the Political heading.

We will now explore in turn each component of the PESTE model in an airline context.

3:2 PESTE Analysis – Political Factors

3:2:1 Terrorism Fears/Political Instability

The years at the beginning of the new millennium have turned out to be some of the most difficult that the aviation industry has ever faced

As we will see in Section 3:3, the industry was undoubtedly heading for challenging times in any case, but there can be no doubt that the events of September 11 2001 caused an unprecedented crisis. Armed hijackers seized four aircraft in the USA, and used these to attack the World Trade Centre in New York and the Pentagon in Washington. Many thousands of people lost their lives.

The effects on the airline industry were catastrophic. For four days, the airspace over the eastern USA was closed, resulting in direct losses to airlines (for which, admittedly, they were mostly compensated). More seriously still, the fear of further terrorism attacks caused a steep decline in demand, both in the USA, on international routes to and from the US, and to a lesser extent elsewhere.

The time since the September 11 attacks has seen little improvement. The American government, aided and abetted by several others, notably Britain, has mounted a so-called 'War on Terror'. This has resulted in seemingly disastrous interventions in Afghanistan and Iraq, and in strong support for Israel in that country's response to what have been seen there as terrorist attacks. This support was at its strongest in the summer of 2006 when many thousands of civilians were killed as war flared up again in the Middle East.

Assessing the longer-term impact of the fear of terrorist attack on the size of the aviation market is very difficult. It is, of course, important to keep personal political opinions out of any analysis as far as possible, but it is this writer's opinion that little was learnt as a result of the September 11 attack, or from those which have followed it. A terrorism threat can only be addressed by seeking to understand and address the underlying grievances which caused the terrorist movement to arise in the first place. The "War on Terror" has simply increased resentment, and has provided the best imaginable recruitment propaganda for those seeking to foment extremism. It has certainly worsened and not solved the problem.

This leads to a thoroughly depressing conclusion. We may have to accept that periodic attacks by the Al-Quaeda organisation, and others that will grow up around it will be a long-term feature. Worse still, the aviation industry will probably be peculiarly vulnerable to these attacks because many airlines are strongly identified with a particular nation. It is also a very high profile activity, meeting the terrorist group's desire for widespread publicity for their cause.

Perhaps the best that can be hoped for is that September 11 2001 will turn out to be an extreme case. New security measures may make the task of terrorist groups a harder one, so they may target aircraft less frequently. However, the summer of 2006 provided a stark reminder of the problem with the apparent uncovering of a plot to blow up a large number of transatlantic aircraft. Weeks of chaos then ensued as new security measures were applied.

We can now reach an overall, difficult conclusion for Airline Marketing. In a very real sense, airlines do not have control over the size of the markets they have available to them because wars and terrorist attacks -- or the threat of them -- can have a sudden, strong and negative impact. Given the growing instabilities in the world political scene, it is unlikely that this fact will change significantly in the industry's favour. The industry will therefore have to accept a growing burden of security costs. It will also have to understand that demand to travel from those who do not have to do so will be held back as a result of some people at least feeling that the airport hassles associated with air journeys just render the whole exercise too difficult and time-consuming to be worthwhile.

3:2:2 Deregulation and "Open Skies"

Throughout its history, the airline industry has been constrained by decisions made by politicians and governments. Governments have controlled where airlines can fly, and aspects of their product planning and pricing policies.[9] They have also had a major involvement in the industry through the ownership of airlines. Finally, political decisions have often affected the extent, nature and geographical distribution of demand. We will consider each of these aspects in turn.

Almost from the inception of the commercial aviation industry, governments regulated airlines. They have always had a role in regulating airline safety standards, a role that remains important and, in principle, relatively non-controversial. Government regulation, though, traditionally went very much further than this. For many years, and in almost all aviation markets, governments controlled airlines' route entry and capacity

---

[9] For a history of government involvement in the industry, see A P Dobson, "Flying in the Face of Competition", Ashgate Books 1995.

and frequency decisions. Very commonly too, and astonishingly by today's standards, governments intervened to stop airlines engaging in price competition.

In recent years, substantial regulatory reform has taken place, giving carriers the challenge and the opportunity of responding to a freer economic environment.[10] We need to look now at exactly what has happened, and the issues which change poses for marketing policies.

In describing the system of economic regulation of the airline industry, a fundamental distinction has always been between the regulation of domestic services, which are solely under the control of one government, and international services, which require the agreement of at least two.

Until relatively recently, almost all domestic travel markets were highly regulated. An extreme case was the USA. Despite the United States supposedly being the home of free market thinking, airlines' commercial freedom was constrained by what now seems a very burdensome system of economic regulation. Between the passing of the Federal Aviation Act in 1938 and the Airline Deregulation Act in 1978, carriers could only enter new routes by going through a cumbersome and extremely slow bureaucratic procedure. A similar process was needed before service could be withdrawn from an unprofitable route. At the same time, regulatory approval was needed before fares could be raised or lowered. The actions of the regulatory body concerned – the Civil Aeronautics Board – ensured that where two airlines competed on a particular route, their fares were generally identical.

Another extreme case of a highly regulated domestic market was that of Australia. For many years prior to 1990, Australia pursued a so-called "Two Airline" policy. Under this, only two airlines were granted access to Australian domestic trunk routes, Ansett Airlines and Trans-Australia Airlines (later renamed Australian Airlines). Even though these carriers were supposed to compete with each other, in practice almost all the areas where competition might have occurred were regulated, including the question of price levels.

The situation with regard to domestic aviation markets today has undergone substantial change, though in one very important sense we are still (with one exception) very far from true "Deregulation".

In terms of regulatory change, the USA led the way with the passing of the Airline Deregulation Act in 1978. This allowed for much greater freedom for airlines to enter new markets and to exploit them free of

---

[10] See: G Williams, "The Airline Industry and the Impact of Deregulation", Ashgate Books 1994 and the same authors', "Airline Competition – Deregulation's Mixed Legacy", Ashgate Books 2002. The subject is also well-covered in R Doganis "The Airline Business" 2nd Edition. Routledge 2006.

constraints on capacity or pricing policies. However, one important regulatory limitation remained – that of ownership. Still today, it is necessary for 75% of the voting shares of an airline to be owned by United States citizens before that airline is allowed to fly domestic routes in the USA. This means that foreign-owned carriers are still denied the much-prized "Cabotage" rights to fly internal routes in the US.

Regulatory reform in the United States has been followed by a similar pattern in many other countries. Today, many countries would claim to have "deregulated" their domestic aviation industries. Still, though, rules on ownership provide a highly significant constraint on the extent of airlines' true commercial freedom-of-action. At the time of writing, Australia and New Zealand provide rare exceptions to the general rule that foreign-owned airlines are not allowed domestic rights. One of the major players in the Australian domestic market, Virgin Blue, was set up by a non-Australian – the British businessman Sir Richard Branson.

With domestic aviation, the European Union now provides an interesting case study. By a progressive process of liberalisation (completed in 1997), the countries of the European Union effectively set up a Single Aviation Market which freed airlines to make their own decisions regarding market access, capacity and fares. In turn, this has led to airlines such as Easyjet and Ryanair establishing a true pan-European presence, which includes many 'Cabotage' domestic operations in other countries.

The situation regarding regulatory change in international markets has inevitably been more fragmented and diffuse, but even here, the state-of-play is significantly different from the one which prevailed only a few years ago. On the horizon, we can now see the possibility for radical regulatory reform, which could transform the structure of the entire international airline industry.

For more than fifty years, international aviation has generally been very tightly regulated indeed. Early attempts were made by the USA to establish a liberal environment at the so-called Chicago Convention of 1944. These were decisively rejected and in the ensuing compromise, the world fell back on a system of controls through intergovernmental Air Services Agreements. Working on a bilateral basis between pairs of governments, these Agreements limited market entry, controlled capacity and interfered (though now, to a much reduced extent) with airlines' freedom-of-action over pricing policy. As a particularly severe constraint, the Air Services Agreement system limited the exercising of traffic rights to airlines that were owned and controlled by nationals of the two countries which signed a particular agreement. This made nationality of ownership as important a constraint in international aviation as it was in domestic services.

Given the all-embracing nature of the Air Services Agreement system, it is almost impossible to exaggerate its significance as a constraint on airlines' marketing and commercial policies. In almost every other industry, it is possible for firms to trade on a global basis. They widely do so, by entering foreign markets and by engaging in cross-border merger and take-over activity. Airlines are denied such freedom. Their route networks (the cornerstone, of course, of the product they offer) largely begin and end in the countries in which they are based. Any wider global presence can only be secured by the unsatisfactory and second-best solution of signing alliance agreements with other airlines (See Section 4:2:3).

Few would disagree with the general proposition that the regulatory system facing airlines today is many years out-of-date and in need of root-and-branch reform. So far, though, efforts at reform have produced results which are fragmented, piecemeal and unsatisfactory.

As we have seen, the "deregulation" of many domestic markets has left the constraint that foreign-owned airlines are prevented from competing in almost all domestic markets. We will not have true free trade in aviation services until these constraints are removed.

In international aviation, the United States began a process, which it presumably regarded as a reforming one, during the 1990s. Beginning with the government of the Netherlands in 1993, the US has signed with foreign governments what it has described as "Open Skies" agreements. At the time of writing, more than seventy of these agreements are in place. They do change the regulatory landscape significantly in the markets where they apply, in that they allow each side to designate as many airlines as they choose. These airlines are then able to fly to any number of gateway points with no limitations on their capacity and pricing decisions. They do not, however, break free of the question of ownership and control. Entry is still confined to airlines which are substantially owned and effectively controlled by nationals of the two countries. Nor do they concede access to internal routes by foreign airlines. Therefore, to describe these agreements as representing "Open Skies" is nonsense.

At the time of the preparation of this new edition (the autumn of 2006), we may have seen the development that, by a long tortuous process, may finally bring about the long overdue process of true regulatory reform. In November 2002, the European Court published a complex, but historic, judgement. In it, the Court ruled that individual member governments of the European Union offended against EU law if they signed Air Services Agreements with other countries which limited the use of traffic rights purely to airlines which are owned and controlled by their citizens. Such rights had potentially to be available to all EU airlines. If they were not, such discrimination was an infringement of the competition articles in the Treaty of Rome.

Following this judgement, it is just possible to conceive of the present system continuing, with individual EU governments removing the now-illegal discrimination in favour of their own airlines. This would almost certainly prove to be impractical. A more likely outcome is a completely new system, whereby the European Commission will take over the negotiation of external aviation relationships with other countries, on behalf of all EU member states.

In a first move in this direction, in 2003, the Commission asked for, and was granted, authority by the EU Council of Ministers for authority to begin the negotiation of a new Air Services Agreement with the United States, an agreement to cover all air routes between the EU and the USA. From the outset, it was clear that this was a highly significant development. Not only is the market between the EU and the USA a very large one in itself, but any agreement there will be watched closely by other significant aviation nations. It is very likely that the principles established by it will be widely followed in other markets too.

Exactly as one would expect, negotiations regarding such an agreement were long and tortuous. From their beginnings in 2003, it was not until November 2005 that a tentative agreement was reached.

The new agreement (if it is endorsed by the EU council of Ministers, which at the time of writing is by no means certain), is a significant, but not complete, step in the direction of true regulatory reform. It does not provide any significant access for EU airlines into the US domestic market, where the attitude of the United States remains stubbornly protectionist. It does, though, provide complete freedom in terms of international Beyond and Fifth Freedom rights, something which is likely to be especially valuable to US cargo operators such as Federal Express and UPS as it will allow them to set up networks inside the European Union. In addition, all restrictions on international designations will disappear, with each side free to nominate as many airlines as they wish to serve each international city pair. There will also be no restrictions at all on the number of gateways points on which service can be provided. Perhaps the most significant reform of all, though, will be in the changes which the new agreement brings to the question of airline ownership and control. The American side have accepted that there will in future be only a rule which says that airlines exercising traffic rights from the European side need only be controlled by European Union citizens. This will mean that for the first time, so-called 'Seventh Freedom' services will be possible, with, for example, an airline owned in Germany being able to fly a route from, say, Manchester to New York. The 'European Union' ownership clause, if, as seems likely, it is adopted more widely, will also allow cross-border merger and takeover activity amongst EU airlines to become a reality. This will then see Air France and KLM cement their already close relationship and may lead to other mergers – one between British Airways and Iberia looks as if it may be the first of these.

The question of the future regulatory scene which will face airlines, is still an uncertain one. It is clear, though, that the trend will be towards an increasingly liberally-regulated or deregulated marketplace. This will in turn require a response in terms of the business and marketing strategies that carriers pursue.

3:2:3 Marketing Policies for a Deregulated Environment

In many aviation markets today, airline managers are facing the challenge of change and adaptation. They were formerly able to enjoy the reassurance of regulated conditions, with limited competition and only a very slow pace of change. Today, economic liberalisation is giving new opportunities which must be exploited if success is to be achieved. It also brings new threats which must be countered effectively.

Given the nature of the challenges facing airlines, it would be naïve in the extreme to assume that these do not impinge on the marketing area of their activities. They most certainly do, with sound marketing policies for a liberal market being quite different for those which might be appropriate for a regulated one.

Above all other considerations, a deregulated situation requires that systems should be in place to enable decisions to be made quickly. New opportunities to enter routes will arise at short notice, and may disappear equally rapidly if another airline is able to react faster and take advantage of the potential first. Equally, it may be necessary to change the specification of the product quickly, if a competitor offers customers better value-for-money. Also, pricing policies will have to be adjusted frequently, with changes often being required on a daily basis or sometimes even more frequently than this. As we will discuss further in Section 6:1:2, a feature of regulated markets used to be that all airlines charged the same fares, and fares only changed infrequently, following an often tortuous set of procedures which needed to be undertaken in order to gain regulatory approval.

The situation in today's liberal markets is in strong contrast. The combination of the ending of regulatory controls on pricing and the advent of the ability to disseminate fares information instantaneously, through the spread of so-called Global Distribution Systems and over the Internet, (see Section 7:3) has meant that millions of fares now often change overnight at times of active price competition. No airline can now afford the luxury of a slow response at such a time.

If airlines are to make decisions quickly, certain conditions must be met. Decision-making processes must be streamlined, with flat organisational structures and, often, a degree of autocracy prevailing in the most successful carriers. Where possible, too, decision-making must be decentralised to the managers of small profit centres, where people will have a better understanding of the detail of local market conditions.

Up-to-date and accurate commercial information will also be needed. In a regulated market, little damage will result from a situation where details of financial performance do not emerge for months, or where such information is of dubious accuracy. In a deregulated market, it almost certainly will. Inaccurate or late information will cause opportunities to be lost and problems to go undetected until it is too late. Not only must information be accurate and timely, it must also incorporate a forecasting capability which allows the state of forward bookings to be monitored and corrective action to be taken where appropriate.

Besides having the flexibility to ensure that opportunities are exploited as they become available, marketing policies for a deregulated environment need to have a defensive component, to enable airlines to fend off potential competitors. Many carriers, particularly in the U.S.A., based their strategies for success under deregulation on the so-called 'hub-and-spoke' principle, whereby airlines set out to dominate as high a percentage as possible of the destinations served and the frequencies provided at a particular airport. High frequencies in themselves gave a protection against the attacks of competitors because they minimised the gaps available for rivals to mount an attractive schedule.

The question of the control of distribution channels is of prime importance in defining marketing policies for deregulated markets. The methods whereby control of wholesalers and retailers can be established are considered in Section 7:2. The firms which are successful in establishing and maintaining control will be those that achieve 'Superprofits', over and above the minimum levels necessary to keep them in business. The instability characteristic of a deregulated market will give many opportunities for the control of distribution channels to be contested and to change. Any airline seeking to be successful must maintain control of distribution.

In a liberal market, carriers also often have to change the basis of their advertising and promotional policies. Regulation means a slow pace of change. Promotional activities can therefore be focussed on long-term aims through corporate and brand-building advertising. In deregulated markets, however, a greater proportion of promotional spending must deal with tactical messages such as those announcing entry into new markets, changes to the product specification or fare reductions. It follows, therefore, that a different set of skills may be needed by the advertising agencies that airlines employ.

A final, but crucial, requirement for marketing success in a deregulated environment is a low cost base. As we have seen, competition under deregulation focuses to a large degree on the question of price. Low cost airlines can base their marketing strategy on the offer of attractive lower fares, and still be profitable. A high cost airline which matches or undercuts these fares will lose money as a result.

The need for low costs poses a special problem for mature, long-established airlines. These carriers had the luxury of developing their operations under regulated conditions, where price competition was either muted or absent. They therefore did not have a great deal of incentive to control their costs effectively. The result has often been that such airlines have carried an inappropriately high cost structure into the era of deregulation. Some have then successfully carried out the necessary changes. Others have taken on the appearance of dinosaurs, earning for themselves the unflattering title of "Legacy" airlines.

3:2:4 Privatisation

Historically, state ownership has always been important in the airline industry. Many governments regarded the existence of a national airline as an essential requirement for nationhood. Besides questions of prestige, an airline might bring benefits as a back-up for national defence capability, in employment, and in balance-of-payments and tourism income.

During the early years of the industry's development, it was often felt that public, rather than private ownership was appropriate. Public ownership allowed governments to insist that their airlines sometimes worked to a wider set of objectives than those associated with the attempt to achieve profits. These wider objectives were designed to ensure that the airline maximised the contribution it made to the advancement of the national interest. It also gave governments the reassurance that their airline would survive, despite the threat of competition from better-established rivals.

Until the mid-1980s, almost all the world's major airlines, with the exception of those from the USA, were state-owned. The Brazilian carrier VARIG and the Korean-based Korean Air were at the time rare exceptions to this general rule.

Since then, the situation has been transformed. The fashion in political and economic thinking has turned full circle, with the emphasis now on the benefits in efficiency likely to result from private rather than public ownership. At the same time, the airline industry has matured. It has become impossible to argue that a global industry such as aviation, now operating on a massive scale, is an infant one in need of the protection of widespread state ownership.

Many formerly state-owned airlines have now been fully privatised. British Airways, Lufthansa, Qantas, and Air Canada are examples. Many others have seen the proportion of their ownership which is state-controlled substantially reduced, to the point where only a minority of the shareholding is government-owned. Air France illustrates this latter change.

For marketing managers, airline privatisation brought both problems and opportunities. For those who worked for a carrier that had undergone privatisation, their task in many senses became an easier one. They needed to have only one objective, to assist their airline in achieving satisfactory profits for shareholders. Often, under government ownership, objectives to cover costs had in practice to be combined with such requirements as ensuring that domestic air fares remained low or that services were maintained on socially-necessary but financially unprofitable routes. Also, beyond argument, privatisation was often accompanied by substantial improvements in efficiency and the elimination of the bureaucracy stemming from political interference in decision-making.

For other airlines, privatisation has changed the competitive scene substantially. Competition with a state-owned airline has always been a different proposition from that with a privately-owned carrier. State ownership has always been a virtual guarantee that an airline would not be allowed to go out of business, with state subsidy being used to cover operating losses. State-owned airlines may, therefore, have been able to take greater risks in defining their business and marketing strategies, a factor which made it more difficult for privately-owned firms to compete effectively. At the same time, though, state ownership brought real problems. Government airlines often suffered from a poor image associated with subsidy and bureaucracy. They also sometimes had poorly-motivated staff, making it very difficult for them to implement changes designed to improve service to customers.

It should be noted that in the crisis that faced the industry after the terrorist attacks of September 2001, we saw the first reversal of the trend towards airline privatisation. Two airlines, Air New Zealand and Malaysia Airlines, were effectively taken back into public ownership. In both cases, it is highly likely that the airlines would have collapsed if they had not been renationalised.

This illustrates a very important feature of the relationship between governments and airlines – that many governments seem committed to maintaining an airline as a "national carrier", and that they will use taxpayers' money where necessary to ensure its survival.

3:2:5 *"State Aid"*

The question of political support given by governments to airlines in the form of subsidies has been a controversial one in recent years.

Following on from the events of September 11 2001, many governments paid compensation to airlines for the losses incurred during the four days after the attacks when United States airspace was closed to all commercial airliners. However, the US government's attitude regarding aid to the American airline industry went very much further than this. Large direct subsidies were paid to all the US major carriers. These were intended to cover not only the immediate losses due to the airspace closure, but also to compensate airlines for the effect of the severe and long-lasting traffic downturn which followed. As a further piece of state aid, US carriers were offered government loan guarantees of significant value. These allowed struggling US carriers to borrow money at much lower interest rates than they would otherwise have had to pay.

Given the nature of these arrangements, there have been accusations made in Europe that they have given US carriers a freedom to behave in a cavalier commercial manner. These accusations have become much stronger as successive US carriers - notably United, Northwest and Delta - have used the protection afforded to them under the Chapter 11 provisions of the US bankruptcy code to substantially restructure their operations.

In Europe, State Aid questions have a much longer history. When agreement was reached to set up the Single Aviation Market of the European Union in 1993, it was argued – entirely correctly – that government subsidies were incompatible with the concept. It was impossible for competition to take place on a level playing field when some government-owned airlines were receiving subsidies whilst privately-owned carriers were not.

Since then, the European Commission has attempted to police State Aid. In doing so, it has followed two principles. Firstly, that when State Aid is given to an airline, it should be possible to argue that the government that pays it is conforming to the so-called Economic Market Investor Principle. This means that a credible argument must be made that the government is offering additional equity capital, which a rational private investor would also have been willing to provide. In practice, the interpretation of this Principle has been that any fresh government investment in an airline must be matched by private sector investors on a 50/50 basis.

The other requirement in State Aid cases has been that additional state funding must not just be there to fund continuing operating losses. It must provide a breathing space for an airline so carry out much needed reforms so that it will be able to survive in the future without additional government support. The history of Air France illustrates this idea. The airline received very large injections of new equity from the French government during the middle 1990s on a "one last time" basis. Within a few years, the airline had emerged much stronger, and in recent times has been one of the more successful of the older-established European carriers.

The market downturn in 2000 and 2001 and especially the after-effects of September 11 2001 brought the question of state aid for European Union carriers into sharp focus once again. In the aftermath of September 11, one European Union airline – Sabena of Belgium – collapsed because it was not possible under the rules for the Belgian government bail it out to the extent that would have been necessary to ensure its survival. Several others – notably Alitalia and Olympic – may find such survival difficult or impossible given the combination of economic circumstances and increasing competition which confronts them, and the likely non-availability of further support from taxpayers. (Though up to the time of writing the Italian government has shown itself to adept at finding methods which seem to circumvent the strict interpretation of the rules regarding State Aid).

3:2:6 Airport Slot Allocation

The schedule of an airline will clearly be one of the cornerstones of the product that it offers. In turn, it will be the question – clearly a political one – of the ways in which airport slots are allocated which will decide on the schedule which can be planned, both in terms of the frequency of flights and their timings. Not surprisingly, slot allocation is a complex and controversial question.

The difficulties begin with the apparently straightforward question of agreeing what a 'Slot' actually is. It can be defined as "a pre-agreed time for a takeoff or landing to take place at a particular airport". This hides, though, a number of complexities. For a landing slot to have meaning, four different capacity constraints must be satisfied. Firstly, there must be capacity in the air traffic control system, to allow the aircraft to approach the destination airport. Runway space must be available, to permit the aircraft to land. There must be parking and apron space, so that turnaround procedures can be completed. Finally, terminal-processing capacity must be sufficient to enable passengers to pass through immigration and collect their bags in reasonable time.

Of course, for a departure, these capacity requirements must be satisfied in reverse. Also, for a departure slot to have meaning, the relevant arrival slot at the destination airport must be obtained, as must a further departure slot for the return journey once turnaround procedures have been completed.

All this brings us to the question of the methods by which slots at airports should be awarded. It might be assumed that because airport operators are responsible for the provision of the terminal, apron and runway capacity which allow slots to exist, they will also be able to decide which airlines use these slots. This is not the case. The only role of the airport operator is to define (in liaison, of course, with the relevant air traffic control authority), the maximum capacity of a given airport. In this way, the number of slots available for distribution is decided.

Once it has been, the actual distribution of slots is carried out by a "Slot Co-ordinator". In the past, it has been traditional for the largest airline operator at a particular airport to carry out the Slot Co-ordination function. This is still the situation that prevails at many airports today. It is, though, a totally unsatisfactory one. It reflects a past time when slot allocation was essentially an administrative function, where there were generally plenty of slots available in relation to the demand for them. Today, the situation could not be more different, with many airports suffering from a shortage of peak-time slots and some, such as London's Heathrow and Orly Airport at Paris virtually full throughout the day. The pressure is on for slot co-ordination to be carried out by more neutral and transparent bodies, and at many European airports in particular, multi-owned airline consortia have been set up to co-ordinate airport slot allocation. In the UK, the company that does this is called Airport Co-ordination Ltd. It is a consortium jointly owned by 13 airlines.

Whatever system is adopted to allocate slots, the fundamental principle which is followed is not in doubt. Slot Co-ordinators are required to award slots under what is known as the "Grandfather Rights" concept. The year is divided into two traffic seasons, "Summer" (in the Northern Hemisphere) from 1 April to 31 October, and "Winter" from 1 November to 31 March. Slots are awarded separately for each season, reflecting different demand patterns.

Once an airline has been awarded a slot, the requirement is that it should be used on a minimum of 80% of the occasions when it is available during the season in question (omitting such times as when it was not available due to weather-related disruption etc) Provided that they do, they will automatically receive the same slot for the next equivalent season. As reputable airlines normally have no difficulty in meeting the 'Eighty Per Cent Rule', it effectively means that slots are awarded to them on an "in perpetuity" basis. It should also be noted that no payment is made following an initial award of a slot. When they are awarded by the Co-ordinator, they are given away free of charge.

The Grandfather Rights principle has many defenders, particularly, as one would expect, from the long-established airlines who benefit most from it. These carriers argue that airlines have a particularly long planning cycle. Once an order for new aircraft has been placed with a manufacturer, two or three years may elapse before the aircraft are actually delivered (at least at times of buoyant demand). Once they have been, modern aircraft may stay in an airline's fleet for a period of 25 – 28 years. It would be impossible, (so the argument goes), to justify risking shareholders' funds on such costly assets, if it was feared that the most crucial requirement of all needed to allow the asset to produce profits for shareholders – the airport slot – could be taken away before the completion of the full operating life of the aircraft.

Though such arguments are powerful ones, they do not, of course, represent the only point-of-view. It is possible to say that Grandfather Rights represent a major distortion of competition in the industry. This is because they give opportunity to long-established (and perhaps undeserving) airlines, and deny such opportunity for fresh, innovative carriers, who might be able to deliver substantially better value-for-money to consumers.

Because of these criticisms, a great deal of thought has been given to the question of alternatives to Grandfather Rights in recent years, particularly by the European Commission. There is, however, little progress to report. An initial Directive on Slot Allocation was adopted by the European Union as long ago as 1993. This was intended to cover a three-year period, to allow time for a final Directive to be agreed. At the time of writing in the summer of 2006, no new agreement is in place and attempts continue to secure a consensus on what it should contain.

There has, however, been one major recent development in slot allocation principles. In 1999, the High Court in the UK gave what has turned out to be a historic judgement about the question of the buying and selling of slots. It has always been possible for airlines to exchange slots on which they hold Grandfather Rights. The 1999 judgement confirmed the legality of taking this one step further, by an airline with a less attractive slot time being able to pay money to another carrier with a more attractive time, to encourage the second airline to undertake a slot exchange.

This judgement has been taken by airlines, within the European Union at least, as a green light to openly buy and sell slots (there can be little doubt that such activity had been taking place on an under-the-counter basis for several years beforehand).

The open buying and selling of slots is being accompanied by yet more controversy. It amounts to the shareholders of airlines benefiting from the sale of assets which they certainly do not own, and which were originally given to them for nothing. It could be argued that airport operators should gain from the sale of the slots that they have created. More convincingly, it could be said that airport slots should be regarded as a national asset. If they are, the proceeds of any sales could go to the government and through this, hopefully, benefit everyone. This is exactly the policy that many governments have adopted in selling off third generation mobile phone licenses.

The other risk with the buying and selling of slots is that a greater and greater proportion of the available slots will come into the hands of a small number of large airlines. We already have a situation today where at many hub airports, a high proportion of the slots are held by just one airline. This is the case, for example, with Lufthansa at Frankfurt, Air France at Paris, KLM at Schiphol and (admittedly, to a lesser degree) British Airways at London Heathrow. It is highly likely that, in the future, these airlines will be able to outbid smaller, new entrant carriers for any attractive slots that do become available. If they can, they will be able to further cement their dominance of these major airports, to the detriment of competition and the consumer interest.

Despite these concerns, the movement towards a Slot Allocation system based on the buying and selling of slots, and with airlines pocketing the money from the slots whose Grandfather Rights they sell, now appears unstoppable. In marketing terms, this will undoubtedly give opportunities for airlines to grow their route networks and increase frequencies which would not have been possible had the old, purely administrative system for Slot Allocation continued. However, these possibilities will be bought at a high price.

3:3 PESTE Analysis – Economic Factors

If there is a clear and important interplay between the world of politics and airline marketing, there is a relationship of equal or even greater importance with economic change and development.

3:3:1 Economic Growth and the Trade Cycle

The demand for air travel is characterised by a very high income elasticity.

Therefore, as the world economy grows, so the demand for air travel can be expected to increase too.

This continuing growth gives both enormous opportunities and great challenges to the airline industry. The opportunities come with the chance to exploit a growing market, something which would be the envy of managers in many other industries. The challenges are to accommodate the growth through suitable infrastructure development and without unacceptable environmental consequences, (we return to this question in Section 3:6), and to exploit the demand whilst achieving the stable profits which the industry has so often found elusive.

Besides a clear pattern of growth, growth rates are uneven through time. Just as one would expect, air transport industry growth rates are tied closely to those in the world economy. If growth in the economy is rapid in a particular year, so is the increase in air travel demand. Periods of economic stagnation see a significant slowing of the rate of increase in demand.

This pattern has immense strategic and marketing implications. It is not sufficient for carriers to implement policies which allow for profits during prosperous periods if these same policies result in heavy losses or bankruptcy during the downturns in the trade cycle.

Unfortunately, the industry's past record is not encouraging. Too often, periods of buoyant demand have seen airlines over-invest in additional capacity. They have also commonly given too much emphasis to the First and Business Class market, a market which tends to be very strong when times are good, but which suffers particularly severely during a downturn when firms require their executives to travel in Economy or Coach Class to save money. A final problem often is that in upswing periods, insufficient attention may be given to the control of costs, particularly labour costs. Pay increases that can easily be financed in good times may turn out to be a crippling burden when, in a downturn, yields are forced lower because of an overcapacity situation, to levels which do not allow costs to be covered.

The upswing of the middle and late 1990s illustrated all these shortcomings. Large orders for new aircraft were placed with the aircraft manufacturers, with many of these planes actually delivered in 2000 and 2001 when market conditions were much less favourable. Labour costs were allowed to rise, with some airlines – notably so United Airlines – leading the industry by granting unprecedented increases in wages and salaries to a number of their work groups. Finally, some airlines changed their entire business strategy during 1997 and 1998, to focus very heavily on the booming market of so-called "Premium" travellers in First and Business Class. The flaws in this strategy became very obvious in 2000 and 2001, when recession ended the growth in this market and made its exceptional growth rates in the late 1990s look very much an aberration, far above any sustainable long-term level. British Airways is an example of an airline that appeared to make this serious strategic mistake.

After September 11 2001, there was a tendency to blame the severe financial problems experienced by many airlines on the New York and Washington terrorist attacks and their aftermath. The impact of these was undoubtedly severe but they merely substantially increased the extent of serious problems which already existed. These problems could be traced to the fundamental error of failure to take adequate account of the trade cycle in setting business and marketing strategies. One could perhaps feel easier about them if there was any sign that difficult lessons had really been learnt. However, the resumption of strong growth in the world economy in 2004 was followed by both Boeing and Airbus having runaway record years in 2005 in terms of the numbers of orders for new aircraft that they received. To some degree, these orders were explicable by the fact that both firms had launched new aircraft projects (the B787 and Airbus A350). Nonetheless, one was left with an awkward feeling that history may be repeating itself. This feeling was reinforced by announcements from several airlines that they were intending to increase the number of 'Premium' (First Class and Business Class) seats in their aircraft, and by the launch of a number of 'All Business Class' start-up airlines targeting exactly this segment of the market.

3:4 PESTE Analysis – Social Factors

Trends in social factors will have widespread consequences for airline marketing – indeed, in some senses, this is the most significant component of the PESTE analysis model as far as marketing policies are concerned.

3:4:1 The Ageing Population

In Europe and North America in particular, the average age of the population is now increasing steadily. Fewer babies are being born, and improving medical provision is allowing more people to live longer. (It should be born in mind, of course, that an ageing population is not yet at all characteristic of many countries in the Third World).

The ageing of the population has some obvious, and some more subtle, implications for Airline Marketing. Clearly, the product that airlines offer will have to evolve, with more provision being made for disabled passengers and those needing help at airports, and medical care services will have to be improved. There may also be opportunities for more specialist brands to be launched, reflecting the needs and aspirations of older people. In the UK, the SAGA brand is already a good example of this.

In terms of subtler changes, the travel industry may have to adjust its promotional policies. In advertising to promote leisure air travel, the industry still overwhelmingly focuses on images of fun-loving younger people. The very fact that such advertising implies that a resort area is likely to be popular with such people is likely to discourage many older people from visiting it.

3:4:2 Changing Family Structures

Just as the population is ageing, so in many Western societies, the traditional structure of the family is also changing. The rise in divorce and an increase in the number of one-parent families are well-established trends, which the travel industry has so far done little to accommodate. Still, holiday brochures overwhelmingly feature on their front cover a "traditional" family of a man, woman and two children. (Without exception, the children are always a girl and a boy). The truth is that there are very important sub-segments to the market, such as those consisting of singles, gays or one-parent families, whose particular requirements from a holiday should be reflected in promotional and product-planning policies.

3:4:3 Changing Tastes and Fashions in Holidays

Partly, but not exclusively, reflecting trends in age and family structures, the modern travel industry is having to adjust to a marked broadening in the range of requirements of vacationers. When holidays by air first began to become popular in the 1960s, most people wanted little more than a relaxing opportunity to sunbathe by a hotel swimming pool. This is not so today. Better education, growing experience of air travel and fears about the health risks of excessive exposure to the sun are all meaning that to a greater and greater degree, holidays must reflect a lifestyle based on individual choice. People expect to be able to pursue their hobbies while they are on holiday, with winter sports, golf, history and trekking holidays all now well-established sub-segments of the market. They expect to be able to take holidays of different lengths in order to fit in with their available vacation time. They also require opportunities to visit new and interesting, often long-haul, destinations.

Overall, the trend in the holiday market is often, and appropriately, described as "de-packaging the package". People increasingly want a holiday experience which reflects their own individual requirements. They do not expect to be treated as part of a herd of cattle, to suit the convenience of the travel provider. We shall return to this theme in Chapter 9, dealing with the subject of Relationship Marketing.

3:4:4 *The Uncertain, Deregulated Labour Market*

Of all the social trends occurring in the 1990s and into the new century, none was of greater significance than the transformation which took place in the world of work. Before this, in many societies most jobs were seen as being secure for a lifetime. Today, the situation could not be more different. Redundancy and job seeking occurs – perhaps several times – in many people's careers. At the same time, pressures at work are far greater as people battle to keep their jobs, often with far less administrative support than they once had.

The changes in the job market have consequences for Airline Marketing policies, in both the business travel and leisure travel segments of demand. In business travel, the fact that people are under greater and greater time pressure means that issues such as the ability to make a day-return trip, rather than take two days, is becoming more important still in short-haul markets. On long-haul routes, for many executives, it is now a thing of the past to expect to take a day off on arrival to recover from tiredness and jet lag. They are now expected to arrive at a destination in the morning and step off the plane into a busy day of meetings. This places a premium on their ability to sleep on board the aircraft, and on facilities for them to shower and freshen up on arrival.

More subtly, greater work pressures are changing business travellers' perception of the role of air travel. Many now see a flight as a haven of peace in an otherwise over-demanding schedule. Issues such as in-flight entertainment are thus assuming greater importance.

For those who lose their jobs, or who perhaps voluntarily decide to take a greater control of their lives, self-employment or working for a small, independent firm are often options to be considered. In the UK, the proportion of the working population which is self-employed has more than doubled since 1980.

As was discussed in Section 2:3:2, self-employment has lead to the emergence of the so-called "Independent" sub-segment of business travel demand, where customer requirements are different from those of the corporate traveller.

The deregulated labour market also has implications for the leisure air travel market. In the 1970s some extravagant, and, with the benefit of hindsight, absurd promises were made that by the 1990s a utopia would have arrived. This was expected to result from the growing automation of industrial processes through the micro-chip, cheap computing power and developments in robotics. The outcome was supposed to be a dream world of increases in leisure time through a shorter day, a shorter working week, longer holidays and earlier, more prosperous retirement.

Now that the 1990s have passed, we can certainly see that the micro-chip has had a dramatic impact, but not in the way these forecasters had predicted. There has certainly been a growth in the aggregate amount of so-called leisure, but this has been unevenly and unsatisfactorily distributed.

For people who have a job, their working lives are now busier than ever before. Working hours are often longer rather than shorter, with working at home commonplace in the evenings and at weekends. Also, whilst holiday entitlements have often risen in principle, many people are reluctant to take their full allowances because of a "presenteeism" philosophy of trying to seem indispensable to the firms that employ them.

At the opposite end of the spectrum, we see people who have large amounts of leisure, but who lack the financial resources to be able to enjoy it to the full. The young unemployed are a clear example of this, as are those who, often despite their qualifications and experience can only find poorly-paid, often part-time, work. Particular issues surround those who have retired from work. In the past it has been fashionable to regard the trend towards earlier and earlier retirement as a very positive one from the point-of-view of the airline industry. It would, we were told, result in a larger and larger group of people with the time, money and inclination to travel by air a great deal. Present trends are sometimes leading to people retiring earlier (often reluctantly, because they cannot find work), and living longer. The result is that a bigger and bigger retired population is relying on a smaller and smaller working one to maintain the value of their post-retirement incomes. Sooner, it seems inevitable that the trends will reverse, with living standards for the retired population starting to fall and people having to retire later rather than earlier. If they do, this will be disappointing rather than encouraging news for air travel demand.

3:4:5 The Female Business Traveller

Until now, the business travel market has been overwhelmingly dominated by men. In the USA, still more than 70% of business travellers are men, whilst in many European countries the percentage is near to 80%.

Today, the role of women in the workplace is changing dramatically in many cultures. It is now usual for women to return to work after childbirth, and to expect to build a career alongside their male colleagues. Because of this, it is certain that the proportion of business travellers who are female will steadily increase. It is expected that a third of the North American business travel market will consist of women by the year 2010.

This is a change which is forcing airlines to re-think a number of components of their marketing. The most obvious areas are in aspects of product detail. For example, most airlines give toilet bags to their First Class and Business Class travellers. Only recently has it become common for separate bags made up for female as well as male travellers to be offered. Also, it has been shown that women are more likely than their male colleagues to check in hold baggage, and less likely to carry large amounts of baggage on board on aircraft. Increasingly numbers of female travellers suggest changes in the demands made on baggage handling systems.

More fundamental are issues associated with airline advertising. In the past, much airline advertising has had sexist undertones, with pictures of beautiful young girls ministering to the needs of men. In many cultures, such approaches will be less and less acceptable in the future.

3:5 PESTE Analysis – Technological Factors

3:5:1 Video-conferencing

Section 2:1 looked at the possible effect of video-conferencing on the demand for air transport. The conclusion reached was that it posed a significant long-term threat. It is unlikely to lead to a decline in the demand for air travel. It will, though, result in future growth rates for business air travel growth which are disappointing by historic standards. Business travel growth will tend to be below the growth rates for GDP rather then above them as has commonly been the case in the past. It will also increase the airline industry's already very substantial vulnerability to downturns caused by trade cycle fluctuations or wars and terrorist activity.

Given the nature of the threat, a progressively greater response will be required from airlines in their marketing policies. In terms of the product which is offered to the customer, greater and greater emphasis will be required on convenience to enable business travellers to fly with the minimum impact on their working time, allowing the benefits of a face-to-face meeting to outweigh the time required to travel to such a meeting. Issues such as a high frequency of direct flights with the right timings to allow for day return trips will become still more important.

Airline advertising approaches will also have to change. In the past, most airlines have simply concentrated on promoting the merits of their services against those of rival airlines. In the future, they will have to accept telecommunications companies as being amongst their most formidable competitors. Advertising will be needed which promotes the benefits of face-to-face meetings as opposed to conducting these meetings via video-conferencing or conference calls.

3:5:2 The Internet

The mid-1990s saw the beginnings of airline interest in the marketing possibilities opened up by the Internet. Since then, the growth in its use has been astonishing. At the time of writing almost all major airlines have websites which they use for promotional purposes, with these sites supplying timetable and product information and also often having an interactive component which allows people make bookings. Sites are also being used as a way of increasing the attractiveness of an airline's Frequent Flyer Programme by permitting programme members to check on their mileage accounts and also by giving the availability of flights with the surplus seats available for redemption. In the field of air freight, firms such as UPS and Federal Express allow customers to track their consignments as they move through the system using the Internet.

The greatest debates about the future role of the Internet in airline marketing concern its use as a distribution channel. Full attention will be given to the many controversies which currently affect the subject of distribution in the airline industry in Chapter Seven. For the moment though, it is worthwhile to note two issues in particular. Firstly, in recent years airlines have become more and more concerned about the amount of commission they have been paying to travel agents and other marketing intermediaries. Secondly, they have had to face the escalating costs associated with the booking fees charged to them by Global Distribution Systems (GDS) companies. Anger at these fees has been especially marked amongst airlines which do not have a shareholding in a GDS (or which have sold the shareholdings that they once had), and which do not therefore have the prospect of dividends on their investment compensating them for the booking fees they pay.

The Internet is now alleviating both these problems. If individuals or firms make bookings direct with the airlines through a personal computer, substantial reductions in both commissions and booking fees are now possible.

3:5:3 *Surface Transport Investment*

Today, many countries have seen a resurgence of interest in surface – especially railway – transport investment. Railway operators have largely won the battle to be viewed as the most environmentally acceptable form of transport. Investment is taking place in both new railways to provide fast city-centre to city-centre links, and in the tunnels to enable railway operators to extend their networks. This investment was especially notable in Europe, where during the 1990s as a whole, investment in railway infrastructure was more than three times as great as that in infrastructure for the aviation industry. This is now a trend which is spreading to other countries, notably so to China, with plans now in place for the construction of a high speed rail link between Beijing and Shanghai.

Surface transport investment provides both problems and opportunities in Airline Marketing. The problems come from the fact that, beyond question, railway investment can have a significant negative impact on the demand for air transport. The evidence from countries such as France, where new railway developments compete alongside formerly busy air routes, is that once rail can offer a city-centre to city-centre journey time of less than three hours, the effect on the air market is a substantial one. Worse still, the traffic that is lost tends to be the so-called point-to-point demand. Those who have been using air services to connect onto a long-haul flight at a hub continue to do so. As discussed in Chapter 6, the pricing practices adopted by airlines almost always mean that point-to-point traffic gives a much higher yield in terms of revenue per kilometre than connecting traffic does. The effect on the profitability of an airline's short-haul routes can therefore be even greater than the decline in demand would suggest.

The opportunities provided by surface transport come with the options which it opens up for airlines to co-operate rather than compete, with railway operators. As will be discussed in the next section, the future growth of the airline industry is now being jeopardised by growing shortages of runway and passenger handling capacity. Also, for most airlines, short-haul services tend only to be marginally profitable. The high incidence of fixed costs such as landing fees has always made it difficult to achieve satisfactory profits on these routes. On the other hand, many long-haul routes tend to be more profitable.

The opportunity of surface transport developments is for airlines to lobby for improved public transport links to major airports. If these come about, they will enable train operators to deliver long-haul passengers to airline hubs, thus freeing valuable airport slots for further long-haul services.

3:6 PESTE Analysis – Environmental Factors

It might be thought that environmental factors would pose broadly strategic questions for airlines, rather than ones with a specific marketing component to them. However, in a number of areas, environmental issues will affect both the nature and characteristics of airline demand. They will therefore have an impact on marketing activities. Also, environmental issues pose an increasingly important issue in terms of airline promotional policies.

3:6:1 Climate Change and Global Warming

Concerns about global warming are very controversial, with arguments continuing about the likely future extent of the current warming trend and its consequences. It does, though, now seem to be certain that in the future, average temperatures will continue to rise, with warmer climatic zones being progressively displaced towards the Poles.

If this happens, the effect on both the extent and patterns of air transport demand could be a substantial one. For example, in the UK, the summer of 2003 was exceptionally hot and settled. The months of May through to September were characterised by almost unbroken hot, sunny weather. Though welcome no doubt to many British people, this turned out to be unhelpful to the air transport industry. In 2003, demand for air-based packaged holidays to Mediterranean resorts fell by nearly 10% It was widely assumed that this was because many people who had left booking their holiday to the last minute (a trend increasingly characteristic of the market generally) decided to take a holiday at home instead of enduring the sometimes doubtful pleasures of a long flight by air.

Global warming may affect other, well-established markets. It now seems clear that one of the effects of rising sea surface temperatures is that tropical storms and hurricanes are becoming more frequent, especially in the Caribbean and the southern United States. This is already making people reluctant to visit these areas during the August to November period, when the hurricane risk is at its peak.

In the longer term, of course, climate change will begin to adversely affect rates of economic growth, with a marked effect in turn on the airline industry's growth and profitability.

Important though such issues are, they do not represent the greatest challenge posed to the airline industry by climate change. The battle for hearts and minds will be a far more important and challenging one. There can be no doubt that air transport is significant in terms of the quantities of emissions of carbon dioxide and the other Greenhouse Gases increasingly being blamed for the warming of the world's climate, and that it is becoming more so. Worse still, the industry is being accused of depositing these emissions high in the atmosphere, where normal meteorological process do not affect them. Their effect on the warming trend may therefore be even greater than the absolute quantity of emissions would suggest.

Not surprisingly, the industry is coming under more and more pressure from environmental groups. These groups point to the frivolous nature of much leisure air travel, and are arguing that people with a genuine concern for the future of the planet should curtail or, better still stop, the amount of air travel which they undertake. With air freight, they advocate that more food should be produced and consumed locally, to avoid the waste inherent in moving foodstuffs around world by air freight.

Winning this battle will not be easy for the world's airlines, nor should it be. At the time of writing, some airlines seem to think that it can be won by a public relations initiative, whereby airlines' role in the problem of climate change can be covered up or denied. Such policies are fundamentally in error, and will come back to haunt those attempting to implement them as the problems associated with climate change worsen.

Instead, the industry will have to demonstrate that it is investing as heavily as it can in the technological developments which will increase the fuel efficiency of aircraft. Every effort will have to be made to improve operating procedures, so that present wasteful burning of fuel because of indirect flight paths is eliminated. Research must being undertaken - and paid for - into alternative and cleaner fuels. Carbon Trading initiatives will also have to be enthusiastically embraced, even if they raise costs significantly.

When, and only when, such initiatives are in place does it become a legitimate role of Airline Marketing to put across a positive message on behalf of the industry. It will also then be sensible to place emphasis on the role that air transport can play in allowing poor countries to develop though tourism and through the export opportunities which air freight can provide.

3:6:2 *Shortages of Infrastructure Capacity*

Over the last three decades, the airline industry has made important progress in one area in ensuring that its activities become more acceptable, in that aircraft have become very much quieter during this time. Unfortunately, the result has not been an easing of the environmental pressures opposing aviation infrastructure investment. The lobby groups responsible for them have become still more vociferous and better organised.

The result of these pressures is that it is not possible, and probably never will be possible, for the aviation industry's infrastructure to be expanded at the pace, and in the locations, that airlines would ideally like. This may mean that some of the industry's growth plans cannot be brought to fruition. In many other cases, compromise and adaptation will be necessary in the face of growing shortages of infrastructure capacity.

3:6:3 "Tourism Saturation"

All tourism-receiving areas have a finite capacity. This may be due to factors such as the limited amount of accommodation that can be provided. More importantly, though, over-exploitation of a tourism area can mean that the reasons for people going there are often destroyed. These reasons may include prestige and status through the exclusivity of a resort, natural resources such as wildlife, or un-crowded access to sites of historic importance.

The so-called "Tourism Saturation" effects of over-exploitation may not affect the total amount of air travel undertaken for leisure purposes. They will, though, have a substantial effect on its geographical distribution, and provide a challenge for all managers of resort areas.

Overall, the marketing environment of the airline industry provides a crucial background against which airline managers must develop their marketing policies. These policies clearly cannot be formulated in isolation. Instead, they must reflect the background factors illustrated by the PESTE analysis model.

SUCCESSFUL AIRLINES ……

+ Are those which conduct a thorough and on-going review of their marketing environment, and take full account of this in preparing their marketing policies.

4 Airline Business and Marketing Strategies

We have now completed our coverage of the essential building blocks in the application of marketing principles in the airline industry. No airline can hope to apply these principles successfully without the understanding of customer needs and the marketing environment which Chapters Two and Three have provided. Once such understanding is in place, the next requirement is the challenging one of the formulation of a sound strategy.

In one sense, the news here is good in that in today's airline industry there is no single, unique strategy which must be followed if success is to be achieved. There is a range of possible strategies available. What *is* essential, though, is that one strategy must be selected from this range. It must then be implemented well, and continued on a long-term basis. The aim of this Chapter is to set out and discuss the types of possible strategy, and their advantages and disadvantages.

4:1 Porter's "Five Forces" and their Application to the Airline Industry

In understanding these strategic options, a useful start can be made by looking at some of the ideas of the Harvard Professor, Michael Porter.[11] Porter states that in different industries, strategic issues are coloured by the interplay of the Five Forces of the rivalry amongst existing firms, substitution, new entry, the power of customers and the power of suppliers. We will examine each of these in turn.

4:1:1 Rivalry amongst Existing Firms

Porter argues that, in many industries, often little of the true competition and the drive for change comes from long-established firms. These long established firms often resemble one another in terms of the strengths which they have, and in their problems and weaknesses. They therefore

---

[11] First set out in his book "Competitive Strategy", published in 1980 by Free Press.

can only identify benefit from aggressive competition at the margins of their activities.

In the air transport industry, the policies of the long-established airlines of Europe illustrate this point only too well, especially in their short-haul markets. As we saw in the last Chapter, there are now no regulatory reasons which preclude intense competition between them. Since April 1997, the airlines of the European Union have competed in a Single Aviation Market where there have been only the very loosest controls over entry, capacity and fares. This represented a major change when it took place compared with the tight regulation characteristic of the previous system. Yet, one would hardly know that this change had occurred if one had merely looked at the reaction of the old-established airlines to it. They continued to fly mostly similar aircraft (usually drawn from the Airbus A320 family), and placed in them identical or near-identical seating configurations. Frequencies and timings remained very similar, with few airlines prepared to allow their competitors a frequency advantage. The on-board products were mostly comparable, and did not change. Finally and most tellingly, until recently these airlines pursued an almost identical pricing policy. Very high fares were charged for seats in Business Class, and for access to Economy tickets which allowed full flexibility. Lower fares were also on offer, but these had had tight restrictions attached to them, restrictions which were mainly designed to prevent business travellers using them.

The result of such policies was that they made it much easier than it should have been for new Low Cost Carriers to grow in Europe, and for them to have a dramatic effect on the economics of the long-established firms. British Airways, for example, lost nearly £250 million on its intra-European network during its 2002/2003 financial year.

4:1:2 Substitution

Porter argues that disturbance to the competitive equilibrium set up by the long-established firms can come from two possible sources, the first of these being that of Substitution. Substitution occurs when firms in another industry find a new and better way of meeting the same customer needs as are being targeted by the existing players.

There are a number of Substitution issues affecting airlines at the present time. Of these, potentially the most serious is the effect of electronic methods of communication on the market for business air travel. As we discussed in Section 3:5:1, videoconferencing, teleconferencing and email all have the potential to mean that business travellers will travel less, and still satisfy their needs for effective communication. At the time of writing, there are worrying signs that this is exactly what is happening, an effect which is likely to increase still further during future downturns similar to the one which followed the September 11 attacks in 2001.

Surface transport, especially by rail, also raises important substitution issues. As we have seen, unlike airlines, railways can provide city-centre to city-centre travel, and have been shown to severely impact the business travel market once these city-centre to city-centre journey times can be brought down below three hours.

The air freight industry is also being affected by Substitution issues. Email is substantially reducing the market for the movement of urgent documents by air. Also, newspapers do not provide the lucrative air freight commodity they once did. They still lose their value completely soon after they have been published. The problem is, though, that today media publishers are increasingly reaching their readers through the Internet, or by setting up satellite printing stations which enable newspapers to be printed simultaneously in a large number of different markets. They therefore no longer have to make use of air freight.

4:1:3 New Entry

The second of the forces which may disturb the competitive equilibrium amongst the existing players is that of new entry.

In some industries, new entry is difficult or impossible. In others, it is commonplace. In the modern aviation industry, the latter is very much the case, especially in short-haul, point-to-point markets. This is because of the many possible so-called "Barriers to Entry", most have become low or are now non-existent.

A first possible barrier to entry may result from regulatory limitations. It is true that, as we saw in Section 3:2, there are still regulatory barriers to entry in many international markets, and airlines are constrained in their market entry policies by out-of-date and anachronistic limitations on ownership and control. However, it is now the case that many of the world's largest domestic markets, such as those of the United States and the European Union, now operate without any significant entry controls, apart from those applying to so-called Cabotage Rights.[12]

In others cases, *resources* may act as a Barrier-to-Entry. If vital resources are unavailable or very costly, entry will clearly be constrained.

In the aviation industry, airport slots provide a classic resource barrier to entry. As long as airport slots continue to be awarded under the Grandfather Rights principle which we discussed in Section 3:2:6, it will be

---

[12] See the "Glossary of Aviation Terms" at the end of the book.

very difficult for new entrants to gain access to attractively-timed slots at congested hub airports.

Significant though slot constraints already are, with a likely worsening of them in the future, radical strategies are possible which find a way round them. In particular, Europe's vibrant low-fares scene - the subject of Section 4:2:2 and 4:2:3 - has largely grown free of airport slot constraints because of the willingness of the airlines to use uncongested airports, sometimes located a considerable distance from the cities they are designed to serve.

Slot constraints may provide some comfort to existing airlines in Europe today, but they can derive little more from the remaining possible resource constraints to entry. Especially during downturns such as the one experienced during 2002 and 2003, resources to underpin entry can actually be remarkably cheap and plentiful.

This is certainly the case with the question of the aircraft fleet that will be needed by a new entrant airline. In a recessionary period, aircraft manufacturers will be prepared to strike very attractive deals for the white-tailed aircraft which sometimes result from order cancellations. Also, there will be large numbers of parked aircraft – many of them owned by leasing companies – where the owners will offer extremely low lease rates in order to get their idle aircraft flying once again.

Staff resources – especially of pilots and mechanics – will also be important. Again, in a recessionary period many trained people will unfortunately lose their jobs, and may well be prepared to take new ones at relatively low salaries and wages in order to obtain employment.

As a final, and, at first sight, odd feature of resource constraints on entry in the aviation industry, it will always be possible for a new entrant to buy the support services, such as maintenance and ground handling that it needs. Many airlines have built subsidiary businesses offering such services and they will be prepared to sell these to a new entrant, even if the new entrant's business plan involves competing with them. They will reason that if they do not meet the need, this will not stop the new entrant. Instead, the required services will be bought elsewhere, denying the first airline some useful revenue.

Several more issues need to be covered in assessing the nature of barriers to entry in the airline business. Some industries are characterised by marked *Economies of Scale*, where lower unit costs can be obtained by large-scale producers. Many heavy industries such as steel, chemicals and car-making are like this. In them, existing firms are likely to be protected against entry because they will have been able to achieve a scale of production which is unlikely to be available to a new entrant.

In the airline business, there are some aspects where existing players are protected against new entry by scale economies. In particular, hubbing operations where short-haul passengers are collected together in order to feed long-haul services are increased in their effectiveness by being undertaken at a substantial scale. It is hard for small new entrants to break in. In point-to-point markets, however, no such protection for incumbents exists. Economies of Scale in areas like pilot training and maintenance quickly run out with increasing size, and are counterbalanced by the bureaucracy and poor staff morale often characteristic of large airlines.

In some industries, incumbents have a lot of protection against new entrants because of so-called *Learning Curve* effects. In them, mature firms achieve lower costs than new entrants because the intricacies of the production process mean that substantial experience is required before optimum cost levels can be achieved. Aircraft manufacturing and aero-engine production both illustrate this from within the aviation industry, with unit costs of production falling steadily as an airframe or engine family matures. Airlines, on the other hand, seem to show the opposite effect, with the concept of *Start-up Economics* a well-established one. Airlines often achieve their lowest costs of operation during the first five years of their existence. Later, costs tend to rise as more staff ascend seniority scales to higher rates of pay, and bureaucracy and declining staff morale start to impact on cost levels. The existence or start-up cost advantages does of course, make the task facing a new airline a significantly easier one.

One final issue with regard to entry into the airline industry is difficult to analyse, but very important. Over the last twenty years, the list of airlines which have entered the industry and then left it again through bankruptcy is a depressingly long one. All the evidence one could possibly require is there to illustrate the point that investing in and setting up a new airline is, at best, highly speculative, with an overwhelming likelihood of failure. From this, one might assume that new entry into the aviation industry would largely be a thing of the past, especially given the depressed state of the industry in the early years of the new century. Nothing could be further from the truth, with the pressure of entry seemingly as strong, or stronger, than ever. One explanation for this apparent contradiction is that aviation is seen as a glamorous and exciting industry by many, and that the dream to set up and own one's own airline is a continuing one for those with large egos and deep pockets. Industries with dirty, unpleasant processes at their heart do not have the same appeal, despite the fact that profits and returns on capital may be much better within them. The English expression, "where there's muck there's brass" is a telling one.

As an overall conclusion to the question of entry, incumbent airlines must prepare themselves for a continuing challenge from new entrants, especially in their short-haul, point-to-point markets.

4:1:4   *Power of Customers*

Porter argues that the power of their customers will be a crucial determinant of profitability for the firms in any industry. In turn, customer power will be related to two variables: the number of customers a firm has, and the existence – or otherwise – of so-called *Switching Costs*.

In principle, the point about the number of customers is an obvious one. If a firm has many customers and some of these defect to the competition, there will still be a large number of customers remaining. If, on the other hand, the firm has only two or three customers, the loss of one of them will result in a third or more of its business being lost. In such a situation, customers will have extreme amounts of bargaining power. They will be able to cut deals on terms which are extremely favourable to them, holding down the profits of the companies from which they are buying.

Despite the unambiguous nature of this point, a series of industry trends during the 1990s suggested that airlines were ignoring it. They allowed the size of their customer base to decline steadily, with serious consequences for their profitability.

This decline resulted from at least three factors. Firstly, as we have seen, there was an increase in the extent to which firms in business travel were prepared to use their bargaining power to conclude corporate deals in which a degree of loyalty was traded for substantial price discounts. This changed the nature of the business travel market. Instead of the airline's 'Customers' being the business travellers who actually flew, they were increasingly negotiating with a relatively small number of finance and purchasing people who had been given the responsibility of negotiating corporate deals.

The structure of the travel agency industry also changed during the 1990s. In many countries, life became harder for the smaller, independent agent. Instead, an increasing share of the market was held by large, often multinational, agency chains, who achieved substantial power as a result of their ability – often exaggerated, but still significant – to switch passengers between airlines according the commissions they were being paid.

Such a trend did not arise by accident. Many airlines adopted a policy of paying so-called over-ride commissions to agents according to the volume of business delivered to them. In the short term, such a policy gained them the greatest amount of revenue. It did, though, give important advantages to large travel agents who could meet their revenue targets for over-rides. These agents were in turn able to use their higher commissions to fund market share battles against their smaller rivals, further cementing their domination.

A further issue regarding the size of the airline customer base concerned the selling of seats to price-sensitive leisure travellers. Again during the 1990s, many airlines tended to opt out of retail marketing of these seats. Instead, this job was increasingly left to so-called *Bucket Shops* and Consolidators, who treated the airlines as suppliers of cheap seats which in turn could be sold on, at a profit, through their own retail marketing outlets. Firms such as Trailfinders in the UK and Eupo-Air in the Far East achieved substantial dominance as a result. As they did so, they were progressively able to change their role from one of selling a small number of otherwise unsold seats, to one where they were able to dictate prices to carriers, negotiating deals which were very attractive to them, but which were much less so to the airlines supplying them.

As we shall see in section 7:2, the last five years have seen a revolution in the distribution channels used by airlines. The Internet has become a very important channel, and from the issues raised in this section, it is easy to see why. The Internet allows carriers to begin the process of broadening their customer base once again, and to make better contact with the true sources of their revenue. They are therefore able to address the problems of escalating commission costs and falling yields, which were a clear consequence of the mistaken polices of the 1990s.

A final question with the size of the airline customer base is in some senses the most worrying of all. Porter warns that if one, or a small number of the firm's customers become too big, they may take the view that it would be more cost-efficient to take on the resources to do the job themselves. If they do, a firm may lose all of the large amount of business currently being obtained from a single source. Worse still, the former customer may decide that there is actually money to be made in the new area of activity. If it does, it will not only cease to supply business to the firm in question, but will actively begin to compete with the firm for its remaining customers.

In the aviation industry, a common situation where a customer turns into a competitor occurs when a tour operator grows bigger and bigger, giving larger amounts of business to existing charter airlines. Often, a point arrives where it will make sense for the tour operator to buy its own aircraft, in order to set up an airline to carry its own passengers and perhaps also the compete in the open market for other airlines' passengers as well. The tax benefits associated with aircraft ownership can be an added incentive to do this, given that tour operators normally do not have significant capital assets to use to offset against their tax liabilities.

The subject of so-called *Integrated Carriers* is also an interesting one with regard to the question of customers becoming competitors. The subject of Integrators is covered fully in Section 4:4:2, but, in summary, they are freight companies specialising in the movement of relatively small, urgent, packages. When they begin service on a new route, it is normal for them to offer substantial amounts of business to existing combination airlines. This helps the Integrators to grow their traffic. Unfortunately for the combination airlines, once they have done so, it has been common practice for them to then put on their own specialist freighter aircraft, cutting out of the equation the airlines that first helped them to grow.

The question of *Switching Costs* is an equally difficult one. In some industries, there are very substantial costs associated with switching from one supplier to another. Airline fleet planning illustrated this point very well. An airline only using, for example, Boeing aircraft will have built up a large investment in Boeing spare parts, Boeing-orientated flight simulators, and in the training of its staff to be familiar with Boeing products. There will therefore be a strong financial incentive to continue to buy from Boeing. If Airbus is to break the stranglehold of Boeing at such an airline, they will have to offer very large discounts on the purchase price of their aircraft, in order to effectively pay themselves for the Switching Costs of moving away from Boeing. They will probably have to offer many other incentives as well, such as large amounts of free pilot training.

The problem for airlines is that they do not have the Switching Cost protection which assists aircraft manufacturers in retaining their customer base. An airline may be getting a worthwhile amount of business from a major customer as a result of having a corporate deal with them. It will be a simple task, though, for another carrier to come along and offer the customer a more attractive level of discount, with the result that the corporate deal with the first airline is cancelled and transferred to the second. This will be easy, because little capital investment or training is required to work with one airline rather than with another.

Of course, the first airline will hope that its Frequent Flyer Programme will be of some value in fending off predatory attacks by its rivals, in that many people who actually travel for the firm in question will wish to continue to build their mileage balance, and retain their privileged status, within the programme. Even this, very limited, Switching Cost protection can be addressed by the predator by a 'Golden Hello' tactic of giving out a large number of free miles and Gold Cards in their programme to these people.

Overall, the question of the Power of their Customers is a very difficult one for airlines to address, and goes a long way towards explaining the poor profit performance of many carriers in recent years.

4:1:5 Power of Suppliers

This depressing conclusion is equally applicable to Porter's remaining point, that of the power of a firm's suppliers.

Porter argues – again, the point is straightforward – that when a firm is totally dependent on monopoly suppliers of crucially-needed resources, these suppliers will be able to charge prices which ensure handsome profits for themselves, but which severely limit profits of the firms that they supply.

For airlines, the list of suppliers who either actually or potentially have this monopoly power is a depressingly long one. Most obviously, suppliers of Air Traffic Control and airport services may have it, with many airlines having no choice but to pay whatever ATC and airport charges are levied on them. It is most noticeable that at the time of writing airline profits have been severely affected in a major industry downturn, but the pain of this is not being evenly distributed across the industry. Many airports are continuing to show strong financial returns, reflecting the monopoly power that many of them have. Often, it has been necessary to regulate landing fees in order to control the use of this power.

Sometimes, airlines' fleet planning can be affected by powerful supplier issues. The Boeing 747 was introduced into airline service in 1970, and was unchallenged by any other aircraft for the next 25 years. If a carrier's requirement was a long-range aircraft with 400+ seats, the 747 was the only option available to them. Not surprisingly, the aircraft became a very profitable project for Boeing. In the future, a similar situation may develop with the 555 seat Airbus A380, though Boeing's recent decision to launch a stretched version of the 747 – the so-called 747-8 – will have been greeted with a sigh of relief by many airlines.

Perhaps the best, and most controversial, example of powerful suppliers in the aviation industry has concerned the so-called *Global Distribution Systems* (GDSs).

Since their inception in the late 1980s, the GDSs have provided the switching technology which allows travel agents to make reservations with hundreds of different airlines, hotels, car rental companies and tour operators through a single computer keyboard.

Unlike airlines, the GDS business is one of immense scale economies. The capital costs of entering the business have been very high, but running costs have been low. Large firms have therefore been able to spread their capital costs over greater volumes of output and achieve lower unit costs. As a result, there are only four significant players in the global GDS industry – the US based SABRE and Worldspan, and European-originating Galileo International and Amadeus. (In December 2006, a plan was announced for a merger between Galileo and Worldspan). All were first set up by airlines or consortia of airlines, though in recent years their ownership has become more diverse. (Very recently, some new entrants, using a different business model, have appeared in the GDS industry. This is a development which we will cover fully in Section 7:3)

Besides strongly concentrated patterns of ownership, the GDS industry has also shown a trend towards the establishment of geographical monopolies. For example, a high proportion of travel agents in the UK use Galileo. An equally high proportion in France and Germany are Amadeus customers.

The GDS companies do not, of course, provide their services free. When they were first proposed, the plan was that the costs associated with them would be shared equally between travel agents and airlines. Travel agents would pay substantial rent to the company which supplied them with a GDS service, reflecting the fact that the GDS allowed them to substantially increase the productivity of their staff. Airlines and other travel firms would pay their contribution to GDS costs through a booking fee payable on each booking made in their reservation systems.

It has not worked out in this way. Because of the Economies of Scale involved, the GDS companies saw it as a major business objective to increase their market share in order to boost transaction volume. They did so by engaging in aggressive pricing, so aggressive in many cases that travel agents were given a GDS service free-of-charge if they switched from one firm to another, or even received incentive payments for doing so.

The result of such a policy has been that the costs of GDS fell disproportionately on airlines, with the current level of booking fee they are paying being between $4 and $4.50 per passenger. This may seem a trivial amount, until it is multiplied by the hundreds of millions of passengers carried by the world's airlines each year.

Not surprisingly, such a situation has been regarded as totally unsatisfactory by many airlines, particularly by those which have not benefited by having a shareholding in a GDS. Until recently, though, it has been difficult for many of them to do much about it. Some carriers, such as the UK firm Easyjet, have from the beginning adopted a radical policy of direct selling, completely by-passing the travel agency distribution system. Besides avoiding commission payments, this policy has also allowed the airline to save on GDS booking fees. This has been something of great importance to a low fares airline given that booking fees are levied on each booking made and thus potentially make up a disproportionate amount of cost for such an airline.

For traditional carriers, the travel agency system has overwhelmingly been their main channel of distribution, with 85 – 90% of their bookings coming from this source. They have not, therefore, been able to refuse to pay GDS booking fees. Had they done so, the GDS firms would simply have removed the schedules and fares information of the recalcitrant airlines from their database, with the result that almost all the bookings they might have received from travel agents would have been lost. Therefore, in Porter terms, the GDS companies were monopoly suppliers of vital resources, and it should have come as no surprise that during the 1990s they were highly profitable. It should equally be of no surprise that as soon as the Internet offered a viable alternative distribution channel, airlines would embrace it enthusiastically. This whole, very controversial area will be reviewed further in Section 7:3.

4:1:6   *"Disintermediation"*

Sometimes, in the application of the Five Forces model, situations arise where relationships between firms change radically. This is especially likely when a particular player or group of players is not adding sufficient value to justify the prices that they are charging. An attempt may then be made to by-pass them, in a process which Porter describes as *Disintermediation*. Two examples, one actual and one potential, illustrate this process in the aviation industry. Returning to the example of the GDS firms given above, the recent rapid growth in the use of the internet as a distribution channel reflects a clear attempt by airlines to disintermediate the GDS companies, one which has already saved them substantial amounts in terms of booking fees.

Another interesting case comes from the freight side of the industry. In recent years, a number of companies have grown up which have specialised in providing so-called *wet-leasing* services for large freighter aircraft (mainly the Boeing 747F). The American firm Atlasair is the most notable of these. By using their services, an airline can offer its customers main deck freight capacity, without the costly overheads of owning and operating freighter aircraft themselves. In particular, they can save money because Atlasair crew salaries are generally very much lower than the often stratospheric rates of pay given to 747 crews by traditional airlines.

The potential problem of such policies is, though, very clear, in that the airlines using wet-leased freighters are adding very little value. Mostly, they are taking pre-loaded Unit Load Devices (ULDs) from air freight forwarders, and loading these onto the wet-leased freighters. Sooner or later, the freight forwarders may decide that it will be more profitable for them to wet-lease the freighters themselves, and employ local handling agents to perform the simple task of dealing with the pre-loaded units.

Indeed, one forwarder, the Swiss-owned Panalpina, is already doing so. Each time they do is a classic case of Disintermediation.

Overall, Porter's Five Forces model provides a valuable backcloth against which to view airline strategic decision-making. Any airline strategy, if it is to be successful, must deal with a complex interplay of often conflicting forces.

4:2 Strategic Families

4:2:1 *Cost Leadership, Differentiation and Focus – The Principles*

Figure 4:1 presents a diagram, again taken from Porter's "Competitive Strategy".

In it, Porter argues that some firms achieve success from what he calls *Cost Leadership* position. Others employ a strategy based on *Differentiation*. A third option is to adopt a *Focussing* position, though here, the focussing expertise may be used either to add value, or to achieve low production costs. Porter also argues that there is a fourth position, called *Lost-in-the-Middle*, from which success is difficult or impossible.

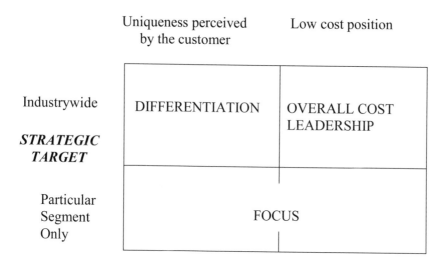

Figure 4:1 Sources of Competitive Advantage

Source: M Porter, Competitive Strategy. The Free Press 1980 p.39.

The diagram is not above criticism. In particular, it suffers from the weakness inherent in any two-by-two format, of attempting to place things in discrete boxes when more normally, relationships are ones of continuum or spectrum. Also, as Porter has recognised in his subsequent writing, a corporate entity may be represented in more than one box as a business becomes larger and more diversified. Finally, in the airline industry, for many years the model failed to work well because government regulation of competition distorted the free interplay of market forces.

Despite these limitations, the model is now a very powerful one in understanding the strategic options open to firms in today's airline industry. In particular, as the forces of deregulation and liberalisation have advanced over the last fifteen years, so the model has fitted the circumstances of the industry better and better.

In order to make use of the model, it is first of all necessary to understand the meaning of the terms contained in it.

A *Cost Leader* firm has a set of clear requirements it must satisfy if it is to be successful. Firstly, it must achieve, and then sustain, significantly lower operating costs than its rivals. If it loses its cost advantage, it will be in serious difficulties. Secondly and crucially, it must correctly identify what its customers are prepared to give up, and what they are not prepared to give up, in order to gain access to cheap prices.

There are many examples of firms which do successfully achieve these requirements. Interestingly, (in terms of traditional thinking in the airline industry), such firms are often highly profitable, despite the low prices which they charge.

In the world of supermarkets, the German firm Aldi has achieved a great deal of success, now having branches in many European countries. This success has been based on the remarkably low prices which it charges. Those shopping at Aldi have to accept, though, that sacrifices will be required if they are to take advantage of the very cheap prices on offer. Choice may be limited, display standards poor, and check-out queues long. There is no loyalty scheme available and even the plastic bags into which shopping is packed are charged for.

In another sector, IKEA is a successful firm in the field of furniture retailing. Again, prices are keen and attractive, but major sacrifices have to be made to obtain them. In particular, most of their furniture is supplied in flat-pack form, with the purchaser required to assemble what they have bought themselves. This condition permits IKEA to make major savings in labour and storage costs, and judging by the firm's growth, is something which its customers accept.

A final example of successful Cost Leadership comes with cheap motel chains such as Travelodge. These chains make available rooms at a very attractive rate. Those using them, though, have to make sacrifices to gain access to cheap prices. The room often has to be paid for on arrival rather than on departure. It may be rather small, and may not have a telephone. Sometimes, the motel does not have its own restaurant, requiring patrons to walk to a nearby fast food outlet. Generally, though, the rooms do have a private bathroom – albeit a very small one. Going without a private bathroom is an example of a sacrifice which most people are not prepared to countenance. If bathrooms have to be shared, the motels would be less popular, even if, as a result, prices could be even lower.

In a sense, the concept of *Differentiation* is a harder one to analyse, in that there are potentially many ways for firms to successfully achieve differentiation. However, perhaps for our purposes, the UK firm Marks and Spencer is a good illustration. Marks and Spencer has been through some difficult times recently, and to some extent has been knocked off its pedestal. For many years, though, it was a great success story.

The secret of Marks and Spencer's long-term success did not come from it being recognised as the cheapest place where one could buy food, clothes or household goods. Rather, it prided itself on occupying the *Value-for-money* high ground. Quality standards were high and proven, and an unequivocal guarantee was given that purchases could be exchanged or the money paid for then refunded if they failed to please.

From the point of view of the airline industry, as we shall see shortly, one of the most interesting aspects of the success of Marks and Spencer (or, for that matter, the British firm Tesco or the French Carrefour) is their very successful exploitation of synergies in order to achieve Differentiation. If a store is stocking 30,000 or more products under one roof, there is a very good chance that, once customers, have entered the store, they will end up buying more than they had originally intended, due to the range of goods on offer. In aerospace, much the same can be said for aero-engine companies such as Rolls-Royce. Rolls defines itself as being in the Power business, and supplies turbines for power stations, ships and military aircraft, as well as for civil airframes. By being in all these sectors at the same time, Rolls presumably hopes that synergies will be available in such areas as research and development expenditure.

The concept of Focussing is one where a firm chooses to give up all these potential benefits of synergy by concentrating on one activity. Their aim is to achieve such expertise in this one area that they will be able to hold off the challenge of those who are benefiting from synergies in either the Cost Leader or Differentiation sectors

By way of illustration, a fashion in the UK at the time of writing is for ethnic – particularly Indian – food. In response, specialist grocery stores are growing up which only sell Indian grocery products. They therefore have none of the synergies available to Tesco or Marks and Spencer. They achieve such strength, though, from their exclusive focus of activity that they are able to hold off the supermarket's competitive challenge. Tesco does have a good Indian food section, but it cannot be as comprehensive as that available in a store which lives or dies by its ability to meet the demand for Indian ingredients.

Of, such a positioning also illustrates the danger of a Focussing approach. If fashions change and Indian food looses its appeal, the firm supplying such food will be in a very difficult position.

Lost-in-the-Middle is, as we have said, a situation where a firm is in none of the major boxes. In many countries the small village store represents this position. As car ownership has grown, it has become commonplace for people to drive to an out-of-town hypermarket, rather than patronise the local store in the town or village where they live. In fighting back, the owners of village stores have few weapons at their disposal. They will not have the buying power of an Aldi which would allow them to offer very low prices, whilst they cannot stock the 30,000 or more items typical of a hypermarket. Finally, there would be insufficient demand in a small town or village for a store which specialised in a narrow area such as Indian grocery products.

The *Lost-in-the-Middle* nature of the village store's position is illustrated by the fact that over the last ten years, many of them have been forced to close. As we shall see, many medium-sized airlines are likely to follow them in the years to come.

4:2:2 *Cost Leadership in the Airline Industry: Background*[13]

The concept of Cost Leadership strategies is by no means new in the airline industry. In 1971, a new carrier, Southwest Airlines, was set up (after a series of drawn out legal battles instigated by incumbent carriers), to serve the intra-state Texan market in the USA. The airline became profitable in 1975, and, remarkably, has stayed profitable ever since. It has remained in the black even during the recessionary periods of 1991-94 and from 2000 until 2005, when the losses made by almost all the other airlines in the USA were very large indeed.

It has been the period since the late 1990s that has seen the rapid spread of the use of Cost Leadership strategies around the world. We now have two large, and rapidly growing airlines employing it in Europe,

---

[13] For further information, please see T C Lawton, "Cleared for Takeoff: Structure and Strategy in the Low Fare Airline Business", Ashgate Books 2002 and Simon Calder, "No Frills: the Truth behind the Low Cost Revolution in the Skies", Virgin Books 2002.

Ryanair and Easyjet, as well as many smaller new entrants. A new airline, Jetblue Airways, has appeared in the USA, and has made a successful beginning. This has been no mean feat considering the sea of red ink which engulfed the US airline industry during its early years. Other examples of new entrant Cost Leader players around the world include Westjet in Canada, Virgin Blue in Australia, Gol in Brazil and Air Asia, a domestic and regional carrier in Malaysia.

Besides these existing players, a high proportion of the start-up proposals being put forward at the present time include Cost Leadership elements in them.

It is instructive to ask the question why recent times have seen this explosion in the use of Cost Leadership strategies, when the success of the pioneer, Southwest, had been obvious for many years.

Regulatory liberalisation is one obvious explanation. The agreement for the setting up of the Single Aviation Market of the European Union in 1993 (and the subsequent completion of the liberalisation process in 1997) gave opportunities for new entry which never existed before. Liberalisation of other domestic markets – notably those of Canada and Australia – has also been helpful in allowing start-up entrepreneurs to fulfil their ambitions. It is notable that those markets which have so far seen the least development of Cost Leadership – for example South East Asia – are also still amongst the most regulated.

The arrival of the Internet as a channel for airline distribution has also been highly significant. Until the late 1990s, distribution was both challenging and costly for airlines, which were mostly forced to rely on one channel of distribution, that provided by the travel agency industry.

The Internet has changed this situation beyond all recognition. For carriers that have been prepared to break with the past and simplify their fares and reservations procedures, the Internet has provided a route to speedy and cost-effective distribution. In using it, airlines have been further helped by the introduction of electronic, rather than paper, ticketing.

The changing nature of the business air travel market provides a final and interesting explanation for the growth of Cost Leadership strategies. Until the late 1990s, traditional carriers were greatly favoured by the fact that business travellers generally paid high prices for expensive, but prestigious travel in Business Class on board airlines which dedicated a great deal of effort to meeting a range of needs centred around prestige and status.

Some of them are still prepared to do this, but a number of changes have now taken place. As we discussed in Section 2:3:3, recent years have seen an increase in the importance of the so-called "Independent" business traveller. These are people who work for themselves or for small firms, and who feel that the price of an air ticket comes out of their own pocket. Even in the corporate travel market, business travellers are being forced to become more price-sensitive by the corporate purchasing of business travel, whereby companies trade lower fares for loyalty. Even travel agents now join in the quest for lower fares as they seek to prove their ability to get value-for-money, in order to retain their increasingly demanding corporate clients.

Whatever the explanation, the interest being shown around the world in Cost Leadership strategies now makes this the most important strategic development in the industry for many years.

4:2:3 Fundamentals of the Business Model

The business principles that underlie Cost Leadership need hold no terrors for the analyst. They are now very well understood, and remarkably straightforward.

Underlying all these principles is one fundamental philosophy – that of *simplicity*. Some of the world's most successful and profitable businesses have taken processes which from the point-of-view of the user were complicated, and simplified them.

Outside of the aviation industry, computing provides a good example. Thirty years ago, the use of computers was restricted to a relatively small and highly trained group. Today, computers are used by almost everyone, because software firms such as Microsoft have taken most of the mystique and difficulties away. The result has been a remarkable virtuous circle. Growing demand for PCs and laptops has led to very large economies of scale in production, which have in turn allowed for further price reductions.

Coming to the airline business, the example of so-called Integrated Carriers is instructive. We will cover these firms in detail in Section 4:4:2, but for the moment what it is important to note is that before their arrival, using air freight for a small urgent package was a complex task, only accessible to experts. Traditional airlines were only interested in the relatively easy job of moving shipments from airport to airport. This left the shipper to make arrangements for collection and delivery, documentation (in itself no mean task in view of the complexities inherent in the documentation requirements dreamed up by airlines) and customs clearance. The result was that large firms called air freight forwarders, grew up to handle air freight shipments, because lay people could not undertake the task themselves. Over the years, forwarders have cost airlines immense sums in commissions and in the consequences of reduced market control.

The situation today for the non-expert who has a small package needing air transportation is very different. Integrated carriers – for example, DHL, FedEx, UPS and TNT – all offer a collection and delivery service. They have simplified documentation, so that non-expert people can easily complete it, and arrange customs clearance. For added peace-of-mind, they also have a comprehensive tracking and tracing service available over the Internet.

The result has been exactly as one would expect. The market for small, urgent packages – the so-called "Express" market – is the fastest growing part of the air freight market. The growth, though, is not benefiting the traditional airlines very much with the complicated demands which they place on the customer. Rather, the market share of the Integrators is steadily increasing, allowing them to further reduce their prices as they benefit from the substantial economies-of-scale inherent in small package operations.

If we turn now to the strategies of traditional airlines on the passenger side, the importance of simplicity – or, rather, the lack of it – becomes clearer still. This is best illustrated in the area of pricing policy. To the passenger, the question "What will the fare be?" for a given journey on a given day, seems to be completely straightforward, but airlines have been incapable of giving a straightforward answer. Often, fifty or more fares are available on a given route. Which one the passenger will actually be able to use will depend on their ability to satisfy a range of conditions around such things as advanced booking, length of stay and cancellation/rebooking opportunities.

The consequences of such complexities are severe. They make the training of new reservations and ticketing personnel a costly and time-consuming process. Even more so, the point-of-sale task becomes a slow and complex one. This in turn often forces the consumer to turn to a travel agent to unravel the complexities, involving airlines in the same commission and market control issues which have arisen on the freight side with air freight forwarders. In turn, the build-up of business obtained over the Internet has been much slower for traditional airlines than it has been for new entrant Cost Leader players with their simple fare structures.

Overall, achieving and sustaining simplicity in business processes is an absolutely fundamental requirement for a successful Cost Leadership strategy. Bearing this point in mind, let us now explore further features of the strategy:

1. Low Fleet Costs

Most successful Cost Leader airlines today are pursuing a so-called "Fleet Commonality" policy, having only one type of aircraft in their fleet. In turn, for many, this one type is the various members of the Boeing 737 family. Whatever this aircraft may now lack (at least according to Airbus) in passenger appeal and the use of the latest technology, it has rugged and proven reliability as its greatest asset. These are exactly the qualities needed by a Cost Leader airline, and both Southwest Airlines (with a fleet now consisting of more that 400 737s) and Ryanair illustrate very well a commonality policy with 737s. By sticking to one type of aircraft, they are gaining substantial economies in such areas as pilot training and maintenance.

Other Cost Leader airlines are pursuing different fleet strategies, but still with the aim of securing low costs. Easyjet began as a 737 operator, but in 2002 signed a very large deal for the acquisition of A319s, a smaller version of the A320. One must assume that the deal offered by Airbus was so attractive that it led the airline's management to conclude that lower acquisition costs would outweigh the costs associated with a mixed fleet. The airline will also be in a good position to play one manufacturer off against the other when it comes to the question of new aircraft acquisitions in the future.

2. Low Landing Fees

Section 4:2:1 showed that the key to successful Cost Leadership was for a firm to establish and sustain a cost and through that, pricing advantage over all its rivals. In order to do so, it must address the "big ticket" cost items, those which will have a substantial impact on unit costs.

Table 4:1 presents cost data for British Midland Airways, a short-haul airline providing a conventional service on UK domestic and regional routes. The cost information is broken down on a departmental cost basis. It shows that landing fees and passenger embarkation charges are a major cost item, accounting for nearly 18% of costs. Any airline which can substantially reduce them will have taken a very successful first step towards a sustainable Cost Leadership position.

Southwest Airlines illustrates the principle well. Throughout its history the airline has pursued a policy of seeking out unused or little-used airports, even if these are old, sometimes dilapidated and unfashionable. At its home base, Dallas, it uses Dallas/Love Field airport, rather than the much larger DFW. At Chicago, it flies to Midway, rather than O'Hare, whilst in the New York region the relatively remote airport of Islip, on Long Island, is used rather than the congested and expensive Kennedy, Newark or Laguardia.

Table: 4:1 British Midland – Cost Structure: Financial Year 2003/04

Cost Category	%
1. Depreciation and Rental	14.5
2. Handling Costs, Parking Fees & Station Costs	10.8
3. General & Administrative	5.8
4. Landing Fees, Passenger Embarkation Charges	17.6
5. Flight Crew Costs	6.7
6. Maintenance & Overhaul	10.3
7. Aircraft Fuel & Oil	10.5
8. Commission	2.9
9. Passenger Services	3.8
10. Cabin Crew Costs	3.6
11. Navigation & En Route Charges	5.0
12. Reservations	3.5
13. Advertising & Promotion	2.8
14. Sales	0.8
15. Specific Cargo Costs	1.3
16. Insurance	0.8
17. Other Operating Costs	
	100.0%

Source: CAA.

In Europe, Ryanair pursues such a policy in an even more exaggerated fashion. Indeed, the airline has stated that in its route expansion policy, the existence of an underutilised airport, even if it is a long way from the city it purports to serve, is the most fundamental requirement.

The benefits of using underutilised airports are very great. The airline gains from very low landing fees, as airport operators reason that they are better off having substantial numbers of passengers (who will, in turn, provide commercial income for the airport from such activities as car parking and shopping) rather than none at all. It will also be able to expand rapidly, free of the slot-availability constraints that bedevil congested hubs.

Interestingly, at the present time, not all Cost Leader airlines are sticking to the "pure" form of the model with respect to airport selection. In strong contrast to Southwest, Jetblue Airways has based itself at Kennedy Airport In New York. Easyjet is making use of some congested European airports – notably Gatwick, Schiphol and both Orly and CDG airports at Paris, though the airline has shown itself to be particularly adept at moving quickly when slots at such airports have unexpectedly become available.

3. ShortTurnarounds/High Aircraft Utilisation

Once uncongested airports have been selected, the Cost Leader airline is well on the way to achieving its next requirement, that of short turnarounds and high aircraft utilisation. Southwest Airlines has always scheduled turnarounds of 20-25 minutes, in contrast to the 50 minutes to one hour which the industry has traditionally used. This greatly helps the airline in its aim of achieving low costs, because it allows additional rotations to be operated each day. In turn, this permits a wider spread of capital costs (in the case of aircraft which are owned), or of lease rentals.

Of course, short turnarounds are not the only requirements. These turnarounds must be engineered so that they can be achieved consistently – otherwise an unacceptable punctuality penalty will result. Thus, for example, most Cost Leader airlines do not use airbridges at airports, despite the fact that this leaves their passengers unprotected in wet or cold weather. The benefit of this is that it allows both the front and rear aircraft exits to be used, speeding passenger enplaning and deplaning. Controversially, many Cost Leader airlines do not pre-allocate seats. This leads to jibes about "Cattle Truck Handling" as passengers rush for the seats they want when the boarding process begins. It means, though, that passengers are far more likely to be at the gate at the boarding time, and that they can be encouraged to sit down by the cabin crew in any available seat once they are on the aircraft.

As a further point, the fact that Cost Leader airlines are generally "no frills" (see below) makes galley servicing a very easy and quick process, as is cabin cleaning. Indeed, many Cost Leader airlines require their cabin crews to clean the aircraft during daytime stops, with a thorough clean only being given overnight. This will not be possible for full service airlines where food and other debris will be more of a problem (and trade union resistance highly likely).

4. Limited On-board Service

The data presented in Table 4:1 is instructive, in that it shows that a short-haul airline, British Midland, spends 3.8% of its costs on "Passenger Services" – the meals and drinks given away free to passengers.

It might at first sight be assumed that Passenger Service costs would only be high for long-haul airlines, where passengers need to be offered generous hospitality because of the length of time they are on board the aircraft. This is not so. Traditional short-haul airlines (especially in Europe) have given passengers a complementary drinks and meal service, even on flights with a duration of only an hour or so. The costs of doing so can then only be spread over a small number of passenger-kilometres, and therefore have a disproportionate impact on unit costs.

Cost Leader airlines have a choice to make with respect to on-board catering. Some have chosen to be completely "no-frills". This allows cheaper aircraft acquisition costs due to the absence of galley space, speeds aircraft cleaning and allows extra seating. Others – in fact, today, most of them – do offer a meals-and-drinks service, but charge relatively high prices to what are captive customers. Passenger service then becomes a worthwhile source of so-called 'Ancillary' revenue rather than a cost item.

5. Point-to-Point Only

One of the most important, but more overlooked, reasons explaining the recent success of the Cost Leader model is that airlines using it have concentrated on point-to-point traffic, eliminating what has hitherto been an unacceptable level of cross-subsidy from point-to-point to connecting passengers.

Any airline offering a transfer and connections product at a hub will incur substantial additional costs. Passengers checking in for a connecting flight will expect to be given a boarding pass not only for their first sector, into the hub, but also for their onward flight. Providing such a service will involve the airline in significant investment in its data processing and communications capability. Passengers will also assume that they can check-in their baggage at their point-of-origin, and reclaim it only at their final destination. All interim baggage handling will be taken care of by the airline, at a substantial cost. Once they reach their hub airport, they will expect to wait for their onward flight in a comfortable and well-appointed lounge.

Important though these costs are, the provision of a connecting product will have still wider – and greater – cost implications. Implicit in the idea of hubbing is that flights will be co-ordinated in banks, so that connections can be made in the shortest possible time. These banks require a peak availability of resources, resources which will be poorly utilised as soon as the peak is over.

The costs of a connections product would be a severe problem in themselves. The problem is made worse, though, by the low yields often obtainable from transfer traffic. A passenger making a connection will generally have a worthwhile choice available to them, because they will be able to travel via the hubs of a range of different airlines. Carriers know this, and will try to entice the passenger to choose their hub rather than that of a rival. Yields are therefore generally poor in the market of transfer traffic.

In the past, traditional airlines have been able to compensate for these low yields by charging disproportionately high prices to people travelling on a point-to-point basis, for whom the hub serves as a local airport. The result has been that it has commonly been cheaper to fly from a point behind the hub, into the hub and then beyond, than it has been to travel on a point-to-point basis. Such absurd and discriminatory pricing practices have led to so-called Cross-Border Ticketing, an "abuse" which airlines have repeatedly tried and failed to eliminate.

Cost Leader airlines have removed all the costs and revenue dilution associated with a transfer product by concentrating exclusively on point-to-point traffic. It is, of course, possible to transfer form one flight to another on these airlines, though the fact that the emphasis is placed on high aircraft utilisation rather than the scheduling of banks of flights makes connecting opportunities less likely. Nothing is done, though, to assist the connecting passenger. When they reach their transfer airport, they will have to reclaim their own bag, and take it to the check-in desk for their onward flight themselves. No luxurious lounges are, of course, provided. With fares and yields, there is no dilution, because the airlines follow a "Sum-of-sector Fares" pricing principle, rather than the complex "Pro-rating" procedures we will describe in section 6:2:1.

6. Simple Fares

Cost Leader airlines follow significantly different pricing practices from traditional airlines in other ways as well. As we saw earlier in this section, the disciplines of Revenue Management have led airlines in the direction of greater pricing complexity, with often fifty or more fares being on offer on a particular route, most of them having different, and confusing, conditions associated with them.

Cost Leader airlines do make use of Revenue Management techniques, but generally with one crucial difference compared to traditional carriers. When someone looks at the website of one of these airlines, at the time they do so there is only one fare on offer for the flight in which they are interested. They are therefore faced with a clear "take it or leave it" choice. The fare on offer will certainly vary through time, being generally low well in advance of flight departure and rising as the departure day nears. The fact that there is only ever one fare available at a particular time makes the whole reservations procedure a very simple one, and, as we move onto now, allows the internet to be the cornerstone of distribution.

7. Low Distribution Costs

Section 7:2 gives full coverage of the changing world of airline distribution.

We will see there that the 1990s saw a rapid and unacceptable increase in the distribution costs of traditional airlines. This was due to the overwhelming domination of one channel of distribution – that provided by the travel agency industry. This near-monopoly caused a rapid increase in the commissions being paid to travel agents, as well as seeing airlines very vulnerable to the pricing practices of the Global Distribution Systems.

Any airline seeking a Cost Leadership position must address the question of distribution costs. If it can eliminate travel agents' commissions, a major step will have been taken towards the establishment and maintenance of a cost advantage, especially when it is born in mind that by the end of the 1990s it was common to find that 12% - 14% of a traditional airline's costs were made up of commissions.

In some sense, the elimination of GDS booking fees has been even more important for Cost Leader airlines. As we saw in Section 4:1:5, the GDS companies have always charged on a flat rate basis, currently about $4.50 per booking made. This is a reasonable policy given the structure of their costs, but it means that booking fees fall disproportionately on low fares carriers. $4.50 on a Business Class return fare of $3000 is an irrelevance. The same booking fee on a $50 fare most certainly is not.

The answer to the distribution problem for Cost Leader airlines has, of course, been to use the Internet. In this regard, the UK airline Easyjet has been the pioneer. From its foundation in 1995, Easyjet has paid no commission to any travel agent, and, because of this, no booking fees to any GDS company. The cost savings it has achieved as a result have been immense.

Easyjet has been followed by the airlines set up before it – Southwest and Ryanair – which have progressively eliminated the use of travel agents, and now have almost as high a proportion of their seats sold direct as Easyjet. Later entrants into the market have almost totally relied on internet-based direct sales.

8. Non-Refundable Tickets

In the past, most airlines have had a policy of making their more expensive tickets fully refundable. This makes them very much more attractive, especially for the business traveller whose exact schedule cannot be predicted very far in advance. It means, though, that these airlines have always had a significant no-show problem, which they have resolved, to a degree, by overbooking.

All the Cost Leader airlines have a policy of allowing no refunds. Bookings can be changed, in return for a substantial fee (in the UK, generally £25 plus any difference between the fare already paid and the current fare available on the flight to which the booking is to be transferred) but no money is ever refunded. This allows the airlines a better and more certain cash flow, which in turn brings useful savings in interest costs.

4:2:4 Cost Leader Airlines: Current Issues

We have now looked at the different policies which airlines in the Cost Leader sector pursue. They illustrate perfectly Porter's principles of Cost Leadership set out in Section 4:2:2. Successful players have to establish and sustain a cost, and through that, pricing advantage over their rivals. They must also correctly identify what their customers will, and will not give up to gain access to cheap prices. Cost Leader airlines have discovered that their customers will give up, amongst other things, service from their ideal airport, complementary meals and drinks, seat selection, the opportunity to buy a ticket through a travel agent and ticket refunds.The consequences of such policies, if correctly applied, are remarkable.

Cost Leader airlines seem to be the ones which have found a way round the chronic airline industry problem of cyclicality. As we will see in Section 4:3:1, the business model of Differentiation in the airline industry has generally allowed carriers to make reasonable returns in the buoyant upswing periods of the Trade Cycle. It has left them hopelessly exposed, though, in slow-down and recessionary times when large parts of the high yielding Business Class market – on which these airlines depend – has evaporated.

The Cost Leadership position, though, addresses such issues through what appears to be a virtuous circle. Low costs allow for profitable lower prices, which in turn substantially increase the size of the market. In times when the economy is strong, this market growth comes from new passengers being brought into the market who would not otherwise have flown. In times of slowdown or recession, Cost Leader airlines also appear to gain as people who are still anxious to fly trade down from the full service airlines as they seek lower prices.

A controversy currently affecting the Cost Leader sector is the question of the importance of customer service standards. The Cost Leader pioneer, Southwest, is a remarkable airline in that despite the fact that it is now a very large and mature carrier, it has retained a high degree of popularity with its passengers. The Department of Transportation in the USA collects, and publishes, data about passenger complaints, with the Major carriers being compared on the basis of the numbers of complaints received per 100,000 passengers carried. Southwest has been the airline with the lowest number of complaints for more than ten years, despite its "no frills" service. The secret seems to be that the airline makes a limited promise but keeps it consistently. It has also made great play on a warm and friendly style of service, and a solid approach to customer service if things go wrong.

Amongst the other Cost Leader players, a different approach is apparent. Ryanair in particular, if media reports are to be believed, takes the view that customer service on the rare occasions when things go wrong is less important. Providing fares are cheap enough, people will mostly keep coming back. Those who desert the airline after experiencing a severe service failure will soon be replaced by new people brought into the market by the airline's very low prices. It will be interesting to see which of these philosophies turns out to be the correct one in the long term.

Another major issue in Cost Leadership at the moment concerns the best way for a Cost Leader airline to be set up. Today, the successful Cost Leader players are all independent, in that they have been put together entrepreneurially, without links with any pre-existing airline. Given the profits that they have enjoyed in recent years, and the threat that they pose to longer-established airlines, it is not at all surprising that these "Legacy" airlines have adopted the philosophy that, "If you can't beat them, join them". A common way for a Cost Leader airline to be set up has been as a subsidiary of a full service carrier.

So far, little success has attended these efforts. During the 1990s, three of the US majors, United, Delta and USAirways set up low fares subsidiaries, using the branding of Shuttle-by-United, Delta Express and Metroair respectively. Within 4 years, each of these airlines had been closed down. In 1995, British Airways set up a Cost Leader subsidiary called Go. Presumably, the airline did not regard this carrier as a success, because it was eventually sold off (to its management, who then sold it to Easyjet), at what seems now to have been a very low price.

In recent years, there has been renewed interest in the idea of full-service airlines setting up low fares subsidiaries in order to try to compete with independent Cost Leader players. For example, Air Canada established two subsidiaries, using the sub-branding of Tango and Zip, to compete, presumably, with the very successful and rapidly-growing Westjet. Delta Airlines carried out a second attempt to enter the Cost Leader business with a new subsidiary branded Song. In Europe, British Midland set up BMI Baby, and SAS announced a Scandinavian no-frills airline under the Snowflake branding. In Australia, Qantas has set up its Jetstar operation, which at the time of writing seems to be faring quite well.

Some of these new initiatives may indeed be successful, but it is impossible to be optimistic. Air Canada has already closed down its Tango subsidiary, and Delta is merging its Song subsidiary back into its mainline activities. The essence of Cost Leadership is that firms are able to establish and *sustain* a cost advantage over their rivals. With low fares subsidiaries of full service (and highly unionised) airlines, concessions may be given in a time of crisis which allow a lower cost base to be established. However, once things begin to improve, it often becomes a major objective of union negotiators to ensure that wages, salaries and conditions of employment at the subsidiary start to move nearer to those which prevail in the mainline operation. The cost advantages are then progressively eroded. Also, the setting up of a low fares subsidiary involves significant branding problems. When someone experiences no-frills service on a low-cost subsidiary it may colour their view of what will happen on their next flight with the full-service parent. Finally, low fares subsidiaries will perhaps allow an airline to compete more successfully with Cost Leader players which are challenging its dominance. Another, less desirable, effect is that the subsidiary may take traffic away from its parent, and lead to criticism of the parent's relatively high prices.

4:2:5 *Cost Leader Airlines: The Future*

The question of the future of the Cost Leader sector is one of the most fascinating in the airline industry at the moment.

In answering it, it is first of all clear that Cost Leadership positions are much easier to establish and sustain in short-haul and regional markets than on long-haul. This is because many of the cost advantages we have been discussing as resulting from the Cost Leadership model are most marked there. The use of underutilised airports to lower landing fees and increase aircraft utilisation is a case in point. Landing fees are clearly a much higher proportion of operating costs in short-haul markets, whilst on long-haul, all airlines can achieve similar, high, aircraft utilisations. Shorter turnarounds do not allow extra rotations to be fitted into the flying day. A no-frills approach is a problem on long-haul, where a meals and drinks service will be regarded as more important by passengers spending many hours on an aircraft. Also a point-to-point only approach is less possible, with few long-haul markets having sufficient density on their own to be viable without hubbing. Finally, GDS booking fees, being charged on a flat-rate basis, are much less of a burden for the long-haul airline.

One could argue that the long-haul services mounted by many of Europe's charter airlines in recent years amount to Cost Leadership in long-haul markets. However, in establishing and sustaining a cost advantage, these airlines have relied on low seat pitches – commonly 28 inches. Such a policy certainly has a dramatic effect on seat-kilometre costs, allowing 25% or more extra seats to be put on an aircraft compared with the more traditional pitches of 32 or 33 inches. However, we may now be getting to the stage where such a lack of seating comfort is becoming an unacceptable sacrifice which people will not make.   Sitting in such uncomfortable seating for many hours is not the same as it would be, for example, on a two-hour flight to the Mediterranean.   Also, growing concern about Deep Vein Thrombosis means that airlines may leave themselves open to legal action if they continue to restrict seat pitches to such low levels.

Overall, it is likely that attempts will be made to spread the Low Cost Carrier concept onto long-haul routes – indeed, at the time of writing, the Canadian carrier Zoom, the Hong-Kong base Oasis Air and the Scottish airline Flyglobespan.com are all doing so.   However, it is unlikely that these carriers and airlines like them will have the same dramatic effect on long-haul markets as Ryanair and Easyjet have had on short haul routes

A further question for the future of the Cost Leader sector concerns safety standards.   Safety is, of course, an absolutely fundamental concern for all airlines, but it has to especially be so for Cost Leader players.   When tickets are extremely cheap, passengers must be wondering, perhaps subconsciously, as to why prices are so low.   Do they reflect the fact that corners are being cut on safety?

Whilst the Cost Leader sector continues to enjoy a good safety record – for example, Ryanair has never had a fatal accident in more than fifteen years of flying – its growth will continue unabated.   However, the experience of an airline called Valujet in 1996 was a salutary one.   At the time, it was a successful and rapidly growing new entrant into the Cost Leader sector, but suffered a tragic fatal accident when one of its aircraft crashed in the Florida Everglades with a large loss of life.   It never recovered, and was shortly afterwards taken over in a near-bankrupt condition.

At the time of writing, the major issue concerning the future of the Cost Leader sector concerns its explosive growth, and the large number of new entrants that are appearing.

Of course, the fact that the market is growing quickly would in any case be likely to induce a great deal of entry.   In this regard, the Cost Leader sector is doing no more than illustrate the principles of the Product Life Cycle which we will further discuss in Section 5:2:1.   However, there are particular factors at work at the moment, which are exacerbating "normal" Life Cycle effects.   As we have seen, resources have been cheap, with leased aircraft plentifully available at low lease rentals.   Also, in the short-haul markets where Cost Leaders operate there are few of the economies of scale which (through hubbing) to some degree protect existing players on long-haul.   In long-haul, as we saw in Section 3:2:2, there are often still regulatory barriers to entry which protect long-established airlines against the threat of entry.

These things are important, but perhaps the biggest factor explaining the current explosion of entry into the Cost Leader sector at the moment, is that entrepreneurs are being drawn to it. It seems to be the one business model which offers the possibility of sustained profitability, in an industry otherwise often characterised by a sea of red ink.

The effect of all these factors is remarkable, and frightening. At the time of writing (summer 2006), many markets, notably so the UK, Germany and Scandinavia, are seeing a rapid pace of growth by existing Cost Leader airlines, and the setting up of large numbers of independent newcomers. At the same time, as we have just seen, many threatened incumbent airlines are introducing their own Cost Leader brands. Even where they are not doing so, they are having to lower the prices to compete with the newcomers, a development we will examine further in Section 4:2:7.

The result of all these developments will be to make the Cost Leader sector a volatile and unstable one over the next few years. It is true that the airlines in it will continue to be able to generate new traffic, but it seems inevitable that there will be significant problems of overcapacity as LCC markets, inevitably, mature. As a result, some of the high profits which are currently being made will disappear, and less well-managed firms will be forced to leave the industry. Those that remain, and succeed, will be those that apply Porter's Cost Leadership model in its purest form. They will establish and sustain a clear cost advantage over their rivals.

The other issues concerning the future of the Cost Leader sector are mainly European, and stem from possible regulatory problems.

To achieve and sustain their success, Cost Leader airlines need very attractive deals from airport operators. To a remarkable degree, they have succeeded in obtaining these deals. Sometimes, though, the deals have been given to them by loss-making airports which are owned by local and regional governments and subsidised by them. This therefore raises the question as to whether or not the airlines, by an indirect routing, have received "illegal" State Aid. Ryanair was accused of doing so in its deal with Charleroi Airport in the south of Belgium and in its relationship with Strasbourg Airport. The result has been a new regulatory policy introduced by the European Commission to limit the scale and duration of payments from state-owned airports to airlines, and to ensure that deals are available to all airlines who might wish to take advantage of them, on a non-discriminatory basis.

Another current regulatory problem concerns the developing argument about Passenger Rights. During the autumn of 2002, a vigorous debate took place in the European Parliament about the need for airlines to compensate the victims of airline service failures – in particular those who have experienced cancelled or delayed flights.   Such compensation schemes would be in addition to those which already apply to a passenger experiencing Denied Boarding as a result of flight overbooking.

Not surprisingly, Cost Leader airlines mounted a strong lobby against such proposals. They argued, with reason, that a person paying a very low price should not be entitled to the same compensation as someone using an expensive ticket, which they would be under the scheme as it was currently proposed. However, their lobbying was not successful. New Passenger Rights rules have been introduced, and a challenge before the European Court mounted by two airline trade bodies (IATA and the European Low Fare Airlines Association) was rejected in January 2006. So far, though, the amounts of compensation paid out have been small.

A final regulatory issue concerns environmental taxation. In some senses, the Cost Leader sector is becoming a victim of it own success, in that it has produced often significant levels of traffic growth. This has in turn brought concerns to a head about the environmental impact of air transport, with the argument being put forward that the growth is only occurring because air passengers are not made to pay for the full environmental impact of aviation. If they are required to do so, through some form of additional taxation being imposed, it would certainly slow growth in the Cost Leader sector, especially if, as seems likely, it was imposed on a flat rate basis rather than as a percentage of the fare. The introduction of a scheme of Emissions Trading for aviation would have a similar, though almost certainly lesser, effect.

Overall, it is impossible to exaggerate the impact of the Cost Leader revolution on the air transport industry. Over the next few years, its implications will become ever more apparent in the markets where its effects have already been felt. It will also spread to hitherto unaffected markets.

4:2:6 "Differentiation" in the Airline Industry

Large numbers of airlines – mainly those which are long-established – in today's airline industry do not seek out a Cost Leadership position for their mainline activity (though, as we have seen, increasing numbers of them have set up Cost Leader subsidiaries). Instead, their argument is that they provide a value-for-money solution to a wide range of customer requirements, exploiting the synergies which become available to a firm producing a range of different products under the same umbrella. Such policies conform very well to the "Differentiation" position of the Porter model described in Section 4:2:1.

In recent years, many airlines in the Differentiation sector have suffering chronic financial losses. This has been especially so amongst the airlines of the United States, and to a lesser extent, Europe. Indeed, in many cases, the term "Legacy Airline" is a good description of these carriers, as they have often seemed to be dinosaurs finding life difficult or impossible in a fast-changing world.

This dire situation has, though, only arisen relatively recently. Whilst financial returns in the Differentiation sector have never been good, the period from about 1996 until 1999 was as prosperous a time as many of them had enjoyed in their entire history. Indeed, at the time it did seem that a business model was becoming established which would allow, at long last, a sound and consistent return for shareholders. We need, firstly, to define this model, and then to come onto the difficult and painful question as to why, in a comparatively short time, it was so disastrously undermined.

In order to be successful in the Differentiation sector it has always been necessary for airlines to be innovative. Indeed it is not co-incidence that two of the most successful airlines in this sector, Emirates and Singapore Airlines, are also the airlines with a strong reputation for innovation. Both are early customers for the Airbus A380 large aircraft, and both have consistently aimed to be at the forefront of new developments in such areas as cabin comfort, in-flight service and in-flight entertainment.

Of course, over time, almost all innovations are capable of being matched by competitors and most of them are. However, Emirates and Singapore Airlines illustrate the concept of so-called "First Mover Advantage", in that they have continued to reap the benefits of innovation even after matching by competitors has taken place. It seems that consumers continue to think well of a pioneer that took the risks and made the investment in an innovation which improves their lot.

Despite the importance of a product which matches the state-of-the-art, the standards of personal service which are offered assume even more significance for a Differentiation airline. As we have seen in Section 2:3:4, the business travel market – of crucial importance to Differentiation players – consists of a relatively small number of people, many of whom travel frequently over a long period of time. They get to know the airlines that give them a warm and caring welcome, and those which do not. Naturally, they prefer to travel, all other things being equal, with carriers which treat them well.

Personal service standards assume an even greater importance because they can provide a Sustainable Competitive Advantage. An airline may find that its standards of seating comfort, for example, have fallen behind those available on it rivals. If it does, it is then a straightforward, albeit costly, task to order and install the new seats which will correct the anomaly. Things are not so straightforward if it has customer-contact staff who are ill-disciplined, poorly motivated and incompetent. Correcting such a state of affairs may take concerted action on many fronts over a long period of time. During this time, the airline will be losing out to its rivals if these competitors do not have the same problems.

Brand building forms another, vital, part of the business model for successful Differentiation in the airline industry. The subject of brands is fully covered in Section 8:2. For the moment, though, it is worthwhile to note that for many airlines, their problem is that they have become commoditised. Passengers tend to feel that all airlines are the same and that there are no strong reasons for choosing one rather than another. A small number of airlines do, though, manage to rise above such generalisations, and to achieve valuable status as a brand. The British carrier Virgin Atlantic is an example, in addition to Emirates and Singapore Airlines.

A further aspect of the traditional business model for Differentiation carriers is that they need to be well-represented in each of the major market segments, those of business travel, leisure travel and air freight.

Such a policy will bring with it the major disadvantage that the airline will be setting itself a complex management task, in which contradictions and compromises will be a major feature. However, the synergies available to the multi-product airline will often more than compensate. A presence in the business travel market will give an airline access to the highest yields, whilst the leisure market is the one which is producing the highest growth rates. Also, almost by definition, the business and leisure markets have complementary demand patterns, as when business travellers aren't travelling because it is a holiday season, there will be a peak in leisure travel.

The synergies available from a strong presence in the air freight market are perhaps even greater. Belly-hold space in passenger aircraft will be cheaply available, and will also allow freight customers to benefit from the frequency and wide route network essentially provided for passengers. Air freight will help airlines' cash flow during the times when passenger demand is affected by wars or a terrorism threat. Also, there is some evidence that air freight helps airlines respond to the challenges of the trade cycle, in that it tends to be affected by a recession earlier, but to come out of it sooner, than the passenger side of the business. It is not co-incidental that both Singapore Airlines and Emirates earn about a quarter of all their revenue from air freight.

Points about the importance of innovation, customer service, brand-building and a synergistic presence in all the major market segments have always been true and remain so today. The other major issue with regard to the business model for Differentiation airlines is more controversial.

During the 1990s a fashion grew up in the airline industry that "Big is Beautiful" – that only airlines with a wide – preferably a global – network had any real hope of survival in a rapidly changing world.

It is easy to see why such ideas should have arisen. In principle, an airline with a wide network is better insulated against risk, in that it is unlikely that traffic will turn down across the whole of a global network at exactly the same time. Too many carriers in practice have their success or failure linked to the fortunes of a single, or at least a small number, of markets.

A wide route network also, by definition, allows airlines to offer a greater number of "on-line" rather than "transfer" connections. An on-line connection is one where the passenger uses the same airline both for the flight into a hub and for the one beyond it. In the transfer case, two different airlines are used.

All surveys of passenger preferences show that on-line connections are preferred to transfer ones. People are more confident that they will get the boarding passes for both sectors when they first check in, removing the need for a visit to the Transfer Desk when they arrive at the hub airport. They feel there is a greater likelihood of the baggage handling system working, and their bag arriving at their final destination at the same time as they do. They may hope that the gates for their two flights will be closer together, avoiding the need for a long walk and, perhaps, an inter-terminal transfer. Finally, they may be more confident that they will actually make the connection, with greater efforts being made to help them if their inbound flight is late.

Where an airline is too small to have a large number of on-line connections, it has to fall back on the expedient of Code-Sharing. This is where it lends its code to other airlines, or borrows theirs, so that connections appear as on-line in Global Distribution System displays when, in practice, they are nothing of the sort. Here, though, the downside may be one of customer alienation if passengers end up flying on airlines they would specifically prefer to avoid.

A final reason why big came to be regarded as beautiful in the airline industry, was because of the introduction of Frequent Flyer Programmes. In principle, the FFP of a large airline is more attractive than that of a small carrier. Points can be earned more quickly, in that there is a greater probability that an airline will have a service to all the destinations to which a passenger will need to travel. Once they have been earned, redemption opportunities for free flights will be greater, in that a wider range of destinations will be available.

Given this range of factors, it was no surprise that the second half of the 1990s saw a trend towards consolidation, as a fashion for wide networks gripped the industry. However, there were strict limits as to how far such a trend could develop. In any "normal" industry, the quest for size would have meant entering new markets and significant amounts of merger and takeover activity. These trends – though they arose – were very muted in air transport because of the ownership and control rules which we discussed in Section 3:2:2. Airlines attempted to grow where they could, but ownership and control issues meant that such organic growth was limited to the domestic markets of the countries in which they were based, and largely to international routes to and from these countries. Merger and takeover activity certainly did occur, but purely with national boundaries. Still, very few examples exist in the airline industry of true cross-border merger and takeover activity.

The United States market was the one where growth and consolidation of the industry was able to proceed furthest, due to the size of the market and the permissive attitude towards mergers and takeovers adopted by successive administrations in Washington. By the middle 1990s, the industry had consolidated to the point where it was overwhelmingly dominated by six mega-carriers – American, United, Delta, Northwest, USAirways and Continental.

The US experience does not lead to a confident view that consolidation is the way to financial success for the world's "Differentiation" airlines. During the 1990s, each of the Big Six became a hotbed of militant trade unionism, with unions finding fertile ground on which to work amongst labour groups who appeared to feel isolated and threatened. Freed of the fear of a strong competitive response by the fact that each of the big airlines held strong, hub-based, geographical monopolies, each airline progressively gave way to demands for large increases in wages and salaries. The result was that by the end of the decade, wages and salaries had risen to unsustainable levels. This left the airlines extremely vulnerable to the business downturn which then began to affect them. Once it did, the airlines showed themselves slow to respond, their sheer size leading to bureaucracy and inertia.

Outside of the United States, the quest for greater size has been just as strong but has been incapable of fulfilment. One attempt was made in 2000 to grow by a policy of cross-border takeover, when British Airways proposed a takeover of the Dutch airline KLM. This, though, merely illustrated the inflexibility inherent in the anachronistic regulatory system, because the proposal had to be abandoned in the face of threats (from the United States in particular) that KLM would have to forfeit its international traffic rights if it became British controlled. KLM did eventually get together Air France, but with a deal where a special structure had to be adopted which in fact left the arrangement well short of a true merger.

As airlines sought the benefits of size through the 1990s and found that they were unable to obtain them through the "normal" processes of organic growth and merger and takeover, they progressively fell back on another expedient, that of alliances.

4:2:7 Airline Alliances

Alliance relationships now have a long, and chequered, history in the industry.

Throughout the history of commercial air transport, carriers have often preferred the comfort of co-operative rather than competitive relationships, but the modern alliance movement can be dated to 1993. Then, KLM and Northwest Airlines announced their wish to set up a strategic partnership. They were able to move ahead once the United States government gave them immunity from the US Anti-Trust laws, which it did following the signing of an "Open Skies" agreement between the US and Netherlands government, a development which we have discussed in Section 3:2:2.

The KLM/Northwest move was followed in 1995 by Lufthansa and United Airlines proposing what has become the Star Alliance. Again, anti-trust immunity was available once the German government had agreed to a US-style Open Skies Agreement. The Star Alliance grew rapidly in terms of the number of members it had, with it currently consisting of 19 member airlines.

A year later, the formation of the OneWorld alliance by British Airways, American Airlines and Cathay Pacific was announced. Although OneWorld has certainly developed since then, its activities have been hampered by the fact that American and British Airways do not have anti-trust immunity due to a long-running and bitter dispute about aviation policy between the US and British governments. This in turn means that co-operative discussions with OneWorld have always had to stop short of subjects of commercial intimacy such as fares and schedules co-ordination.

The evolution of the modern alliance scene was completed in 1999 when Air France and Delta Airlines formed the Skyteam alliance. Skyteam initially followed a different policy from Star, in that limited itself to a smaller, but, arguably, more manageable number of members. Now, though, attempts are being made to bring Continental and Northwest Airlines into the alliance, with bitter battles being fought to win what is seen as being the necessary anti-trust immunity.

It now seems that we are reaching a mature airline alliance scene consisting of three global alliances, Star, OneWorld and Skyteam. There does not seem to be room for a fourth.

There is one final element of the current alliance scene which should not be overlooked. Some airlines have not joined any of the global alliances. Virgin Atlantic and Emirates are both examples. Emirates, in particular, has taken a strong position of preferring to maintain its independence rather than become enmeshed in what the airline's chief executive has called the straitjacket of membership of a single alliance.

Overall, it is clear that the formation and growth of alliances has been a central theme of the airline industry over the last decade. It is not hard to see why. A combination of theory and practice shows that, potentially, alliances can bring their members significant benefits to their bottom line. We will look first at these benefits, before considering the – often overwhelming – problems of alliance relationships.

Theoretical principles show us that the benefits of greater size – which airline alliances are essentially aiming to tap into – can be divided into two: *Economies of Scale*, which consist of cost reductions achieved through size, and *Economies of Scope*, which reflect the revenue benefits of co-operation, normally brought about by increased marketing muscle-power.

In investigating each of these areas in today's aviation industry, we are immediately faced with the difficult question of "What is an alliance?" The word is used very loosely. It can mean anything from the most distant and loose of code-shares to a situation which is as near a merger as the present ownership and control rules allow. It also may, or may not, involve the partners in minority equity stakes.

Having said this, it is clear that airlines which enter into co-operative alliance relationships are seeking cost reductions as a result of doing so. They may engage in joint purchasing activity (though, as we shall see shortly, this is often easier said than done). A common expedient is co-operation in ground handling. If alliance partners can negotiate together, this may increase their bargaining power with the often-intransigent suppliers of airport services. Sometimes, airlines have attempted to save money by an agreement to give up being self-handling at out-stations, leaving such activity to their alliance partners. In turn, they will handle the partners at their own home base. Finally, sometimes, airlines will agree to save money by combining their sales teams, although history says that such agreements are normally only of short duration. They usually fail as soon as one of the partners finds that its revenue is falling as a result of the fact that it is no longer represented by a sales force solely motivated to promote its services.

Each of these possible areas has the potential to be important, but they are often overshadowed by the cost advantages of Code-Sharing.

Code-sharing activity between airlines can be divided into two types: that designed to cement traffic feed, and that which, however it is presented, is actually meant to reduce the intensity of competition on a route.

Code-sharing to control feed is, mostly, a legitimate activity from the consumer viewpoint. Two or more airlines may agree to share their codes, so that their connections will appear as on-line in the GDS displays. Ideally, they will then co-ordinate their activities to provide, as far as possible, genuinely seamless connections for each others' passengers. All airlines will then benefit. In particular, long-haul airlines will gain feed from short-haul markets. It may not be possible for them to fly these short-haul routes themselves, because of ownership and control rules. Even if they can, it will often make more sense to rely on a specialist short-haul airline, with a more appropriate cost structure, to do so.

Code-sharing to reduce the intensity of competition is, inevitably, much more controversial, carrying, as it does, connotations of collusion between supposed market competitors.

Such activity has a long history in the airline industry. Prior to the development of Code-Sharing in the late 1980s, airlines commonly formed "Pooling Agreements" whereby all the revenue on a route was put into a single pot and divided up at the end of each year according to a pre-agreed formula. Modern Code-Sharing agreements, in their extreme form, are little different. All the flights on a route carry the codes of both the "competitors" and are jointly marketed by both the airlines.

It is certainly possible to argue that such arrangements bring benefits to the consumer. The airlines are able to engage in co-operative rather than competitive scheduling, giving the passenger a better spread of flights throughout the day. Also, larger aircraft may be employed, giving lower seat-mile costs and the promise of lower fares. Nonetheless, these benefits must be offset against the lower intensity of competition on a route. Generally, the consumer interest is best safeguarded by competition, rather than collusion. We will return to this point shortly.

Economies-of-Scope may deliver further bottom-line benefits of airline alliance activity. For example, a group of airlines in an alliance may co-operate in marketing by offering corporate customers deals whereby if the customer will offer loyalty to the alliance, even more attractive discounts will be available. It is believed that the Star Alliance has been active in this area. Unfortunately, securing agreements amongst the alliance members may prove very difficult because of the fact that there will still be many cases where they are competing with one another. Such activity may even turn out to be of doubtful legality, at least within the European Union. It may be challenged as an abuse of a dominant position within the terms of the competition rules of the EU.

The question of alliance co-operation strengthening airline Frequent Flyer Programmes is a more telling one. Indeed, it can be suggested that in many senses this is the glue which has held the alliances together through all the difficulties that they have experienced – to be discussed shortly.

When an airline joins an alliance, it normally agrees to offer the benefits of its FFP to the programme members of all the other carriers. Thus, for example, if someone has a Gold Card issued by one of the other airlines, the new member airline will allow them to use its airport lounges. Reciprocal benefits will also be on offer to its own members. Even more importantly, alliances are able to offer the benefit of "Earn-and-Burn" rights. These mean that someone flying on any of the airlines in an alliance can earn miles in the FFP of which they are a member. They can also use these miles to obtain free flights on any alliance airline.

There is no doubt that "Earn-and-Burn" is a very significant marketing advantage. It is certainly a powerful argument in favour of joining an alliance, and it is the aspect of alliances which independent airlines outside of them find hard to deal with.

Despite the undoubted benefits that alliances have brought to those airlines that have joined them, one's sense of unease remains. We are now nearly ten years into an alliance-dominated industry, yet only a relatively low proportion of the gains which were hoped for in the early, optimistic years have actually materialised. At the same time, problems have appeared which are likely to put a permanent damper on the enthusiasm for alliances, and which many mean that they end up constituting merely a transient phase in the industry's development.

In understanding why this should be so, it should first of all be emphasised that strategic alliances are, fundamentally a difficult form of business organisation, because nobody is in overall charge. There is a constant risk that an alliance will end up using a so-called "Lowest Common Denominator" form of decision-making. This means that relatively unimportant decisions are given a disproportionate amount of time, because everyone can agree on them, whilst difficult, but vitally necessary decisions are put off, because they involve concession and compromise. Also, there is a great deal of evidence – the airline industry supports this point well, as we shall see shortly – that the more members an alliance has, the more intractable are the problems which will arise. The number of problems tends to increase exponentially with the number of members, rather than just arithmetically.

With airline alliances, perhaps the most fundamental criticism to be made of them is that they illustrate a mindset which has bedevilled the commercial airline industry almost since its inception. When faced with a tough competitor, it has nearly always been the airlines' instinct to form collusive, rather than competitive, relationships. The enthusiasm shown by airlines for so-called "Tariff Co-ordination" within IATA(when this term was largely just a euphemism for price fixing) was an illustration of this, as was the widespread use of Pooling Agreements referred to earlier in this section.

Such enthusiasm would have been understandable had it been successful in solving the perennial problem amongst "Differentiator" airlines of inadequate levels of profitability. There is no evidence at all that it did. The reason is all too clear. Without the challenge of strong competition, airlines do not work sufficiently hard to control their costs, particularly their labour costs. They therefore quickly eat up all the guaranteed revenues which collusive behaviour gives them, leading to calls for a further diminution of competition.

It is instructive in this regard to look at two air transport markets where, historically, levels of profitability have generally been better than amongst the "Differentiator" airlines. These are the markets of charter airlines in Europe and the "Cost Leader" sector we analysed in Section 4:2:6. In both cases, these sectors have been characterised by an almost complete absence of collusive behaviour. In both cases, too, profitability has been stronger, and far less cyclical, than amongst "Differentiator" airlines. This is because airlines within these sectors have always known that cost control and cost management was a core business function, and failure to address it would be likely to result in bankruptcy. The result has been that their wage and salary rates have generally been more reasonable, and their labour productivity far higher, than has been the case amongst "Differentiator" airlines.

Overall, one is led to a cynical, but inevitable conclusion: the much vaunted cost savings that airlines are thought likely to experience as a result of alliance membership will turn out to be illusory. For all the cost savings which *are* achieved, there will also be cost increases as a result of the very substantial costs of the bureaucracy associated with running the alliances. Also, alliances will be the cause of a leveraging up of labour costs amongst their members.

It is true that in recent years labour cost pressures in the industry have abated, due to the disastrous state of airline finances and the fears of redundancy and job losses which this has engendered. However, there were clear signs of this leveraging effect before the crisis struck, with high salary increases for pilots at United Airlines being followed by labour unrest at Air Canada and Lufthansa, both Star Alliance members alongside United. It may soon come back if the present signs of a long overdue recovery continue. Of course, advertising messages may not help. The Star Alliance in particular has put out large amounts of advertising emphasising the way in which passengers should view its airlines as a single entity, working together as one to improve the passenger experience. The more it does so, the more it invites the riposte from the unions within each member airline that wages and salaries should be comparable across the alliance. Naturally, this will lead to a leveraging up, rather than a leveraging down, of labour costs.

The other problem of airline alliances is a particularly pressing one at the moment. There are too many differences in financial performance and product standards amongst the alliance members. Again, the Star Alliance illustrates this problem in its starkest form. Amongst the Star Alliance carriers is Lufthansa, a carrier with high product standards and considerable financial strength. At the opposite end of the spectrum is United Airlines. United was in Chapter 11 bankruptcy for over three years, only emerging from it in the spring of 2006. Its balance sheet is still in very poor shape. How can United finance the investment which will ensure that it at least closes the gap between its product standards and those of Lufthansa? Also, how can the Star Alliance carriers generally engage in strategic discussions about developing their long-term co-operation, when they must all know the possibility exists that United may not survive? For United itself, inevitably the priority will have to be the raising of cash in the short term to meet obligations and stave off liquidation, rather than planning for the strategic strengthening of co-operation within Star. The Brazilian carrier Varig has been another Star airline which has had to deal with severe financial problems – indeed, at the time of writing it appears unlikely to be able to stay in business.

If all this sounds overly negative, it should be born in mind that alliance relationships can be successful ones in the aviation industry. For this to happen, though, the number of alliance partners must be kept small and manageable. There must be a powerful enemy, strong enough to ensure that the alliance members have to overcome their mutual animosities and stay together. Each alliance member must know that they cannot take on the enemy alone.

In the airline industry, Airbus illustrates this point well. Since 2001, Airbus has been constituted as a fully-integrated business, but for the first thirty years of its life it was a strategic alliance of German, French, Spanish and British aerospace interests. Harmony did not always characterise relationships within the consortium, but its members always knew that they had to stick together, because no individual firm could take on the common enemy – Boeing – on their own and hope to win.

The world of GDSs also shows this "common enemy" principle. Both Galileo and Amadeus were formed in the late 1980s by different consortia of European airlines, and neither had an easy birth. The two consortia did, though, stay intact through the 1990s, because they needed to do so. In the background was the SABRE GDS, then wholly owned by American Airlines. It was no secret that American had aggressive plans to move SABRE into a globally-dominant position, and that they had such a head start that no GDS owned just by one other airline could prevent them from doing so. The Galileo and Amadeus consortia therefore had to stay together, in order to thwart American's plans. Now, with airlines mostly having sold off their GDS shareholdings, it is instructive that some of the most impressive examples of successful airline alliance co-operation are coming with the strong position being taken by each of the alliances in their attempts to secure reductions in GDS booking fees.

No such conditions of an overwhelming common enemy exist to underpin the difficult world of airline alliances when they are dealing with the fundamental question of where they should compete and where they should co-operate with each other. This writer's experience is that whatever they may say in public, airlines generally regard their so-called alliance 'partners' as actually being amongst their most significant competitors.

The likely way forward for the alliances is that they will continue for the time being, bringing to their members some, but far from all, of the net benefits which were hoped for by their founders. Eventually, though, the restrictions on cross-border ownership of airlines – the driving force behind the formation of airline alliances – will be eased and may eventually disappear. When they are, alliances will become largely a thing of the past. They will be replaced by global airlines.

Whether this will solve the airline industry's seemingly perennial financial problems must be a matter for conjecture. As we have seen, there has already been one market, the US domestic market, where consolidation into a small number of mega-airlines has been permitted. One of the arguments used by regulators for allowing this to happen was that it would lead to stability through improved airline profitability. The reverse has actually happened, with rising labour costs amongst the de-motivated workforces of large, amorphous and remote carriers a primary reason. There is no reason to think that true global airlines would not go the same way. Nonetheless, the movement for consolidation is likely to prove unstoppable. If it is, it will be interesting to see if the existing alliances turn out to be the basis of any global airlines that emerge. It is possible that new groupings will come through, perhaps driven by the animosities which have arisen within the existing alliances.

4:3 "Differentiation" Airlines – The Future

4:3:1 The Concept of the "Legacy Airline"

In Section 4:2:8, we looked at the business model employed by the world's "Differentiation" airlines. We saw that, during the second half of the 1990s, whilst profitability was still inadequate, these airlines were generally doing as well as they had ever done. Good returns were being earned by the industry's traditionally stronger airlines such as American, Delta and British Airways, whilst even some of the weaker players (such as the Belgian carrier Sabena) moved into the black after years of losses.

Only a few short years later, the picture could not have been more different. The losses amongst the once–strong airlines of the USA were staggering, whilst in Europe airline profitability was generally weak. Some airlines were unable to survive, notably so Swissair and the aforementioned Sabena. Only in south east Asia did the traditional business model still seem to be working well, for such carriers as Singapore Airlines and Cathay Pacific. They were being joined by some of the carriers of mainland China where strong traffic growth was assisting them in joining the small elite of Differentiation airlines which were still achieving profits. Then, the SARS epidemic interrupted even this favourable trend.

In looking for any explanation for this rapid and catastrophic turnaround in airline financial fortunes, the managements of the airlines concerned would no doubt have liked us to look to factors wholly outside their control.

To some extent, we would have been right to do so. The terrorist attacks on New York of September 11 2001 dented the confidence of travellers, notably US travellers. This confidence took a long time to return. The subsequent "War on Terrorism" and the allied attack on Iraq worsened the problems of depressed demand, as passengers feared reprisal attacks on civil aviation. In turn, the need for increased security checks at airports added to the hassles associated with air travel, making the discretionary traveller who did not have to make a particular trip much more likely to stay at home. For the business traveller who chose not to fly, they could, of course, continue their business much more easily than before because of advances in electronic forms of communication.

External factors associated with wars and terrorism were a part, but by no means the whole, explanation for the woes of the Differentiation airlines which they experienced between 2001 and 2005. These airlines would also want us to use as an excuse the economic slowdown which began in the United States in 2000, and subsequently spread to other markets.

Airlines are never likely to find things as easy in a recession as they do in prosperous times, but we should be wary of giving too much credence to arguments that the economic slowdown is an "external" factor about which airlines can do nothing. During the boom years of the 1990s, many airlines pursued aggressive expansion programmes, despite the fact that the evidence of history suggested that the world economic boom then in progress was overdue for a correction. Even more unforgivably, they often based their expansion plans on a concentration on "Premium Traffic" – that in First and Business Class cabins. It is schoolboy economics to say that this was a mistake, because all the evidence one could possibly require is there to say that this is the type of traffic most severely affected by the onset of recession. British Airways is but one airline of many at which the criticism can be levelled that its strategy involved an extremely risky concentration on the Premium end of the market.

Of course, as we have seen, at the same time as Differentiation airlines struggled in a recession-hit market, many Cost Leader airlines saw little effect on their growth and profitability. This is because their business model showed itself to be far more resilient in the face of the ups and downs of the Trade Cycle.

Aside from "Terrorism" and "Trade Cycle" issues, Differentiation airlines were affected by fundamental changes in customer needs and market segmentation. The rapid rise in the importance of the "Independent" business traveller, who regarded the price of the ticket as being much more important than their corporate counterparts, was one factor in this, depressing yields significantly. The increase in the amount of business travel sold on the basis of corporate dealing (see Section 2:2:4) had a similar effect. It is not convincing, though, for airlines to argue that they were the innocent victims of these trends. It is certainly possible to argue that successful carriers are always likely to be those which anticipate change and are ready when it occurs. Unsuccessful carriers are often those which wait for change to happen and then make a belated response to it. In many ways, the problems endured by many traditional Differentiation airlines illustrated exactly the latter failing.

Table 4.2 Staff Costs 1999(Average Annual Remuneration, USD)

Airline	Pilots & Co-pilots	Cabin Attendants
1. Air Portugal	$144,570	$44,215
2. British Airways	$121,153	$30,815
3. British Midland	$ 94,995	$28,721
4. Iberia	$188,091	$59,340
5. Lufthansa	$141,646	$50,017
6. SAS	$129,445	$58,441
7. Virgin Atlantic	$ 85,048	$18,810

Source: ICAO.

Other criticisms of these airlines are in a sense even more damning. Table 4:2 presents data giving average salaries for selected work groups at a number of European airlines at the height of the boom in the late 1990s. By any standards, some of the numbers are excessive, and reflect the fact that, as we have seen, airlines had little incentive to control their costs when regulatory protection meant that they had nothing to fear from the potential threat of lower cost new entrants. Nor could such high rewards be said to reflect what people might be entitled to expect from working for highly profitable and successful businesses.

Of course, high wages and salaries need not indicate high unit costs, if they are offset by extremely high productivity. Southwest Airlines has always prided itself on not being a sweatshop. All the work groups at Southwest are rewarded at market rates, or at levels which are even somewhat above the average. Its remarkable ability to maintain low unit costs, even now when it is a very large and mature airline, reflects the fact that its labour productivity is very high.

The same conclusion cannot be reached for most traditional airlines. For example, the rules governing pilots' hours as set by the various regulatory bodies are complex, but in summary allow pilots to work a total of 900 duty hours in a year. Many European airlines had agreements with their pilots which require them to work only two-thirds or even a half of the permitted maximum. Not surprisingly, Ryanair has made it a condition of the jobs offered to pilots that they will be rewarded at market rates, but that they should expect to work the full number of hours which the regulators allow.

Besides having a cost base which was no longer sustainable in difficult, changing, market conditions, there are two other aspects of the traditional business model of Differentiation which rendered it under threat, especially in short-haul markets.

We have already referred to the way in which Cost Leader airlines concentrate on point-to-point traffic, avoiding the extra costs and revenue dilution associated with connections and transfers. The whole of the traditional business model of Differentiation was based on transfer traffic and hubbing. Fares were kept extremely high for point-to-point passengers who had few choices available to them. Much lower prices were offered to connecting passengers to encourage them to use the airline's hub, rather than the connecting possibilities offered by other carriers.

There is an economic defence to be offered for such a pricing policy. Hubbing passengers, even though they are low-yielding, contribute to the spreading of overheads and allow for frequencies to be increased over a wider route network. They also permit larger aircraft to be used, which may allow the passenger to benefit from the lower seat-kilometre costs associated with bigger planes. The model is, though, entirely dependent on high fares being paid by point-to-point passengers if overall costs are to be covered. In that sense, it can be argued that it is based on cross-subsidy from point-to-point to connecting passengers.

In recent years, this aspect of the business model of traditional airlines has ceased to work. As we have seen, the Cost Leader players specialise exclusively in point-to-point traffic, and their fares do not contain this element of cross-subsidy. They have taken away a significant proportion of the point-to-point traffic of rival airlines, meaning that, overall, the business model for short-haul routes is no longer offering the prospect of adequate profitability.

A final set of criticisms can be made of airline Revenue Management policies. Pricing and Revenue Management is the subject of Chapter 6 of the book, but it can be stated that a sound Revenue Management policy will have many components. One aspect will be to vary prices according to people's willingness and ability to pay.

Traditional airlines took such a policy too far. On short-haul routes prices were kept extremely high for people who needed a flexible ticket. Much lower fares were available, but on a strictly controlled basis whereby those using them had to comply with tight conditions regarding (sometimes) an advanced booking requirement, length-of-stay rules and restrictions on cancellation and re-booking. The result was that those using flexible tickets paid prices which to the airlines charging them were extremely high yielding.

The fact that they were was long regarded by Revenue Management professionals as a triumph. People who had to travel, often at short notice were paying prices which reflected their very low price elasticity.

Unfortunately, it is now clear that these policies were having another, less desirable effect. They were responsible for a strong feeling of resentment against the airlines whose pricing policies were actually reflecting the fact that those using high priced tickets had no choice. All traditional airlines were using the same pricing policy, and regulation was preventing the entry of new airlines into the market.

Now, the situation is very different, with the explosion of entry of Cost Leader airlines. In turn, this entry has shown up what could be described as the "water behind the dam" effect of airline Revenue Management policies. Those who paid very high fares before were not "willing" to pay them as the jargon of Revenue Management would suggest – rather they were "forced" to pay them by the lack of choice. Once a choice became available, many have taken a particular pleasure in voting with their feet and transferring to Cost Leader airlines, partly to punish those whom they believed had exploited them. Overall, one can say that the attitude of consumers to high air fares changed for all time. Cheap point-to-point fares became regarded as the norm, and high prices as exceptional and unjustified.

Overall, we are forced to a depressing conclusion about the business model of Differentiation in the airline industry. Only a short time ago, this model was earning reasonable returns for the better-managed airlines. Then, there was a long period when it failed to do so. Wars and terrorism fears depressed demand, and may do so again, at any time. The business model was shown to be incompatible with the ups and downs of the Trade Cycle, with airlines hoping against hope for an early resumption of strong economic growth to rescue them. Market segmentation and customer needs changed, lowering yields and giving opportunity to rapidly developing competitors from the Cost Leader sector. The business model of the airlines was also shown to be built on the sand, being based on the charging of unacceptably high prices to supposedly "captive" business travellers, and on cross-subsidy from point-to-point to connecting passengers.

Of course, at the time of writing, (summer 2006), things might be held to be different. 2005 and the first half of 2006 have seen signs of improvements in the finances of even some of the world's most troubled airlines, despite the problem of continuing high oil prices. We may, though, be in a fool's paradise, with financial improvements being driven largely by the buoyancy of demand, fuelled in turn by strong growth in the world economy. This boost will disappear when growth slows again. It is interesting, too, that the airlines have responded to the short term improvements in financial performance by ordering new aircraft in staggering numbers. Both Boeing and Airbus had record years in 2005 in terms of the number or orders they took for new aircraft. Will airlines never learn?

Such a litany of problems would be very serious indeed for carriers trying to navigate their way through challenging times with fully competitive cost structures. Unfortunately, long-established airlines have often had a high cost legacy built up during times of state-ownership and the absence of price competition or, in the case of US airlines in particular, during a time of strong union militancy in a then-buoyant market.

In recent years, a new term has come into common usage to describe many of these carriers – "Legacy Airlines". It is an appropriate one. They have attempted to navigate extremely difficult waters with a set of problems left over from a time when circumstances in the industry were very different. They have had competition from newer airlines that have had the priceless advantage of setting out in recent competitive market conditions. They therefore had no legacy from the past to deal with.

Given this litany of problems, it is not at all surprising that recent years have seen a great deal of discussion of the strategic options open to the Legacy sector.

4:3:2 "Legacy Airlines" – Strategic Options

For these airlines, it should be emphasised that their situation is by no means hopeless. They carry with them some very valuable strengths today, and have worthwhile opportunities which will open up for them in the future. For example, the very fact that they are long-established means that they have Grandfather Rights on airport slots which often stretch back many years. They will retain these rights into the future, unless the industry radically changes the methods used for slot allocation, something which, at the time of writing, appears unlikely. Also, and despite the criticisms of hubbing made in the previous section, their hubs do give them opportunities to gather in traffic from a wide geographical area, and provide a worthwhile fortress against new entrants. As we have seen, their Frequent Flyer Programmes are valuable, and pose a difficult competitive issue for smaller newcomers. Also, despite the criticisms made in Section 4:2:6 about airline alliances, one has to concede that to some degree alliance membership should be seen as a strength, particularly when it comes to negotiating with 'common enemy' outside suppliers.

Perhaps of greatest value to these airlines is that they still have a defendable position in long-haul markets. As we have seen, it is much harder for Cost Leader approaches to succeed on long-haul routes, because of the difficulties such airlines have in establishing and sustaining a substantial cost advantage.

Finally, the very fact that "Legacy" airlines are long-established allows them to make the branding claim that they are "proven". A carrier with an unblemished safety record stretching back for many years is likely to be able to persuade the nervous traveller to choose them rather than a new entrant, whose safety promise must be taken on trust. Unfortunately, for British and American airlines, the fact that they may have a proven safety record may not be enough to stave off the perception that they are a possible target for terrorist attack, following on from the Second Gulf War of 2003. and the so-called 'War on Terror'.

Despite these strengths, the Legacy airlines have had to change their strategies. Indeed, those that have not done so have simply gone out of business, or have become dependent on state handouts and protection. The question is, what strategic options have been open to them? Fortunately, there have been a number. No single option has provided all the answers. Carriers have had to select the best parts of each one in order to define an overall strategy.

A first option might be described as a "Retreat to Core" strategy. As we have seen, the Legacy carriers still have a defendable position in long-haul markets. Also, despite the radical nature of the developments which have taken place on short-haul, they have not affected every passenger. There is still a hard core of business people who will pay high prices for a flexible ticket and a seat in a comfortable Business Class, even on short journeys. Has it been possible to retreat to this core of high-yielding and hopefully profitable business? Certainly, at the present time all the Major US airlines are trying to increase the emphasis which they are placing on long-haul international services, while shrinking their involvement in the American domestic market, where competition from Low Cost Carriers is at its most intense.

Strategies of retrenchment are notoriously difficult to implement in the airline industry. They require, to begin with, a complete re-planning of the fleet around smaller aircraft. Those high yielding passengers who constitute the supposed core will normally be business travellers, who will in turn be extremely frequency-sensitive. Airlines will also need to maintain frequency to ensure that there are sufficient numbers of connecting passengers feeding into their long-haul services. Fortunately, there are now suitable aircraft available. The smaller versions of the B737 and Airbus A320 families are well-proven, if less than optimal, aircraft. Embraer is now introducing its 170 and 190 families of new aircraft with around 100 seats.

Although these aircraft have good operating economics, inevitably their seat-kilometre costs are quite high, especially given the generous salaries normally paid to pilots by Legacy carriers. These salaries are, of course, especially punitive when spread over only the hundred seats or so of a small aircraft.

This aspect of "Retreat to Core" strategy is one aspect of a more general problem. Such a retreat involves cutting back on the scale of an airline's activity. The reduction in revenue will be immediate. Far more problematic will be the carrier's ability to reduce overhead costs at the same rate, or, hopefully, faster, than revenue declines. Achieving this in the airline industry is notoriously difficult. A far more likely situation is that the decline in overhead will be less than the decline in revenue. Each passenger who remains will then, through the fares that they pay, have to cover a greater proportion of overhead if overall profitability is to be achieved. Given the long term trend in the industry for yields to decline rather than rise, it is unlikely that they will.

The other major problem of "Retreat to Core" strategies is that they can leave market opportunities open to competitors. The situation in the UK aviation industry illustrates this problem well. Many short-haul destinations have been served from both London's Heathrow and Gatwick Airports. Generally, profitability has been much better on the routes from Heathrow. If an airline is making money by serving a destination from Heathrow, whilst incurring losses on the equivalent route from Gatwick, the solution appears to be obvious. By cutting out the Gatwick service, the profitable core can be identified and overall profitability achieved. Unfortunately, in practice, the situation may not be so simple. Giving up a route may involve the relinquishing of airport slots which under the "Grandfather Rights" rules described in Section 3:2:6, can then be awarded to another airline on an "in perpetuity" basis. This airline may then use the slot to sharpen its attack on the rival which gave it up in the first place. This may involve beginning service on the specific route abandoned by the first airline. If the challenger has lower costs and more attractive fares than its competition, traffic may be attracted from the "core" route, turning it from profit into loss-making.

The second strategic option is a very clear one, and has been dealt with in Section 4:2:4. If "Legacy" airlines find that their position in short-haul markets is being undermined by "Cost Leader" players, it seems the most obvious of initiatives for them to fight back by setting up Cost Leader subsidiaries of their own. The jury is still out on the question as to whether this is a sound strategy or not. So far, the results produced by it have been, at best, mixed. Those airlines which have recently decided to use it will no doubt argue that lessons have been learned, and that we should now be talking about "second generation" Cost Leader subsidiaries which will achieve much better results. In the month before this new edition was completed, both South African Airways and Iberia announced that they were intending to set up new Cost Leader subsidiaries, so the area is certainly still an active one.

It is interesting to note that some airlines have examined and rejected the idea of a Cost Leader subsidiary. Aer Lingus has never set up such an airline, despite being the first European airline to face competition from a Cost Leader player (Ryanair is based in Dublin), and to face it in a particularly severe form. As we have seen, British Airways set up a Cost Leader subsidiary called Go, but sold it in 2001. If the public statements of the present BA Chief Executive are to be believed, they have no plans to re-enter the sector.

All Legacy airlines, whether they have set up a Cost Leader subsidiary or not, have had to follow the third strategic option. They have had to do all they could to reduce their cost base. If they can reduce the often enormous disparity between their costs and those of the newer Cost Leader airlines, they are then in a position to lower their fares themselves. They may also be able to regain some of the passengers who may be unhappy at the sacrifices the Cost Leaders require them to make to gain access to their cheap prices.

Some of these cost reductions have been achieved relatively painlessly. All airlines have undoubtedly leant on their suppliers and demanded concessions from them. In a recession-hit industry, these suppliers have had little choice but to agree, especially if airlines pursue tough policies to reduce the number of their suppliers so that they are able to exercise the maximum amount of buying power over them. Commission costs and GDS booking fees have come down everywhere as airlines have relied on such initiatives as electronic ticketing and selling over the Internet. A growing self-service culture has been encouraged through useful developments as self-service or, more recently, on-line check-in. Finally, some successful attempts have been made to cut out some of the complexities which Legacy airlines have traditionally built into their business model. This has in turn allowed for lower costs as a result of a reduction in overhead expenses.

Important though such initiatives have been, they do not address the key question. As always, has been those airlines that have successfully dealt with the perennial Legacy airline problem of labour costs that are now the best placed to face what is bound to be very rough weather in the future.

Labour costs are vital to Legacy airlines because they are the biggest single input cost item for them. Commonly, 30% or more of their costs are made up by wages, salaries and benefits. Addressing labour costs therefore has the greatest single impact on unit costs. Unfortunately, in doing so, airlines have been faced with the fact that their unions are generally in a very powerful bargaining position. The list of work groups who can paralyse an airline through strike action is a very long one. As service businesses, carriers have no opportunity to build up inventory with customers in advance of a strike. Once it begins, the effect of a strike on cash flow will be immediate. In the case of one work group – pilots – airlines have to deal with people who are generally articulate and intelligent and with a long record of militancy at many carriers. Finally, in the view of this writer at least, airlines have worsened what would in any case be a difficult labour relations environment by their continuing belief that big is better. Too often, people working in large airlines feel isolated and threatened, providing fertile ground for trade union militancy.

In some cases, carriers have resorted to extreme measures to bring down their labour costs. The US Chapter 11 bankruptcy code allows a firm to receive, for a period of time, court protection from its creditors. Several airlines have used time in Chapter 11 to radically change their labour contracts, emerging from bankruptcy with a much lower cost base. USAirways did this in 2002/3. Air Canada used the Canadian equivalent at same time. United Airlines and Delta have done so subsequently. Others have used the possibility of bankruptcy as a threat. American Airlines in March 2003 obtained significant concessions from its normally militant unions by suggesting that a bankruptcy filing would take place if these concessions were not granted. The unions knew, of course, that they would be taken anyway if American had gone in Chapter 11.

More generally, it often proves possible for airlines to lower labour costs in a time of crisis. The threat of bankruptcy, or at least of large job losses, will usually be enough to focus minds. The problem, of course, is that demands will be made for the old conditions of service to be re-instated once happier times return. In the meantime, customer service standards will slip, if the workforce becomes punch-drunk and demoralised.

A further possibility for addressing labour cost issues is to make a proportion of the rewards available depend on company performance through stock options and profit-sharing schemes. Such methods have been used by some of the new entrant Cost Leader airlines, where profits have been good and share prices rising. They are of no relevance, though, to Legacy airlines where share prices have fallen to very low levels and profits are non-existent. In any case, the whole question of employee shareholdings has been discredited by the experience of United, where for a number of years the employees actually owned a majority of the company's shares. This did not turn out to be a recipe for harmonious labour relations – much the reverse. The experiment was finally abandoned in March 2003.

Overall, we can say that if there was an easy, miracle solution to the problem of labour costs and labour productivity at the Legacy airlines, it would have been found by now. Moving forward on the labour cost front has, though, been vitally important, and inaction has not been an option. Further progress will depend on the correct policies being pursued in a wide range of areas. This author believes that the most important factor will be inspiring, sympathetic and considerate leadership, by a leadership team which convincingly demonstrates that it does not have its own snout in the trough whilst asking others to make sacrifices.

If costs *can* continue to be brought down, and the reductions maintained on a permanent basis, exciting new opportunities will appear. We have looked in Section 4:2:3 at the successes of Cost Leader airlines, but it is clear that from the consumer viewpoint, flying with these airlines does have its drawbacks. People may have to use an inconvenient airport, accept a "no frills" on-board product or be denied a seat-selection service. Most importantly, some of the Cost Leader airlines appear to be taking a gamble on questions of customer service. If things go according to plan – and they usually do – passengers benefit from remarkably cheap fares. If things go wrong, though, the passenger experience may be very different. The European press and media regularly carry horror stories about the problems experienced by passengers whose flight is badly delayed or whose bags are lost. Once such a severe service failure has been experienced, is a passenger's view of Cost Leader airlines changed for all time, and will they become willing to pay more to fly on an airline which does give appropriate attention to customer service? If they do, full service airlines can be expected to benefit from the gradual build-up of a so-called "Army of the Disaffected", of those who feel that they have been let down by the Cost Leader sector.

It would be wrong to exaggerate the importance of this trend. There will be no return to the days of extremely high airfares. Sound standards of customer service may, though, allow the Differentiation airlines to hold prices a small amount above those of the lowest pricing Cost Leaders. For those that can reduce their costs down to these levels, a return to profitability for their short-haul services may still be possible.

A strategic option which has been followed by many Differentiation airlines has been to subcontract some of their short haul feeder services to airlines with a more appropriate cost structure. As we have seen, service on thinner routes often presents traditional airlines with particular problems. Pilots unions have generally successfully made the case that pilot salaries should be higher for flying bigger aircraft. They do not usually accept the corollary that if an airline introduces smaller planes, salaries should fall.

The result is that carriers often end up flying regional jets on the basis of high pilot salaries, making profitability on thin routes impossible.

The answer to this problem is to ensure that the thinner routes are flown by regional airlines with better cost structure, using Code-Sharing and franchising relationships. Though such expedients raise questions about brand integrity, the policy has generally turned out to be a sound one. The large airline gains the benefit of feed onto its long-haul routes without the costs of trying to do the job itself. The smaller carrier also benefits through such aspects as membership of the major carrier's Frequent Flyer Programme.

Despite the usefulness of franchising, there has been a limit on the extent to which it can be employed. Strong resistance has been encountered from pilots' unions, who have interpreted it – often correctly – as being a device to reduce the number of highly paid pilot jobs, as regional subsidiaries or franchise partners take over an increasing proportion of short-haul flying. The result has been their insistence on "Scope Clauses" which limit the number of small regional jets that can be flown to a fixed, small, percentage of the aircraft in use by the mainline airline. The disastrous financial state of many airlines in recent years has given opportunities for these clauses to be renegotiated along more flexible lines.

A last strategic option open to threatened Legacy airlines might be described as "Jugular Marketing". If the position of a long-established airline comes under attack from new entrants, it may respond aggressively. Fares may be cut to the levels of the newcomers, or even below them. Capacity may also be added so that there is a glut of seats in the market. Such a policy will be designed to drive the new entrants out of the market, and also to send a clear message to others to keep away. Lufthansa's policies in Germany towards Low Cost Carriers do, at the time of writing, seem to reflect exactly these principles.

Such tactics now have to be employed with caution. It will depend on the particular legal jurisdiction under which the airline is operating, but they may well be interpreted by the courts as representing an "Abuse of a Dominant Position". None-the-less, the dividing line between what is an abuse and what is a legitimate (and, from the consumer viewpoint, desirable) response to a competitive challenge will always be a fine one. Established airlines cannot be expected to do nothing, nor should they be, as the ground is taken from beneath their feet.

This has been a difficult section of the book, and it will be a relief in the next one to reach happier ground. The facts, though, cannot be avoided. The undermining of the position of many once strong Differentiation airlines has been the major strategic trend in the industry over the past five years. The best managed of these carriers certainly do have a future, but they have had to radically reform their ways of doing business.

4:4 "Focus" Strategies

4:4:1 Types of Focussing in the Airline Industry

In Section 4:2:1 we looked at the two-by-two diagram developed by Professor Michael Porter to describe different business strategies. Using the diagram, he suggests that there are two possible Focussing positions. They both involve the same principles – giving up all benefits of synergies by concentrating on one single activity. Sustainable Competitive Advantage can then be found through the expertise built up in one area. Where focussing works successfully, this expertise will be so great that the firm will be able to use it to hold off the competitive challenge of the so-called 'Industrywide' Differentiation players, who often will base their pursuit of Competitive Advantage on the synergies available to the multi-product firm.

In the diagram, Porter proposes that successful Focussing can come about in two ways. Some Focussing firms achieve a defendable position by adding a great deal of value, which allows them to cover high production costs and still sustain profitability. Others use their expertise to achieve very low costs.

The airline industry illustrates both of these positions.

4:4:2 "Value Added" Focussing

A very good example of "Value Added" focussing in the airline industry is that of "Integrated Carriers" such as Fedex and UPS. Both these firms are now long-established, and both have modified their basic business strategies in recent years to reflect changing market conditions. They have, though, always had a strong emphasis on a single activity – the provision of guaranteed next-day delivery services for shippers who need to send small, urgent packages.

Such a service cannot be provided cheaply. Indeed, capital investment needs are enormous. Integrators need to invest in very large fleets of freighter aircraft. They generally cannot rely on the services of existing airlines, which, on short-haul routes at least mainly provide capacity in the daytime, in passenger aircraft belly-holds. They also must construct and run costly sortation centres at their hubs, centres which are capable of dealing with millions of packages in a short two-or-three hour window in the middle of the night. Huge investment will be needed in the surface transport vehicles which they will need in order to offer the collection and delivery part of their service. They will also be involved in heavy spending on Information Technology in order to provide the tracking and tracing options which their customers expect.

Such large capital requirements provide a formidable barrier-to-entry. It now looks likely that UPS and Fedex will be the leading players in the duopoly which has always been likely to be the mature structure of the integrated operations industry. It is possible, though, for those that make the investment to cover their costs and achieve profitability because of the uniqueness of their product and the substantial amount of value that they add. Prior to the arrival of the Integrators, the shipper of a small urgent package was required to solve most of their problems themselves. Traditional airlines were only interested in the undemanding task of moving goods on an airport-to-airport basis. Collection and delivery had to be arranged by the shipper, normally using the services of an air freight forwarder. In addition, it was rarely possible to achieve the late afternoon collection, early next morning delivery ideal because, as we have seen, combination airlines relying on belly-hold capacity had most of their freight space available in the daytime. Little was available at the dead of night, as it would need to be if true overnight delivery was to be available.

Another value-adding Focussing proposition has been tried frequently in the airline industry, but appears to offer a much poorer chance of sustainable profits. This proposition is based on the idea of focussing exclusively on meeting the needs of the business air traveller.

At first sight, the strategy appears to be a promising one. Market surveys amongst higher status business travellers show that they expect such things as high standards of seating comfort and in-flight service from the airlines they choose. Sometimes, though, an additional factor emerges. Business travellers often say that they dislike flying with those on vacation, who may be noisy and disruptive. They say that they would prefer their own airline, where their needs and status can be properly recognised.

Given such apparently fertile ground, there has been a regular supply of start-up airlines focussing purely on the market of high status business travellers. MGMGrand Air was a United States example – it ceased trading in 1995. From 1995 until it closed in 1998, Fairlines was a European equivalent, flying all First Class services from its Paris base.

In October 2005, two new, very interesting, airlines both began flying the route between JFK Airport in New York and London's Stansted Airport. Both have been employing an 'All Business Class' strategy, though there have been substantial differences in the detail of the strategy that each has adopted. The first, Maxjet, has been flying a Boeing 767, with good, but not exceptional, standards of seating comfort – each aircraft has been configured with just over 100 seats. Eos Air, in contrast, is using a single-aisle Boeing 757, but has placed only 48 seats in the aircraft. These offer truly remarkable standards of seating comfort, with each seat folding down into a flat bed, and provision for another seat to be available so that business meetings can be held during the flight.

Despite their popularity with start-up entrepreneurs, no business travel focussed airline has yet stood the test of time This is firstly because the concept is based on a misunderstanding of the priority of need of the business traveller. Business people certainly appreciate high standards of in-flight service and the benefits in terms of status and exclusivity which having their own airline can give them. Their most important needs, though, are more mundane. They must have a high frequency of conveniently-timed flights over a broad route network. They also appreciate the personal gains available to them (using their employer's money) of a Frequent Flyer Programme. All these needs can be better met by Differentiation airlines, exploiting the synergies available from carrying both business and leisure travellers. Indeed, one of the great problems of business traveller focussed airlines is the question of what they do with their aircraft during holiday periods and over the weekend when the business market falls away.

The second problem with the All Business Class concept is that it is as far away as can be imagined from a niche strategy designed not to provoke a damaging competitive response from stronger and more powerful rivals. Eos Air in particular is targeting well-established rivals – British Airways, Virgin Atlantic, United Airlines and American Airlines, on one of their most important and profitable routes. It is also seeking to take market share away from them in the most important market that they have – high yield passengers in the First and Business Class cabins. In doing so, it is provoking these airlines into a competitive battle that they simply cannot afford to lose. Sadly, a bloody and (for Eos) fatal confrontation looks to be a serious risk.

Of Eos and Maxjet, perhaps one can be more optimistic in the case of Maxjet, and it is possible that this airline will set a new template for a successful 'All Business Class' strategy. Its fares (and unit costs) are much lower than those of Eos, and it appears to be aiming at the much larger market for full economy and 'Premium Economy' passengers (to use Virgin Atlantic's jargon). It may be able to find profitable uses for its aircraft on charter work during slack times for business travel. Finally, by choosing a wide-bodied rather than a narrow-bodied aircraft, they will have air cargo as a potential source of revenue, given that the airline's concentration on business travellers and relatively small number of seats in each aircraft will mean that little belly hold space will be taken up with passenger's baggage. Its prospects will look particularly bright if it can find working relationships with the Low Cost Carriers which dominate short-haul flying out of London's Stansted Airport.

Despite one's reservations about Eos Air, there may be one possible way in which a business traveller Focus may work and that is under the umbrella of a full-service airline. In many senses, the Concorde flights of Air France and British Airways were exactly that, being focussed on the tiny "tip of the pyramid" market. Both airlines continued with them for a long period, so one must assume that a profit was made, though "profit" has a doubtful meaning when the airlines received the aircraft free of charge from their respective governments. The services, were, of course, terminated in October 2003, largely due to technical problems with the aircraft and their increasing age.

Concorde services have come to an end, but an experiment has recently been mounted by the German carrier Lufthansa which may have interesting possibilities. Both Boeing and Airbus offer corporate jet versions of their narrow-bodied aircraft, Boeing with its 737 and Airbus with the A319. In essence, because corporate jets do not need large amounts of belly-hold space to be available for passenger's baggage, the manufacturers have used some of the belly-holds of their aircraft to install the extra fuel tanks necessary to give corporate customers the long ranges which they expect.

During 2002, Lufthansa entered into an arrangement with the Swiss-based corporate jet operator Privatair that Privatair should provide corporate jet services on three routes between Germany and the USA, with the aircraft configured with 48 all-Business Class seats. The services are branded by Lufthansa and sold through the Lufthansa marketing system. Users are given privilege and exclusivity, but have all the back-up in terms of frequency and network of Lufthansa's "normal" services. They are also able to gain points in the Lufthansa "Miles and More" Frequent Flyer Programme. An additional selling point is that Dusseldorf Airport is used, rather than Lufthansa's main hub at Frankfurt. This allows passengers to escape from most of the delays and security hassles that they might otherwise encounter. In any case, it would not be possible to mount the services from Frankfurt because of the slot shortages which exit there.

Since 2002, Lufthansa has continued with these services, and has expanded the number of destinations served. One must therefore assume that they are satisfied with the financial results. Also, Swiss International Airlines (now closely associated with Lufthansa), has begun similar services out of Zurich. Air France has also started a comparable co-operation with Privatair, though its All Business Class services are mainly on new routes (to oil-related destinations) that the airline has not previously served.

A final example of *Value Added* focussing in today's airline industry marks the policies being pursued by many smaller airlines from tourism receiving countries. Airlines such as Air Mauritius and Air Seychelles could be said to be engaging in a form of "Geographical" focussing. They cannot set out to conquer the world, but they can claim to know the particular country where they are based better than anyone else. Someone on holiday choosing them might feel that their vacation was beginning sooner than would be the case on, say, British Airways or Lufthansa where the flight to their holiday destination would be just like any other.

4:4:3 "Low Cost" Focussing

The airline industry does show one good example of firms which use their Focussing expertise to achieve very low costs, rather than to add value.

Europe has a long tradition of aviation activity by "Charter" airlines. Originally, these airlines developed because of a gap in the regulatory blanket enveloping European carriers, whereby Charter carriers were given much more freedom than Scheduled airlines, providing they kept to the so-called "Inclusive Tour" principle. This meant that they could not retail seats direct to the public. Instead, they were limited to a wholesaling role, wholesaling seats to tour operators. The tour operators would then add in the accommodation and other elements to make up a packaged holiday, and undertake the retailing of these holidays. The rules were essentially introduced as a compromise which allowed the Charter sector to develop, whilst giving a measure of protection to Scheduled carriers with their supposed obligation to provide year-round on-demand services

Today, these regulatory limitations have been completely removed (at least within the European Union) but the business model to which they gave rise persists. European charter airlines developed a way of working which saw them focus on one single activity – the wholesaling of blocks of seats to tour operators. In order to attract the business of these tour operators, they had to achieve one thing above all others – low seat-kilometre costs.

Such costs were achieved in a number of ways. The airlines used relatively large aircraft, because their customers were not seen as being frequency sensitive. Aircraft as large as the Airbus A330 became common in the fleets used by Europe's Charter airlines. Seat pitches were kept low, commonly at only 28 or 29 inches. Aircraft utilisations were pushed to remarkably high levels of 4200 – 4300 hours per year, spreading ownership and lease-rental costs. Achieving such figures was especially challenging because the market had a clear winter off-peak period. During the summer peak, aircraft were often flown throughout the night as well as the day, reflecting the fact that a proportion of package holiday customers were prepared to use "dead-of-night" departures providing that fares were low enough. Also, and in advance of the "Cost Leader" revolution which is now affecting them so much, Charter airlines kept with the idea that the provision of food and drink on board the aircraft need not be on a complementary basis. Instead, it was made a source of revenue.

Today, the situation facing Europe's Charter airlines is a very challenging one. The industry has mostly consolidated into two huge, vertically-integrated firms under the leadership of the German-based TUI and CNTouristic groups. This has made life hard for smaller independents. Also, customer needs have changed radically. Many people do not now require rigid package holidays containing the three elements of airline seat, accommodation and surface transfers. They certainly will not if they have their own accommodation with a villa or a timeshare, but generally now people are more experienced and adventurous, and are often prepared to put together their own holidays using the Internet.

In many ways, the newer Cost Leader airlines are better suited to these trends than the rigid model of traditional Charter airlines, and the Charter carriers have had to respond. Some have set up their own Cost Leader subsidiaries – My TravelLite and Hapag-Lloyd Express were both examples of this, although both have now been re-integrated into their parent airlines. Almost all of them have now set up web-sites to enable at least a proportion of their capacity to be retailed direct to the public. Monarch Airlines and Excel Airways are UK-based examples of carriers which have taken this initiative. In doing so, they have one crucial advantage over the Scheduled airlines. Because competition amongst the Charter carriers has been intense for a long time, these airlines generally do have the low operating costs necessary for them to compete. If they can maintain them, the Charter airlines of Europe do have a sound future, even if their business model will have to be substantially modified.

Overall, the history of the European Charter sector illustrates very well both the advantages and disadvantages of a Focussing approach. By focussing on a single activity, the Charter carriers were able to achieve a great deal of expertise in their single area of activity – expertise which for many years allowed them to hold off the competitive challenge of the 'Industrywide' airlines. This was despite the latter having many synergies available to them as a result of being in different markets and offering different products under the one corporate umbrella. The Charter airlines have, though, been vulnerable once demand began to move away from the product that they had become so expert in providing.

4:4:4 "Lost-in-the-Middle"

Porter's Competitive Advantage model has one more concept we need to consider in the context of today's aviation industry – that of the "Lost-in-the-Middle" firm.

Porter argues that there are firms that do not fit into any of the boxes. Their costs are too high for them to pursue Cost Leadership and there is too little about them which is distinctive for true Differentiation to be achieved. They are also too broadly-based in their activities to gain the benefits of expertise through Focussing.

Sadly, the airline industry today has an almost endless list of firms to which this description can be applied. As we have seen, the structure of the industry has always been distorted by ownership and control issues, with the result that there are many more airlines in the world today than would be the case if market forces had been allowed to prevail. If ownership and control constraints are eased in the future, (which is now looking increasingly likely), many of them will not survive, especially if rules about State Aid for struggling airlines are more rigidly enforced.

4:5 Airline Business and Marketing Strategies – Common Mistakes

We have now almost completed our survey of the strategic options open to carriers in today's airline industry.

Unfortunately, the world's smoothest diplomat could not argue that the industry presents a picture of strategic success. Periods of severe loss-making have occurred regularly throughout the industry's history and, as we have seen, between 2003 and 2005 these losses were at a catastrophic level for many airlines. Bankruptcy has been a common feature, whilst a large number of carriers would not have survived without substantial government handouts.

When an airline fails, it is, of course, a tragedy for those affected. A bankruptcy does, however, at least give an opportunity for lessons to be learned. The problem with the airlines is that they rarely are. Each airline failure does, of course, reflect some unique circumstances, special to a particular case. What is so depressing, though, is that the same issues, mistakes and problems seem to arise time and again. In this last section of the chapter, we review some of these common mistakes made by failed airlines.

4:5:1 Objectives

The writing of classical economists suggests that firms should be viewed as rational entities, lead by entrepreneurial managers whose objective is profit maximisation. In the airline business, such a theoretical position is often far from the true one. Airlines are set up and run for many reasons, which often make the achieving of satisfactory profits impossible. Sometimes, these objectives may be imposed from the outside. Equally, they may reflect the failings of the firm's senior managers.

This situation presents itself most clearly in the case of many state-owned airlines. Almost all governments which still own airlines presumably expect that the carrier should be run to make a profit, to ensure that it is not a burden on the taxpayer. The problem is that either explicitly or implicitly, it is set a series of objectives which make profitability difficult or impossible. Amongst these is the need to maintain services on unprofitable routes for social or political reasons, or to assist economic development of backward regions. Also, airlines may be required to keep domestic air fares artificially low, due to the desire to control inflation, or to maintain unnecessary high levels of staffing because the government wishes to minimise unemployment. Even worse, though not strictly related to the question of objectives, governments often seek to interfere with airline management appointments, with senior management jobs being given to political supporters who have few qualifications to fill these demanding positions. A final, but sadly common problem in the developing world is that government employees and supporters travel a great deal on the national airline, but the government does not then pay the bill for this transportation. Ironically, many state-controlled airlines in developing countries are owed millions of dollars by the governments that own them.

The question of conflicting objectives is most obvious in the case of state-owned airlines, but as an issue it is not confined to them. Many private airlines are in practice operating to a mixed and confusing set of objectives.

Some privately-owned carriers are ego-trips for their owners. This is because aviation is a high profile activity where it is normal to achieve easily a great deal of media coverage. It is remarkable in the airline industry how many small airlines have grandiose names playing on the themes of an "intercontinental" or "world" presence. It is also noticeable that these airlines are often based in an impressive head office described as a "global headquarters" building. A further indication of an airline being driven forward by its owner's ego is that the owner then ensures that their name is incorporated in the name of the airline and that it is painted on the side of each aircraft in large letters.   Ego-driven airlines are rarely successful because they tend to grow based on the owner's desire for more publicity and a still higher profile rather than on opportunities for profit. Even if the owner has very deep pockets, there will come a point where losses can no longer be sustained.

A further problem with some airlines is that they are essentially hobbies for those that set them up. Besides being a business, aviation also provides a fascinating hobby for many people. It is one thing to pursue this hobby by plane-spotting. It is quite another to take it to the extent of setting up an airline. Hobby-based carriers only tend to survive if the owner is extremely rich and prepared to lose a great deal of money.

A final, difficult objective for an airline to pursue in practice is that of being a vehicle for revenge. There have been a number of cases where someone who has been fired from one airline sets up a rival carrier designed to allow them to get even with the people who dismissed them. Again, emotion rather than economics will be the driving force behind decision-making and success will be very difficult to achieve.

All-in-all, the foundation for a successful airline must be that the carrier must be profit-based in terms of the objectives it is pursuing. It must also have a clear and agreed strategy, based on the principles which have been discussed in this chapter.

4:5:2 Diversification vs Specialisation

Successful airlines are often those which successfully strike a very difficult balance between over-diversifying and over-specialising.

Over-diversification can take on a number of different forms. In the past, some airlines have diversified into travel-related businesses such as hotel and car rental. At first sight, this appears to be a sound move, allowing carriers to trade on the synergies resulting from being a "One-stop Shop" for the business traveller. It has, though, mostly turned out to be a mistake. It has resulted in a dilution of the top management attention being given to the demanding task of running the airline, and has provided competition for financial resources. More seriously still, it has meant diversification into industries which have exactly the same cyclical problems as the airline business. If airline seats are unoccupied in a downturn, hotel rooms will also be vacant and cars unrented, because suppliers are relying on the same person for each of these activities.

If there is an argument for an airline to pursue a diversification policy into other industries (which is doubtful), a stronger case could be made that they should concentrate on counter-cyclical activities which are likely to remain resilient in a downturn.

Another aspect of over-diversification occurs when an airline tries to cover too broad a route network with too few aircraft. If each route in a network is only served at a low frequency, a great deal of opportunity will still be available for competitors to invade the firm's markets. Southwest Airlines now has a fleet of more than 450 aircraft, but it still only serves 62 cities in its route network. It has always had a clear policy to build frequency as quickly as possible on a new route, to cement its control of the market. "Do the job properly, or not at all" is a sound maxim.

Despite these arguments, over-specialisation can be an equal problem. It occurs when an airline bets its future on success in a single market. For example, in the past, some airlines (notably so the now-forgotten UK carrier British Caledonian) have tried to build a route network concentrated on serving oil-producing regions. Such a policy will work well when (as at the time of writing) the oil price is high, but will fail disastrously during times of oversupply and low oil prices.

4:5:3 Pace of Expansion

A difficult issue with regard to successful strategies is that of the appropriate rate of growth which the airline should aim to achieve.

It will be hard to ensure success without growth, for two reasons. Firstly, as they mature, airlines tend to find that their costs rise. This is mainly because many groups within the airline are paid according to salary scales which means that their pay increases each year that they remain on the payroll. Growth means that new members can be recruited at relatively low salaries because they will join at the bottom of their pay scale. Secondly, unless an airline grows it will not be taking advantage of new market opportunities as they become available. Besides a possible loss of profit, there is a strong likelihood that these opportunities will be taken up by competitors who will use them to further build the strength of their competitive challenge.

In the airline industry there is another, peculiar factor ensuring that growth opportunities need to be taken, reflecting the way in which airport slots are allocated. If an airport still has slots available, there is strong pressure on an airline to grow and use them because, once they have been obtained, they will be almost certainly be kept forever under the in-perpetuity principle of 'Grandfather Rights' which underlies slot awards. Much the same applies to the route licenses which are still necessary to take advantage of international Traffic Rights negotiated under the terms of Air Services Agreements.

Growth rates can, though, easily become over-ambitious. If a carrier attempts to grow too quickly, it will run the risk of becoming dependent on borrowed rather then equity capital. In turn, this may mean exposure to exchange rate and interest rate fluctuations. Also, over-rapid growth may mean that an airline falls apart operationally. Airlines are a very complex interacting system where all aspects of the system much be functioning well together. If one component is fails, then the whole is at risk. At the extreme, this may manifest itself in a poor safety record and the disastrous consequences of a fatal accident. A less severe, but still serious, problem might, for example, be that potential customers are unable to make bookings because of a shortage of reservations capacity.

Of all the airlines that fail, a proportion do so because they do not grow fast enough. A far greater number, though, go out of business because of over-rapid expansion – a salutary lesson, perhaps, for those European Cost Leader airlines which, at the time writing are attempting to grow at rates exceeding 30% a year.

4:5:4 Competitive Response

Successful airlines tend to be those that manage their competitive strategies well, and unsuccessful ones those that fail to do so. This is especially a problem for new, small carriers.

When a small, start-up airline first begins to fly, it poses a difficult problem for its larger, more powerful rivals. These carriers may launch a vigorous competitive response, and make life very hard for the newcomer. If they do though, they will be spending a great deal of money to deal with what is a minor threat to them. In particular if larger airlines respond with aggressive pricing, they will certainly be competing with a smaller rival. What they will also be doing, though, is offering discounted fares to the many customers who would have flown with them anyway. Because of this, they may be reluctant to respond strongly at first to any challenge. They may also fear that, if they do, they will be exposed to court action over allegations of anti-competitive behaviour.

Because of these factors, a small new airline may often find that its early days of flying are marked by considerable success. On the basis of this, plans are then formulated for rapid expansion. These plans are usually helped by aircraft manufacturers being willing to offer large numbers of aeroplanes at low prices, and by suppliers of finance being quite happy to accept risk based on the asset value of these aircraft, or to lease aircraft on flexible terms. Unfortunately, once the expansion has begun, the new airline changes from an irritant to a significant threat to its more powerful rivals. It must then anticipate a strong competitive response, a response which will be especially serious if it coincides with a cyclical downturn as the industry enters a recession.

As we have seen, the aviation industry never seems to have a shortage of start-up entrepreneurs, wanting to set up airlines. Even severe recessions do not dampen this enthusiasm – indeed they may increase it due to the cheaply-available resources which are on offer at such times. All the evidence of history, though, says that most of these airlines will fail, many after a very short time. Since the liberalisation trend began with so-called US domestic deregulation in 1978, the proportion of failures has exceeded 90%. Many have failed because they underestimated the response of threatened, more powerful competitors. 'Don't get into a bleeding match with a blood bank' is a sound and necessary piece of advice.

4:5:5 "Control"

The "DotCom" excesses of the period from 1998 – 2000 demonstrated many important lessons for airlines. Too often, the entrepreneurs who set up dot.com businesses were seduced by the lifestyle that sudden wealth made possible, and lost sight of the fact that any business needs to meet a worthwhile set of customer needs and to charge profitable prices. The trappings of a supposedly successful business such as expensive cars and prestigious offices make no contribution to this.

Airlines have just as much to fear. Some have failed because large sums have been spent on building an expensive head office building and on funding the lifestyles of the Directors and Senior Managers.

4:5:6 Over-optimism/Fall Back Position

No-one who chooses to work in the aviation industry should be under any illusion. It will be a roller-coaster ride. Periods of relative prosperity will alternate with times of real difficulty, with recessions and now wars and the threat of terrorism providing daunting challenges.

In such an industry, the most fatal business plan of all will be one which is based on the principle, "if everything keeps going our way, we'll be fine". Business plans have to be resilient to deal with sudden increases in uncontrollable costs such as the price of fuel. They have to address the likelihood that demand and particularly yield will from time-to-time fall away badly as a recession bites or a destabilising war or terrorism incident affects the industry. They especially have to deal with the likelihood that a whole set of unfavourable circumstances may arrive at the same time, as they often do.

In order to be able to do so, they need to have a fall-back position, the components of which will include a number of expedients. They may, for example take a proportion of their aircraft on relatively costly short-term operating leases, allowing for the return of aircraft to lessors if trouble strikes. Also, a proportion of support services can be bought in on a sub-contracted basis, allowing contracts with suppliers to be renegotiated in a down-turn.

This chapter on Airline Strategies has inevitably been long and involved. The whole subject, though, is of vital importance. No airline can hope to implement successful marketing policies unless these are underpinned by a sound strategy.

SUCCESSFUL AIRLINES ......

✈   Are those which design and implement a sound strategy

5 Product Analysis in Airline Marketing

Once an airline has its strategy in place, attention needs to shift to the translation of this strategy into the product design process. This Chapter looks at the theory of product analysis in Marketing and discusses the ways in which it can be applied to Marketing in today's airline industry.

5:1 What is the "Product"?

At first sight, it might be thought that applying theoretical product principles to the airline industry is inappropriate. These principles have mainly been developed for industries dealing with tangible consumer products. The airline industry's "product" is, of course, an intangible one which is instantly perishable and cannot be stored.

This is an argument which can be rejected. The airline industry's product may be intangible and many-facetted. It is still capable of providing – or failing to provide – customer satisfaction. It is also the case that many of the analytical models developed for analysing products in Fast Moving Consumer Goods industries can also be used in the air transport industry. They do, though, have to be used in an analogous way, to take account of the intangible nature of the airline product.

In this chapter we shall begin by looking at questions of product innovation and product management using the theoretical principles that can be derived from the concept of the Product Life Cycle.

5:2 The Theory of Product Analysis and its Application to the Airline Industry

5:2:1 The Product Life Cycle

In all areas of marketing, the processes of product development, product innovation and product management need to be continuous and never-ending. The reasons for this are derived from the model illustrated below.

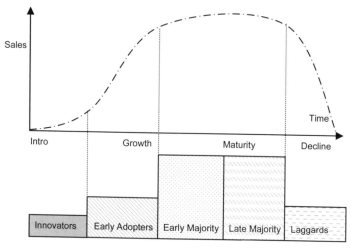

Figure 5:1 The Product Life Cycle

When a new product is introduced into the market, it is inevitable that it will first go through the so-called Introductory stage of the Product Life Cycle. The product is new, so there will not have been time for advertising and promotional work to come to fruition. Also, the product will not benefit from so-called "Imitative Buying", because few people will know about it, and fewer still will be using it.

The Introductory stage will be a crucial stage in the life of a product. Some pass through it and go on to be successes. A far greater number do not. Instead, sales are disappointing and the product has to be withdrawn from the market after a short time. Somewhere between 60% and 80% of new products eventually come into this category.

Sadly, the aerospace industry illustrates well some of the risks involved in product innovation. For example, Concorde was completely unsuccessful in achieving commercial sales and had to be withdrawn from production as a marketing disaster. The only aircraft operated commercially were those given to Air France and British Airways under the most favourable terms. A more recent case was the Advanced Turbo-Prop of British Aerospace. This aircraft, a 64 seat propeller-driven plane, was abandoned after fewer than 40 had been produced. Even re-naming it the Jetstream 61 failed to change its fortunes. The Saab 2000 aircraft had a similarly short and disappointing Life Cycle, again being withdrawn after very few had been sold. In 2005, Boeing had to stop production of its 717 aircraft after only a relatively short time.

Airline marketing also illustrates the perils of innovation. Many airlines have the experience of launching a new route amidst great optimism, only to find that the financial results are so disappointing that it has to give up very quickly. Some have made an innovation in their in-flight product, only to find that this is unpopular with passengers and has to be quickly withdrawn. An example of this came in 1990 when Lufthansa up-graded product standards in the rear cabin of its aircraft in Europe, and re-named the whole of this cabin "Business Class". It was a change which was unacceptable to those passengers who had paid higher fares and who felt that they were entitled to greater recognition. Innovation can also be risky in terms of selling or distribution concepts. For example, in the late 1980's British Airways invested in a new chain of up-market travel shops in Britain's high streets using the branding of "Four Corners Travel". Again the concept had only a short life. It was soon discontinued, with, presumably, substantial losses having to be written off.

An example of a failed product innovation which combined together issues in both aerospace and airline marketing occurred in 2006. Earlier, Boeing had launched an initiative to offer airlines the opportunity to give their customers onboard access to email and the internet. This was done using the brand named of Connexion by Boeing. Unfortunately, it did not turn out to be a success. The necessary equipment proved to be costly and unreliable, and added significantly to aircraft weight – a problem which was particularly serious at a time of high aviation fuel prices. Eventually, Boeing had to bow to the inevitable and withdraw the product from the market, after it had been responsible for accumulated losses of more than three hundred million dollars.

There is now substantial literature in the theory of marketing about product innovation. This has largely been derived from the work of the US marketing professor, E. M. Rogers. Using Rogers' principles, it is possible to suggest that new products must show at least the following characteristics if they are to be long-term successes:

1. Relative Advantage
Clearly, new products must be substantially better value-for-money than those they are replacing, in order for consumers to accept the risks of using them.

2. Compatibility
An innovation is unlikely to be successful if it is a very radical departure from the existing ways in which business is done in the market sector in

question, or if it is incompatible with prevailing ethical or moral standards. At the time of writing, this might apply to products which were seen as having an unacceptable environmental impact. For example, if Boeing had moved ahead with the plans announced in 2002 for a so-called 'Sonic Cruiser' (an aircraft with a significantly higher cruising speed than today's aircraft, but with a much higher fuel consumption) Compatibility questions would certainly have affected the likelihood of a successful product launch.

3. Complexity

Some innovations fail because they are perceived as being extremely difficult to use, requiring purchasers to invest a great deal of time and effort in becoming familiar with them. As we have seen, part of the appeal of Low Cost Carriers has been that making flight bookings with them over the internet has been so easy.

4. Divisibility

It is often easier to persuade consumers to take a series of short steps, rather than one very large and risky one. Each small step can then be portrayed as a trial, the successful completion of which allows confidence to be built. For example, in aerospace marketing, it may be much easier to persuade an airline to buy a large fleet of a particular aircraft if short-term leases of one or two aircraft have demonstrated that the aircraft will perform well in the airline's particular operating environment. The principle of Divisibility is also very well illustrated by the growing popularity of so-called Fractional Ownership schemes for business jets. Here, the manufacturers of these jets hope that experiencing the product through a Fractional Ownership plan will result in a company or an individual eventually buying their own aircraft

5. Communicability

Customers are unlikely to be persuaded to buy a product if the benefits this product will bring cannot be communicated to them persuasively.

If these features illustrate some of the requirements of successful product innovation in air transport marketing, it is equally instructive to look at some of the common mistakes that lead to product failure. Products will fail if the size of the market for them has been over-estimated through poor or non-existent market research. They will also fail if the product cannot be delivered on time, or does not perform well even when it is. Mistakes can also be made in pricing policy, with the product either being offered at a price which is too high relative to the benefits it will bring, or too low (in the case of so-called "Status Goods") to give the necessary aura of exclusivity. Finally, promotional or distribution policies may be poorly thought-out. For example, advertising campaigns may offend rather than excite potential customers, or the incentives which are given to distribution channel intermediaries may not be enough to encourage them to push the product strongly.

All in all, product innovation represents an extremely challenging part of the product management process, with the range of possible mistakes explaining easily why so many products fail to get beyond even the Introductory stage of their Life Cycle.

Let us now make the assumption that a new product *does* get beyond this stage, and enters the so-called Growth phase of the Cycle. Here, sales accelerate markedly as advertising and promotional work comes to fruition, and the product benefits from imitative buying as consumers see it being bought and used by others.

Clearly, the onset of the Growth phase is good news for the innovating firm. Substantial amounts of cash will begin to flow in, allowing the original research, development and promotional costs invested in the product to be recovered. Also, production volumes can be increased, bringing the Economies of Scale and Learning Curve effects which will permit lower unit production costs.

The Growth phase does, though, hint at some of the problems which will have to be addressed during the later, much more challenging, stages of the Cycle. When it begins, there will be the task of ensuring that production rates are increased to meet the rapidly-rising volume of demand. If they cannot be, there is a risk that a major marketing opportunity will be lost if potential customers are not prepared to wait in order to take delivery. Later in the Growth phase, there will almost certainly be the first worrying signs of a classic problem of product management: the firm's competitors will see the success of the innovation, and will begin the research and development of their own rival products. In a sense, they will not have to carry out their own market research or demand forecasting exercise. The innovating firm will have done this for them.

The leading firm will hope that the Growth phase will go on for as long as possible. It cannot, though, continue forever. Eventually, the Maturity stage of the Product Life Cycle will arrive. Here, firstly, the growth in the size of the total market for the product begins to slow, Most of the people who can be persuaded to buy the product have already done so. The market therefore begins to progressively change from one of growth to one of replacement. Replacement sales are rarely enough to maintain, let alone expand, the volume of demand.

The other change of the Maturity phase is more serious still. By this time, rival firms will have had time to complete the research and development of their own, competing products. These will be introduced into the market, probably in rapid succession. Worse still, these firms will have had the benefit of being able to study the product of the innovator. They will have been able to isolate its weaknesses and, almost certainly, to develop a product which will leapfrog the standards set by the innovating firm.

The Maturity phase of the Cycle is a very challenging one. By this stage, the market is no longer growing rapidly. It is also becoming saturated with competition. Strong product management skills will be needed if the success established during the Growth phase is to be continued in Maturity.

In responding to the challenges of Maturity, the situation is by no means hopeless. By this stage, the original costs of developing and introducing the product will have been recovered. It will therefore be possible to make profits at lower prices. Also, the firm should be getting the maximum benefits from production Scale Economies and from the Learning Curve effects which make production more efficient. Again, these factors will increase financial flexibility. The task in managing mature products is to use this flexibility in the most telling way.

The keys to doing so lie in the "4Ps" of marketing discussed under the heading of the Marketing Mix in Section 1:1:2. A first possible response is to invest money in the product itself. This can be used to improve its specification so that it catches up with and preferably overtakes the value-for-money on offer from the products which have arrived in the market later. It can also be used to modify the product so that it can be used to exploit other, hopefully less saturated, markets.

Alongside investment in the product, discounted prices can be offered as a possible way of ensuring that growth in the total market resumes, or that a greater share of the existing market is obtained. Also, increased investment in advertising and promotion can be sanctioned with the same two purposes in mind. Finally, greater incentives can be offered to firms in the distribution channel through higher commissions or greater mark-ups.

If the right balance of these measures are correctly applied, there is no reason why the success of a product established during a Growth phase cannot be continued for a considerable time once the onset of Maturity has begun. For many products, though, such success cannot be prolonged indefinitely. They will eventually reach the Decline phase of the Life Cycle. This is where market growth comes to an end, and the product is overwhelmed by newer rivals, Once Decline sets in, there is no choice but to abandon the product and take the resources devoted to it and use them for more rewarding purposes.

The inevitability for many products of a Decline phase poses another challenge in product management. If a firm wishes to continue in business and expand, it will be making a grave mistake if it leaves investment in research and development of new products until the Decline phase of its existing products sets in. If it does, the result will be a disastrous period of poor sales and loss of reputation. Instead development and innovation of new products must begin whilst existing products are still doing well.

5:2:2 Product Life Cycles in the Aviation Industry

The Product Life Cycle is well-illustrated by applications which can be found both in the aerospace industry, and, by analogy, in airline marketing as well.

In aerospace, a very good illustration of successful product management comes with the world's biggest-selling commercial aircraft, the Boeing 737. The 737 family has a long history - the first 737s were introduced in 1967 - but it continues to sell well today. It does so because, at all stages of its Life Cycle, Boeing has managed the product skilfully.

It is now often forgotten, but when the first 737s were delivered in the late 1960s, there were no signs at all of the enormous success that the aircraft would become. Early sales were slow, and the initial aircraft – designated 737-100s – performed poorly. Such was the scale of the early disappointments that, when it faced a financial crisis in 1972, Boeing came very near to withdrawing the aircraft and stopping production. Thus the 737 was close to being one of the many product innovations that fail to get beyond the Introductory stage of their Life Cycle.

Boeing did not do so, though. Instead, an improved version of the aircraft, the 737-200, was put on the market. This entered a very clear Growth phase in the 1970s, achieving more than 1000 sales during the decade.

By the early 1980s it became clear that the success enjoyed by the 737-200 could not continue indefinitely. The aircraft was not especially fuel efficient at a time when fuel prices were very high. It was also noisy, when environmental resistance to aircraft noise was increasing and the first signs were appearing that excessively-noisy aircraft would be banned. Finally, the early 1980s saw Boeing's increasingly-confident European rival Airbus planning what has become the highly-successful A320 family. The B737 was clearly reaching the Maturity stage of its Product Life Cycle.

The reaction of the company was a very positive one. Instead of ceasing production as they might have done, Boeing invested further by introducing three new versions of the aircraft, the -300, -400 and -500 series. These featured a fuselage stretch (in the case of the -300 and -400.

The 737-500 was the same size as the -200), a more up-to-date cockpit and quieter, more fuel-efficient engines. These new models revitalised the product, to the extent that more than 2000 aircraft were sold between the beginning of the 1980's and the early 1990s.

By 1994, the 737 was again under threat as the Airbus A320 family expanded and became better established. Then, though, Boeing launched further developments in the form of the -600, -700, -800 and -900 737's. These aircraft have again sold well, confirming the 737 as by far the most successful aircraft family ever in terms of the number of units sold. Boeing is currently in the process of extending the family still further with another stretch of the aircraft, but the company knows that even its Life Cycle will come to an end eventually. Early plans are being made for the development of an all-new family of aircraft to replace the 737 sometime during the next decade. It is clear that Airbus will also introduce a replacement for the A320 at around the same time.

A second, equally convincing, illustration of Product Life Cycle concepts in the aviation industry can be found in the history of Frequent Flyer Programmes. FFPs are a major issue in Airline Marketing today, and will be fully covered in Section 9:3.

The first programme, the AAdvantage scheme, was introduced by American Airlines in 1981. It was, of course, then perfectly possible that this would turn out to be an unsuccessful idea, unpopular with customers and abandoned quickly. It did not, though. The programme passed quickly through the Introductory stage of its Product Life Cycle and entered a rapid Growth phase. Soon, the programme had many millions of members and was having a significant impact on choice-of-airline decisions in the US domestic market.

Once this had happened, it was certain that American would not be left alone to enjoy its success. The very extent of this success meant that its rivals had no choice but to follow. They did so, first in the US domestic market and then, progressively, internationally as well. At the time of writing, FFPs are at the Maturity stage of their Life Cycle. Almost all airlines are participating in FFPs either by running their own programme or by forming partnership and franchising agreements with those who do. Also, most of the programmes are now similar in terms of the benefits they offer – a clear sign of the commoditization one would expect at Maturity.

There are now early signs that FFPs may be reaching a Decline phase of their Life Cycle. The programmes are becoming increasingly unpopular with corporate travel purchasers, who argue that they tempt irresponsible employees to take unnecessary journeys to accumulate extra mileage or to protect their programme status. FFPs also make it more difficult to implement changes in corporate travel policy due to "Switching Cost" effects, a subject which was covered in Section 4:1:4. Many Corporate Travel Managers are now insisting that FFP points are awarded to the company, or are not given at all. Instead, they require increased levels of corporate discounting. All these factors may, in some cases, make FFPs less important in airline marketing in the future then they are today. Also, airlines are now moving to neutralise their effects. The growing links between the different FFPs within airline alliances mean that often passengers can obtain mileage points in the programme of their choice, irrespective of the airline they actually choose to fly. This is, in reality, an admission by the airlines concerned that the effect of FFPs on market share is increasingly a neutral one, but one which comes at a high cost.

A third, and especially fascinating, illustration of the application of the Product Life Cycle comes with the marketing of leisure air travel and of vacation resorts. It requires an understanding of a further aspect of Life Cycle theory.

At different stages, of a Life Cycle, different types of customer are buying a product, because people vary in their attitudes to new products. When a product is at the Introductory stage of its Life Cycle, the people who are most likely to buy it are known as *Innovators*. Innovators are people who have relatively high disposable incomes. They tend to be well-educated, confident, and adventurous in terms of their willingness to experiment with new purchases. They are also often insecure and status-conscious, anxious to impress their friends and acquaintances.

Because of these characteristics, a particular marketing mix will often be required at the Introductory stage of a product's Life Cycle, if the Introductory period is to be negotiated successfully and lead to a profitable Growth phase. The product must be positioned as fresh, innovative and exciting. Advertising and promotional policies must emphasise it as status-enhancing, and something which only the smartest of consumers are yet able to appreciate. Often, a high price will also be needed as a further way of emphasising a product's exclusivity.

Late in the Product Life Cycle, a completely different type of customer will need to be targeted. By this time the product will be seen as old-fashioned by Innovators. Instead the target market will consist of so-called *Laggards*. Those people who will only buy a product when it is very well-proven. They will usually have only a relatively low disposable income, and will often be poorly-educated and also be fearful of the risks involved in buying a new and, to them, untested product. They may be less status-conscious than Innovators.

Bringing Laggards into the market requires a significantly different Marketing Mix, compared to the one which will need to be used to attract Innovators. The product must be positioned as well-tested, tried, and proven to work. Sometimes, even shame will be used as a marketing weapon by pointing out how widely used the product is and how behind-the-times non-users are. Testimonials from satisfied customers will also be a common tactic. Prices will have to be kept low, reflecting the generally-lower disposable income of Laggards.

The theory of Innovator and Laggard behaviour should be applied in Airline Marketing to the marketing of holiday destinations. When choosing their holiday, Innovators will often be prepared to travel to new, untried places, because of their adventurous spirit. They will also want to visit somewhere that is status-enhancing. A new resort area will therefore find a readier audience amongst Innovators. The problem that then arises, though, is that Innovators make up only a small percentage of the population – perhaps only 5% of people show true Innovator characteristics. There is always a temptation on the part of those who manage resort development to aim at a move into mass tourism, to bring greater benefits in terms of employment and balance-of-payments gains. The problem of doing so is that once a resort becomes known as a destination for the mass market, it will at the same time become unattractive to Innovators because "everyone" is going there. This is serious because, although small in numbers, Innovators usually have very high disposable incomes.

The history of visitors to some of Spain's holiday resorts illustrates this use of the theory of the Product Life Cycle very well. In the 1960's Spanish resorts such as Benidorm, Torremolinos and Lloret del Mar were seen as exciting and different at a time when most people were still taking their holidays close to home. By the 1980s the reverse was the case. The resorts were associated with noise, congestion and unruly behaviour, and were no longer visited by the well-off travellers who could contribute the most to the local economy. During the 1990s it became necessary to spend large amounts in cleaning up the resorts in an attempt to reverse these adverse trends.

5:2:3   *Managing a Product Portfolio – the "Boston Box"*

The management of Product Life Cycles is important in Airline Marketing today. It does not, though, provide the sole basis for effective product management. Most firms do not deal in only a single product. Indeed, any that do are probably dangerously over-specialised. Many firms have a range, or portfolio, of products which may run into hundreds or even thousands of different products. They need a framework which will guide their decision-making so that the contribution of each of the products to corporate profitability is maximised.

The classic method for analysing a Product Portfolio is known as the Boston Box, because it was developed by the US Boston Consulting Group. It was first introduced in 1963, and has remained a cornerstone of product management policies ever since. It is illustrated in its most basic form in Figure 5:2.

Market
Growth

WILDCAT	STAR
DOG	CASH COW

Market Share

Figure 5:2 Product Portfolio: The Boston Box

The model classifies products using two variables: the size of the total market and the share of the market held by the product of the firm in question. (In some versions of the product then the second variable is the share held relative to the share of the market leader). This allows a division into so-called *Wildcats*, *Stars*, *Cash Cows* and *Dogs*. Each of these types of product needs to be managed in a different way.

Wildcat products are defined as those where the firm's product only holds a low share of the market, but the overall market is growing quickly. The message the model gives is a clear one: invest, to gain market share. Though such investment will be risky, if it is managed properly a return will be obtained because of the rapid growth taking place in the total market. It can take the form of spending on any of the "4Ps" of the Marketing Mix. Investment can be made in the product, to ensure that its specification meets, or preferably overtakes, that of the market leader. Advertising and promotional work can be used to gain market share, or competitive pricing can be employed. Lastly, the firm's distribution channel intermediaries can be incentivised to push the product harder through increased commissions or mark-ups.

In Airline Marketing, an often very instructive use of the Boston Box is to apply it to an airline's route network. By analogy, this can give some very useful messages as to how each route should be managed.

A Wildcat route is one where the traffic as a whole is growing strongly, but where the airline concerned has only a small share of this rapidly growing market.   Wildcats require both patience and continuing investment. Patience is needed because in the short-term a Wildcat may be a loss-maker. If the growth prospects of the route are good enough, these losses should be accepted and a presence maintained. This is especially so given the regulated nature of competition in many air transport markets, and the ways in which airport slots are allocated. In international markets, if an airline withdraws from a route, it may lose its status as its government's designated carrier on the route in question, with the relevant Traffic Rights instead given to another airline.   It may also have to surrender some airport slots, with the risk that these again will be given to another airline. The overall effect may then be that when it wishes to re-enter the market it will not be able to do so.

For many airlines, routes to India and China are currently exhibiting 'Wildcat' characteristics. The rapid growth being experienced in these countries means that carriers should maintain a long-term presence, even if short-term losses are incurred.

The Star situation is one where the overall market is growing quickly and the firm's product has a good share of the market. Star products are obviously strong ones for the firm in question, and they should be a significant source of profit. They do, though, require intensive and costly management. This is because the rapid growth in the total market will provide a continuing incentive for new competitors to enter them. Established firms will therefore have to spend heavily to defend their position.   This spending will need to encompass continuing product investment and substantial efforts in the direction of advertising and promotion.   Pricing will also probably be very keen, with thin profit margins.   All-in-all, Star products are often those which provide a high proportion of a firm's sales volumes, but a significantly lower proportion of its profits.

The aero-engine market illustrates the principle of Star products very well.   The market for big-fan engines powering large jet aircraft is a huge one.   The competition, though, between General Electric, Pratt and Whitney and Rolls-Royce is intense.   All three firms have to spend large amounts on continuous product development and improvement. (Because of this, General Electric and Pratt and Whitney have combined forces in part of the market, to form the so-called Engine Alliance)   Pricing is so keen that it is believed that often engines are sold for less than the cost of producing them. The manufacturers then hope to obtain a return on sales of spares and product support through the lifetime of the engine. For each manufacturer, the big fan engine market produces large sales revenues, but often only relatively thin profit margins.

For Cost Leader airlines, intra-European routes illustrate Star principles well. The market is very large and growing rapidly, but the growth has attracted an explosion of new entry that, increasingly, is likely to hold down profit margins.

The next the Boston Box category is the Cash Cow. This is the one where the product in question still has a good share of the market, but where the total market is no longer growing strongly.

The fundamental difference between Stars and Cash Cows is that the Cash Cow market will no longer be an attractive one for new entrants. Established firms will have invested to gain their place in the market, and should be able to continue to exploit it successfully. New entrants, though, will have to spend especially heavily if they are to challenge the existing players. Entering a new market will always be costly. It will be particularly expensive, though, to enter a market which is not growing. A growing market allows a new firm to hope that it will be able to become established on the basis of new demand rather then by having to take existing customers away from their suppliers. This will not be possible in a stagnant market. Success will only be possible for a newcomer if it succeeds in taking market share from other firms. We shall see in Section 10:2:1 that growing with a market can be achieved relatively cheaply. Growing by taking share from others will always be a costly and risky activity, one which is unlikely to yield a return to a new entrant.

For existing firms, of course, Cash Cows should be a major source of profit, because they will not have to protect themselves so much from the activities of newcomers. The problem will often be that though the milking of Cash Cows may be extremely profitable, the lack of growth in the total market means that these milking opportunities may not continue for long.

The aero-engine market again provides a good illustration. We have already seen that in this market, the big firms have to invest heavily to maintain their position. For some years, one of the firms in this market, Rolls-Royce, appeared to have a product which conformed to Cash Cow principles.

Alongside its larger engines, Rolls-Royce offered its Tay product, a small engine of 15,000-17,000 lbs of thrust. The Tay was itself a relatively unambitious investment based on the core of an older Rolls engine, the Spey. The Tay, however, enjoyed a favourable position, because General Electric and Pratt and Whitney for a long time offered no engine in this class. The Tay therefore had a virtual monopoly in the three markets where it was used, for the Fokker 100 and Fokker 70, the Gulfstream business jet, and in the re-engining of older noisy jets. One's guess is that Rolls enjoyed strong profit margins on Tay sales.

The Tay also illustrates the point that Cash Cow products may not be available to milk for very long. The Fokker company went into bankruptcy in 1996, and production of the Fokker 70 and Fokker 100 stopped. It has never resumed, despite efforts being made to bring this about In addition, recent years have seen many Fokker aircraft parked, removing from Rolls the income from spares and support.

For airlines, Cash Cow situations occur on any route where future growth prospects are poor. An example at the moment is the is routes between London and Paris and London and Brussels. These routes have been affected by railway competition as a result of the opening of the Channel Tunnel. This competition will become more intense once a fast rail link has been completed between London and the Tunnel in 2008. This will reduce city centre to city centre journey times to below the critical three hours duration.

Because of these poor growth prospects, it would be a foolish airline that decided to enter these markets today. With little traffic growth, they could only establish their position by taking market share from some very strong established carriers. With new entry therefore unlikely, these established airlines should be able to exploit the available demand relatively unchallenged. There may come a time though, when the effect of surface competition means that the route changes from a profitable Cash Cow into the next Boston Box category, the Dog.

Dog products are those where the total market is not growing and the firm has only a low share of the existing small market. Once a product has been finally classified as a Dog, there is a clear product management message. It should be abandoned and the resources which might otherwise have been spent on maintaining it and on attempts to improve market share should instead be devoted to much more promising Wildcat situations.

We have already referred in the last section to British Aerospace's decision to withdraw its ATP (later, Jetstream 61) aircraft from the market. They presumably did so because it matched the characteristics one would expect of a Dog very well. The ATP was a 64 seat turboprop aircraft. Growth prospects for the market of turbo-props in this size bracket at the time were poor. The reason was that regional jets of similar size were being produced in increasing numbers, and these aircraft seemed to have a clear edge over turbo-props in terms of passenger appeal. This meant that more and more airlines were choosing them, despite their somewhat higher operating costs. At the same time, the ATP achieved only a low share of the market with sales being dominated by its rivals the Franco-Italian ATR 72 and Canadian Bombardier Dash-8 (Ironically, at the time of writing, turbo-prop sales are reviving, with their operating economics looking especially good with fuel prices high).

For airlines, the use of the Dog category is, by analogy, the route withdrawal decision. Almost all airlines find from time-to-time that they have routes where traffic is not growing, where they have a poor market share, and where losses are being incurred. They must give up service on these routes and take the resources used to serve them to more promising situations.

5:2:4 Balancing Risk and Opportunity — the Ansoff Matrix

The Boston Box allows for some important rules for product management to be defined. One further model is, though, very useful in the search for a complete range of decision-making tools.

All firms have to balance risk and opportunity in their product planning decisions. The firm's profits will be a reward for its risk-taking, and too conservative an approach will mean that profits will be foregone and market opportunities will be left open for competitors. At the same time, if too many products are introduced which are risky, the result will be financial disaster if things go wrong.

The model which is used to guide decisions about risk and opportunity is known as the Ansoff Matrix after its US inventor. It is illustrated in figure 5:3.

MARKETS

	Existing	New
Existing	1	2
New	3	4

PRODUCTS

Figure 5:3 The Ansoff Matrix

The Matrix suggests that products can be divided into four categories. The first is illustrated by Box One in the Matrix. It is where the firm offers its existing products to its existing customers. In the short term, this will be a low risk solution. The markets are ones which the firm knows, and the products are presumably proven successes. It does not, though, provide a basis for the long-term development and growth of a business. The existing products will go through their Life Cycle, and will eventually reach the Decline phase. At the same time, new opportunities will be appearing which the firm will be ignoring. These will be available to the firm's competitors who will use them to build their strength to eventually challenge the firm in its core activities.

If what is effectively a "Do-Nothing Case" is unacceptable, firms must do more than simply offer existing products to existing customers. To do so, they must balance risk and opportunity in the way described in Boxes Two and Three of the Ansoff Matrix. Box Two describes taking existing products and offering them to a new market. For example, a firm having a successful range of products selling well in a domestic market might decide to move into exporting. Box Three is the situation where new products are developed for markets where the firm has a sound knowledge of customer requirements and established customer loyalty. For example, we have already referred (in Section 4:4:2) to Lufthansa's introduction of All-Business Class corporate jets on routes where it already had a strong presence in the business travel market through its conventional services.

The most interesting case in the Ansoff Matrix is that described in Box Four. This is where the firm takes a completely new and unproven product and offers it to a totally new and undeveloped market. It carries almost limitless opportunities, but also usually a very high degree of risk. The result is that new businesses which adopt this philosophy sometimes achieve great success. More commonly, though, the risks are unsustainable and the result may be a disastrous bankruptcy.

We have already referred in Section 4:2:6 to one aviation situation where an entirely new product was offered to an entirely new market, and the result was a remarkable success story – that of Federal Express. When Mr Fred Smith (Fedex's founder) introduced his idea of overnight guaranteed door-to-door deliveries of small urgent shipments, it was a new idea tapping a hitherto unexploited market. It is true that some of FedEx's growth can be explained by the fact that it has taken the existing small shipment market away from the established airlines and the US Post Office which had been serving it so poorly. To an equal or greater degree, though, FedEx developed new traffic flows as a result of firms realising the opportunities for business growth which the FedEx concept gave them.

Mr Smith did, though, take an enormous risk. The fact that he was successful should not be taken as meaning that in all comparable cases, the result would be the same. The concept requires a heavy investment to be made before significant cash flows can be obtained. Funding the investment and sustaining early operating losses can often prove fatal, especially if it coincides with a cyclical business downturn. The timing of such downturns, of course, cannot be accurately predicted.

The overall message of the Ansoff Matrix is a clear one. To achieve the correct balance between risk and opportunity, firms must have products which fit into each of the four boxes of the Matrix. There must be established products and markets which provide for profits in the short term. The business must grow and develop using examples drawn from Boxes Two and Three. If it can do so, there may be room for some much riskier products drawn from the Fourth Box. It must be accepted that some of these products will fail. Others may cause large early losses before becoming long-term winners. The business must be certain that current profits are sufficient to cover these possible losses.

5:3 Fleet and Schedules-Related Product Features

In the book, we have already spent considerable time looking at the product from the point-of-view of the customer. Section 2:3:3 examined the product requirements of the business air traveller and Section 2:3:5, those of the leisure customer. In this section, we will focus more on the supply side of the product, by examining the product decisions that airlines must take. In doing so, they fact a dilemma. They presumably wish to offer a product which is as attractive as possible to the customer. However, an attractive product will often be an expensive one to produce. Therefore, decisions must often be based on a complex tradeoff between product quality and production costs.

In making this tradeoff, the overriding factor to be taken into account will be the business strategy of the airline concerned. Optimum decision-making for an airline in a Cost Leadership position will be quite different from one aiming at multi-product Differentiation.

The work is divided into two. In this section, product features which relate to the aircraft and the way in which it is used are considered. In the next, we will look at more general customer-service related product decisions. In all cases, we will be seeking to define the current areas of controversy and to define the ways in which an airline can achieve a Sustainable Competitive Advantage.

5:3:1 Cabin Configuration and Classes of Service

The principle of trading off product quality against production costs is well-illustrated by this first area of decision-making.

An airline seeking the lowest costs of operation will configure its aircraft in a single class, and will place as many seats as possible in each plane. Safety considerations will give an absolute limit. These will reflect both the structural capabilities of the aircraft and the need to meet standards for emergency evacuations. The other question will be that of passenger comfort. There seems to be an acceptance in the industry that a seat pitch of 28 inches is the minimum which passengers will accept. Even with modern, lightweight seats this represents a poor standard of comfort, and most airlines do not go as far as this extreme. 29 inch or 30 inch seat pitches are usually given, even by airlines focusing on the European leisure air travel market where low production costs have been a traditional pre-occupation.

Decisions about basic seating comfort standards have a very significant impact on unit cost levels. For example, leisure-orientated airlines will usually place 235 seats into one of their most commonly-used aircraft, the Boeing 757. This results from a mix of seats at 28 and 29 inch seat pitches. Raising the seat pitch to 33 inches – typically used by scheduled airlines – reduces the number of seats that can be placed in the same aircraft to around 180. Thus a decision about cabin comfort can affect unit costs by 30%.

An airline whose marketing strategy is based on targeting both the business and leisure traveller cannot rely on a cabin configuration aimed at producing the lowest operating costs. Instead, they must develop a multi-product philosophy, one of the manifestations of which is the need to have different classes of service on board their aircraft. The cost implications of doing so are substantial, and are becoming greater all the time.

The problem is that as they search for competitive advantage, many airlines are making the cabin configuration of their First and Business classes more and more attractive. They are doing so by using new and costly seats, and also by giving substantially more space to each passenger. This in turn is forcing their rivals to match or exceed their product specification. The result is what at the moment appears to be a never-ending and fruitless search for competitive advantage. One airline may establish such an advantage, but this does not turn out to be sustainable. The very fact that customers like its new cabin configuration forces its rivals to respond with something equally or even more appealing in order to protect their market share. The end result of a round of competitive innovation in seating comfort standards is that market shares remain the same, but all the airlines which have taken part in it have significantly higher unit costs.

The history of First Class and Business Class cabin configurations illustrates this point well. Today, a competitive long-haul First Class cabin will have seats which fold down into horizontal beds. In order to accommodate this, a seat pitch of around 70 inches will be needed. In Business Class, a competitive seat pitch is now around 55 inches, an increase from the 38 or 40 inches typical of only ten years ago. At the time of writing, there is a growing trend to extend the flat-bed principle to Business as well as First Class. It will be hard, though, to get a return on this investment, particularly during times when a business slowdown reduces the size of the Business Class market.

In some cases, airlines have opted out of at least some aspects of competition over cabin service. In particular, many carriers have withdrawn from the First Class market entirely and have instead put their faith in a much-enhanced Business Class product. Air Canada, Aer Lingus, KLM and Northwest are all examples of airlines which have made this decision. They risk losing some of their highest-yielding business, but have much greater freedom of action. In particular, they can improve their Business Class so that it is fully competitive with the highest standards, without the concern that by doing so, they will be competing with their own First Class market. Airlines that stay with First Class often find that by improving their Business Class to keep up with market trends, they succeed in persuading some of their own First Class passengers that it is no longer worthwhile for them to pay the First Class premium.

On short-haul routes, questions of cabin configuration and classes of service are rather different. On these routes, almost all airlines outside of the U.S.A have given up First Class, on the grounds that it has become harder and harder to persuade passengers to pay the higher fares for sectors of only an hour or so. In Europe Swissair and Lufthansa were the last airlines to withdraw First Class, doing so in 1993. Instead, short-haul flights now are usually based on a two-class cabin, divided between Business and Economy seating.

Until very recently, airlines that had such a cabin configuration used a uniform standard of seating comfort throughout the aircraft. Seat pitches were the same throughout at 32 or 33 inches, as was the number of seats abreast. On Boeing and Airbus single aisle aircraft such as the 737, 757 and A320, this meant six-abreast seating with three seats either side of the aisle. (McDonnell-Douglas aircraft such as the MD-80, being slightly narrower have been used at 5-abreast. This has also been the case with the Boeing 717). The division between Business Class and Economy Class was made by using a flexible cabin divider which could be moved up and down the aircraft according to the relative demand for Business and Economy seats.

Such a philosophy gave the airlines the benefit of valuable operational flexibility, but it was probably only sustainable in the tightly-regulated market that then prevailed. The problem it gave was that seating comfort standards were very poor in Business Class, particularly for those people who on busy flights had to sit in the middle seat of three. Business passengers came to feel that not enough was being done to recognise the fact that they had paid very much higher fares – often four or five times as high – as those who sat in the rear cabin.

The solution which has been adopted recently is to install convertible seats. These seats are expensive and also rather heavier than standard seats. They do, though, allow a row of six-abreast seating to be converted into one of four or five-abreast very quickly, during an aircraft turnaround period. This is an expensive option because, besides the capital costs of the seats, it also means that fewer seats are available for sale on busy peak-time flights. It is probably an inevitable move though, given the changing competitive scene in the industry.

The other current controversy with cabin configuration and classes of service is a similar one, but it applies to airlines' long-haul rather than short-haul routes. When three classes were adopted as the standard configuration on these routes, the principles appeared clear. First Class would accommodate passengers prepared to pay high fares for extravagant standards of comfort. Business class would be for all other passengers who paid full, flexible fares. The Economy cabin would offer only a low product specification for passengers paying discount and promotional fares.

As time has passed, these principles have become blurred. Business Class product specifications have risen steadily, and, in an attempt by airlines to get a return on their money, the fares that allow passengers to sit in Business Class have been very substantially increased. In turn, market demand has often meant that lower flexible fares have been introduced. These fares permit passengers to travel without restrictions. They only allow seating in the Economy Cabin, though.

The problem is that despite the fact that flexible Economy Fares are lower than Business Class Fares, they are still very high in comparison with restricted discount fares. They again mean that a passenger who has paid a relatively high fare can end up sitting next to someone who has paid very much less.

The answer to this problem may be a four-class aircraft, with the Economy cabin sub-divided so that a section of the aircraft is available exclusively for those people paying the higher economy fares. British Airways has introduced this idea with its World Traveller Plus cabin. More may do so as the Airbus A380 is introduced.

5:3:2 Network, Frequencies and Timings

The planning of an airline's schedule is again one where compromise between product quality and cost will be needed. There will also be many practical constraints which may mean that the carrier's freedom of action to meet the requirements of its customers will be significantly affected.

We saw in Section 2:3:3 that for business travellers, a broad network of direct flights is central to their product requirements. These are the features which will give them the flexibility they need. It will not be easy, though, to decide on exactly what should and should not be offered.

In terms of the practical constraints, route entry decisions are still often limited by government regulation of market access. On international routes, it may still be necessary for an airline to gain designation by the home government under the terms of the relevant Air Services Agreement. Even if such designation is obtained, decisions about capacities and frequencies may also be constrained by regulatory factors. Many Air Services Agreements are still written in a way which is designed to ensure that airlines do not compete on capacity, with equal amounts provided by airlines from each country.

Airport slot availability is an increasing number of cases a constraint on route entry and scheduling as was discussed in Section 3:2:5. At the moment, the industry bases slot allocation at congested airports on the 'Grandfather Rights' principle. Opportunities to land and take off at particular times are retained by established airlines on a more-or-less permanent basis, from one season to the next. This can mean that there will be significant difficulties for a new airline wishing to begin services at a congested airport where all the attractively-timed slots will be in the possession of incumbent airlines. Even if slots can be obtained to allow services to begin, they may be at unsuitable times. It may also be difficult to get sufficient slots to allow the frequencies of established airlines to be matched.

Environmental factors are often another practical constraint. Many airports now impose restrictions on the amount of night flying they allow, and some ban it altogether. Whilst many airlines try to avoid 'dead-of-night' arrivals and departures because of their unpopularity with passengers and difficulties with airport access, night flying is still a way for leisure-orientated airlines to boost aircraft utilisation and lower their unit costs.

In terms of current controversies regarding network and schedules planning, airlines are having to make a number of difficult decisions, many of which involve the familiar tradeoff between costs and product quality.

On long-haul routes, a very clear passenger preference has emerged in recent years. Passengers prefer non-stop flying to flights involving intermediate stops. To meet this requirement, aircraft manufacturers have responded by producing families of aircraft with longer and longer ranges, and the opportunities provided by such planes have been taken up by some airlines. Many markets have now been transformed in terms of the ways in which carriers serve them. For example, almost all services between

Southeast Asia and Europe, and Southeast Asia to the West Coast of the USA are now non-stop, and any airline which attempted to serve them with an intermediate stop would find itself at a serious competitive disadvantage.

The industry's appetite for longer range non-stop services still appears to be significant. Airbus offers a variant of its A340 family – the A340-500 – which is able to fly non-stop over routes requiring 16-17 hours of flying time. Boeing is marketing an comparable long-range variant of its 777 family, known as the B777-200LR.

In principle, non-stop flying helps airlines to achieve low operating costs, but only up to a point. Non-stop flights allow for higher aircraft utilisation and of course the landing fees and turnaround costs associated with the intermediate stop are avoided. The very long ranges now being used, though, are on balance a higher cost option for the airlines that offer them to their customers. Very large quantities of fuel have to be carried early in a flight for use later on, in turn raising aircraft weight and fuel burn – something of great significance with oil prices in excess of $70 a barrel, as they are at the time of writing. Also extra crews have to be carried to permit proper rest periods. This increases costs and takes up seating capacity.

The other main area of controversy involves debate over the related issues of hub-and-spoke networks and so-called 'market fragmentation'.

Many airlines have based their strategic response to the competitive challenges of deregulation on the hub-and-spoke principle. The idea is a simple one. The airline selects an airport with a good geographical location relative to major traffic flows. Its flights in-and-out of this airport are then co-ordinated in carefully-timed "banks", so that passengers can transfer from an in-bound flight from their origin to an outbound flight to their destination.

Passengers benefit substantially from networks based on the hub-and-spoke principle. On each of the spokes, frequencies can be much higher because the airline is carrying the traffic heading to the end destination from all the origin points, rather than just passengers in one city-pair market. Also, it should be possible for larger aircraft to be used, giving access to lower seat-kilometre costs. This may in turn result in lower fares.

From the airline's point-of-view, hub-and-spoke concepts allow them to exploit a far larger number of origin-and-destination markets than they could do with a route network based on the point-to-point principle. It also protects them from competitive attack. The dominance they achieve at the hub airport and the higher frequencies achievable on each of the spokes both help in this regard.

Despite these advantages, the role of hub-and-spoke networks is becoming increasingly controversial. It is now clear that they are unpopular with passengers because of the delays and congestion associated with changing flights at the hub. They are also extremely resource-intensive. Because of the need to group flights together in co-ordinated banks, at some stages of the day a hub airport will be the scene of frenetic activity. At others, it will be almost deserted, and costly resources in terms of staff and equipment will be idle.

It is instructive to note that one of the most successful carriers of recent years, Southwest Airlines, is not a hub-and-spoke operator. Instead, it uses a network based clearly on line-haul, point-to-point principles. This means that the airline has to use a relatively small aircraft, the Boeing 737. It does, though, achieve low unit costs through the intensive utilisation of resources. It also appears to be a remarkably popular airline with passengers.

The viability of hub-and-spoke networks is now being affected by another factor. Increasingly, aircraft manufacturers are producing smaller jet aircraft with reasonable operating costs. One of the main markets for these is airlines seeking to attack their rival's hubs with a so-called "hub overflying" strategy. The regional jets produced by Bombardier and Embraer are current examples of these aircraft.

On long-haul routes, similar trends can now be seen, though they are usually referred to as the trends towards market fragmentation rather than hub overflying.

During the 1970s and 1980s, a passenger wishing to fly from, say, a smaller city in Europe to one in the USA often faced a difficult and tiring journey. They had to fly from their home city to a European hub and from there to a gateway hub in the USA. There, they had to pass through immigration checks, reclaim their bags and clear customs as it was their point-of-entry into the USA. Their journey was only completed when they finally took a connecting flight domestically in the USA.

Again, this system brought advantages to both the airlines and their passengers. It allowed Boeing 747 aircraft to be used between the two hub airports, with a daily or better then daily frequency. As a large aircraft with low seat-kilometre costs, the 747 in turn allowed airlines to offer lower fares than might otherwise have been the case.

During the 1980s, though, a revolution in airline fleet planning began to take place. Controversially, the rules governing over-water flying with twin-engined aircraft were progressively relaxed, a relaxation which allowed airlines to choose a more-or-less optimum flight path for all their trans-Atlantic flights whether they were using two, three or four-engined jets. The Boeing Company in particular responded by producing longer range versions of its 767 aircraft, and by investing in a new twin engined family, the 777. Airbus produced a competitor to the 777, the slightly smaller A330, although interestingly it stayed with the four-engined principle for its A340 family.

All these developments meant that airlines had access to a series of aircraft which were smaller than the 747 but which had attractive seat-kilometre operating costs. This, when combined with the substantial growth which had taken place in the market and a growing trend towards regulatory liberalisation, permitted an increasing number of direct non-stop services to be introduced, services which linked two secondary cities on either side of the Atlantic. In turn, these allowed more passengers to fly point-to-point, without the tiresome hub interchanges referred to earlier.

Of the different airlines flying the Atlantic, the one that exploited the situation most fully was undoubtedly American Airlines. Despite having more than 20% of its activity in the international, rather than the US domestic market (a proportion which it is now seeking to increase still further), American has never had Boeing 747s in its fleet and appears very unlikely to order the Airbus A380. Instead it has focussed exclusively on the use of smaller aircraft on its long-haul services.

The controversy about aircraft downsizing on long-haul routes continues. As has been noted, Airbus is now introducing a new large aircraft, the A380. The initial version of this aircraft has around 550 seats in a mixed-class configuration. It will certainly be stretched, though, and later versions may have 800 or even 1000 seats.

Alongside the Airbus innovation, Boeing, after much hesitation, has launched a stretched and up-dated version of the 747, which will be known as the 747-8.

The reason Boeing was so hesitant in deciding on a stretched 747 was an interesting one. Both Boeing and Airbus have agreed that the crucial market for new large jets is that from Asia/Pacific markets to Europe and, especially to North America. Many of the airports in the region will suffer from runway congestion in the future. The disagreement between Boeing and Airbus is regarding the extent to which the fragmentation trends which have affected Atlantic routes will spread to Asia/Pacific markets. Boeing stated that it has come to accept that such a spread is inevitable, and that this will significantly undermine the demand for large aircraft, at least in the short and medium term. Airbus, seeking every opportunity to undermine Boeing's dominant position with the 747, argues that if fragmentation did occur to some extent, it will not eliminate the urgent need for a larger aircraft with, in their case, the technological edge available from an all-new design. To some degree, Boeing's decision to launch begin development of the 747-8 shows a change in the company's position, though, in fact, a large measure of the justification for investment in the new version derives from forecasts of sales of a freight version of the aircraft. Boeing would also point to the considerable early success of the new 787 aircraft as an indicator that its fragmentation predictions will still be proved accurate.

5:3:3 *Punctuality*

Planning to ensure high standards of punctuality is a central product issue for all airlines. It is true that some of the punctuality problems being experienced by airlines at the present time reflect outside factors such as airport and air traffic control congestion. Still, many trade-offs exist where airlines that are prepared to spend more may fare significantly better than those which opt for the lowest possible costs of operation. In turn, these carriers will have an important advantage in securing long-term customer loyalty.

An important first area for these tradeoffs is in airline fleet planning. Generally, an airline will obtain the best punctuality performance if it operates new aircraft of proven technology. This means that an airline seeking the best possible punctuality performance should avoid being a launching customer for a new aircraft containing significant amounts of new technology. An especially difficult situation is when both the airframe and systems and the aircraft engines are entirely new. It will, though, lose opportunities to take advantage of the attractive discounts manufacturers always offer to launching customers.

The airline should also have a policy of replacing aircraft with new planes after a few years. Some airlines - Singapore Airlines is an example - do so, and appear to gain significant punctuality benefits from it. This is because aircraft despatch reliability tends to decline with the age of an aircraft once a certain threshold has been passed.

A further punctuality-related decision is whether or not an airline should invest in the automatic landing capability which will enable its aircraft to operate in conditions of poor visibility. Heavy costs will be associated with such a decision. Besides the capital costs of buying the equipment and maintaining it, flight crew training costs will also be significantly raised both in initial training and also because of the regular opportunities which must be given for crews to practise their blind landing skills. As a further difficulty, it is an investment which for many airlines will be poorly utilized. Few airports in the world have a problem with low visibility for more than ten or fifteen days per year, meaning that for almost all the time, a blind landing capability will not be needed.

Despite all these problems, investment in automatic landing is now a necessity for many airlines. Customers now realise that fog need not delay an aircraft unduly, and competition has forced more and more carriers to make the required investment.

Maintenance is another area where trade-offs between cost levels and punctuality performance will need to be made. An airline seeking to achieve the best possible punctuality record will need a substantial line maintenance capability, to ensure that technical problems can be corrected as soon as they arise. Also, a considerable investment in spares will be required, for the same reason.

It is in the area of schedules planning where the most significant trade-offs have to be made if an airline is to achieve a good punctuality performance. A carrier aiming at the lowest possible cost of operation will develop a schedule which will give a high annual utilization of each aircraft in the fleet. Such a policy will lower costs because it will result in the fixed costs of aircraft ownership or lease rentals being spread over the greatest quantity of output. Very high aircraft utilization will, though, often bring significant product penalties. It will result in some customers having to accept inconvenient departure and arrival times, because high utilization will require aircraft to be kept flying continuously except for essential maintenance and turnaround periods. Even more significantly, a policy of high aircraft utilization may bring problems with punctuality. This is because once an airline experiences an initial delay, there will be no slack in the schedule to allow the delay to be made up. Thus, if an aircraft is delayed early in the day – perhaps for reasons outside the airline's control such as air traffic difficulties – all the remaining flights it is due to operate during the day will also be late. The only way around such difficulties seems to be to use uncongested, often remote, airports, where delays due to congestion are less likely to occur. This is the policy adopted by many Low Cost Carriers - notably so by Ryanair. When it is combined with careful attention to the detailed analysis of the aircraft turnaround process, it does indeed seem to be possible to combine high aircraft utilisation with a good punctuality performance.

Similar considerations apply to the question of the time which an airline allows in its timetable for a flight to be completed. A punctual departure is, of course, reassuring for passengers. However, it is a punctual arrival which matters to them even more, especially if they are trying to make a connection. If an airline allows a generous time in its schedule for the completion of flight, a punctual arrival is much more likely. It will also mean that a flight will arrive punctually even if it runs into stronger-than-expected headwinds. A slack schedule will, though, bring a cost penalty if it reduces the number of aircraft rotations that can be flown in a day.

5:4 Customer Service-Related Product Features

5:4:1 *Point-of-Sale Service*

Point-of-sale service is the term used to describe service offered to the customer at the point where they are actually making a booking. It is an area where revolutionary changes have occurred over the last five years.

Point-of-sale service has always been difficult for airlines because of the large number and wide variety of sales outlets they have used. In the past, some airline customers have wished to deal with them direct. The traditional methods to allow this have been downtown ticket offices, airport ticket desks and call centres. In addition, airlines have had to make themselves accessible to travel agents, with over 80% of bookings traditionally being obtained through agents. A final source of business has been from other airlines on an interline basis. Though the nature of interline relationships is now changing, it is still the case that a passenger wishing to book a multi-sector journey using several different airlines can do so by contacting only the first carrier (assuming that they are proposing to use a relatively expensive flexible ticket). This airline will then contact the others to make the necessary bookings.

Given this range of outlets, the point-of-sale task would always have been difficult for airlines. There can be little doubt, though, that by their own policy decisions traditional 'Legacy' airlines made it a great deal harder. In particular, by adopting very complex fare structures and reservations procedures, they increased point-of-sale transaction times and also ensured that the systems could only be accessed by trained experts. In turn, this further increased the proportion of bookings coming through the travel agency system and raised commission and booking fee costs.

To try to address the problem, the response of many airlines was to invest large sums in the development of so-called Global Distribution Systems such as Amadeus and Sabre, which we will cover fully in Section 7:3. Though to some degree these arrested the rise in processing costs by improving staff productivity, they proved costly and controversial. They were also to a large extent addressing the symptoms of the problem rather than the problem itself.

It has taken the Cost Leader revolution we referred to in the last chapter as well as the growth of widely-available internet access, to radically change the situation. As we have seen, by making fares and reservations procedures very simple, these airlines have been able to move to a "self-service" approach, with a high proportion of their bookings being made on-line by passengers themselves. This has resulted in very large cost savings in terms of commissions and administration, and is a policy which many traditional airlines are now belatedly following.

5:4:2 *Reservations and Overbooking*

For most air travellers, a pre-booked reservation they can rely on remains an integral part of the product that they expect from airlines Today, the availability of cheap computing power means that most of the technical problems associated with providing them have been resolved.

There is still one air transport product where a reservation is not offered. This is with the pure form of the so-called Shuttle concept. Pioneered by Eastern Airlines in the USA in 1961, the idea of the Shuttle is that passengers do not need to book in advance. Instead, the airline guarantees to fly all those who report for a flight. They can do so by keeping back-up aircraft and crews, which are called into action if the number of passengers checking in for a flight exceeds the capacity of the aircraft allocated to it.

The Shuttle concept brings a number of theoretical advantages. Passengers are saved the trouble of making reservations, and airlines the cost of recording them. Also, most Shuttle passengers pay at the airport. The business therefore comes direct to airlines with a useful saving in commission costs and some cash-flow benefits. It also helps to cement market control.

Shuttle concepts continue to be used in the USA, with, for example, US Airways and Delta still flying Shuttle flights between New York, Washington and Boston. The concept is in decline, though, in other markets. It requires a very large commitment of resources of aircraft and crew. These only achieve poor utilization because of the rarity with which back-up aircraft will be needed outside of the peak periods. Also, airport slot constraints are becoming more and more severe. In order to protect their so-called "Grandfather Rights" on the slots they have been allocated, airlines need to use them on a minimum of 80% of occasions during a given traffic season. There can be no certainty that they will do so if these slots are allocated to Shuttle back-up flights. Finally, through the advent of very capable Revenue Management systems (dealt with in the next chapter), carriers are now much more successful at selling seats on off-peak flights at low, but still profitable, prices. It is therefore often a worthwhile option to fly a route with an aircraft which will cater for all the peak time full-fare demand. Though this aircraft will then be too big for the level of such demand at off-peak periods, lower fares and careful capacity management can be used to produce worthwhile returns even on these flights. This may well be a cheaper and more profitable option than flying all services with a relatively small plane and augmenting peak-time capacity with a costly back-up aircraft.

An illustration of changing attitudes towards Shuttle services came in the UK domestic market in 1997. British Airways had flown domestic trunk services from Heathrow using the Shuttle principle since 1975. In 1997, though, the guarantee of a seat for all those reporting for a particular flight was discontinued, with all passengers expected to make a reservation. At the same time, the making of reservations was made easier by the adoption of "ticketless travel", a development discussed fully in Section 7:2:2.

If reservations are to be required in almost all cases, airlines still have to address another difficult problem: many passengers do not turn up and use the reservation they have made. The proportion of occasions where this is so varies from market to market, but it is quite common to find 10% of bookings coming into the "no-show" category. There are many reasons for this. Some passengers fully intend to get to the airport to check in for their flight but are prevented from doing so. They constitute *accidental* no-shows. Last minute illness or death will be an obvious reason for accidental no-showing. Other reasons will include traffic delays on the way to the airport and the passenger experiencing a late in-bound connecting flight.

Not all no-shows are accidental, however. Many are *deliberate*. For example, business travellers who are uncertain about the time at which their meetings will end may book seats on several flights with different airlines. They will then have a convenient return flight whatever the actual finishing time. Another problem may occur when an unscrupulous passenger is holding a Standby ticket for a particular flight. They have an incentive to phone the airline a number of times making false bookings using fictitious names. The result will be no-shows, meaning that the Standby passenger will be accommodated.

Given such a significant no-show problem, it might be argued that airlines are themselves creating the problem by an over-generous attitude to those who book but fail to check-in for a flight. All service industries face the same problem as airlines, that their output is instantly perishable and cannot be stored. Some – cinemas are a good example – require customers to pay at the time of booking and no refunds are given if they fail to show up for the actual performance. As mentioned in Section 4:2:3, many Low-Cost Carriers take a similar approach. They will only deal with customers who have credit or debit cards. Card details are taken by the airline when a reservation is made and the card is automatically debited. This gives the carrier a guaranteed income and removes the necessity to overbook. Other, less radical airlines are increasingly making some of their lower fares non-refundable.

Despite the attraction of this idea, it is not a practical one for airlines in all circumstances. In particular, business travellers often regard the right to no-show as an important part of the flexibility they are buying when using an expensive fare. If one carrier unilaterally made such fares non-refundable in the event of a no-show it would lose significant market share to its rivals.

If a degree of no-showing is inevitable, airlines have a strong incentive to overbook, and, perhaps perversely, their passengers will also benefit as a result of such a policy. By overbooking, load factors can be increased, which will in turn allow fares to be lower. Also, overbooking permits more passengers to travel on the flight of their choice. If an airline did not overbook, it would only accept reservations up to the number of seats on an aircraft. All other requests for bookings would be refused. However, if, as would be very likely, there were no-shows, the flight would take off with some of the seats unoccupied. Ironically, there would then be passengers using later and presumably less convenient flights who could in fact have taken the flight of their choice.

There are thus clear advantages which will accrue to the customer if an airline practises overbooking which will be lost if it does not. Despite this, overbooking remains unpopular. Of course, an airline should use historical records to help fix the amount by which each flight should be overbooked. If a conservative estimate is made, on almost all occasions there will be no problem. The number of no-show passengers will exceed the amount of overbooking and all passengers will get on the flight. However, no matter what degree of care is exercised, there will be occasions – hopefully rare – when difficulties arise. Then, the random element present in patterns of no-showing means that the number of passengers reporting for a flight exceeds the capacity of the aircraft being used for it. Some passengers will therefore be "bumped".

In the past, airline approaches to this problem were totally unsatisfactory. Too often, the passengers selected for bumping were the last ones to check in. This was expedient, in the sense that these passengers would not have baggage already loaded into the aircraft lower holds, which would otherwise have to be retrieved for security reasons. However, these late-arriving passengers would often be business travellers. They would therefore be commercially important to the airline. Also, as business travellers, it would often be vital that they should get the flight on which they are booked, because they had meetings to attend, or onward connections to make.

Today, better-managed airlines are more sophisticated at handling bumping situations. Their aim is to identify, and to compensate, the passengers who are prepared to accept a delay. These are clearly unlikely to include business travellers. If such a passenger is, for example, flying to negotiate an important contract, no amount of compensation will be sufficient to make up for the fact that they miss their meeting. Many leisure travellers, though, will find the offer of compensation an attractive one. It may not matter to them a great deal whether they reach their destination today or tomorrow, especially if they receive a cash payment in compensation. Airlines should therefore seek volunteers for off-loading on those flights where they expect to have problems. In doing so, they can provide a valuable protection for their commercial reputation. A further incentive for them to do so, at least in the European Union is that now substantial compensation has to be paid to passengers who are involuntarily bumped from a flight and face a substantial delay as a result.

5:4:3 Airport Service

As in all other areas of product design, airline decisions about the level of airport service they offer to their customers will be a reflection of their overall business strategy. Low-fare airlines will find airport service a major area where they can achieve economies to ensure that their low fares will be profitable. They often use uncongested airports, which may sometimes impose inconvenience on passengers by being far from the cities they are designed to serve. They may insist on longer check-in times to enable a smaller number of check-in desks to be used, or, increasingly encourage check-in to be undertaken in advance on-line. A simple bag-drop facility is then all that is needed at the airport, though even here, charges are now often made for each piece of checked baggage, both as a way of producing additional revenue and to encourage people where they can to limit themselves to hand baggage only. No special lounges are provided, resulting in a significant cost saving. Finally, the boarding process will be a usually be a simple one on a "first come, first served" basis with no pre-allocation of seats.

For airlines aiming to penetrate the market of frequent business travellers the task could not be more different. Major efforts have been made in recent years to establish airport service as a significant area of product differentiation. Some carriers now provide limousine services to pick up premium-fare passengers at their home or office to bring them to the airport – Virgin Atlantic, Continental and Emirates are examples. Once there, kerbside check-in facilities may be on offer to remove the necessity of carrying heavy baggage into the terminal. If they do come into the terminal to check-in, a separate, uncongested desk will be provided. There may then be provision for a preferential channel for moving through passport and security formalities, before the passenger is invited to use what will generally be an extremely luxurious lounge with hospitality and business facilities available free-of-charge. At the arrival airport, business travellers can now expect preferential baggage service with their bags arriving on the baggage carousel first. There may also be an arrivals lounge allowing them to freshen up before going to their meeting.

All these advances in airport service do not come cheaply. They involve investment in extra staff and equipment, and in rental payments to the airport operator in respect of lounge space and extra check-in desks. It is essential therefore that airlines are able to raise their fares to pay for them or increase their share of the business travel market as a result of better airport service. It may be harder to sustain higher fares in a recessionary period, whilst increases in market share may only be transient if rival airlines also offer enhanced airport service.

5:4:4   In-Flight Service

Many of the points we need to discuss with regard to in-flight service have been made in earlier sections. Section 2:3:3 looked at the question of customer requirements in this area, and in this chapter, Section 5:3:1 considered issues associated with classes-of-service decisions. There are, though, a number of additional aspects which will affect the nature of passengers' in-flight experience.

One of these areas is the question of an airline's fleet planning policies. Naturally, all aircraft manufacturers argue that selecting their aircraft will in turn allow airlines to give their customers a superior in-flight product. For example, Airbus claim that their A320 family is better than the B737 because it has a wider fuselage cross-section, allowing for wider seats and wider aisles. Equally, though, Boeing argues that its B767 is superior to the Airbus A330 and A340 because it is designed for 7-abreast rather than 8-abreast seating in the Economy cabin. Airbus replies that its A330 and A340 are optimised at 6-abreast seating in Business Class, in contrast to the 7 abreast of the B777. The latter therefore results in a 'prisoner', in the middle seat of three in the centre of the cabin.

For smaller aircraft, manufacturers of regional jets might argue that these aircraft bring significant benefits compared with turbo-props, at least over longer routes because they give a smoother flight, usually at higher altitudes, though these advantages are reduced with the latest generation of turboprops such as the Bombardier Dash 8-400.

There are, of course, many costs associated with in-flight service. However, despite what they spend on items such as food, drink and in-flight entertainment, airlines find that the main costs are those associated with cabin staffing in terms of the salaries paid, the allowances given and the costs of hotel accommodation for flight attendants. The usual linking between the correct policy and airlines' overall business strategy applies.

For low-fare airlines, there might appear to be a temptation to dispense with cabin staff altogether. Because these airlines are generally "no-frills", the cabin service task is in any case a limited one. Such an option is not, though, a possibility. The primary function of cabin staff is that of ensuring safety on board, and regulatory bodies insist that a minimum number of qualified cabin staff are carried. The rules are rather complicated, but in essence they mean that there must be one cabin attendant per 50 passengers up to 200, and one per 25 passengers over 200. A "no-frills" airline will, though, work with the minimum legal number of cabin staff as will a typical charter airline.

Scheduled carriers will generally have a greater number of cabin staff than the minimum, to ensure more attentive cabin service for First and Business Class travellers. Some airlines, especially from the Far East, will greatly exceed the minimum number. For example, a typical European or North American airline will budget for 14 or 15 cabin staff on a B747. Carriers such as Thai International use 22 on this same aircraft.

Whatever the number of cabin staff employed, a significantly greater issue for airlines – and their passengers – will be the attitudes displayed by cabin staff towards the passengers in their care. Warm, friendly and confident attitudes will constitute a major marketing advantage, whereas uncaring attitudes will be a serious handicap, especially amongst regular business travellers who will fly often enough to be able to compare the reception which they receive on different airlines.

Ensuring the right approach from cabin staff is one of the industry's intractable problems at the present time. Cabin crew are entitled to expect a career structure like everyone else and in highly unionised carriers in Europe and North America at least, trade unions have often been successful in negotiating this for them. However, there is then a risk that people stay in what is a difficult and exhausting job for too long, when cynicism has long ago replaced the initial enthusiasm that they may once have felt. Also, in recent years, at many airlines, cabin crew have seen their salaries and allowances reduced, as carriers have battled to restore profitability. Though such changes have often been a regrettable necessity, they have hardly helped to improve motivation and commitment.

5:5 Controlling Product Quality

Quality control is an essential part of the product design phase of marketing for any airline. Without it, the carrier cannot know which parts of its product are weak, and where improvements are needed.

Many aspects of the airline product can be quantified. For example, with point-of-sale service, modern telephone equipment can provide statistics on the proportion of calls answered within a given time period. It can also give information about the proportion of calls that are lost at busy times, in the sense that callers become tired of waiting for someone to help them and abandon the call.

Baggage service – or the lack of it – can also be quantified. The proportion of bags which are mishandled and fail to arrive at the destination at the same time as their owners is one necessary statistic. Also, baggage delivery times can be monitored by recording the time taken for the first bag and the last bag to reach the baggage delivery carousel.

Punctuality and regularity performance should also be studied carefully. The proportion of flights departing and arriving within prescribed limits of the scheduled time is a fundamental measure, with on-time to within 5 minutes a suitable standard for short-haul routes, and on-time to within 15 minutes for long-haul. In terms of regularity (the proportion of flights advertised in the timetable which are actually operated), the standard should, of course, be near to 100%.

Monitoring of customer compliments and complaints should also be undertaken. All airlines receive fraudulent or unjustified complaints. Although these require vigilance, the number of them should be relatively constant. Therefore, comparing the number of customer compliments with the number of complaints will provide a first quality control statistic. Airlines should also investigate the nature of the complaints they receive. If these focus to an increasing degree on only a small number of product components, this will be a strong indicator of the areas where management attention is needed.

We have already discussed in Section 2:3:2 the use of in-flight and airport surveys as ways of collecting information about customer requirements. They can also form part of a quality control programme. An in-flight survey will have the advantage that passengers are actually experiencing the product at the time they fill in their questionnaire. If they are questioned at the airport of arrival their memories of the flight will still be fresh. In either case, asking passengers their opinions can have a valuable Customer Relations function, of convincing them that the airline is interested in continuous product improvement.

A further area of quality control work is one which should never be ignored – the opinions of the airline's own customer contact and sales staff. These people will regularly come into contact with customers and will have to listen to their complaints. Their reports can provide an accurate barometer of the airline's performance.

5:6 The Air Freight Product

Airlines with an interest in penetrating the air freight market need to spend a great deal of time in detailed planning of the freight product. There are, of course, many differences between the air passenger and air cargo businesses which were set out in section 2:4:1. The basic principles of product planning are, though, exactly the same. Successful airlines will be those that identify correctly their customer's requirements and then make the difficult tradeoff between product quality and costs.

5:6:1 Air Freight Capacity

With questions of air freight capacity, we have discussed in Section 2:4:1 the advantages from the customer's point-of-view of an airline investing in pure freighter aircraft. These will allow capacity to be provided on the routings that the freight customer wants, at times which suit their demand pattern. They also offer a greater certainty that goods will actually be flown on the flight on which they are booked.

If it is decided that the provision of freighters will be worthwhile, a decision will have to be made about the type of aircraft to be selected. In deciding this, airlines will need to bring in some of the same considerations they will employ when selecting a passenger aircraft. For example, they will need information on the payload/range capabilities of the different aircraft types in comparison with their route networks and traffic flows. They will need data on capital and ownership costs, fuel consumption, field-length performance and available operating costs. In addition, though, there are two pieces of data which are unique to freight operations and which can be crucial in plane choice. First, *cabin door size* and *cabin cross-section* of the main deck of the aircraft will decide what size of consignment can be accommodated. All narrow-bodied jet freighters (such as the freight version of the Boeing 757) can only accept consignments of up to 86 inches in height through their cargo doors. They cannot, therefore, accept the 8 feet by 8 feet rectangular cross-section of International Standards Organization (ISO) standard-sized containers. Of the wide-bodied aircraft, the freighter version of the MD-11 cannot accommodate two of these containers side-by-side in the main deck. The B747F and the A380F are the only freight aircraft at the moment which can do so. The 747F has the added advantage of a nose-loading capability, providing carriers are prepared to accept the higher capital and maintenance costs of an aircraft equipped with this facility.

The second important performance measure for a freighter is its *design density*. Freighters do not only have a weight-limited payload. They also have a fixed volumetric capacity. If an aircraft only has a small volume relative to its maximum payload it will often become volumetrically full before its maximum payload is reached. Older narrow-bodied jets such as the B707 and DC-8 all had significant design density problems because of their inadequate cabin volumes. The Boeing 747 has a design density approximately 40% below that of the 707. This aircraft, though, has a very large payload/range potential so in practice it can only be used on the busiest long-haul services, as can the A380F.

The airline specialising in the air freight market will have to decide which types of freighter aircraft it is to employ. Total market airlines aiming to penetrate both the air passenger and air freight markets must decide whether or not they will use freighters at all. They need not do so. It is part of the synergy available to the total market airline that in providing passenger service it also produces lower-hold freight space. With narrow–bodied planes such as the B737, lower-hold capacity is not especially useful because these aircraft have belly-holds which are awkwardly-shaped and comparatively small. They can therefore carry only a small amount of freight, even when operating a flight where the passenger and baggage load is limited. The freight they do carry also poses time-consuming problems of loading and unloading. Wide-bodied aircraft, though, are much more capable. The B747 can carry 25 tones or more of containerized and palletized cargo in its lower hold. Other wide-bodies such as the A330, A340 and MD-11 have a freight capability of 12 tonnes or more, depending on the passenger payload and the fuel needed for a given sector.

Given that it will have large amounts of freight capacity available in its passenger aircraft, a total market airline operating wide-bodied planes can consider relying exclusively on lower-hold space. It will still be able to offer a good flight frequency, and it will not have to bear the heavy costs of operating a freighter fleet. Indeed, in the past an investment in freighters has rarely been a successful one for such airlines, especially in markets such as the North Atlantic where freight yields have generally been low.

Despite the attractions of not employing freighters, it is unlikely to be a viable option for an airline with a serious interest in the air freight market. To many customers, an exclusive reliance on belly-hold capacity will significantly reduce the quality of the product. For example, a shipper of hazardous cargoes may need freighter service because industry safety rules forbid the carriage of many types of hazardous goods in the lower holds of passenger aircraft. Also, freighter capacity is very important to the shipper of large consignments. The main deck of the B747F, the largest freighter currently in common use, can accommodate shipments of over 100 inches in height.

A further problem with a freight product based only on belly-hold capacity is that it fails to take into account shipper's requirements for space. Air freight peaks strongly at night, following production during the working day, and at the end of the working week. There is a pronounced trough in demand on Sundays and Mondays. Some belly-hold capacity will therefore be provided at times of the day or the week when little freight is moving. At other times, though, there may be a chronic shortage of capacity, especially on Friday evenings.

In the longer term, a policy of relying purely on belly-holds may be untenable for another reason. It ties the amount of freight space offered to passenger demand. Generally, air freight demand is growing more quickly then that for passengers, in itself likely to lead to a shortage of belly-hold freight capacity. Also, passenger demand growth is generally faster in the leisure rather than the business travel segment. Leisure-orientated flights tend to be on routes to holiday resorts where the quantities of air freight moving may be relatively small.

A final factor jeopardising a belly-holds only policy may be that in the longer-term, aircraft developments may mean that less space will be available for freight. The Airbus A380 is a double-decked aircraft in terms of its passenger cabins, in order to keep its overall dimensions within those necessary for airport compatibility. This means that a large increase in the passenger carrying capabilities of the aircraft, without corresponding growth in belly-hold space. Consequently, a greater proportion of the belly-hold capacity will be taken up with passengers' bags, and less will be available for freight.

Overall, airlines with a major interest in building their presence in the air freight market will have to operate a fleet of freighters. They may operate these aircraft themselves, or wet-lease them from specialists such as the US firm Atlasair. If they choose to operate the aircraft themselves, an attractive option may be to use conversions of obsolete passenger aircraft, rather than buy new and very expensive specialist freighters from the manufacturers. This will especially be the case if the passenger aircraft are comparatively new but have become obsolescent because of a lack of range. With freighters, shorter ranges are less of a problem because the aircraft can simply land and take on more fuel. Both Airbus and Boeing are offering freight conversion programmes for used aircraft, both as a way of providing a service to airlines and as a way of hopefully protecting the residual values of their older aircraft.

With questions of air freight capacity, there is an interim solution possible, with the use of so-called "Combi" and "Quick-Change" aircraft. A Combi is an aircraft where the main deck can be divided between passengers and freight with a moveable bulkhead to separate the two. A

Quick-Change (QC) aircraft is one which can be converted from a passenger to a freighter aircraft quickly – generally in less than an hour. This is because the seats can be removed in a short time as they are placed on pallets.

Both Combis and QCs are more expensive and heavier than equivalent passenger aircraft because they need a large cargo door and a strengthened floor. Theoretically, though, both can bring significant benefits. Combis have allowed routes to be opened up where there has been insufficient passenger demand to allow a service to begin at a marketable frequency. They have also permitted carriers to enter the large-shipment market without the risks associated with investing in pure freighters. QC aircraft have sometimes been valuable in short-haul operations. Here, passengers have not generally wished to travel at night, so aircraft have had to be left on the ground then, with a significant penalty in annual utilization. Converting the aircraft into a freighter allowed for extra, night-time flights to be operated.

Despite these advantages, Combi flying has declined recently whilst the QC concept has never achieved the popularity for which the aircraft manufacturers must have hoped. Combis have generally been unpopular with passengers, resulting as they do in a smaller-sized passenger cabin. Recent years have also seen the introduction of new fire suppression rules which have caused increases in both capital costs and aircraft weight. These in turn have challenged the economics of Combis.

With QC aircraft, these have generally been opposed by the passenger departments of airlines. Using an aircraft as a night-time freighter may mean that there will delays to early morning passenger flights if technical problems have occurred overnight. Also, in the past, QC aircraft have suffered from the way in which the nightly conversions have damaged aircraft interiors.

Besides questions of freight capacity, an airline hoping to penetrate the air freight market will have to make decisions about the ground handling systems to be employed, and the investment to be made in information technology.

In the late 1960s and early 1970s a number of airlines installed sophisticated on-airport automated freight handling systems. These were intended to allow them to lower their ground handling costs and to improve the service they offered to their customers. This early move to highly automated cargo handling was not successful, though, largely due to the unreliability and inflexibility of the systems.

During the later 1970s, many airlines discontinued automated on-airport handling and returned to labour-intensive methods. By this time, the advent of wide-bodied aircraft meant that more and more freight was loaded into aircraft in containerized or palletized form. As this trend developed, airlines found at least a short-term answer to their handling problems by offering concessionary rates to those air freight forwarders who were prepared to take the Unit Load Devices (ULDs), load them and present them to the airlines in a ready-for-carriage form. This process, operating under the so-called Bulk Unitization Programme, rescued airlines from otherwise intractable problems of on-airport cargo handling. It did, though greatly increase the number of expensive Unit Load Devices which they needed to purchase. The Programme also raised the bargaining power of air freight forwarders relative to the airlines. It was therefore significant that during the 1980s and 1990s large integrated carriers such as FedEx, UPS and DHL grew rapidly. These firms adopted a policy of substantial investment in airport handling facilities, and largely chose to by-pass the forwarding industry. It is also the case that some airlines – British Airways and Air France are good examples – have now invested again in automated on-airport handling, despite having their fingers badly burnt in the industry's first move in this direction. They are relying on the fact that the state-of-the-art in cargo handling has advanced considerably since then.

The design of the freight product is an interesting aspect of airline marketing. The total market airline can use the synergies available from the belly-hold space in its passenger aircraft. It can therefore offer flight frequency and cheaply available capacity as its main advantages. The pure freight airline, on the other hand, can supply capacity which will meet the needs of the freight customer without any requirement for compromise. It is these advantages that are becoming increasingly important.

SUCCESSFUL AIRLINES ......

✈   Appreciate that product development is a continuous, never-ending process, using the lessons of the Product Life Cycle.

✈   Analyse products and routes, using the Boston Box model to guide their investment decisions.

✈   Correctly make the difficult decisions which balance risk and opportunity, using the guidelines provided by the Ansoff Matrix.

✈   Appreciate that adding product frills rarely produces long-term gains in market shares, because frills can easily be matched by competitors.

✈   Work towards ensuring that the highest standards of personal service are delivered to customers – something which *can* boost market shares.

✈   Establish a rigorous quality control system for their product, and work to ensure that the weaknesses shown by this system are corrected through a process of continuous improvement.

6 Pricing and Revenue Management

Of all the different facets of airline marketing, none has changed further or faster in recent years than the question of appropriate pricing policies. Today's airline managers are having to learn and apply skills which were either unknown or not needed by their predecessors, and where some of the fundamentals which have served the industry well in the past are being brought into question. It is also a high profile area, where mistakes can result in large losses in a very short time.

6:1 Building Blocks in Airline Pricing Policy

6:1:1 Pricing - A Part of the Marketing Mix

In studying the question of appropriate policies for airlines it is first of all necessary to emphasise that pricing decisions cannot be made in isolation – they can only be seen in the context of the Marketing Mix model presented in Section 1:1:2. In particular, product and pricing decisions must clearly be made together. In recent years, many airlines have invested large sums in improving the specification of their First and Business Class products, with costly investments having been made in such things as better (usually flat-bedded) seats, higher quality catering and greatly improved in-flight entertainment. At the same time they have generally – and correctly – raised the prices of First and Business Class tickets in real terms, to provide a return on the investment that has been made. As we have discussed, whether or not they will be able to maintain these higher prices and the same return when recessionary conditions re-assert themselves is another question.

6:1:2 Deregulation

Until recently, the question of government regulatory policy was a major constraint on airlines' pricing freedom in international aviation. Almost all intergovernmental Air Services Agreements were written in terms which were designed to stop airlines competing on price. The airlines designated under these agreements were required to meet together, agree on what the fares should be, and file these fares with their respective governments for approval. Assuming that this approval was forthcoming – and it normally was – the airlines in question would implement a fare structure based on the principle that all those on a route would change exactly the same fares. Even in domestic markets – notably so in the USA – government regulation was imposed to prevent price competition, presumably in the hope of maintaining a stable industry.

The situation today is totally different. Many domestic markets have been completely deregulated with regard to price, with airlines free to price as they choose. In some international markets, too, a virtual deregulation of pricing has taken place. This is notably so with respect to the so-called Single Aviation Market of the European Union.

Even in markets where the old facade of price regulation nominally remains, the situation today has still changed a great deal from that which prevailed only a few years ago. In these markets, it had been one of the functions of the International Air Transport Association (IATA) to run the Tariff Conferences at which fares have been agreed. The machinery of so-called Tariff Co-ordination has become more flexible. Airlines have gained the freedom to innovate with their own promotional fares, with Tariff Co-ordination activity confined to the highest, interlinable fares. Even where fares still fall within the responsibility of the Traffic Conferences, it is an open secret that airlines have engaged in a great deal of under-the-counter tariff discounting, with IATA having discontinued what were described as its Compliance efforts. There were designed to ensure that carriers implemented the fares policies to which they had agreed.

It is impossible to exaggerate the significance of the moves towards less regulated pricing. They have allowed many airlines to develop a low cost/low fares philosophy, something which they could never have done under the old regulated pricing regimes. This in turn has challenged incumbents to become more efficient and innovative. At the same time, managers responsible for pricing policy have had to develop a completely new set of skills. Under the former regime, the skills required were those of attending often-interminable IATA Tariff Co-ordination meetings and engineering a compromise between supposed competitors. Today, the skills are those of forming an appropriate rapid response to the pricing initiatives of these competitors, and deciding when the airline should lead the market in a change of pricing policy.

6:1:3 Dissemination of Fares Information

Until relatively recently, the pace of change in airline fares was slow. Regulated competition meant that all prices were a compromise, and reaching such a compromise was usually a drawn-out affair. At the same time, the system for disseminating fares information precluded rapid changes. The method for such dissemination was a printed tariff manual. Preparing these manuals ready for a fares change would in itself take many weeks, as would distributing them to the travel agents who needed them. (The delivery of the tariff manuals to agents was a task generally undertaken by the airline's field sales executives). The effect of all these factors was that the fares were only changed once a year or once every two years.

Again, the situation today could not be more different. The development of Global Distribution Systems (see Section 7:3) has meant that almost all travel agents have instant access to a fares database which is up-dated (by the GDS firms) several times a day if necessary. At the same time, an increasing proportion of airline tickets are being sold through carriers' own websites, where the process of tariff updating can be even more rapid if necessary. The result of both these trends is that it the fare structure is now highly unstable at times of active price competition. Such competition will be especially prevalent during recessionary periods, when supply exceeds demand and airlines are fighting to fill otherwise empty seats. It will also break out in the autumn of each year on many routes as the summer peak period comes to an end and airlines compete for their share of the declining market.

At times such as these, millions of fares in the industry's main fares databases may change every day, challenging airline pricing managers not only to get their pricing decisions right, but to make these decisions quickly and under great pressure.

6:1:4 Revenue Management Systems

Clearly, the pricing environment today is a far more challenging one. There is, however, one major change which has made it much easier for airline managers to develop sound pricing policies – the advent of sophisticated systems for managing the sale of seats (and, increasingly, of cargo space).

In deciding on pricing policies which will optimise financial returns, carriers must decide on the number of seats they will sell, at what prices and in what currencies. They must also make often difficult decisions about traffic which will be accepted, and which refused on the grounds that the yield obtained from it is too low.

Twenty years ago, there were no tools that would allow this process to be controlled effectively. Today, there most certainly are. Modern airline reservations computers allow the capacity on board each aircraft to be divided up into a large number of booking classes – currently 26 in the more sophisticated systems with larger numbers than this likely to be possible in the future. Decisions can then be made about the number of seats to be allocated to each class, and the time at which these seats will be made available for sale. These decisions will reflect different patterns of demand. For example, for a flight leaving to a business destination on a Monday morning, few if any seats will be allocated to those classes allowing for early sale at low prices. Almost all of them will be in classes where sale will only be permitted at high fares, with many bookings only being made a relatively short time before flight departure. In contrast, a flight leaving to such a destination early on a Sunday morning will be given a completely different profile. Here, almost all the seats will be allocated to booking classes allowing for sale at low prices (or for their use by people redeeming Frequent Flyer Programme credits) as the airline attempts to obtain at least some revenue from seats which might otherwise remain empty.

A particular problem in airline revenue management at the moment concerns the question of connecting versus point-to-point traffic. Generally, airlines earn a better yield on short-haul routes from passengers who are only flying out and back on the route, rather than from those who are using the short sector to fly to a hub, from where they will connect onto a long-haul service. Unless a Revenue Management system is monitored carefully, there will be a tendency for long-haul connecting traffic to be turned away, and point-to-point passengers to be accepted. This will improve the apparent financial performance of the airline's short-haul routes whilst worsening the carrier's overall financial results because of the loss of so-called network revenue. In terms of the development of Revenue Management technology, many airlines are now attempting to produce the systems which will allow them to optimise revenue through taking account of the true origin and destination of passengers. This is, though, a challenging problem of software development.

6:2 "Uniform" and "Differential" Pricing

6:2:1 The Principles[14]

Table 6:1 presents data which describes the present pricing structure of one of the airlines on the Heathrow – Toronto route. This route has not been selected on account of it having any special features. The situation there is a typical one, replicated on thousands of different routes around the world.

Table 6:1 Fare Structure, Heathrow – Toronto, October 2005

Fare Type	Fare Level	Conditions
J	£4,163 RTN	-
S2	£1.171 RTN	Point-to-point only
"World Offer"	£543 RTN	Saturday night stay required Mid-week travel only £50 fee to change reservation

The situation presented is one of considerable complexity. Prices vary enormously from the seemingly outrageous levels of Business Class fares down to the very low so-called "World Offer" fare. They also vary in terms of the conditions attached to each fare, with some fares – the more expensive ones – being fully flexible, and others having tightly restrictive limitations attached to their use.

To some degree, such wide differences in price levels are easy to explain and understand. In particular, the very high prices charged for seats in the First Class and Business Class cabins reflect substantial, tangible differences in the product supplied. As already discussed, a modern state-of-the-art First Class cabin will have seats which fold down into full-length beds. These will require a Seat Pitch of 70 inches or more. First Class passengers benefit from extravagant standards of in-flight service and entertainment. It is also generally the case that airlines operate their First Class cabins at low average load factors. Figures of only 40-50% are

---

[14] For a theoretical review of these principles, see N Hanna, H R Dodge "Pricing Policies and Procedures". Macmillan 1995

typical. Amongst the reasons for this is that First Class cabins are generally not overbooked as airlines regard the risk of having to off-load such commercially important people as unacceptable. It is clearly correct, though, that First Class passengers should pay both for the seat they occupy, and also for the empty seats in a low load-factor operation.

Though the specification of a typical Business Class is still somewhat lower than for First Class, it is still a very expensive one for airlines to provide. A typical Business Class seat pitch is now over 70", to permit the seat to be folded down into the flat bed that the state-of-the art requires should be made available. The passenger also benefits from better food, a higher ratio of cabin staff to passengers, and more choice in terms of in-flight entertainment.

Overall, whilst First Class and Business Class fare levels appear very high, it is at least possible for airlines to justify them in terms of differences in the product offered. It is much harder for them to do this for Economy Class fares. Here people paying very different prices will sit in the same part of the aircraft, in the same type of seat, and will experience exactly the same in-flight service and entertainment. Not surprisingly, there have been complaints that the existing fare structure is discriminatory. Those people who pay the higher fares argue that they are overcharged in order to subsidize the losses made on "below-cost" cheap fares.

It is possible to refute such arguments to a degree, but they should not be dismissed lightly. Both those who pay high fares and those who pay lower fares may benefit from a properly-applied Differential fare structure. This is obvious in the case of low-fare passengers who are able to travel at a price they can afford. It is less obvious, but can still the case, that the high-fare payers also gain from Differential pricing.

The critic of differential fares might argue that airlines should instead adopt a uniform approach to pricing in the Economy cabin. For example, the data given in Table 6:1, stated that people in the Economy cabin could be paying a fare somewhere between £1,171 and £543 for a return ticket. A uniform approach to pricing would require that everyone should pay the same. The high fare would be lowered – perhaps to £700, and the lower fares would be raised to the same level.

Whilst such a situation might appear to be an ideal one, this might not be the case, for two reasons. Firstly, Economy passengers do not all have the same needs, despite the fact that they all sit in the same cabin. In particular, business travellers often have a requirement for flexibility which is absent in the typical product needs of the leisure traveller. Those flying on business may sometimes have a requirement to obtain a booking shortly before a flight departs, because of an unexpected business crisis arising. They may also need to cancel a booking once they have made it and rebook on another flight due to their plans changing. Leisure travellers, on the other hand will generally book weeks or months before they fly and will only need to alter or cancel a booking on rare occasions due to factors such as illness.

If an airline is to meet these two sets of needs effectively it must adopt a quite different philosophy for capacity management in the part of the aircraft given over to business travellers, compared to that occupied by leisure flyers. If business travellers are to be given the flexibility they need, a relatively low year-round load factor will be inevitable. This is because the pattern of demand from such people has a random, unforecastable component to it. If seats are to be available at the last minute for a high proportion of the people who need them, substantial numbers of seats will have to be kept back in the airline's capacity management system - a number well in excess of the average demand for such seats. This will, of course, result in empty seats at take-off on days when the actual demand is low.

Overall, an airline successfully offering last minute seats and full ticketing flexibility to those of its customers who need them will do well to achieve a year-round load factor of 65-70% in the part of the aircraft allocated to this segment of the market. In contrast, an airline not seeking to give an on-demand product will be able to operate at much higher load factors, often in excess of 90%. Indeed, the charter airlines in Europe which are certainly not in the "on-demand" business do achieve these very high load factors consistently.

These differences in load factor give a first, important clue as to why fares may need to vary in the Economy cabin, despite all the passengers there experiencing the same tangible product features. The tangible features are indeed the same, but the intangible one of flexibility is not. Prices can reflect the costs of providing these different degrees of flexibility.

Some of the arguments in favour of Differential pricing can thus be based on questions of costs. Others, and ones of greater importance still, can be derived from the nature of airline market segmentation.

The advocate of a Uniform approach to pricing might argue that such an approach would be an optimal one because people currently paying high prices would pay substantially less. This, however, is a false view. They might actually in the long run end up paying more, for an inferior product.

If we return to the data given in Table 6:1, the suggestion is that Uniform pricing would see the fares charged to those paying the higher fare fall from the current level of nearly £1,200 down to, say, £700. They would no doubt be pleased by this, arguing that this represents the amount by which they are now being overcharged. The situation would be less happy, though, for those passengers who are currently paying the lower fares. The proposition for these people is that their fares would have to rise to the Uniform level, reflecting the end of the cross-subsidy of their fares by those currently paying higher prices.

In such a situation, it is most unlikely that the people concerned will simply pay the extra in order to continue travelling with the airline concerned. As discussed in Section 2:3:5, most leisure air travellers have a high price-elasticity, reflecting the fact that they are paying fares out of their own pocket. Because of this, a sudden steep increase in ticket prices would result in some not travelling at all. A much greater number will continue to travel, but will choose an airline which is continuing to offer attractive low fares as part of a Differential fare structure. Overall, an airline changing over from such a fare structure to one of Uniform pricing might easily find that the number of passengers it carried fell by 40 per cent or more.

The first reaction of business travellers to such a development might be to welcome it. They might argue that their air trips will be more enjoyable without revelling holidaymakers. They might also see it as a vindication of their arguments about cross-subsidy. Once the over-charging of business travellers to provide such cross-subsidy ceased, large numbers of leisure travellers could no longer afford to fly.

Such an attitude could be short-sighted. There is a synergy available to airlines which carry significant numbers of both business and leisure travellers, and the business flyer is a major beneficiary of this. In particular airlines which participate in both the business and leisure markets are able to maintain a much broader network, with a better flight frequency than those which do not. As shown in section 2:3:3, network and frequency are two of the prime product requirements of the business traveller. Also, such airlines are able to maintain frequencies whilst using larger aircraft. Aircraft show Economies of Scale whereby lower seat-kilometre costs can be obtained from larger planes. These cost advantages can in turn be passed on to passengers in the form of lower fares. Finally, all airlines have a proportion of their costs which must be regarded as fixed overheads. Expenses such as those associated with the reservation and revenue accounting systems, and brand-building advertising, come into this category. Larger and larger numbers of passengers permit these costs to be spread more widely, again allowing fares to be lowered. On the other hand, a substantial fall in the numbers of passengers carried would almost certainly not be followed by a pro-rata fall in overheads. If passenger numbers fell by 40%, an airline might do very well to reduce overheads by, say, 20%. The result would be that the remaining passengers would each have to cover a higher proportion of overhead costs if the airline is to achieve a profit. This will in turn lead to higher, rather than lower, fares.

Overall, the risk is that Uniform pricing might result in business travellers paying still higher prices for a worse product than they currently receive. It is not in their interests that such a pricing policy should be adopted, despite its superficial attractions.

The situation regarding air services across the Atlantic between the UK and the USA helps make the case for the advantages of Differential pricing. Twenty years ago, there were only a small number of gateway points in the USA for travellers from Britain. Direct services were available from the UK only to New York, Washington, Boston, Chicago, Miami and Los Angeles. Any passenger whose final destination was away from these cities had to take a tiring and time-consuming domestic flight in the USA. In addition, flight frequencies were sometimes poor, with some of the gateways served only on an inconvenient less-than-daily basis.

The situation today is substantially better. The number of gateways receiving direct service has increased to over 20, with almost all of them served with frequency of a daily flight or better.

The reason for the improvement is that during this time, the market has grown, by a factor of more than 4 times. Some of the growth has admittedly come from increased amounts of business travel, but a far greater proportion has been the result of a rapid growth in leisure air travel. This has in turn been stimulated by an increasing availability of low fares as airlines have adopted a Differential pricing policy and have refined their ability to control the resulting low fares through more sophisticated Revenue Management systems.

We have now made the case that airlines should base their pricing policies on the Differential principle. Despite all these potential advantages, though, an airline decision to adopt a Differential pricing system should not be taken lightly. Indeed, competitive conditions in the industry today suggest that in the past, Differential pricing has been applied in too extreme a form, and that many of the problems being experienced by today's 'Legacy' airlines result from the fact that this has been done. We will now look at some of the counter-arguments.

The first drawback of Differential pricing is that, inevitably it leads to tariff structures that are very complex. The watchword adopted by the revenue manager is often that they should 'Capture the Value' available in the market – in other words, that each segment of the market should be charged a fare which is as near as possible to its willingness-to-pay. This will mean many different fares, reflecting the varying demand elasticities of the different segments. Worse still, as we shall discuss in the next section, in this mix of fares, all the lower fares will need to have restrictive conditions associated with them. If these are not in place, people with a higher willingness-to-pay may take advantage of lower prices aimed at more elastic segments.

It is almost impossible to exaggerate the drawbacks that a complex tariff brings. Airlines will be faced with a very costly training task. The typical time taking to train a new reservations and ticketing agent joining a 'Legacy' airline in the past has been a matter of several weeks, all needed to explain to the new recruit how to use reservations, ticketing and pricing concepts the airlines themselves have dreamed up. Once they have been trained for such a long time, these people rarely stay for more than a year or so, such is the boring and repetitive nature of the work they are asked to do.

Tariff complexity also gives airlines a very difficult selling task. When someone wishes to buy a ticket, they will presumably seek out the best value-for money. In trying to find out which fare will give them this, they will have to assess not only the level of prices, but also the availability of reservations and the extent to which they can meet the fare conditions applying to each of the different prices which are available. This will mean either a time-consuming phone call, or the need to navigate an airline' website. The latter is a notoriously difficult thing to do when each of the cheaper fares on offer may have a page or more of restrictive conditions associated with it.

In such circumstances, it is hardly surprising that in the past many people have decided that the effort is just not worthwhile. Instead, they have turned to a travel agent to do the hard work for them. In the past, this will generally have been an off-line agent, but increasingly today (as we will discuss in the next chapter) there are a large number of on-line agents which can be used. In both cases, the customer can expect a 'best-buy' recommendation, based on a survey of the whole market. From the airline viewpoint, though, such activity can only lead to an increase in the cost-of-sale as incentives have to be offered to the travel agents and search engine firms to ensure that the 'best buy' proposition goes in their favour.

As we have seen in Section 4:2:3, it is instructive to look at the approaches to pricing that have generally been taken by Low Cost Carriers, in comparison to those adopted by their Legacy competitors. LCC's certainly vary their fares over time. In order to gain access to the cheapest prices – certainly to the prices which these airlines publicise in their media advertising – a passenger will probably have to book weeks or even months before the flight that they want departs. Near to flight depart time, these carriers may be low cost, but their fares are often surprisingly expensive. There is, though, one crucial difference in their approach. At the time someone looks at the airline's website to ascertain how much it will cost them to travel on a particular flight, there will only be one price available. The customer can therefore make a simple 'take-it-or-leave-it' choice. This is in strong contrast to the situation of looking at the site of an airline attempting to take full advantage of the 'charge-at-the-willingness-to-pay' principle which has underpinned Revenue Management approaches at so many Legacy airlines for so long. It is not coincidence that the whole basis of the business model of the Low Cost Carriers has been an almost exclusive concentration on on-line sales, which have in turn resulted in enormous savings in commissions and booking fees. It is an example of where there has been a close interplay and tradeoff between pricing policies and distribution strategies.

Important though the arguments about training and distribution costs are, they are not the most important reason why in today's very competitive industry environment, Differential pricing in its extreme form must be used with a great deal of caution.

As we have seen, the assumption of revenue managers in the past has been that pricing at the willingness-to-pay of different segments of the market will produce an optimum revenue situation for the airline. Such arguments now appear dangerously out-of-date. They will work well in any situation – at least in the short-term – where entry into the market is highly regulated, as of course it was during long periods of the industry's evolution. They will continue to do so even when entry controls are relaxed, providing all the carriers in the market follow the same pricing policies. They are likely to do so if they all have similar high costs, where the yield premium of charging high prices to supposedly price inelastic segments will be valuable for all of them.

The situation changes when new entrant carriers appear, with much lower costs. For them, the use of Differential pricing by Legacy airlines presents an irresistible target. They can take advantage of the fact that past 'Legacy' views of Revenue Management have been based on one fatally-flawed building block. The assumption has always been that some segments of the market – those mostly made up by business travellers – have a very high willingness-to-pay. They often don't have. Instead, their using of high fares has reflected the fact that they have had no choice. All the airlines in the market have adopted the same policies of charging very high prices for flexible tickets of the kind that business travellers often need, and have limited the value of lower priced tickets by such expedients as the length-of-stay rules and cancellation penalties which we discuss in the next section.

It is now clear that the use of extreme forms of Differential pricing by Legacy airlines has had the effect of building up a great deal of resentment amongst business travellers who have been forced to pay very high prices under a Differential pricing policy. Most would accept that there is a pricing premium to be paid if a flexible ticket is needed very near to the departure time of a flight. What has angered them is that if they have booked far in advance – and for many business commitments such as regular board meetings advanced booking is certainly possible – they have paid very much more than a leisure passenger would pay who had booked on the same day, simply because of what they regard as absurd and discriminatory conditions being placed on the lower fares on offer.

Once such levels of resentment have been established, the task of Low Cost Carriers seeking to invade the markets of the Legacy airlines becomes a very easy one. They offer choice, which passengers are only too ready to exercise given their anger at past pricing policies.

The early months of 2005 saw some interesting developments in the pricing policies of the Major airlines in the United States. The period before this had, of course, been one of incredible financial bloodletting by once strong and confident airlines. In January 2005, one troubled carrier, Delta, announced a radical reform of its pricing policies. There were actually several facets to this reform, but the most notable change was that Delta announced a unilateral reduction in most of its highest domestic fares, and an ending of the length-of-stay restrictions on many of its cheaper tickets.

The Delta move was widely attacked by other US Legacy airlines. Delta's Legacy competitors all accepted that they would have to respond to its move, and they argued that it would significantly lower their yields in what was already a disastrous revenue situation. However, there can be little doubt that Delta's policy was sound, and that its new concept represented its 'least bad' option. It was under severe attack from new entrant Low Cost Carriers, notably so from the very aggressive Jetblue Airways. Jetblue was already finding it easy to appeal to former Delta passengers, who were attracted by fully flexible fares which were a fraction of those available from Delta. Worse still, the continuing existence of very high prices on routes where Delta did not yet face Low Cost Carrier competition meant that in many cases it was only a matter of time before it did. The abandonment of extreme forms of Differential pricing was therefore an essential defensive measure.

This has been a long, involved, but necessary discussion on the merits or otherwise of Differential approaches to airline pricing policy. It will always be necessary for airlines to vary their fares over time, to even out variations in demand and to ensure that they fill as high a proportion of their seats as possible. Some efforts to take advantage of varying demand elasticities between market segments are also justified – we will continue with the theme of how this can best be done in the next section. However, it is now clear that in the past, Legacy carriers have taken these measures too far. They have done so because extreme Differential pricing offered them the advantage of the maximisation of short-term revenues, something which they needed because of the fundamental weakness of their position – as 'Legacy' airlines their costs were too high. They are now having to accept that their cost problem must be addressed directly, and that it cannot be hidden by the fig leaf of suitably high yields gouged out by Differential pricing.

6:2:2 *Management of Discount Fares*

If, at least to a degree, a Differential pricing policy is to be employed, it needs to be managed and controlled properly. If it isn't, excessive amounts of so-called 'revenue dilution' will occur when too many people use the lowest fares in the range, and too few the higher prices.

Decisions about price levels must be made in an increasingly deregulated market, where airlines must both respond to the pricing initiatives of their competitors and decide when they should lead the market by a pricing initiative.

Control of discount fares is exercised in two ways. Firstly, and to an increasing degree, the Revenue Management system is used to decide on the number of low-fare seats which are available on different flights. As was discussed in Section 6:1, on off-peak flights, a large number of seats will be made available at low prices, reflecting the low marginal costs of filling seats which would otherwise be flown empty. On peak-time flights, however, few if any low fares will be offered, forcing people who need to travel on these flights to pay higher prices.

The second way in which control should be exercised is through the setting of restrictive conditions on discount fares. With these conditions, the best of them do not aim to simply make a fare unusable by business travellers whom in the past airlines have assumed would then pay them more. Instead, they should make a fare available to all who are prepared and able to meet the condition, and ensure that, if the correct cost allocation methods are used, that the passenger who pays a lower price is carried at a genuinely lower cost We now move on to discuss some of the more common conditions associated with discount fares, in the light of this requirement.

1. *Minimum Stay Conditions*
Many discount fares in the past have required passengers to spend a minimum amount of time at their destination. On short-haul routes, a Saturday night stay has often been specified. This has meant that passengers could not make return journeys earlier than the Sunday morning following their outbound trip. On longer routes, a minimum period of days

– usually seven – which must be spent at the destination was sometimes defined. In both cases, passengers could return early if they wished to do so. However, they would have to pay the full fare.

These conditions, whether set as a Saturday night stay or a period of days, all had the same purpose. They were designed to restrict the business travellers' freedom of action. The Saturday night stay condition meant that they had to use the full fare to spend the weekend at home. Also, business trips usually last for only a few days in any one place. Indeed, a salesperson on a sales tour may visit several countries on a two or three week business trip. The Minimum Stay Conditions on the cheaper fares ensured that they had to buy a full fare ticket in order to obtain the flexibility they needed.

To some degree, length-of-stay conditions met the criterion set down in the last paragraph, of being cost-related. In particular, A 'Saturday Night Stay' rule could be said to do so. Most airlines find that their flights on the evening before the weekend begins are very full, but on Sundays generally loads are much lower. Therefore, a condition which encourages at least some passengers to delay their return may have the beneficial effect of lessening the extent of a peak, whilst lower prices may generate additional trips at off-peak times which will fill otherwise empty seats at lower, but still profitable, yields.

Generally, Minimum Stay rules are amongst the most effective of the conditions designed to protect airlines' high yielding traffic, providing they are strictly applied.

2. Maximum Stay Conditions

Maximum Stay Conditions define a maximum length of time that passengers can stay at their destinations and still return home using a cheaper discounted fare. If they stay longer than the stipulated maximum – 45 or 60 day periods are often allowed – they will have to pay the full fare to return.

Generally, Maximum Stay Conditions are a less effective way of controlling discount fares and their usage by airlines has declined in recent years. They may, though, have some effect in controlling dilution in that sometimes someone who is travelling to a destination and staying for several months may not be on holiday. Instead, they may be travelling on a business contract, in which case their employer will be paying the fare. They may be able to pay a higher price as a result.

3. Advanced Purchase

Advanced purchase rules are still sometimes applied to discount fares. They mean that passengers must book and pay for their ticket a defined minimum period in advance. They must also accept that there will be a substantial penalty if they wish to alter or cancel their booking once they have made it.

Advanced Purchase conditions bring airlines a number of advantages. They improve cash flow. They also ease the task of capacity management in that they force low yielding demand to come forward at an early stage. Their most telling advantage, though is again that they make it difficult for the business traveller to use a lower fare. Many business trips arise in response to last-minute emergencies and cannot be planned far in advance. Even where they can be, business executives often cannot accept the limits on their flexibility that a cancellation or rebooking penalty will cause.

4. Standby

Standby fares can be booked at any time. They do not, though, guarantee the passenger a seat on a particular flight. Instead, the passenger must report for a flight and wait. If there is an empty seat, they will travel. If there isn't, because the flight is full with higher yielding demand, the Standby passenger will not be given a seat. Instead, they will have their money refunded, or will have to wait for a later flight.

Standby fares bring a number of advantages. They are a genuinely cost-related lower fare, in that they are profitable as long as the fare paid exceeds the passenger-related costs of filling an otherwise empty seat. Also, they are often sold at the airport or at an airline's downtown ticket offices. Therefore, no commission has to be paid on them. They permit airlines to exploit a market for last minute, unplanned leisure travel decisions. Advanced booking requirements do not allow this. Of most importance, though, is the fact that, if properly managed, Standby fares protect airlines from revenue dilution. Except in the circumstances discussed below, a business traveller who has to attend an important meeting is unlikely to use a Standby fare to reach it, in view of the uncertainty involved.

Despite these advantages, the use of Standby fares remains controversial, and many airlines have backed away from them in recent years. They are certainly unpopular with airport operators, because of the risk they carry that airport terminals will become crowded with people holding Standby tickets waiting for many hours – perhaps days – for flights on which they can be offered a seat. Also, a passenger holding a Standby ticket for a particular flight has an incentive to phone the airline to make extra bookings using false names, addresses and contact phone numbers. Finally, business travellers may find it surprisingly easy to take advantage of a Standby ticket. All they need to do is to buy a full Economy ticket in advance of their flight. On arrival at the airport they check to see if the flight is fully booked. If it isn't, they then buy a Standby, fully confident that they will be offered a seat. The full-fare ticket is, of course, refundable. They would merely keep this ticket to claim their refund at a later date. Had they found the flight full, they would have used their full-fare ticket in order to get on it.

A final point about Standby fares is a particularly important one. Airlines should not offer Standby fares on their off-peak flights. This is an apparent contradiction. Off-peak flights are those with the greatest number of empty seats, which the Standby fare can help to fill. If, though, Standbys are allowed on off-peak flights, the dilutionary effects of doing so will be severe. Passengers who need to take the flight in question will still have a very high probability of getting it, despite the fact that they only hold a Standby ticket. In contrast, Standbys bought at the peak season will carry with them a significant risk that a seat will not be available. Business travellers in particular may not therefore be able to use them.

5. "Preferential" Fares

Airlines today still offer many types of cheaper fare which are only available to named groups of passengers. These fares can be divided into two types. First, what are known as *stage-of-life* fares. Examples include the special low fares offered to children, young people and to senior citizens. Second, airlines offer many *occupation-related* cheaper fares. Special fares are, for example, often given to seamen, to military personnel and to diplomats.

These "Preferential" fares (they are sometimes, and better, described as "Discriminatory" fares) give preference to named groups. Unfortunately, it is impossible to support them as a form of pricing for airlines. Those carriers that use them often find that they are offering an increasing number of discounts to a wider and wider range of their passengers. The reason is, of course, that once a discriminatory discount has been offered to one group, there are no reasons of principle to deny it to others. Airlines will therefore be subject to constant lobbying, to some of which they may eventually have to give way. Also, after a discriminatory discount has been introduced, it will be very difficult for airlines to withdraw it. Once a particular group has known the privilege of cheaper fares on a preferential basis, they will fight hard to retain this right.

6. Fares Only Available as Part of a Tour Package

These conditions limit the sale of fares to wholesalers, who are then supposed to add in the accommodation and other features which make up a packaged holiday. Only these complete holidays should then be retailed. If these rules are complied with, again the proposition becomes an unattractive one to the business traveller.

6:2:3 *Pricing Response and Pricing Initiatives*

Today, in price-competitive markets, pricing managers will be constantly faced with situations where they have to decide whether or not to respond to the pricing initiatives of their rivals. This may involve questions of responding – or not doing so – to the fares discounts that a competitor introduces. There may also be opportunities to lead the market either in terms of discounts, or in the raising of prices to improve yields.

In all these situations, it can, of course, be argued that every case is unique. Whilst this is undoubtedly true in principle, it is an unhelpful proposition in terms of airlines deciding on what their pricing policy should be. Instead, it can be argued that there is a series of questions which should always be asked. The answers to these questions will ensure that there is at least a consistency in an airline's pricing philosophy.

If we begin with the situation of a rival airline coming into a market with discounted fares, the most fundamental question of all is to decide why they are doing so. There is a wide variety of possible reasons for an airline to offer discounts, reasons which will explain whether or not the initiative may be limited and short-term – in which case it may be possible to ignore it – or substantial and long-term, demanding action from competitors.

In terms of possible reasons for lowering fares, by far and away the most common is that the airline is suffering from an overcapacity problem. It may have taken delivery of an aircraft type which is too big for the prevailing demand, or over-ordered in terms of the number of planes entering its fleet. Such mistakes may be exacerbated by the Trade Cycle entering a downswing, so that forecast increases in demand – which might have filled the new capacity – do not materialise.

In such a situation, other airlines will have little alternative but to respond to the challenge with which they are being faced. By responding, they will risk running into a loss-making situation. By not doing so, though, the fall in their market share may cause even worse problems.

Closely related to price discounting caused by overcapacity is the situation where an airline cuts fares in order to raise cash in the short term. A carrier on the edge of bankruptcy will need to find the cash in order to pay off its most demanding creditors. If it cannot do so, these creditors may insist on the liquidation of the company, seeing this as the best hope of securing at least some of the money they are owed.

This type of pricing is often characterised as the "Dash-for-Cash". It poses an awkward problem for other airlines challenged by it. Their first reaction might be to respond fully by matching or even undercutting the lower prices of the failing airline. By doing so, they would hope to speed its decline into bankruptcy, resulting eventually in the removal of the competitor from the market altogether.

Today, such a reaction might be over-hasty. If an airline disappears, it will certainly be replaced by another, probably stronger, carrier. The long-term result of a weak airline going into bankruptcy may therefore be that a favourable competitive situation is replaced by an unfavourable one. It is often better to allow a weak airline to raise sufficient cash to stay in business, by not fully responding to any desperate pricing initiatives it may undertake. Such a conclusion may be especially true in the USA where Chapter 11 of the bankruptcy code may allow an insolvent airline to survive for a considerable time using the expedient of court protection from its creditors. Whilst it does so, it may be able to price in a cavalier and destructive fashion because it knows that only its short-term creditors (in order to persuade them to continue to forward necessary supplies) rather than its long-term creditors will need to be paid.

There are other reasons why an airline may offer lower prices. A start-up airline may do so, in order to gain useful publicity and to persuade people to try its services. Equally, a mature airline might do so when launching a new route serving a market where it is not well-known. In both cases, established players will have difficult decisions to make. If they match, or even undercut the newcomer they will undoubtedly make life very difficult. They will, though also dilute the yield obtained from the large number of passengers who would have continued to fly with them anyway, despite the newcomer's presence. They may also (within the European Union at least) risk court action being taken against them, with the accusation that they have abused a dominant position under the terms of Article 82 of the Treaty of Rome.

Once a view has been taken as to why a competitor is engaging in fare discounting, other questions then come into play.

The question of appropriate action will be very different in the situation where the price leader is a dominant player rather than a minor market participant. A large airline in its home market will have sufficient power to ensure that whatever pricing initiatives it takes, these will almost certainly have to be followed by its rivals. A minor player, though, may well be left alone if its overall impact on the market is small.

A further question is that of the number of seats made available at discounted prices. Modern Revenue Management systems allow a precise control to be kept not only on the prices which are offered, but also of the number of seats available at each price in an airline's Differential pricing structure. There have been accusations from time to time that some carriers use advertisements describing attractive offers of lower prices in an unscrupulous way. These offers are designed to encourage people to contact the airline seeking the very low prices described in the advertisements. In fact, the airline ensures that very few seats are available for sale at these prices. Those making enquires are told that all the very low-priced seats have already been sold, but that seats are still available at a significantly higher fare. The aim is to "bait and switch" these people into buying higher priced tickets.

Whilst the morality of such tactics is open to question, their implications for pricing policy are clear. Rival airlines should not over-react to the prices placed in newspaper advertisements. Rather, they should base their reaction on the number of seats being made available at the different fares. This can easily be checked by calling the airline in question or visiting its website and making enquiries about seat availability.

A final issue with the question of response to a discounting competitor is the need to study past situations where price discounting has occurred in a particular market. Such discounting often has a seasonal component to it. It commonly breaks out at the end of the summer peak season as airlines position themselves for the quieter winter period. Careful study of the effect on market share and yield of past decisions to match or not to match rival's fare initiatives will certainly have a bearing on the question of appropriate responses to any current challenges being laid down by competitors.

The other major question airlines need to address in managing pricing is when they should take the risk of leading the market in terms of a price increase.

Sometimes, it will be possible to do this in consultation with rival airlines. In some international markets, it is still possible for competitor carriers to meet together at the Traffic Conferences organised by IATA These conferences can be used to discuss the levels of the higher, fully flexible, fares with hopefully (from the airline's point-of-view) agreement being reached that these fares should be raised in tandem. In other situations, all the different airlines serving a market may unite in a so-called Yield Improvement Programme (YIP), with again the questions of reduced availability of discount fares and fare increases on the agenda.

Today, the evidence is that such multi-airline approaches to tariffs management are only effective in situations where capacity and demand are in some sort of equilibrium. When they are not, one or two airlines will always break ranks in pursuit of their own commercial objectives. Once they have done so, any agreement will quickly break down due to the pressures of market forces. Of course, too, airlines must be very careful *not* to discuss raising prices in any situation where this will break applicable competition laws. British Airways was reminded of this in the summer of 2006 when investigations were begun to decide if it had colluded with its competitors over the question of fuel surcharges.

In a situation where airlines are under pressure to raise their prices, it will often be the case that the requirement to do so is dictated by poor profitability. In turn, low profits or losses may be caused by cost increases. If they are, it will be vital to decide whether these increases are in "Controllable" or "Uncontrollable" costs.

"Uncontrollable" costs are those which airlines can do little or nothing to influence. Examples are the price of aircraft fuel and the level of landing fees. If these rise, they will affect all airlines more-or-less equally. Presumably all carriers will then welcome the opportunity to raise prices on order to, hopefully, allow their financial position to recover. At the time of writing, this is happening as carriers attempt to respond to rapid increases in oil prices.

"Controllable" costs are those which are within the control of airline management. By far the largest component of them for almost all airlines is that of labour costs. Typically, 30 percent of a carrier's total costs will be made up of these costs. In pricing terms a very worrying situation is that where an airline fails to control its labour costs effectively by conceding an over-generous wage and salary settlement, or by allowing changes in work rules which damage productivity. Then, rival, better-managed carriers will not be affected to the same degree. They may in turn see competitive advantage in not matching any fare increases which might be put in place to cover higher costs, instead seeking to improve market shares on the basis of sustainable cheaper prices. Beyond any question, in a market where active price-competition is taking place, effective management of these controllable costs is one if the central tasks which management must address.

Other factors to be taken into account in deciding whether or not to lead the market with a price increase, are the questions of the stage of the Trade Cycle, and the degree of market dominance which a carrier has. Generally, it is possible to raise prices much more easily in the up-swing period of the Trade Cycle when demand is recovering and deliveries of new aircraft comparatively small (due to airlines only ordering small numbers of planes during the preceding recession).

This was well-illustrated by the upswing period in the mid-1990's when many airlines were successful in raising prices. They were able to do so to such a degree that yields improved in real terms for the first time in many years. Something similar has occurred during the period of buoyant growth in the world economy during 2004 and 2005.

With regard to market dominance, generally it is a strong airline in its home market that will decide when prices will rise in such a   market. Smaller players will often have little choice but to follow the initiatives taken by their stronger rival.

All-in-all, the questions of pricing response and pricing initiatives illustrate the enormous changes which have come about in the skills required to manage pricing in the airline industry. Today, it is a question of judging, quickly, the pricing decisions which need to be made, in the ever-present knowledge that mistakes will result in large financial losses.

6:3 The Structure of Air Freight Pricing

Pricing policy for air freight is just as controversial as that on the passenger side of the industry. It is also an area where considerable, and long-overdue, change has come about in recent years.

Air freight pricing policy has in principle to encompass almost all of the problems which occur on the passenger side of the business. In addition, a way must be found to taking account of significant differences which are unique to air freight. For example, air freight shipments vary in size from very small packages to consignments of 30,000 kilos or more. Costs, though, do not vary in the same way. Many costs, such as those of documentation and customs clearance are fixed irrespective of consignment size. Also, commodity types vary, often with an impact on cost levels. Some commodities may need extra security. Perishable goods will need refrigeration, whilst especially fragile items may need special handling. Pricing policy must as far as possible reflect these differences. A further problem is that of density. Airlines must charge shippers of low density freight on a volumetric basis. If they do not, they run the risk that they will attract excessive amounts of low density cargo which will fill the volumetric capacity of aircraft without their payload potential being fully exploited.

All these issues are important in air freight pricing. Perhaps the most difficult problem, though, is to find a cost base for pricing in a situation where airlines are using different types of capacity to carry freight.

Where freight is carried in a pure freighter aircraft, the appropriate cost base is clear. Airlines must aim to recover all the costs of operation including such items as depreciation, maintenance, crew salaries and landing fees. When the belly-hold of a passenger aircraft is used the situation is by no means as obvious. Then, some of the costs will clearly be attributable to freight, such as those of freight handling and selling, and the costs of extra fuel burnt as a result of the weight of freight carried. Many costs of these flights will, though, be joint costs. This will be the case, for example, with costs such as those for crew salaries, maintenance and landing fees.

Many airlines now attempt to apportion these costs between the passenger and freight output of a particular flight. This may make some sense at peak times for freight, and on long-haul routes, where it might be argued that the use of belly-hold space saves the costs of the airline's freight department from operating pure freighters. It does not do so at off-peak times, or on routes with little freight demand. Then, the freight department would not operate services at all if it was free to make its own commercial decisions.

In seeking a cost base for pricing, airlines must clearly never offer prices which fall below the level of the marginal costs of freight handling and selling. They must, though, aim to do a great deal better then this. Freight must make a significant contribution to the total costs of flights where a substantial proportion of the aircraft's potential payload consists of belly-hold freight capacity. This will especially be the case if the airline is also operating freighter aircraft. Prices based merely on marginal belly-hold costs will come nowhere near the levels necessary to cover the operating costs of a freighter.

Given these various constraints, it should not be surprising that the subject of air freight pricing has been a controversial one.

In the past, it was possible to divide freight pricing into two distinct parts. Firstly, airlines offered so-called General Cargo Rates. These were pitched at a very high level, with an even higher Minimum Charge for the smallest shipments. Discounts were then offered for larger consignments, to reflect lower documentation and handling costs. The highest rates applied only to shipments weighing 45 kilos or less.

The second part of the traditional air freight rate structure was much more controversial. In addition to General Cargo Rates carriers offered a range of lower so-called Specific Commodity Rates. These were usually available only for larger consignments. Also, they could only be used for specific, named types of freight. IATA set up a complex system to allow its member airlines to define the commodities which would, and would not, be charged a lower rate.

The Specific Commodity Rate system was fundamentally in error. It was based on the principle, comparable to that used on the passenger side of the industry, that if price-sensitive users could be brought into the market, the size of the total market could be expanded with benefits to all customers. The mistake was to equate price sensitivity to commodity type, rather than to the urgency of the shipment. By using commodity type, airlines were faced with insoluble problems of commodity definition, problems that made the industry a laughing stock. For example, should a Specific Commodity Rate covering "footwear" allow socks, bandages or indeed anything else that might be worn on feet to be set at the concessionary rate, in addition to shoes? Also, the system produced a classic problem, encountered in many discriminatory pricing systems. Once a concessionary rate had been offered for one type of commodity, there were few arguments of principle to deny them to shippers of other types of freight. As a result, the role of Specific Commodity Rates changed. They were originally intended to provide a supplement to the General Cargo Rate system. Instead, on some routes (notably the North Atlantic), they came to dominate the rate structure with a high proportion of all cargo moving under them. The implications for average yields then became significant.

In recent years, the emphasis of airline's freight pricing policy has altered. The introduction of the so-called Bulk Unitization Programme was dealt with in Section 5:6. It largely changed the basis of air freight pricing from one of discrimination by commodity type to Freight-of-all-Kinds (FAK) instead. Bulk Unitization rates were available for any type of freight, provided it was pre-loaded into an aircraft Unit Load Device (usually a container), or stowed onto a pallet. They were therefore fairer, and much simpler to administer. The problem with them was that they gave excessive power to the air freight forwarding industry, because it was only the largest shipments (which the forwarders could provide through their consolidation activities) which qualified. They also did not differentiate between shipments in terms of urgency.

Today, most airlines by-pass the old, cumbersome structure of air freight rates. Rates are set through negotiation between customer and airline, with rates rising and falling in recognition of the balance between supply and demand in the market. Substantial discounts are generally offered to customers willing to accept deferred delivery, because this often allows airlines to fly their goods during the off-peak period at the beginning of the working week rather than at the busy time at the end of it when there may be shortages of capacity.

In the so-called "Express" market of small, urgent shipments, pricing policies have been led by the integrated carriers such as UPS, Federal Express, DHL and TNT. As was discussed in Section 4:2:6., these firms have not relied on the air freight forwarding industry for their traffic. Instead, they have invested in building strong brands, and promoting these heavily to the retail market. The brands have been divided between those which offer guaranteed next-morning delivery at a premium price, and ones which give a slower, but still time-definite, delivery. Again, this allows carriage to be delayed from peak into an off-peak period.

Such a product-based approach to pricing is simple to administer and essentially fair between different types of customer. Not surprisingly it has been followed by many combination airlines which have launched their own branded products in an attempt to compete with the Integrators. Generally, though, these have been offered on an airport-to-airport basis with the ground transportation provided by air freight forwarders who have been encouraged to sell the products on a commissionable basis.

All-in-all, the field of pricing is one of the most rapidly changing and most challenging in the whole area of airline marketing activity. Only by a flexible adherence to a set of clear principles can costly mistakes be avoided.

SUCCESSFUL AIRLINES ......

✈ Appreciate that the old days of regulated pricing have passed and will not return, and accept that the central skills now required of pricing management are those related to pricing in price-competitive markets.

✈ Acknowledge that different pricing strategies will be needed depending on the airline's business strategy.

✈ Accept that pricing in the Economy cabin must conform to a Differential rather than a Uniform principle, and that airlines must be able to justify the concept of Differential pricing to those who pay higher fares. The use of such pricing, though, must not go to the point where it raises training and selling costs to unacceptable levels, or where it leads to customer alienation.

✈ Control the use of discount fares by imposing, and enforcing, appropriate conditions on these fares, and by developing a state-of-the-art Revenue Management system.

✈ Develop and apply consistent guidelines about when a response should be made to a competitor's pricing initiatives, and when the airline should take pricing initiative.

7 Distributing the Product

In all areas of marketing, links must be made between the customer and the product. These links are known as Distribution Channels. Airlines use a variety of these channels. All of them are giving rise to particularly intense debate at the present time, because the different channels result in different costs, and because they vary in the extent to which they allow airlines to exercise proper and necessary control of the market. It is also an area where radical and controversial change is occurring, as carriers become increasingly adept at exploiting the potential open to them from on-line distribution,

The purpose of this chapter is to consider these controversies, and to analyse current developments in the field of airline distribution.

7:1 Distribution Channel Strategies

7:1:1 Types of Distribution Channel

In any industry, firms can choose from different types of distribution channel. Some may opt for the *direct* route. This is where the producer makes direct contact with the final customers for its product, without any intermediaries being involved at all. This channel philosophy is normal in the industrial marketing of big-ticket capital goods. It certainly has been usual in the field of aircraft manufacturing, though the rise of the specialist operating lease companies has now in many cases provided an intermediary between the aerospace firms and their final customers, the airlines.

In marketing activities involving less costly items a direct approach can still be adopted. For example, some firms choose to deal direct by selling their goods through mail order, backed by extensive advertising aimed at final customers, or increasingly, over the Internet.

Direct channels bring the advantage that no mark-ups or commissions have to be paid to channel intermediaries. They also allow producers to keep complete control of their marketing activities, and to be in touch with the true sources of demand for their products. The problem is that they may make it difficult for the producer to achieve sufficient geographical coverage, though in many areas (for example, insurance), this is being overcome as a result of peoples' increasing willingness to buy over the telephone or on-line. In many industries, producers make use of *wholesalers*. These are firms which buy in bulk from a range of producers, using their buying power to gain appropriate discounts. They then in turn sell on the goods, either by adopting a direct sell policy themselves, or by in turn using *retailers*. Retailers buy from wholesalers, and sell to the final customer for the product.

The essence of both wholesaling and retailing from the producer's point of view is risk-taking. Discounts will have to be given to allow an opportunity for mark-ups to be added and profits to be made by the intermediaries. In turn, though, the producer's risks are reduced because once the goods have been sold to a wholesaler or retailer, unsold goods cannot normally be returned.

The remaining type of channel relationship is that of the *agency*. Such a relationship is common in service industries where there is only an intangible rather than a tangible product offered for sale. In such industries, producers often require wide geographical coverage, but find it costly or impossible to provide this in their own. They therefore use agents, who are paid commission each time they sell on behalf of a particular firm. The agent is able to make a living by selling a variety of products on behalf of many firms, in what should be a mutually beneficial relationship. The problem, of course, is that because agents are selling on behalf of many firms, they may be tempted to use their market leverage by working harder to sell the products of the firms which pay them higher commissions. Suppliers may in turn leapfrog each other's commissions in an attempt to secure agents' support, resulting in an inexorable rise in commission costs. Exactly this process was prevalent in airline marketing in the 1990s.

The aviation industry illustrates all of these different forms of channel relationship. In many ways, the role of the aircraft leasing company is that of a wholesaler. Firms such as ILFC and General Electric Capital Aviation Services buy large numbers of aircraft from the manufacturers and are given substantial price discounts for doing so. They then lease out these planes to their customer airlines, and in buoyant times make substantial profits as a result. They do, though, assume significant risks. In a market downturn, large numbers of aircraft may be returned to them by lessees, and, due to a glut of capacity in the market it may be difficult or impossible to place these aircraft with new customers or sell them in order to realise their residual value. Indeed, in the major recession of the early 1990's, the then-largest operating lease company, GPA, could not survive and was taken over on the edge of bankruptcy.

Another example of a producer/wholesaler relationship has been that between charter airlines and tour operators in the European package holiday industry. The principle here has been that airlines have produced plane-loads of capacity which have then been sold to tour operators. In turn, the operators have added accommodation, surface transfers and other features of a holiday such as cultural tours or sporting opportunities, to make up a complete package. The tour operators have then been responsible for retailing these packages to the final customer.

In terms of agency relationships, it is of course the travel agency system which has been the dominant distribution channel for airlines in the past, and it remains so in many less developed aviation markets. The percentages are now declining markedly in many countries, but for many years airlines found that over 80% of their tickets were sold by travel agents. The trend until recently was in fact for this percentage to rise, with the forces of deregulation allowing the travel agency industry to cement its position as the industry's dominant distribution channel. Deregulation often meant rapid changes in airlines' schedules and fares. Often, the bemused consumer was forced to turn to an agent in order to find up-to-date information without the chore of contacting each of the airlines serving a route individually.

In recent years, of course, direct selling has become more and more significant as traditional airlines have supplemented direct selling through sales shops and call centres with an increasing emphasis on web-based business. New airlines have appeared which largely or totally ignore the travel agency industry.

7:1:2 The Concept of "Super-Profits"

A significant section of this book will be devoted to the question of distribution channels, and the casual reader might ask why this should be so. The reason is simple: control of distribution channels is one of the most powerful drivers of profits in any industry, and this is especially the case in the airline business.

The concept of the control of distribution channels is a straightforward one. In any channel where wholesalers, retailers or agents are involved, producers must ensure that they are in a position to control the rewards received by these channel intermediaries. If a wholesaler, retailer or agent is in a powerful position, they will not be able to do so. Instead, the intermediaries will be able to play one producer off against another, only supporting those who outdo the others in terms of their offer of mark-ups or commissions. In turn, producers will receive only the rewards needed to keep them in the business from year to year. The "Super Profits" – profits over and above these basic rewards – will accrue to the intermediaries who are able to exercise control.

There are a number of danger signals which indicate a probability that producers will lose effective channel control. One is that each intermediary controls a significant share of the market. For example, in the UK grocery market, the scene is dominated by three giant supermarket chains, Sainsbury's, Tesco and Asda/Wallmart. Today, any producer of grocery products has to ensure that it goods are stocked by these firms. If they are not, then they will not be able to reach something like 70% of the UK market. The supermarket firms are thus in a strong bargaining position, a position emphasised by their robust profit performance in recent years.

The other worrying indicator of problems for producers is that their product is perceived as a "Commodity" rather than a "Brand". The subject of Brands Management is now a crucial one in Airline Marketing and the whole of the next chapter is devoted to it. Briefly, though, a commodity situation is one where customers perceive the products of competing suppliers to be identical. The brands case is the opposite of this, where customers see significant differences between the products of alternative suppliers.

The commodity situation is the ideal one for wholesalers, retailers and agents seeking to establish and retain control of a distribution channel. This is because customers have no strong preference as to which firm's products they buy. Therefore the intermediaries will be in a perfect position to play one supplier off against another, because it will be irrelevant from the customer's point-of-view as to which producer is supported.

In some industries, commoditisation of the product has become so complete that the only way forward for producers wishing to protect their "Super-Profits" is to own, or at least franchise, their own distribution channel. This is the case, for example, in the petrol (gasoline) industry where in most countries the firms which refine petrol also own (or franchise)a network of filling stations. It is very difficult indeed for a stand-alone refiner of petrol to earn a reasonable return, given the clear perception of many people that petrol is a commodity. One's car run exactly the same whichever brand of petrol is put into it.

Another sector where ownership of the distribution channel by producers has become the norm is in that of the European package holiday/charter airline area. Seats on charter airlines are often perceived as a commodity by vacationers, in the sense that very few will specify the airline with which they wish to travel when booking their holiday. Indeed many people do not know the identity of their airline until they arrive at the airport on their day-of-departure. Because of this, it is difficult for independent airlines which have no links to their distribution channels to survive. Such airlines can often make reasonable profits when demand is buoyant and capacity limited, as will generally be the case during the up-swing period of the Trade Cycle. They will find life much more difficult in a recession, when capacity will exceed demand and where market power will swing strongly to tour operator intermediaries. These firms will easily be able to play the independent charter airlines off against each other because passengers have no great preferences as to which airline they fly. The result will be strong profits for the tour operators and weaker ones for the airlines, to the point where some of the airlines may not be able to survive. A case-in-point was the UK airline Dan-Air, which disappeared (through a take-over by British Airways) in the recession of the early 1990s, for exactly the reasons described.

A better situation in the market of airlines and tour operators is where the airline either owns, or is owned by, its distribution channel. For example, the UKs biggest charter airline, Thomsonfly, Thomson Holidays (Britain's largest tour operator) and Lunn-Poly, the travel agency with the biggest high-street presence, are all subsidiaries of the same parent company (the German firm TUI). The airline therefore knows that through such vertical integration it has a guaranteed outlet for its production even at times when market conditions are difficult.

One final point needs to be made in this introductory section about distribution channel management. In almost all sectors of the economy there are very substantial differences in the capital invested by producers and by intermediaries. This is certainly the case in the field of travel. Airlines have to invest truly vast amounts in aircraft in order to grow and develop their businesses. For example, today the purchase of just one wide-bodied aircraft, may involve an outlay of perhaps $180 - $200 million. A fleet of these planes will require a risky investment of billions of dollars. In contrast, investments made by tour operators and travel agents will be tiny by comparison. This is becoming even more the case as the travel agency business becomes an increasingly on-line one without the need to invest in costly high street shops. It is absolutely essential that airlines should be in control of their distribution channels so that they can earn the "Super-Profits" which will give their shareholders a fair return on their money. As we shall see, there are now worrying signs that the rise of search engines such as Google provides an even more potent threat to this control than has existed in the past.

7:2   The Travel Agency Distribution System

7:2:1 Advantages and Disadvantages

Having established the general principles, it is now necessary for us to look in more detail at the particular issues raised by the past general reliance on the travel agency distribution channel in the airline industry.

In this context, it cannot be emphasised too strongly that this reliance always brought airlines very important benefits. Exactly as one would expect with an agency relationship, one of these was geographical coverage. An airline would have found it prohibitively expensive to have its own sales shops in every high street and shopping mall around the world. Yet some passengers liked a personalised source of tickets, and someone they could turn to for advice and help. A travel agent provided such a presence by selling tickets on behalf of all airlines and tour operators, and by also offering services such as hotel, car rental and theatre bookings. Agents could – and still can – identify and explore specialist niche markets such as those dealing with hobbies like golf and winter sports, and those focussing on particular ethnic groups.

A second advantage of agency relationships was that they were not a heavy overhead burden on the airlines. It is true that all airlines had to incur the costs of agency support in the form of such things as training for agency staff and special telephone lines to deal with agents' enquiries. The principle though of the agency relationship was that the airline only had to reward the agent when the agent concluded a piece of business on its behalf. This was in contrast, say, to an airline-owned-and-operated sales shop in a city centre, which was an overhead cost burden on the carrier at all times, whether or not any business was actually being transacted.

A final point about the traditional airline/agency relationship was that agents undoubtedly relieved airlines of a great deal of the costly administrative work associated with air travel. For example an agent would issue tickets, assist with visa applications and deal with passengers' queries about airport check-in times, baggage rules etc. If they had not done so, carriers would have had to employ extra staff and resources. Generally, too, airlines paid their staff higher salaries than the poor levels of pay which were generally prevalent in the travel agency sector. Travel agents could therefore probably carry out this work at lower costs than would have prevailed if airlines had done it themselves.

Despite these obvious and strong advantages, the airline/travel agency relationship was the subject of increasing disquiet during the 1990s, and is now undergoing revolutionary reform.

Table 7:1 presents data on the commission costs of British Airways between 1990 and 2004. It is especially valuable data, because it separates out commissions from other selling costs. Normally, it is not possible to do this, as many industry data sources only present an aggregate cost category of "Ticketing, Sales and Promotion" which includes reservations and advertising costs alongside those of commissions.

Table 7:1 British Airways: Commission Costs 1986 – 2004

YEAR	BRITISH AIRWAYS		
	Total Operating Expenses £m	Commission £m	%
1986	2,644	223	8.43
1987	2,947	269	9.12
1988	3,559	332	9.32
1989	4,029	391	9.70
1990	4,373	467	10.67
1991	4,444	506	11.38
1992	4,772	563	11.79
1993	5,289	650	12.28
1994	5,580	768	13.76
1995	5,878	821	13.97
1996	6,612	916	13.85
1997	7,421	864	11.64
1998	7,339	847	11.54
1999	7,210	825	11.44
2000	7,702	817	10.60
2001	6,857	627	9.14
2002	6,491	524	8.07
2003	6,434	431	6.70
2004	6,682	365	5.46

Source: CAA Annual Statistics.

The Table shows that during the 1990's the situation was a disturbing one, and one which was typical of almost all airlines. During the 1990's, commissions increased in absolute terms of monetary payments. They also rose sharply as a proportion of the airline's operating costs. (Admittedly, partly because other costs fell, especially the costs of aircraft fuel).

There were a number of reasons why this should have happened. As has already been stated, during this period the proportion of tickets written by agents rose still further, as the travel agency industry was able to use the confusion associated with deregulation to further cement its control. Also, this was when more and more tickets were being paid for using credit cards, and carriers were having to pay out increasing commissions to credit card companies. Nonetheless, we are safe to draw a conclusion that for UK airlines at least, the travel agency distribution system became very expensive. The same conclusion could be reached for the US domestic market, another where disaggregated data were available.

Rising commission costs were in themselves worrying. They might have been justified, though, from an airline viewpoint, if they had resulted in investment going into improving the distribution channels so that carriers were being better served by them. Unfortunately, one's suspicion was that this was not the case, or at least that the level of investment by the travel agency industry was inadequate to sustain such a conclusion. Increasing commissions were often used by travel agents to finance an intensive market share battle between themselves rather than for investment to provide airlines with better distribution services. Such competition took on two forms. Firstly, in pursuing market share in the business travel market, agents were often prepared to pass on a proportion of the commission they earned to their retail customers in the form of discounts, either to build the loyalty of their existing clients, or to buy that of the clients of other agencies. Secondly, with sales to the leisure market, the manifestation of higher commissions came in the form of a proliferation of sales outlets as firms opened more and more retail shops to strengthen their geographical presence in the market relative to that of their rivals.

In both cases, airlines' money, paid out in higher commissions, was used to finance agents' battle for market share. This was not an acceptable situation, especially bearing in mind the huge investments (mainly through aircraft purchases) made by airlines in the future of the industry, and the comparatively small investments made by agents.

All in all, the situation of airlines with respect to their distribution channels was a very mixed one by the end of the 1990s and was ripe for reform. The travel agency distribution system brought them important advantages, advantages emphasised by the domination of travel retailing which the system achieved. There were, though, significant problems too. The question for airline business strategy was therefore very clear. How could distribution channels be developed so that the advantages were retained, whilst the problems and shortcomings were alleviated?

7:2:2 Today's Distribution Channels

The situation regarding distribution channels today can be traced to a process of reform which dates back many years. In 1996, some airlines began to make radical changes. Market conditions at the time were very buoyant, something which is always likely to favour producers at the expense of intermediaries. At the same time, it began to become clear that the Internet held out the promise of being an alternative distribution channel which could challenge the dominance of the travel agency system. It was already being used by some of the new entrant Cost Leader airlines, which were achieving substantial cost savings as a result, further increasing the pressure on traditional carriers.

The first signs of change came when Delta Airlines announced that for domestic ticket sales in the USA, payments of commission would be capped at a maximum of $50, whatever the percentage calculation of the fare might be. The effect of this was to significantly reduce the amount of commission paid on expensive First Class and Flexible Coach tickets. Within a very short time, Delta's initiative was followed by all the other major airlines in the USA, and, despite many predictions to the contrary, it stood the test of time. Indeed, the process of reform has been both strengthened and widened. Commissions have been reduced or eliminated in many markets today. Where travel agents are still being rewarded directly by airlines, this is now often done using the so-called "Task Based" approach. With this, agents are not paid a percentage of the price of the ticket they sell. Instead, flat rate payments are made for each task the travel agent has undertaken – so much for making the booking, for issuing the ticket (an increasingly rare payment, as the use of electronic tickets proliferates) and for dealing with payment. The effect of such policies has been to reduce the travel agents' rewards significantly, again especially on First and Business Class tickets, and on Flexible Economy fares, where high prices had meant especially high payments to agents.

The overall effect of such reforms has been little short of revolutionary. The proportion of airline tickets being sold by traditional travel agents has fallen, as airline websites have become more popular and a new breed of on-line travel agents has appeared (a development to be referred to in the next section). At the same time, the relationship between airlines and travel agents has changed fundamentally, as agents have had to seek new sources of revenue.

This has been especially the case in the business air travel market. Here, in many markets, agents have changed their role into being one of a travel consultant for their clients, rather than an airline sales agent. They have argued, justifiably in some cases, that they have specialist skills in booking travel, in negotiating corporate deals with airlines and other travel suppliers, and in tracking and tracing travel spending to ensure that the firm gets the best value-for-money from its travel expenditure. In return for such skills, travel have asked for, and have been paid, management fees by their commercial clients.

Reflecting this change, many former travel agency firms have now re-christened themselves Travel Management Companies, to better reflect the working methods that they now employ.

The changeover from commission-based rewards to management fees paid by clients has had mixed results for airlines, but on balance it has proved to be a correct policy. It is true that agents are no longer the airlines' ally in selling higher-yielding tickets. Any form of reward for intermediaries based on commissions can be annoying for those who pay them, with often a feeling that the commission does not accurately reflect the work done. Commissions do, though, give a common interest to both principal and intermediary to secure the highest possible revenue. Management fees can have the reverse effect. In order for a travel agent to justify their work, and to ensure that they retain their travel accounts, they must show their commercial clients that they have managed the travel budget well, and that they have achieved the greatest possible cost savings. This may mean that they encourage booking on low yielding promotional fares, even if restrictive conditions apply to them, or book people on Cost Leader airlines via these airlines' websites, even though they receive no commission for doing so.

Despite this possible adverse consequence, changing the basis for the rewarding of travel agents has been a necessary and long overdue reform. As the data for the later years included in Table 7:1 suggests, it has saved airlines large sums of money which they otherwise would have lost to the travel agency industry, and has given them a better control over their distribution channels than would have been the case had the reforms not come about.

7:2:3 The Future of Distribution

Despite the changes of recent years, the question of distribution channels for airlines is one which is still in a state of flux. Can we yet forecast what the mature situation will be?

It is already clear that the future is going to see a greater proportion of airline seats sold using direct distribution channels. Airline call centres, sales offices and airport ticket desks will continue, but the growth in direct sales will not be explained by them. Clearly, most of this growth will come from the increased use of airline websites. Internet access is spreading rapidly around the world, and use of the Internet is now a regular part of daily life for hundreds of millions of people. These people are, of course, drawn disproportionately from groups who are likely to be regular air travellers. Also, airlines are increasingly adopting the simpler reservations and ticketing procedures, which are necessary to make internet booking commonplace. The newer Cost Leader airlines have always done this, and the "Legacy" airlines that they are threatening are increasingly responding.

Having said this, it is not the case that the future will see an end for the travel agents' role in airline distribution. Many better-managed agents will be able to defend their position by adopting policies which their clients will perceive as adding value. We have already looked at the business travel agents who are repositioning themselves as travel consultants rather than airline sales agents. On the leisure side, the better agents may be able to find niche positions by specialising in particular activities such as winter sports, golf, trekking etc. Clients may then continue to support them because they value their expertise.

The best opportunities for the travel agency industry in the future will stem from the one advantage that they will continue to hold over airline websites. When a passenger consults an airline site, they will only usually be told about travel options and fares on that airline (and, perhaps, on its codeshare partners). In order to find out the best option out of the many that are available, they may have to spend a considerable amount of time looking at the websites of all the competitor airlines in the market. If, however, they consult a good travel agent, the travel agent will be able to display all the flight and fares options that are available and make a "best-buy" recommendation.

This is a service which a traditional off-line travel agency can offer in some form, but it becomes an even more powerful one when it is made available over the Internet. Recent years have seen the rapid growth of a number of very large and well-capitalised on-line travel agencies such as Travelocity (begun by American Airlines, but subsequently sold) and the Expedia service pioneered by Microsoft. This has in turn raised disturbing possibilities for airlines. Their websites have allowed them to loosen the formerly very tight hold that large travel agency chains held over them, but the rise of firms such as Expedia and Travelocity has raised the spectre of a new domination, this time by on-line rather than off-line agencies. Such a threat induced airlines to respond. In both the USA and Europe, consortia of airlines set up what amounted to their own on-line travel agencies, branded Orbitz in the US and Opodo in Europe, though again in both cases, these firms have now been sold by the consortia that owned them, presumably as a way of raising cash. In a wider number of cases, airlines have taken the apparently bizarre course of displaying not only their own flights on their websites, but also those of their competitors. They have done so as a way of providing their customers with a comprehensive booking tool, and as a way of countering the claims of on-line travel agents that only they can do so.

Overall, it is possible to reach a more optimistic conclusion about airline distribution (at least on the passenger side of the industry) than would have been possible only a few years ago. The use of the internet and the reform of the reward systems for travel agents have both made useful contributions to the correcting of what was formerly a totally unsatisfactory situation.

7:3 Global Distribution Systems (GDSs)

7:3:1 History and Background

For nearly twenty years, the subject of so-called Global Distribution Systems has been a controversial one in the airline industry, and it remains so today. The purpose of this section is to examine the reasons for this debate and to look at the future of GDSs.

Until the early 1970s, contact between airlines and their distribution outlets was mainly by telephone. As was noted in Section 5:4:1, this was both time consuming and costly, and became unsustainable as the industry grew. As the 1970s proceeded, the first, pioneering, carriers set out to automate airline/travel agency contact. In order to do so, direct links were provided from each agency location into the airline's reservations computer. Instead of phoning, agents could use the keyboard of a Visual Display Unit to make bookings direct with the airline concerned. Besides saving a great deal of time, this also gave the agent visual confirmation that the required reservation had been made.

In the USA, the leading airlines behind this move were United Airlines with its Apollo system, and American with SABRE. By the end of the 1970's these airlines had been joined in Europe by carriers such as Lufthansa (with START) and British Airways (with BABS).

By today's standards, these systems were extremely basic. They were, though, accompanied by controversy almost from the beginning. It was soon learnt that they provided a cast-iron way for the airlines which owned them to increase their market share at the expense of their rivals. The reason was that travel agents had a clear tendency to book their clients if they could from the first screen of information about the flight options in a given city-pair market. Indeed, booking was made from the first screen on over 90% of occasions. Over 50% of the time, the booking made would be that of the flight at the top of the first screen.

Given these facts, the option for the owner of the system was obvious. They needed to make sure that their own flights were the ones which were displayed most prominently. By doing so, they could obtain a handsome return on their investment through an increased market share. Generally, therefore, they were prepared to provide the systems free, or for a nominal rental, to the agents who used them. Also, though the flights of other airlines were shown, generally bookings were made on these airlines in small numbers, and little or no charge was made for such bookings. Indeed, other airlines' flights were only included because of the agent's requirement for a comprehensive system which would enable then to book all their client's requests on one system.

By the mid-1980s, the question of these early, biased, systems was becoming a controversial one. In the USA in particular, the airline industry had by this time been deregulated, and complaints were made by some airlines that bias in Computer Reservation Systems was significantly hindering the operation of the supposed free market in aviation. This complaint was, of course, raised most vociferously by the airlines which did not have a significant presence in the GDS industry. At the same time, those that did have such a presence – notably American Airlines – argued that the returns they were getting through biased displays merely reflected the investment they had made and the risks they had taken.

The outcome of the debate was that GDS displays – ironically in a supposedly deregulated industry – became subject to regulation by the US government, a move subsequently followed by the European Commission in respect of GDS operations within the European Union. The regulatory regime in both cases had essentially the same purpose, though there were differences in detail – to ensure display neutrality. This purpose was largely achieved. Though the question of the fairness of the rules continued to be debated, any subsequent bias in the systems was at a far lower level than was the case during the 1980s.

Once displays became regulated, it was inevitable that a further issue would arise. Airlines which had invested heavily in GDSs – and American Airlines was by this time claiming that it had spent more than a billion dollars on SABRE – expected to get a return on their investment. If biased displays were ruled out, how was this return to be obtained? The answer soon became clear. The system owners began to charge other airlines substantial fees for every booking made, at an initial level of about $2.80 per flight sector booked

The effect of booking fees was dramatic. Suddenly, Global Distribution Systems were transformed into highly profitable businesses, with American Airlines in particular soon conceding that its involvement in GDS was the most lucrative of all its activities – much more so than the airline itself. At the same time, booking fees provided American with the resources it needed to continue to invest in SABRE. At that time, more than 40% of the travel agents in the USA were using SABRE, giving the system considerable power in that market. There were rumours circulating of American's intention to achieve such dominance on a global basis. Had they done so, their ability to levy higher and higher booking fees would have been immense.

To address the perceived threat of SABRE, it was necessary for other airlines to make counter moves, and in Europe two groups of carriers came together to form consortia, each with the aim of setting up a system with the functionalities and customer base necessary to compete with SABRE. The result was the formation of the AMADEUS and GALILEO consortia in 1987. Both these systems were up and running by the early 1990s, when a series of mergers and acquisitions finally lead to the emergence of a mature industry structure. As one would expect in an industry where there are very large Economies of Scale, this structure was an oligopolistic one. SABRE was a dominant player, as were GALILEO and AMADEUS, both having strengthened their position through mergers with US-based systems in the early 1990s. The fourth and smallest player was WORLDSPAN, a system jointly set up by three US airlines, Delta, Northwest and TWA. (As has been noted, Worldspan is now soon to disappear in a merger with Galileo).

The most recent developments have seen changes in the ownerships of the GDS industry. Airline enthusiasm for the internet as a distribution channel – brought about in part because of the high charges they were incurring in GDS booking fees – has resulted in a lower proportion of bookings coming through the traditional travel agency/GDS channel. This has ended what might be called the "golden age" of GDS profitability. At the same time, airlines having an ownership stake in one of the GDSs have been under pressure to raise cash in order to maintain liquidity. The result has been that these stakes have almost all been sold off. In some cases, this has been through an Initial Public Offering (for example, with the American Airlines holding in Sabre), or through a trade sale (Galileo is now a wholly-owned subsidiary of the US-based Cendant Corporation).

The selling off of airline stakes GDS's has given the industry a degree of unity of purpose about them. Before, those airlines which had an equity stake in a GDS (and which were therefore benefiting from the substantial dividend income they were then receiving) took a different attitude to the question of booking fees than those who did not. Today, almost all airlines have a common interest in lowering booking fees to achieve more cost-effective distribution. Recently, too, in America at least, the GDS industry has been deregulated, with in particular an ending of the requirement that GDS owners must treat all airlines equally. This, together with a reduced regulation of displays, has allowed negotiations to begin around questions of trading display standards and content against booking fees.

7:3:2 Current Issues

Though the subject of bias in Global Distribution Systems is now somewhat less controversial than it was, there are still some substantial debates in progress.

Amongst the most contentious of these is the question of funding of the GDSs. Airlines now argue that they pay, through their booking fees, a disproportionately high level of total costs, whilst the travel agency industry pays far too little.

In principle, both airlines and travel agents benefit from the availability of a GDS. Airlines certainly gain from the wide distribution of their product, but agents also find that their costs are significantly reduced because of the much greater staff productivity they can achieve. The original suggestion was that GDS costs should be met to an equal degree by airlines and agents, reflecting these mutual benefits. This has not turned out to be the case. With the economics of a GDS so dependent on the volume of throughput, the GDS firms have had every incentive to try to steal market share from their rivals. In order to do so, it became a common tactic to allow travel agents the use of a system for a very low rental or, in many cases, if throughput in terms of the number of bookings made is sufficient, for the GDS companies to actually pay them for using their system. The result was, in many countries, an intense market share battle, with agents being offered bigger and bigger incentives to switch from one firm's system to another. In turn, a larger and larger share of GDS costs have in practice been paid by airlines through booking fees – current estimates are that more than 90% of GDS income is being derived in this way.

The dominance of airline funding of Global Distribution Systems has in turn led to two further controversies. The travel agent will often have a deal which ensures that the GDS will be made available free-of-charge, or for a nominal rent providing a sufficient number of bookings are made. Then, the agent with a sense of humour will have a clear incentive to make false and fictitious bookings if the number of true bookings they have is insufficient to reach the relevant break-point. Not surprisingly, such practices have provoked outrage on the part of those airlines that have been the victims of them, for the booking fees levied by the GDS companies have been based on the sectors booked, not on the number of passengers carried. Because of the controversy, the GDS firms have had to divert significant resources to policing false and passive bookings and, because they have done so, the problem now seems to be more under control.

The same certainty cannot be said for the second major problem associated with GDS funding. We have already seen how the travel agency system dominated airline distribution channels, and that until recently the system was costing airlines more and more. Because of this, it became a clear policy objective for many carriers to reduce their sales through travel agents. As discussed in Section 7:2:2, the use of the Internet, and the development of electronic ticketing are the technical developments which have made this possible.

As we have seen, in responding to this challenge to their dominance, better-managed travel agency firms are making what is, for them, an entirely logical move. They are repositioning themselves as travel management firms, able to assist corporate customers not only in the making of bookings, but in the negotiation of deals with airlines and other principles, and in the subsequent policing of expenditure to make sure that those who travel using the firm's money abide by its corporate travel policies.

Such a repositioning requires the travel agent to have a number of tools available in the form of computer systems to aid effective travel management. The GDS firms have been only too willing to develop these tools, hoping that by doing so they will be able to cement their relationship with their existing travel agency customers and also hopefully attract some new ones from rival GDSs. By a supreme irony, though, these system developments have largely been funded by airline booking fees, with the actions of the GDS firms helping travel agents to retain at least a proportion of their hold on airline distribution channels at exactly the time airlines have been seeking to reduce it.

A final issue for the GDS firms reflects the emergence of the so-called "Cost Leader" airlines referred to in Section 4:2:1. Airlines such as Southwest in the USA and Ryanair and Easyjet in Europe have grown significantly in recent years. Their strategy had been based on a low cost/low fares proposition. In order to lower their costs to the level which will make their low fares profitable, they have tried to simplify the product they have offered. In particular, they have generally use simple fares and reservations procedures, and have not offered interline or transfer services to their passengers, working purely on a point-to-point basis.

In the strongest contrast, the GDS firms have been proud to point to the sophistication of the services which, through the travel agent, they can provide to the passenger. A passenger today can contact their travel agent and make a very complex multi-sector booking on any number of different airlines, dealing at the same time with issues such as seat selection and special meal requirements. They can be given information about any fare which is on offer, as all the GDS firms maintain enormous fares databases. Finally, they can book any extra requirements they may have for such services as car rental or hotel accommodation.

Of course, the GDS firms argue that such sophistication comes at a price and they would claim that the booking fees charged represent very good value-for-money given the range of services on offer. The problem is that the customers of the low fares airlines do not need this level of sophistication yet are being asked to pay for it, because booking fees are levied on a flat-rate basis. Worse still, the booking fee, were it to be paid, would represent a very significant component of the fare the passenger had paid.

The upshot of this controversy is that, as we have seen, the GDS industry had been shunned by the low fare airlines. The oldest of them, Southwest Airlines, pays only for a low level of participation in one of the GDSs, SABRE and has no relationship with the others. It also tries to actively encourage bookings which allow it to avoid booking fees completely, through its own call centres or the Internet. In Europe, Easyjet is an example of a direct-sell airline, avoiding completely the travel agency distribution system. Through doing so, it has also avoided any need to be displayed in the databases of the GDS firms and has been able to add the elimination of GDS booking fees to the savings on commissions which it has achieved.

In such a changed world, the GDS companies have been shaken out of their complacency and are adopting a number of expedients. One of them, Amadeus, has embarked on a major diversification policy and now makes a considerable proportion of its income from the work which it does in the field of airline Information Technology consulting. It has also built a business in assisting airlines in their website development, thereby obtaining at least some revenue as a result of the Internet revolution. Each of the firms is also developing products with lower levels of functionality which, they hope, can be sold to the Low Cost Carrier sector. Though there would seem to be little prospect of them doing so to airlines - like Ryanair - which take the low cost theme to its extremes – they may be successful with airlines such as Jet Blue and Air Berlin that may come eventually to have at least some relationship with travel agents and corporate travel buyers.

As has been noted before, the final area where the GDS firms are having to respond to the new market realities is with respect to their booking fees. It has always been a subject of debate between the airlines and the GDSs as to who needed who the most. The GDSs have argued that without them, airlines cannot sell effectively.   On the other hand, without airlines releasing their schedules and fares through the GDS system, no GDS business could exist. It is vital that the GDSs (and on-line travel agents for that matter) should be able to claim that the lowest fares available can be found on their sites. If passengers lose confidence in this proposition, they will stop visiting the sites.   Because of this, airlines have now found a potent negotiating tool, by only allowing their lowest fares to be sold through GDSs in return for significant reductions in their booking fees. By a supreme irony, one of the carriers most active in pursuing this policy has been American Airlines.   It was, of course, American, when it owned SABRE, which originally developed the business model for GDS pricing.

There is one final development now taking place in airline distribution policy which has the potential to put all previous arguments about GDS pricing, bitter though they have often been, into the shade – the rise of search engines, especially Google.   There seems little doubt that the firms that run these engines are already in a position of considerable power, and that this power is going to steadily increase. When someone begins a search by entering such things as 'Cheapest fare to........', or 'Best airline to........, what the search reveals will be highly significant in the booking that they finally make. It seems inevitably that airlines will have to pay large sums to the search engine owners to ensure that references and links to their sites are properly displayed.

7:4 Distribution Channels in the Air Freight Market

The question of product distribution is no less controversial on the freight side of airlines' activities – indeed it could be argued that airlines are further away from finding a solution for their freight distribution problems that they are for those on the passenger side.

We have seen that the equivalent to the travel agent in air freight is the air freight forwarder. Forwarders provide the same sales agency function as the travel agent does. They also have an important role to play in the handling and consolidation of freight.

As we saw in Section 6:3, forwarders have only a small role in the so-called "Express" market of small urgent packages. The Integrated Carriers that dominate Express have built powerful retail brands and have invested large amounts in ground handling systems, which largely negate the role of the forwarder. In the remaining markets of so-called "Heavy Freight", though, the domination of the forwarding industry is almost total. The proportion of heavy freight in the hands of forwarders is well over 90%.

Such a reliance on a single channel of distribution would be unhealthy in itself, but the structure of the forwarding industry makes it worse still. Forwarding appears to be an industry where there are substantial Economies of Scale, and where important advantages accrue to the largest firms. Fewer than 15 global forwarders now dominate the market, with this number tending to reduce steadily through time as a result of what appears to be almost continuous merger and takeover activity amongst the leading players. The degree of consolidation is now increasing still further as the Integrators and the largest forwarders begin to link together.

The result of airline reliance on one channel of distribution is entirely as one would expect. Profits in the airline sector of the air freight industry have been under great pressure in recent years. A serious market downturn in 2000 and 2001 was followed by overcapacity and falling yields on many routes with only a modest improvement coming about in 2004 and 2005. In the strongest possible contrast, reported profits of publicly-quoted air freight forwarders during this time had never been better. Overcapacity amongst the airlines benefited them as they were able to play one carrier off against another, lowering the rates that they paid and in turn increasing the profits they made on their consolidations.

Rather than getting less, forwarders ability to play one airline off against another may be increasing. A number of airlines are now forming consortia, the aim of which is to streamline the process of booking in the air freight industry by the use of the Internet. At the moment, booking is mostly an archaic process using the telephone and appears ripe for reform. Internet platforms such as that provided by the GFX company are revolutionary. They are certainly achieving a streamlining of the process, though the charges rendered by GFX promise a controversy comparable to that generated by Global Distribution Systems on the passenger side of the industry. The charges made by the GFX organisation on the airlines that use it have been high enough to discourage many carriers from joining, whilst the question of the display which each carrier's flights are given in the system is likely to be controversial. Most seriously of all, GFX may complete the commoditisation of the air freight product, with forwarders able to make an immediate comparison between the rates on offer from the different competitors in a market. Great power will then accrue to the lowest-pricing airline, giving an endemic tendency towards rate cutting, especially in an over-supplied market.

It is easy to conclude that the present situation with regard to distribution channels for air freight is unsatisfactory. Airlines have too little market power despite making the bulk of the capital investment in the industry. They have also failed to make the progress seen on the passenger side in recent years, where the situation today is a good deal better than it was in the late 1990s. Unfortunately, arriving at solutions to the problem will not be easy.

In the past, some airlines have attempted to address matters by buying into the forwarding industry, or by setting up subsidiaries to compete with forwarders in such areas as off-airport ground handling. These attempts have generally not been successful. Whatever benefits they may have brought in terms of improved market control have been outweighed by the fact that remaining independent forwarders have generally reacted angrily, regarding such moves as an invasion of their territory. The commercial damage that they have been able to inflict has generally outweighed the benefits.

A more promising initiative has been taken in recent years, most notably by Air France. This airline appears to have learnt from the computer chip industry, and the strategies of Intel. Intel does not manufacture its own computers, but maintains a strong position with those who do by investing a great deal in the development of a powerful brand for its microprocessors. Air France has developed brands in air freight based on time-definite deliveries and different segments of the market. The airline clearly hopes that these brands will be requested more when shippers and forwarders are contemplating which airline to use.

Overall, questions of distribution strategies are today amongst the most contentious in the whole field of Airline Marketing. It is essential that airlines should control their distribution channels as it is largely their money that is at risk through these channels. The problem is that safeguarding long-term channel control may conflict with short-term objectives to maximise revenues, especially given the powerful positions that the industry's wholesalers and retailers have been able to build.

SUCCESSFUL AIRLINES ......

✈   Acknowledge that effective control of distribution channels is one of the most important drivers of profitability in the airline industry, and act to establish and sustain such control.

8 Brands Management in Airline Marketing

Brands management is receiving increasing attention in Airline Marketing today. There is optimism that by adopting branding concepts developed in other industries, carriers will be able to both add value to their product (and thereby reverse or at least slow the long-term decline in average yields), and secure better control of their distribution channels. The author's experience is, though, that the subject is one where there is a great deal of misunderstanding in the industry. This chapter's aim is therefore to clarify the issues, and to set out the ways in which airlines can make the best use of branding techniques.

8:1 "Brands" and "Commodities"

8:1:1 What is a "Brand"?

In terms of understanding the concept of a brand, it is best to think in terms of a spectrum. At one end of the spectrum, there are products which customers perceive as pure "commodities". At the other, there are situations where they recognise the existence of powerful brands.

A "Commodity" can be defined as any situation where customers do not perceive significant differences in the products of competing suppliers. Such situations are common. As has already been noted, in the UK at least, the petrol (gasoline) market is a good example. Few drivers have strong preferences as to the type of petrol they put in their car. Instead, they take into account a range of factors when deciding which filling station to use, none of which are related to the qualities or lack of them in the different types of petrol on offer. Many people will pull into the next garage they see after deciding they need to fill up. Others will choose the garage where the petrol is cheapest. Some – especially those with company cars where the petrol is being paid for by their employer – will select the garage with the best loyalty scheme where payments for petrol can be translated into gifts through an awards programme.

Commodity situations are fundamentally unhealthy from a marketing viewpoint. Because buyers have no strong preferences, they can be attracted only by price discounts or incentives. Commodity markets are thus ones characterised by intense competition and often, low profit margins.

The aviation industry has at least one classic commodity market – the aeroplane seat included in packaged holiday arrangements. This is especially the case in Europe, where the industry is dominated by charter airlines, few, if any, of which have a significant brand presence. Most people when booking their holiday specify the destination they would like to visit. If a brand is quoted, it is normally the brand of the tour operator organising their holiday. It is almost never that of the airline that will fly them there.

It is possible for producers in commodity markets to make satisfactory profits, but those that do are almost always those that are vertically integrated with their distribution channels, either owning or being owned by the firms that make up these channels. This is certainly the case in the petrol market, where, as we have discussed, the firms refining the petrol from crude oil generally also own or franchise a network of filling stations. They are able to earn significant profits from such outlets. A concern for them, though, is the increasing proportion of petrol being sold through supermarket filling stations, with now about a third of the UK market in the hands of these outlets. They have no formal links with the refiners of petrol, but have substantial and increasing bargaining power with them. As a consequence the refiners are finding it much more difficult to achieve acceptable profits in the supermarket-controlled sector.

If commodity situations bring significant problems, it is clearly better in many cases for firms to achieve "Brand" rather than "Commodity" status. A Brand is defined as any situation where customers *do* perceive significant differences in the products of competing suppliers. The reasons why they do are of vital importance in understanding the concept of Brands Management.

For many products, some of the reasons for their brand status can be found in so-called *Tangible* brand differentiators. These are features of a product that can actually be experienced through the senses of taste, appearance, smell etc. For example, someone might have a preference for a particular type of soup because it is thicker than other brands, or for a make of car because they believe it has a superior air conditioning system.

Tangible brand differentiators are important for almost all brands. Indeed, those that lack them, or possess them to an insufficient degree, often have to face problems of counterfeiting. (This is because it is all too easy to reproduce the product and sell counterfeit items in competition with genuine ones). It is rarely possible, though, to build powerful brands on the basis of Tangible differentiators alone. The reason is that a Tangible brand differentiator may produce only a transient marketing advantage, because it can often be matched or over-ridden very easily by the firm's competitors. The manufacturer of thicker soup may obtain some short-term growth in its sales, if consumers prefer thick soup to thin. The very fact that they do will force rival firms to thicken up their own soups, something they will be able to do very easily by a slight adjustment to the recipes they use.

The airline industry certainly has its share of easily-matched Tangible brand values. This is especially so in such areas as seating comfort and catering standards. Recent years have seen a steady stream of airlines re-launching their Business Class products. The cornerstones of such re-launches are normally better seats with a greater seat pitch and improved catering. Providing the airline's investment is large enough, a short-term improvement in market share can often be obtained. The fact that it can, though, forces other airlines to respond with their own product up-grades which normally surpass, rather than just match, the standards achieved by the innovating carrier. The end result is higher costs for all the competitors, without a significant long-term change in market shares.

The fact that Tangible brand values can often be easily matched means that powerful brands cannot be based soley on them. Brand power is normally dependent on *Psychological* brand values, which cannot be quickly matched by rivals. If they are to be matched, this can only be done after the expenditure of a great deal of time, money and effort.

With Psychological brand values, very common and very powerful ones relate to the pride, status and aspirations of those that use a particular brand. In many markets, BMW or Mercedes cars have exactly this appeal. The BMW driver does, of course, benefit from Tangible brand values relating to such things as engineering excellence and interior comfort, and would no doubt point to such factors as the dominant ones in their decision to buy the car. They may also feel, though, that driving a BMW is a sign that they have made a success of their lives, and that they are someone to be looked up to and envied by those less prosperous than themselves. Similar aspirational brands are Rolex and VanCleef and Arpel.

Another, increasingly common Psychological brand value is that of fun. In many ways, the success of McDonalds as a fast food brand could for a long time be attributed as much to its customers' perception that McDonalds stores were fun places to go as to the food and drink actually on offer there. Disney is a fun brand in the entertainment industry, with the Virgin brand having a similar strength, though it has now been stretched to encompass a much wider range of products than was the case in its original base in the entertainment industry. The subject of Brand Stretching is further discussed in Section 8:3.

Some brands attempt to position themselves as being trustworthy. This is especially so with long-established firms such as Marks and Spencer. For them, trustworthiness is a powerful psychological brand differentiator because it allows them to defend their strong position against the attacks of newer rivals. A perception of being trustworthy can only be established and sustained after a long period of customer-friendly trading. It is not usually a credible claim when made by a new entrant.

A final, interesting, example of a Psychological brand value which has grown in importance recently is that of greenness and environmental awareness. The UK cosmetics firm Body Shop has been an example of a brand built on the proposition that it trades ethically, with a proper concern for issues such as the environment and animal welfare. The US ice-cream firm Ben and Jerry's achieved a similar positioning.

This discussion of the fundamentals of branding has been a necessary one. It shows that branding is a complex and difficult subject. The fact that it is raises the question of why brands can be useful to airlines, and the methods that should be used to build and position brands. These issues form the subject of the next two sections.

8:1:2 Why Brands?

Strong brands bring firms two benefits. Firstly, they can add value to the product, allowing branded products to be sold at a premium price compared with those that are merely perceived as commodities. Secondly, they assist firms in establishing and maintaining control of their distribution channels.

The ability of brands to add value is substantial and still, despite some threats which have arisen in recent years, beyond dispute. For example, BMW cars sell at a substantial price premium compared with other cars with a comparable product specification. People pay very much more for trainers with a strong brand associated with them than for those without such a name. As airlines wrestle with the problem of a long-term decline in their average yields, they can reasonably expect that emphasis on Brands Management will at least make a contribution to slowing this trend.

The contribution that brands can make towards securing control of distribution channels is less clear, but still of vital importance. To understand it, we need to revisit the concept of "Super-profits". These are the profits earned which are over and above the "normal" profits needed to keep a firm in business. They accrue to the firms which are able to establish and maintain control of a distribution channel through the exercise of market power. Generally, such control is disputed between manufacturers, wholesalers, retailers and agents.

In many markets today, it has been wholesalers and retailers who have been able to establish distribution channel control, at the expense of manufacturers. As we have seen, this has been especially so in fields such as grocery retailing, where retailers such as (in the UK), Tesco, Sainsburys and Asda dominate the market. As they have done so, they have invested a great deal in the development of "own-brand" products, whereby goods are bought in from outside manufacturers and the retailers' own-brand labelling added prior to sale in the supermarkets and hypermarkets which now constitute most of the grocery retailing scene.

Own-brand goods can be sold at relatively low prices (helping the firms to defend and expand their market share), whilst still permitting high profit margins. The reason for this is that the retailers are in an excellent position to play one supplier off against another, enhancing their own profit margins through "Super-Profits" whilst restricting the profits of the suppliers to the levels necessary to keep them in business. In this regard, it is instructive to note that the early 1990s was a period of serious recession in the UK, with profit margins of most firms significantly affected by poor trading conditions. During this time, Tesco and Sainsburys, the two largest supermarket retailers, continued to make record profits at a time when their suppliers' returns fell significantly. This is because they had successfully established control of their distribution channels. Similar trends have been apparent in more recent years, when the success of the major supermarkets has continued unabated.

Despite the widespread dominance of "own-label", there have been significant sectors where its advance has been successfully resisted. A notable case of this has been in the retailing of cigarettes. The major supermarket chains have each launched "own-brand" cigarettes, presumably of acceptable quality and at prices well below those of the manufacturer-based cigarette brands. The penetration achieved by own-brand cigarettes has remained small, and very much lower than has been the case in most other sectors of supermarket retailing. The reason, of course, is that the cigarette market is occupied by some of the world's most powerful brands, with brands such as Marlboro, Camel and Lucky Strike still overwhelmingly dominant. Because of the strength of these brands, they are asked for by name at supermarket tobacco counters. The supermarkets therefore have no choice but to stock them, despite the fact that they cannot achieve the same profits from them as they can in the own-brand sector because they do not have the same degree of distribution channel control.

As we saw in the last chapter, battles to take control of distribution channels are very prevalent today in airline marketing. Such control is disputed between the airlines themselves, tour operators and other wholesalers, and the travel agency sector. It is absolutely essential that airlines should establish and maintain control of their distribution channels because, overwhelmingly, it is their money which is at risk. If an airline can ensure that when people go to a travel agent, they demand to be booked with that carrier and no other, they will have taken a significant step towards proper channel control. This is because the agents' ability to play one supplier off against another in searching for the best deal for themselves, will have been eliminated.

Overall, investment in brands can bring airlines very worthwhile advantages, and make a real contribution to the achievement of satisfactory profits.

8:2 Brand-Building in the Airline Industry

8:2:1 Foundations for Brand-Building

In developing a brand-building strategy, airlines must first of all decide on the basis which will be used for brand development. Here, it is useful to distinguish between Corporate and Sub-brands.

Corporate brands are those which are based on a firm's principle trading name – Ford cars, Philips electrical goods etc. The extent to which they are emphasised varies from industry to industry. In some – the airline business is a good example – almost all of the brand-building activity is carried out around Corporate brands. In others, such brands are of little or no significance. For example, in the cigarette market, smokers are often unaware of which company has actually manufactured the cigarettes they are smoking. It is, for example, unclear as to which of the major brands are Philip Morris brands and which are from RJ Reynolds or BAT Industries.

Sub-brands are those which exist under a corporate umbrella. In the car market, for example, some of the brand values are corporate, but some relate to individual models under the corporate umbrella. Ford is in itself a major Corporate brand, but models such as Mondeo, Focus and Fiesta (to use the UK brand-names) are aimed at different segments of the market and each has different brand values associated with it.

In the airline industry, there have been few successful developments of sub-brands. Many airlines have tried to launch sub-brands based on cabin classes, particularly on their business classes, but few of these have made a real impact. Exceptions are the British Airways Club World brand and also the Upper Class brand developed by Virgin Atlantic.

Another attempt at sub-branding in the airline industry has been to build such brands on the basis of a service concept. "Shuttle" became a well-recognised brand both in UK domestic markets and in the north-east of the USA, whilst the Air France "La Navette" service concept is similar both in the nature of the operation it describes and the way in which the initiative has been made to try to build a sub-brand around the concept of high-frequency short-haul services. At the opposite end of the market, Concorde was an example of a Sub-brand for Air France and British Airways until it was withdrawn from service in the autumn of 2003.

An early, and very impressive example of sub-branding in the airline industry was that of the "Skytrain" brand developed by Laker Airways for North Atlantic services in the late 1970s. Laker Airways was lost to bankruptcy in 1982, but whatever faults there were lay outside the area of brand-building. "Skytrain" was a powerful and well-recognised brand, backed by a strong mixture of both Tangible and Psychological brand values. The successors to Skytrain have been the brands which some airlines have developed around low fares subsidiaries such as Delta's Song and SAS's Snowflake, although these have mostly turned out to be unsuccessful initiatives.

At the time of writing, the relationship between Corporate and Sub-branding in the airline industry may be undergoing a significant change. We have already noted in Section 4:2:3 the trend towards airlines to come together in a small number of large global alliances. If these alliances are to stay together and to achieve what the airlines which are members hope will come from them, branding may have a crucial role to play. Until now, airlines' names have tended to form the Corporate brands, with, as we have seen a very limited development of Sub-brands under the corporate umbrella. In the future, the brands of individual airlines might come to be perceived as the Sub-brands, under the umbrella of an alliance-based Corporate brand. The first alliance to move in this direction has been the Star Alliance, although recently the Skyteam alliance has begun a similar programme. It is a point of controversy as to the extent to which alliance-based brands should subsume the brands of individual airlines within an alliance, a topic to which we will return in Section 8:3.

8:2:2 Positioning Brands

Once a decision has been taken as to the basis for brand building, airlines must decide on the values that will position their brand. These must encompass a proper mixture of Tangible and Psychological brand values, so that the brand is both powerful and defendable.

The starting point in the brand positioning process is, of course, the airline's business strategy. Some airlines target mainly the business air traveller. Others are more leisure-market orientated, or operate purely in the air freight business. Many carriers aim at a presence in all the major market segments, a strategy which carries with it especial brand positioning problems which we will discuss shortly. The correct brand positions for these different types of airline will themselves be very different.

This point becomes especially clear when we introduce the next factor that should be taken into account – the needs of customers in the airline's selected target market segments. Section 2:2:2 dealt with the question of customer needs, and laid especial emphasis on the difference between "Apparent" and "True" needs. "Apparent" needs were defined as the needs which the person concerned will willingly admit to if asked. "True" needs are deeper, and represent the true motivation for the customer's buying behaviour.

In terms of customer needs, there is one that all of them have in common, that of safety. It can be said that all passengers are frightened of flying. There is simply a spectrum stretching from those who are mildly concerned about it to those who are terrified of the whole experience. Because of this, all airlines have to build their brands on the basis of a brand value of safety, and those that do anything to compromise this (for example, by becoming involved in the sponsorship of a dangerous sport such as motor racing) make a serious mistake.

Once the fundamental value of safety has been accepted the variety of customer needs give airlines significant choices when positioning brands. For example, an airline targeting the business air traveller will have to focus on Tangible brand values such as punctuality, reliability and frequency. In terms of Psychological values, it is known that many business flyers are prestige and status-conscious. An airline seeking to attract them must in turn position its brand in such a way as to suggest that it is the carrier of choice for successful people, who know the sort of airline they like to be seen to be flying. Exactly this attempt is being made at the time of writing by the transatlantic 'All Business Class' airline, Eos Air.

For airlines targeting the leisure market, they will know that many of their customers will have the price of the ticket as a prime factor in making their choice-of-airline decisions. Therefore, airlines have to position themselves as the value-for-money choice, offering the cheapest fares possible whilst maintaining safety standards and giving acceptable levels of punctuality and passenger amenities. Southwest Airlines illustrates exactly this positioning.

With regard to passenger needs, the most difficult brand positioning problems are faced by the many airlines which are seeking to be well-represented both in business travel (because of its high yields) and in leisure travel (at least partly because of its higher-than-average growth rates). These carriers have to present themselves as the airline of choice for the status-conscious business traveller, and as the value-for-money solution for the leisure flyer looking for a cheap fare. These two positions represent a contradiction, one that has not often been dealt with successfully. British Airways has perhaps been as successful as any with the launch of its "WorldOffers" Sub-brand. This enabled cheap-fare offers to be separated from advertising, promotion and brand-building aimed at the business traveller.

As in many other aspects of Airline Marketing, the question of the Trade Cycle has to be brought into discussions about brand positioning. People's sentiments about spending money tend to be very different in the up-swing times of the Cycle compared with times of slowdown or recession. In prosperous periods, spending in an extravagant, conspicuous way may be commonplace. It will not be during recessions. Some poorly-positioned brands have brand values which are suitable for up-swing periods, but leave the brand badly exposed when things get tougher. Examples might be some of the car and jewellery brands which suffered during the recession of the early 1990s, and are did so again in the early years of the new century.

The question of market gap analysis is a crucial one in successful brand positioning. The essence of a brand is that it is perceived as being unique and different from the offerings of rival suppliers. Such a perception is unlikely if customers believe that all features of competing products are similar. In positioning brands, firms need to carry out studies into the ways in which rivals are perceived, and to position their brand in such a way that it is focused on areas where they are seen as strong and their rivals weak. One can assume that this was the thinking behind the brand positioning adopted by the airline Lauda Air when it was set up by the former racing driver Nikki Lauda. Lauda positioned itself as a light-hearted "fun" brand, in strong contrast to the rather stolid image of its main rival Austrian Airlines.

A final factor to be considered in the correct positioning of a brand may be that of the national interest. This will be of obvious importance to a state-owned airline which may be in need of continuing financial support from taxpayers. Even for privately-owned airlines, however few can operate successfully without a measure of favourable support from governments. This may be needed in such areas as the granting of international route rights, or in favourable access to capacity at a congested airport. Branding messages that the airline is behaving patriotically, or providing substantial benefits to the national economy may then be especially useful.

Whatever criteria are used, the pr[...]
will be a complex and demanding proce[...]
should be based on proper research and an[...]
guesswork.

8:2:3 *The Brand-Building Process*

One of the greatest misconceptions is that brand building is a[...]
and that it provides a speedy and cheap panacea for a firm's p[...]
Once agreement has been reached on the values that will position the [...]
it is essential that the process concentrates on the delivery of the prom[...]
which are implicit in its positioning.

This crucial requirement is most obvious with the question of Tangible brand values. Clearly, it will be a brand-building disaster if an airline has a fatal accident, or, worse still, a series of such accidents. All airlines have to make absolute safety the cornerstone of their brand, and failure to deliver this product feature will be very serious. Punctuality is also a good example. Many carriers have tried to position themselves as the "on-time airline", yet, as we saw in Section 5:3:3, punctuality is one of the most difficult product features for carriers to deliver in practice, and many fail to do so.

With product weaknesses in the area of Tangible brand values, it should be born in mind that their effect will not be a neutral one. An airline with a poor punctuality record will always alienate its customers every time a flight is late. The effect on customer perceptions of the airline will, though, be especially serious if the carrier has been attempting to get across a branding message with a media advertising campaign based on a slogan such as "Europe's most punctual airline".

With Psychological brand values, delivery, or the failure to do so, may be more subtle, but still important in the building of a brand. For example, an airline might choose a positioning based on the proposition that it is a "Winner" – a successful company with which successful people will want to be associated. It would then be a significant mistake to get into a sponsorship deal with an unsuccessful football team that lost every game it played.

Once, and only once, an airline is confident that it can deliver on the values that will position its brand, it can then proceed to the next stage of brand-building, that of marketing communication. This subject is fully covered in Sections 10:3 and 10:4. For the moment, though, it should be emphasised that almost all marketing communication can play a role in brand-building, and that very substantial spending will almost certainly be necessary if a powerful brand is to be built and sustained. Media

s messages that reflect
tabase marketing activity
e an especially powerful
ed in the right way. If it
e impact on a brand. This

an airline's marketing
dia relations. The airline
y media owners and editors.
have a potentially disastrous
are sustained on a long-term
ly beneficial effect, and the
dia will be of great importance
d-building.
at strong brands are rarely built
ckly). It is of vital importance

per positioning of an airline brand
It is certainly a process that
ysis, rather than hunch and

simple task,
oblems.
rand,
es

quickly
that firms adopt a suck ... emphasising strong, core brand
values on a very long-term basis. One only has to look at the power
achieved by the Marlboro brand, where the core values have been
unchanged now for nearly 40 years to see the truth of this statement. In the
airline industry, Singapore Airlines gives an equally good illustration of the
importance of consistency in successful brand development.

8:3 Brand Strategies

The discussion has now reached the point where we have covered the
fundamentals of positioning and building brands. All firms have to make
strategic decisions about managing their brands and this next section aims
to address these decisions.

A first area of debate in many industries is whether investment should
be directed towards the development of new brands, or the purchase of
existing ones from other firms. Development of a new brand allows the
firm to start with a clean sheet of paper, and to use the brand values which
exactly match its business strategy and capabilities. It may also be that the
end result of the process is a significant asset, which might in turn be sold
at a later stage. The problem is that brand building is a risky, time-
consuming and expensive business. For all the new brands that are
introduced and eventually become valuable successes, there are many
others which turn out to be costly failures.

Building new brands is so risky that in many areas of the economy,
established brands are bought and sold, rather than new ones being

developed. This may occur as a specific transaction, or it may be the driving force behind merger and take-over activity. An example was the take-over of Rolls-Royce cars by BMW of Germany in 1999 – a clear case where the price paid by BMW was significantly above the value of Rolls' tangible assets. This extra payment essentially represented the value placed by BMW on the Rolls-Royce brand.

Such activity is rare in the airline industry. There are few examples where a brand owned by one airline has been sold to another as a standalone transaction. This reflects the emphasis in the industry on Corporate rather than Sub-brands. A case where this might be said to have taken place was in 1988 when Pan American, desperate for cash and in a near-bankrupt condition, sold its Shuttle routes in the north-east of the USA to USAirways. The price paid was significantly above the value of the tangible assets transferred, with it being possible to argue that the extra payment was for the Shuttle brand.

With merger and take-over activity driven by brand acquisition, the ownership and control rules which still dominate the aviation industry mean that mergers and take-overs are in any case much less common that in a "normal" industry. Where mergers and take-overs do occur, they only do so on the basis of airlines from the same country merging (or, in the case of the European Union, carriers within the same trading bloc).

When airline mergers and take-overs are proposed, it is certainly not generally the case that they are driven by the desire of the bidder to acquire the brand of the airline it is attempting to take over. Indeed, the commonest situation is for the brand of the airline being taken over to be dumped, and all trace of it to disappear in the shortest possible time. This was certainly the case, for example when USAirways took over Piedmont Airlines in the USA in the late 1980s. The Piedmont brand was abandoned completely, despite the fact that its reputation had been a good one – probably better than that of USAirways.

The buying and selling of brands in the airline industry may be rare, but we have seen a number of examples of *brand repositioning*. The most extreme example of this has been when airlines with a significant presence in the leisure air travel market try to reposition their brand to help them achieve penetration of the business travel segment. There are certainly factors which might lead them to attempt this. Business travel yields are higher, and it also tends to be more of a a year-round activity – with resulting cash-flow advantages – rather than showing the acute seasonality normally characteristic of leisure travel. Generally, though the problems of doing so have been insuperable, with questions of brand positioning amongst the most difficult.

Two well-known airlines which attempted such a transition at almost exactly the same time were the Canadian airline Wardair and the British-based carrier Air Europe. Both had built a strong presence in the leisure market with their emphasis on charter flying for the holiday traveller. Both in 1987 made announcements that they were going to radically re-position themselves, with the business traveller the future target market. In each case, the move was a complete failure. Wardair was soon taken over in a near-bankrupt condition by Canadian Airlines whilst Air Europe went into receivership in 1991. (A former franchise partner still survives in Italy and uses the Air Europe name).

Amongst the problems both airlines had was the enormous investment required to make the transition. They recognised – correctly – that they would need a new fleet of smaller aircraft so that they could boost frequencies to the level required by the business traveller. Ironically, both selected the Fokker 100 and made a large commitment to acquire new aircraft from Fokker. Unfortunately, this required a huge cash outflow before the products could be introduced which would make the airlines attractive to the business market. At the same time, they were handicapped by a brand which was perceived as leisure-orientated and, in the case of Air Europe, associated with young, rowdy and poorly-behaved holiday travellers. Their brands were unlikely to appeal to status-conscious business flyers, and in truth it came as no surprise that they were overwhelmed by their financial difficulties before the brand repositioning could bring its hoped-for rewards.

Brand strengthening obviously needs to be a constant strategy in any sound brands management process. Many brands run into difficulty from time-to-time, because of the inability of the firms that own them to deliver the brand values consistently. When this happens, the delivery problems must be addressed, and then, and only then, marketing communication work to bring the brand back to its former strength must be undertaken.

Two interesting issues in brand strategy are those of *Brand Stretching* and *Co-branding*. A Brand Stretching strategy is one where the brand values developed around one product are used to market others. Such strategies have become increasingly common in recent years, notably so in the cigarette industry where brands originally developed for cigarettes are now being used to market such things as outdoor clothing and travel.

In the airline industry, the use of Brand Stretching has so far achieved only mixed results. Three airlines – Virgin Atlantic, Virgin America and Virgin Blue – are in fact themselves an extension of the Virgin brand which began life in the entertainment industry. Many carriers have attempted to stretch their own brand into travel-related businesses, such as hotels and tour operations. There are currently some suggestions that lucrative areas for investment might be in travel-related financial services products such as travel insurance and traveller's cheques.

The potential benefits of Brand Stretching are clear, in that it leverages investment made in the brand. The problems, though, are equally telling. A Brand Stretching exercise amounts to a giant house of cards where if the essential values related to the core brand are undermined, the whole house collapses. Also, Brand Stretching runs the risk that management time and the firm's financial resources will be diluted, by businesses about which the firm knows little and where there are few synergies between the new activities and the core business. Where such synergies may be argued to exist – between an airline and, say, a chain of hotels – the value of the synergy may be reduced by the fact that both the businesses are vulnerable to the same downswings in the Trade Cycle.

In some ways, a better approach to the leveraging of brand investment is that of Brand Franchising. Franchising has a long history in the airline industry, having begun in the USA in the 1970s. It did, though, become much more common in the 1990s, and can be seen as part of the trend towards consolidation and the emergence of global alliances which was discussed in Section 4:2:6.

The essence of franchising relationships as they have developed in the airline industry is that a smaller airline contracts with a larger one by renting its brand. This buys the small carrier respectability, in that passengers are likely to perceive it in a better light with regard to technical aspects such as safety and punctuality. The small airline also benefits because it is able to join the Frequent Flyer Programme of the major carrier, and share its GDS code (so that it can appear to offer on-line service to its connecting passengers). Finally, the small airline benefits too because its partner will act as its global General Sales Agent and a substantial increase in bookings should be the result.

For the large airline, the advantages are also clear. It will be able to charge substantial franchising fees, and such fees will constitute useful incremental revenue. Even more significantly, it will gain important feed into its long-haul traffic system, without the costs of providing such feed itself. Large airlines generally find it difficult to achieve competitive costs on thin routes, mainly because these routes require small aircraft which in turn do not allow high operating costs to be spread over a large number of seats. Smaller airlines, with lower pilot salaries in particular, will be much better placed to be cost efficient suppliers.

Despite these advantages, franchising brings disadvantages, to both the small and the large airlines who engage in it. The smaller airline has to accept the payment of franchising fees, and a loss of a great deal of its independence. Its larger partner will dictate such decisions as aircraft livery, staff uniforms, seating comfort and service standards. Often, control will also be exercised over the routes which can and cannot be flown. For the larger airlines, the issues mainly centre around the question of brand integrity. If someone books with a major airline, they expect the service to be provided by that airline, using a jet aircraft. With franchising, they may arrive at the airport to find that they are actually flying with the regional partner, and perhaps in a turbo-prop aircraft. However wrong it may be, turbo-props are still regarded by some people as being slow and old-fashioned, and they may feel that the brand promise has not been kept if they have to travel in one.

Overall, it is impossible to exaggerate the contribution which can be played by sound Brands Management in airline marketing today. Brands can add value, and give carriers the best possible opportunity to establish and sustain control of their distribution channels. It is a subject that should be given the greatest possible emphasis.

SUCCESSFUL AIRLINES ......

✈   Are those which understand the differences between "Brands" and Commodities.

✈   That spend the large amount of time, money and effort that will be needed to build powerful brands.

9 Relationship Marketing

We come now to one of the most demanding aspects of Airline Marketing today – the attempt to apply relationship management concepts. Theoretically, the segmentation of the air travel market means that airlines should be well placed to take advantage of some of the techniques of Relationship Marketing. As they have attempted to do so, though, very substantial costs have arisen, costs which make the question of the return being obtained on their investment a controversial one.

9:1 Fundamentals of Relationship Marketing

9:1:1 Some Definitions

A common error in the airline industry is to assume that "Relationship Marketing" is just a more impressive way of describing an airline's Frequent Flyer Programme. This is fundamentally wrong. An FFP may well be part of a sound investment in relationship building – indeed at the moment it almost always is – but Relationship Marketing approaches should encompass much more than simply a mileage programme. Let us begin with a definition:

> Relationship Marketing is a marketing philosophy whereby a firm gives equal or greater emphasis to the maintenance and strengthening of its relationships with its existing customers as it does to the necessary search for new customers.

The last part of the definition should certainly not be disregarded. All firms – airlines included – will lose some of their customers every year. A small number of people will sadly die, whilst in business travel, others retire from work. Some customers will be affected by the – hopefully small – number of service failures which the firm will inevitably have. They will no longer purchae from it as a result. Finally, some people will desert the firm for no logical reason – they just decide to change. Therefore, the search for new customers will have to be an intensive and continuous one.

Despite this, it is the earlier part of the definition which is of still greater importance to airlines. As we saw in Section 2:3:4, the business air travel market consists of a relatively small number of people who each fly a great deal. Indeed, in many countries, the average number of trips taken each year is often more than ten per person. In addition, each person will probably be part of the business travel market for many years. They may be promoted to a job requiring extensive travel in their middle or late twenties, and do that job, or similar ones, for twenty or thirty years. To use the jargon of Relationship Marketing, this means that they have an extremely high Lifetime Value. An airline gaining the passenger's loyalty when they begin business travel will gain substantial sums if it can retain such support throughout the person's career. Equally, an airline failing to gain such loyalty should regard it as a severe loss.

Besides the amount of money at stake, relationship-based approaches often bring with them the advantage that once loyalty has been established – a process which admittedly may be costly – subsequent, incremental business can be obtained quite cheaply. Once someone has decided on a particular airline, that airline only has the task of persuading them to continue to make the same choice. This should be relatively easy, because it will be a question of reinforcing in their mind the correctness of their original decision. If on the other hand, a carrier needs to persuade someone to fly with them who until now has been travelling with a competitor, they will have to convince them that their original choice was wrong. Human nature being what it is, few of us readily admit our mistakes. Attracting business away from competitors will therefore need powerful persuasion, and such business may have a much higher marketing cost associated with it.

Two remaining definitions are important – those of "Advocate" and Destroyer" relationships. Until a few years ago, the principle concern of marketing in the airline industry was simply to divide those people who were customers of an airline from those who were not. Today, much more attention is being given to the nature and strength of the relationship between the firm and its customers.

An "Advocate" relationship is where someone not only buys from the firm in question, but they act as the firm's advocate by strongly advising other people that they should do so too. A "Destroyer" relationship is one where a potential customer does not buy from the firm, and also does all they can to persuade other people not to do so by pointing out the firm's many inadequacies. Clearly, having a high number of Advocates will be a significant advantage, whilst the existence of a large body of Destroyers will be a large – probably insuperable – handicap. The question of building Advocate relationships is thus at the core of Relationship Marketing for all firms, notably so for airlines. It is to this aspect that we now turn.

9:1:2 Building Advocate Relationships

In any industry, Advocate Relationships only result if a number of basic philosophies are followed. Of these, *straight dealing* is the most fundamental. For example, few people cheated over the purchase of a second-hand car will return to the same dealer that overcharged them. In the airline industry, people will feel angry if they subsequently find that an airline had a much lower fare was on offer than the one they actually paid – an increasingly common cause of complaint. Such overcharging could well turn out to be a mistake if the extra money obtained had to be set against the loss of the customer's loyalty because they felt they had been dealt with in an unacceptable way.

A second, crucial aspect of relationship-building is that of *delivering promises*. Airlines are generally not shy of making claims in their advertising and promotion. Indeed, if one looks at the advertising of many airlines with a poor reputation, the proposition seems to be that travelling with the carrier will be the most wonderful, faultless experience with on-time flights, comfortable seating, excellent food and, especially, the warmest of welcomes from the airline's customer service staff. Those actually choosing to do so may find in practice that there are delays, that aircraft are dirty, the food inedible and that customer contact staff are rude and unmotivated. If they do so, they will feel a sense of betrayal, because of the false claims that have been made, and are likely to form a Destroyer relationship with the airline that will be hard to shift.

Closely alongside the delivery of promises will be the question of *caring*. People tend to form Advocate relationships with firms where they feel the firm cares about them as individuals. Caring can, of course, take on many different forms in addition to the delivery of promises mentioned in the last paragraph. People may feel that the firm is showing a caring attitude if it keeps them informed about new service developments or offers which they may find attractive. They will especially do so if they feel that the firm makes a positive response if they have a cause to complain.

Service beyond reasonable expectations can be especially valuable in building Advocate relationships. People give an airline little credit for a meal being served or a cup of coffee being offered – they expect such things by right. The may feel very warm towards an airline, though, if they see a cabin staff member making a particular effort to calm an anxious or distressed passenger.

A further important point is that customers should find a firm *accessible*. No-one likes to find that it is impossible to make contact with a supplier because of clogged phone lines, or long computerised messages about which phone key to press, especially if they are being forced to use a premium rate phone line at the time.

A final, crucial, fundamental of relationship-building is that of *gratitude*. If someone buys loyally from a particular firm, they will have a reasonable expectation that this loyalty should be recognised. Such recognition may come in the form of a reward scheme. Of equal, or greater importance, though, will be simple, unqualified expressions of thanks for the business they have given to the firm in question. Such expressions are surprisingly rare.

Given the complexity of the relationship-building task, it can only be approached strategically. An airline seeking to build strong relationships with its customer will need to move forward on a wide front. How they should do so forms the subject of the next section.

9:2 Components of a Relationship Marketing Strategy

The cornerstone of a relationship-building strategy is that the firm should know who its main customers are, and the exact nature of each customer's relationship with the firm. This will mean substantial investment in capturing and managing data.

In terms of the data that will be needed, clearly airlines will need to know demographic information about their customers. This will include obvious things about name, address, job title etc. Such information must be accurate, up-to-date and de-duplicated in order to be useful. In addition, information will be required about customer needs. Today, it should not be necessary for airline customers to spell out their particular requirements every time they make a booking. They expect airlines to know their preferences with respect to such things as special dietary requirements and preferred seating.

A second area where data will be needed is that of so-called activity information. This describes what the customer buys from the firm in question, where and when. Airlines need to know the routes that people fly, the class of service in which they travel and the fare types that they use. Only if they do can they put out marketing communication material which will be relevant to each customer's particular set of requirements.

A final, more difficult area of database management is the integration of demographic and activity data with Customer Relations information. From time to time, passengers may have cause to complain to an airline. We will consider further in Section 9:2:3 the question of an effective Customer Relations policy to handle the situation when they do. For the moment, though, it is important to emphasise that Customer Relations information must be integrated into the airline's overall customer database.

If it isn't there is a risk of severe damage to relationships occurring. For example, someone who had just complained about a delayed flight will be furious if shortly after having done so they receive a circular letter or email from the airline claiming that it has a very high standard of punctuality.

The only good news about database management in the airline industry today is that computing power to store and process data is now much cheaper than it used to be. Obtaining and entering the necessary data and ensuring proper systems integration will still be a very costly and demanding task.

In terms of demographic information about actual and potential customers, by far the best data is that which people volunteer about themselves. As we shall see shortly, the great benefit that Frequent Flyer Programmes bring to airlines is that they provide a ready source of database information which people give voluntarily. These people also help airlines to keep information up-to-date by letting carriers know when they change their address. It should also be easy to produce an integration between such demographic data and activity data by asking people to quote a reference number every time they make a booking or check-in for a flight. They will generally be very willing to do so, because they want to make sure that the appropriate credit is given to their mileage account. Of course, it will still be necessary for the carrier to work hard to capture the data, by ensuring that their own customer contact staff always enter the data when necessary, even at times when they are very busy.

9:2:1 The Management of Quality

We have already seen that the keeping of promises is the cornerstone of a relationship building strategy. If airlines deliver what they promise in terms of issues such as safety, punctuality, aircraft cleanliness and baggage handling they will have achieved a great deal in terms of establishing and sustaining Advocate relationships with their most important customers. If they fail to do so, they will quickly become known as the airline to avoid.

Quality management poses especial problems in service industries generally and in the aviation industry in particular. In service industries, output is instantly perishable at the time it is produced. It is not possible to produce the product and then check it over before delivery to the customer as can be done, for example in the car or electrical appliance industries. In aviation, there is not only the problem of perishability of output. The production process itself is a complex one, where the activities of many different departments have to come together in the right way and at the right time if product quality is to be sustained. This is especially so in areas such as safety and punctuality.

There is now widespread recognition that effective quality management comes from the top of an organisation, and that it is a continuous, never-ending task. Circumstances change, and a continuous adaptation to such changes will be needed. Standards will also inevitably decline through time unless a constant effort is made to ensure that they do not do so. Generally, this will mean ensuring that things move ahead by small increments, over a broad front, steadily, though time. The grand initiative may occasionally be needed if things have slipped very badly, but short-term thinking often leads to an immediate improvement which, however, is quickly lost as standards fall back again.

9:2:2 *Customer Relations*

Customer Relations policies are an area where substantial progress towards more enlightened thinking has been made in recent years, with a growing recognition of the fact that a sound investment here can make a substantial contribution to a relationship-building strategy.

In the past, the tendency amongst airlines was to regard people who complained as a nuisance, to be got rid of as quickly as possible. The Complaint Handling department was often seen as a career backwater, populated by poor quality and unmotivated staff. Today, better carriers see this function as an important opportunity, where relationships can be repaired, and strengthened for the future. They also recognise it as a Marketing, rather than an Operations, function. Old attitudes based on leaving the task to the Operations department on the grounds that 'They cased the problems, they can sort them out', are no longer appropriate.

All airlines will experience service failures from time to time. Of course, if these failures are frequent, they show that there is a serious problem which needs to be addressed through a quality management programme as discussed in the last section. Such programmes if properly applied can make service failures rare events, but it is only being realistic to say that they cannot eliminate them entirely.

When a service failure occurs, the passengers who are affected are divisible into two: those who complain and those who do not. In the past the tendency was to look more favourably on those who did not complain rather than on those who did. This was quite wrong. People who are dissatisfied but who do not complain are most unlikely to buy again from the firm that has let them down. Worse still, they will probably take on a "Destroyer" role with respect to that firm, telling everyone who will listen to them how bad it is. In contrast, those who do complain, and whose complaint is dealt with properly, often do buy from the firm again and their relationship with that firm may in fact be strengthened rather than weakened by their bad experience.

There are a number of rules which must be followed in an effective Customer Relations policy. Firstly, customers must find it easy, rather than a challenge, to make their views known. Here Freephone numbers can be valuable, assuming that their existence is given wide publicity, as can dedicated email addresses.

Secondly, once a complaint has been received, a prompt acknowledgement should be made. If the complainant leaves a phone number, they should be called on the day their call or letter is received, and an unequivocal deadline stated as to a date by which they will hear more. This date must, of course be kept to.

In terms of the exact response that should be made, the most important requirement is that the airline should, if at all legally possible, give a clear apology. This apology should include ownership of the problem. Customers are not interested in a detailed post-mortem where the airline attempts, say, to lay the blame for a delayed flight on the catering company which failed to deliver the meals to the aircraft on time. They feel that if a carrier is receiving poor service from its suppliers, it should change them for ones which are more reliable.

Once an apology has been given, attention can be directed to re-establishing the strength of the customer's relationship with the airline. Doing so might entail giving financial compensation or – a particularly attractive incentive – offering a free ticket on an off-peak flight where the airline knows it will have empty seats and where unhappy passengers can, hopefully, be shown the airline's normal, and much better, standards of service. A further possibility is that the passenger should be offered bonus miles in their Frequent Flyer Programme account.

Such a response should go a long way towards addressing the passenger's concerns. A further, follow-up letter should, though, be sent after a period of a few weeks, asking people if they are fully satisfied with the airline's response.

Such a generous approach to dealing with complaints does, of course, lead to the possibility of abuse. There is a clear risk that people will complain without a worthwhile reason, hoping for compensation. This may be an especial risk once an initial complaint has been made which has been treated favourably.

Dealing with this problem will be a question of emphasis. Fraudulent claims may become a significant issue if a Customer Relations policy is over-generous. Equally, though, there is a likelihood that valuable customers will be alienated if it isn't generous enough. Of these risks, the second should be regarded as much the more serious, and some losses through fraud should be accepted as inevitable. However, in order to minimise them, database information needs to be collected on each person who complains. It should soon become evident who is doing so on a systematic basis.

9:2:3 Marketing Communication

The question of marketing communication forms the subject of the next chapter, when substantial attention will be given to the question of using databases for targeted messages. For now, though, it is most unlikely that anyone will form a positive relationship with a firm unless that firm takes the trouble to communicate with them.

As we shall discuss in section 10:3:2, the question of using databases in a marketing communications strategy is now a controversial one, with consumer resistance to what they see as "junk mail" and "spam" seeming to increase inexorably. Proper use of a database in this way can, though, significantly strengthen a relationship. It can be used to provide customers with useful information. It can allow firms to make attractive offers to present and possible future customers. Finally, it can be used – though it very rarely is – so that firms have an opportunity to express their gratitude to their customers for their continuing support.

9:2:4 Loyalty Schemes

This chapter began with the correct statement that "Relationship Marketing" is about much more than a Frequent Flyer Programme. It has to be acknowledged, though, that probably no relationship-building strategy in air transport can achieve its full potential without involving a loyalty scheme of some sort. Such schemes have proliferated in many areas of retailing in recent years, with loyalty marketing now, for example, a major aspect of petrol, grocery and credit card marketing. It is, though, airlines through their Frequent Flyer Programmes who were amongst the pioneers of this form of marketing and who have, arguably, developed it to its fullest extent. The whole of the next section is therefore devoted to FFPs.

9:3 Frequent Flyer Programmes

9:3:1 History and Current Status

Frequent Flyer Programmes now have a long history in the airline industry. As was mentioned in Section 5:2:1, the first programme was introduced by

American Airlines as long ago as 1981. It was an immediate success, and American's lead was soon followed by all the other major airlines in the USA.

In the rest of the world, the take-up was rather slower, At that time, competition was still muted in many markets as a result of government regulation, whilst many airlines were fearful of the costs which FFPs might bring with them – fears which to a considerable extent have turned out to be justified. There was a turning point, though, in 1991 when Pan American (soon to disappear into bankruptcy) and TWA lost their positions as the leading US carriers on the North Atlantic. They were instead replaced by American, United and Delta, three airlines with well-established and powerful Frequent Flyer Programmes. Recognising the intensity of the competitive threat that these airlines would pose, European carriers, led by British Airways and Lufthansa, quickly launched their own programmes. They were in turn followed by many airlines in the Far East. At the time of writing the situation is that, outside of the Low Cost Carrier sector, almost all significant airlines have their own FFP, or are partners in a joint-venture programme. Furthermore, Frequent Flyer Programmes are now very much bound up with the trend for the airline industry to consolidate into alliances, with the alliances offering FFP members so-called "Earn and Burn" rights. These allow passengers to be awarded miles in 'their' programme, even if they are travelling on a service of another alliance member. Similar opportunities exist to use the services of other alliance carriers when they are redeeming miles to obtain free tickets.

Today, Frequent Flyer Programmes are at the heart of marketing in the airline industry. Indeed, it is much easier to isolate the airlines which do not have a programme rather than those that do.

Given their all-prevailing presence in the industry, it might be imagined that FFPs have become a non-controversial element in Airline Marketing. Nothing could be further from the truth. Carriers are faced with the challenges of keeping their programmes competitive in an increasingly mature and saturated marketplace. There are also a number of new controversies which are now appearing, and which will decide the future role to be played by FFPs.

In order to investigate these issues further it is necessary first to look at the difficult balancing act which constitutes the cornerstone of running a successful FFP today. In order to be competitive, airlines must make their programmes sufficiently appealing to attract and retain members. The problem is that, if they do so, they run the risk that the programme will become excessively costly to administer. We will now assess how this balance should be struck.

9:3:2 FFPs – Programme Member Requirements

For a programme to attract members, it must clearly be one where credits can be built quickly, so that rewards become available at an early stage. For this to happen, generous credits must be available when someone travels on the airline's own flights, especially if they use an expensive First or Business Class ticket. At the same time, the airline will have to sign extensive partnership agreements with other airlines which serve routes that the first carrier does not. This will allow credits to be collected on any flight that the person takes. They will also expect opportunities to collect miles when staying in hotels, renting cars, or using their credit cards. In some programmes now, points can be obtained when shopping for such things as clothes, petrol and groceries.

Once the points have been collected, the programme member's requirement is that there should be no time limit on their validity. This allows them to be used either for a small, but more immediate reward, or for a major project for which many years' collection may be needed.

Clearly, a generous reward structure will also be attractive. Free flights have always been and remain, the principal reward on offer from an FFP. Here, the programme member's expectation is that there will be ready availability of seats, even at peak holiday periods when it is most likely that they will want to fly. They also expect to be able to use points to obtain up-grades to Business or First Class when they are travelling. In both cases, they will require the airline to have agreements with other airlines so that miles can be used on other carriers, giving a wide choice of destinations. As we have seen, through alliances, such agreements generally are in place.

Besides free travel rewards, today FFP members expect reward opportunities which are not necessarily travel-related. If someone flies, say, thirty times a year it may not be a very attractive temptation for them to take a tedious thirty-first flight. The offer of such a flight is often referred to as the "Walking Holiday for the Postman" effect. Instead, non-travel rewards such as golf lessons or a balloon flight may be much more appealing and a modern FFP must have a wide variety of rewards on offer if it is to be fully competitive.

Besides the rewards available when people are redeeming miles, today FFP members expect extensive benefits to be available to them when they are travelling on business. They will be attracted by a separate phone line when they are making bookings, by a separate check-in desk and especially by airport lounge facilities which will allow them a suitable ambience whilst they are waiting for their flights. They will also expect a tiered membership structure which will allow them access to more and more privileges as the amount of flying they do increases.

These points make up the major ones which will attract members to join and support a Frequent Flyer Programme. There are, though, some less important, but still significant issues which should also be taken into account. For example, programme members expect the right to give away or sell credits to other people – most FFPs forbid this, because of airline fears that it will result in a loss of revenue. They also require airlines to keep records accurately, and object strongly if they find that they are continually having to contact the carrier because their flights are not being recorded properly. Finally, they expect regular statements of their mileage balance to be sent to them, or – better still – for such information to be available on-line. The process of redeeming miles should, of course be easy and straightforward rather than a battle.

9:3:3 *FFPs – Airline Requirements*

Given the competitive nature of the FFP marketplace, airlines need to keep an especial close control of their programmes. If they fail to do so, the costs associated with them will quickly become excessive.

Fundamental to a cost-effective programme is the question of the control of capacity. The airline's Frequent Flyer Programme must be fully integrated with its revenue and capacity management systems so that, as far as possible, people redeeming miles for free tickets use seats on off-peak flights which would otherwise be flown empty. Ideally, a target should be set for this. A typical target would be that on 95% of occasions the FFP redeemer should occupy an otherwise empty seat.

Alongside the control of capacity, the greatest possible emphasis should be given to the acquisition of database material. When joining the programme, new members should be asked to provide extensive, useful database information. If they refuse to give it, then they should not be allowed to join, because effective use of the database for database marketing is now the key to airlines obtaining value-for-money from FFP investment.

At the same time as database information is collected, every opportunity should be taken to build the Frequent Flyer Programme into a profit rather than a cost centre. This can now be done because Loyalty Marketing is in vogue in many industries, and firms in these industries are always looking of innovative ways in which to reward their best customers. Beyond any question, free travel is a very attractive incentive, especially for people who do not travel for their work. An increasing number of airlines now sell mileage credits to other businesses, and are earning worthwhile revenue from doing so. Of course, if they do so it puts strong pressure on them to have credible redemption offers to provide their trade customers with a value-for-money incentive programme.

In terms of airline requirements, time limits on the validity of FFP credits remains controversial. They may certainly make a programme less attractive for someone to join and support, but they mean that the programme is far more likely to produce genuine loyalty as those people who do join will know that they will have to take all their flights with one airline if they are to obtain a good reward within the three years' validity that the credits have typically had in the past. However, most programmes now have no time limits, because of competitive pressures. Others state that miles will continue to be valid as long as the person concerned takes at least one flight each year with the airline in question.

Another factor in the imposition of time limits are the requirements sometimes placed on airlines by their auditors. Mileage credits which have been issued by an airline but not yet redeemed represent a liability which, arguably, should be included on an airline's balance sheet. This is especially so in the case of a carrier which is on the edge of bankruptcy, because the holders of the credits are likely to try to redeem them quickly, and all at once, in such a situation. They will know that if the airline goes into receivership and its assets are liquidated, they will be no more than unsecured creditors, with few rights, of the bankrupt company. This was exactly the situation that arose with Pan American in the early 1990s, and may be the case with Delta Air Lines at the time of writing.

Today, airlines have mostly successfully resisted auditors' demands for the inclusion of unredeemed FFP credits as a liability on their balance sheets, though most do now include an estimate of the liability as a note to the accounts in their annual reports. They have done so by sometimes introducing time limits on the validity of credits to limit the build-up of the liability, but more so by arguing that the advent of modern revenue and capacity management systems allows them to control the use of capacity very closely. They can prevent a rush of FFP redemptions even in circumstances that might otherwise give rise to one.

Tiers of membership are now an essential component of a state-of-the-art Frequent Flyer Programme. Typically, programmes have at least three generally-available tiers, with each one granting progressively higher levels of privilege to those who fly more. Proportionately greater recognition is given to those who use First or Business Class tickets. Many programmes also have a fourth, and highest tier, which can only be awarded by the airline's CEO or other senior managers to those whose favour the carrier is especially anxious to court.

Tiered memberships in many ways improve the attractiveness of the programme, and it is always a pleasant experience for a member of the airline's sales team to inform someone that they have been promoted to a higher tier of membership. It is essential, though, that people are demoted as well as promoted, with demotion occurring if they do not travel sufficiently, even though this will often cause a reaction of outrage. The reason is that if this is not done, the higher tiers become a devalued currency. Also, people may remain loyal to one airline until they have obtained that carrier's Gold Card, but then change to another to see if they can collect further cards.

A final, interesting, airline requirement from a Frequent Flyer Programme is that it must be made quite clear to people when they join that the airline reserves the right to change the programme's rules through time. Market conditions in the airline industry change markedly according to the state of the Trade Cycle. In buoyant times, airlines can grow with the market. During more difficult periods, they can only increase their business at the expense of others by raising their share of a stagnant market. Because of these factors, the terms of a Frequent Flyer Programme may have to be more generous during downswing periods, but can be correspondingly less attractive, and less costly, around the peak of the Cycle.

9:3:4 The Future

We have now discussed a range of issues affecting the attractiveness and costs of a Frequent Flyer Programme today. Marketing is, though, a dynamic and changing subject, and this is especially the case with Frequent Flyer schemes. We must now turn to the question of their future.

A first point of debate is whether they have one at all. We have already seen (Section 2:2:4) that the recent years have seen a marked change in the ways in which business travellers bought their seats. Previously, the "Customer" was usually the person who travelled, who had an absolute right to choose the airline with which they flew. Progressively, though, many firms changed their policy, in order to be able to use their bargaining power to gain discounts. More and more business travel is now bought corporately, with the people who fly required to choose airlines on a list of those giving attractive, low, corporate rates to the firm in question.

This change has made executives such as the firm's V-P of Finance or V-P of Purchasing very important, because these are the people who are often given the task of negotiating corporate deals with airlines. As we have seen, as general rule, such people oppose the existence of Frequent Flyer Programmes, because they make the task of enforcing changes in corporate travel policy a more difficult one. It is one thing for a Vice-

President of Purchasing to negotiate a deal with a new airline which has the potential to save their firm a great deal of money. It may be quite another to police the change once it has been made, and ensure that the firm's business travellers book on the new rather than the old, preferred airline. They may be reluctant to do so. They will have built up large mileage balances with the first airline and will wish to continue to fly with it in order to reach the levels of mileage necessary to obtain awards of free tickets. They will also already have elite status in the carrier's FFP, and will want to protect this.

The pressure today from corporate travel purchasers is for Frequent Flyer Programmes to be abolished, and for the resulting cost savings to be translated into still higher levels of corporate discounting. If the programmes must continue, then they would argue that the awards should be made to firms rather than to individuals so that they can be used to offset the costs of future business travel.

A further issue regarding the future of FFPs is that of taxation. Until now, in most tax jurisdictions there has been a reluctance for governments to tax Frequent Flyer awards. This is despite the fact that they are clearly a benefit-in-kind, comparable to company cars, the value of which is now generally heavily taxed.

The reasons for this reluctance are that it would be difficult to place a value on a free ticket, given the complexity of airlines' present-day pricing policies. Also, governments, particularly in the USA, have been wary of upsetting frequent travellers who make up a large and influential group of voters.

A further, but unlikely, threat to the continued existence of FFPs is that they might come to be regarded as an abuse of a dominant position by competition regulators. In principle, Frequent Flyer Programmes do constitute a significant barrier to entry in the aviation industry, in that, as we have seen, the programme of a large airline will be a much more attractive one than that of a small carrier. This has led to the argument that they should not be allowed to continue because they make life much harder for small, new entrant, airlines. Whilst there is still significant truth in this, the fact that, at a cost, small airlines can buy into the programmes of larger carriers through such expedients as franchising has reduced the strength of the argument.

Despite the possible significance of the issues discussed so far, the biggest drivers of the future development of Frequent Flyer Programmes will be the growing concern about their effectiveness in building and cementing customer loyalty, and the growth of the alliance movement between airlines.

We have already discussed Frequent Flyer Programmes in the context of Product Life Cycle theory in Section 5:2:1. Beyond any question, FFPs worked very well in helping airlines to establish loyalty when only a few airlines had them. The situation today, though, is one of a mature and saturated marketplace where all airlines have a programme of comparable attractiveness. Now, FFPs may indeed help carriers in Loyalty Marketing in their home market where they are dominant. Unfortunately, they have made things more difficult in other markets where, in turn, another airline will have the benefit of home-market dominance. It thus becomes a contentious point as to whether or not the aggregate effect on market loyalty is positive or negative. This factor certainly explains why airlines have been so ready to sign up to the 'Earn-and-Burn' elements of FFPs which are such a feature of the agreements drawn up for membership of today's alliances.

Such agreements point to the way in which airlines will view FFPs in the future. It will be acknowledged that, on their own, the marketing benefit they bring will lessen. What they *will* still do – and do to an increasing degree – is allow airlines to capture crucial database information about their customers. It will be the carriers who capture, process and use this data effectively in well-thought-out database marketing campaigns which will gain the real benefit from their investment in FFPs. The subject of database marketing therefore becomes one of crucial importance, and is considered in full in Section 10:3:2.

Airline alliances will be the other factor which will affect the future developments in FFPs. We have already discussed in Section 4:2:6 the way in which during the last ten years the world's airlines have consolidated into three major alliance groupings. These alliances generally had a difficult birth, but it has been said with a great deal of justification that Frequent Flyer Programmes are the glue which has held them together. Progressively, there may possibly be a re-alignment which will see individual airlines abandoning their individual programmes and instead subscribing to a global FFP based on the alliance brand. At the time of writing the co-called Star Alliance led by Lufthansa and United Airlines appears to have moved furthest in this direction whereby each Star Alliance partner recognises both points and status built up on flights with other alliance members. Even this alliance, though, does not yet have a single homogenous programme. The development of such a programme would require the sharing of a great deal of commercially-confidential data, so a deep degree of trust would be an essential pre-requisite if it were ever to go ahead, and airlines would need to be absolutely confident that all the alliances members would stay in it, rather than succumbing to the temptation to leave and join another one.

In summary, the last decade has seen a remarkable change in the philosophy of marketing employed by many airlines. Today, the correct emphasis is on identifying, understanding and meeting the needs of a carrier's most important customers, in such a way that a strong, positive relationship is built and maintained. Airlines that succeed in doing so will reap a worthwhile reward in terms of added value and improved control of their distribution channels.

SUCCESSFUL AIRLINES ......

→   Are those that accept and embrace fully the concepts of Relationship Marketing, and acknowledge that this requires a broad, strategic approach rather than merely the handing out of incentives through a Frequent Flyer Programme.

10 Airline Selling, Advertising and Promotional Policies

We are nearly at the end of our survey of marketing principles and their application to the airline industry, but one crucial step remains for discussion. The subjects addressed so far show how airlines can analyse their markets and their marketing environment, plot a sound strategy, and, following on from this, put in place correct product, branding, pricing and distribution policies. In order to be successful, though, they must convince and persuade potential customers to buy from them rather than from their rivals. The early stages of marketing should certainly make this process easier. It will always be more straightforward to persuade people to buy value-for-money products which will meet well-understood customer needs, rather than those which do not. In no sense, though, is the sales task an easy one, given the levels of competition which now prevail in the industry. A great deal of planning and hard work will be needed, and this Chapter will discuss the necessary skills.

10:1 The Anatomy of a Sale

10:1:1 The AIDA Model and the SPIN Cycle

In order to understand the sales process as a whole, it is essential to look at some of the theoretical principles which underlie selling in any field. We will then apply these principles to the airline industry.

In all selling situations, it will first of all be necessary to identify the prospect and gain their *Attention*. This may be done using methods such as advertising, direct mail or the telephone. Once this has been achieved, a sales can only result if the salesperson is successful in awakening the *Interest* of the prospect.

It might be thought that the best way of arousing interest would be for them to launch into a long description of all the attractive features of their product. This is not so. Successful selling results from every effort being made to find out about the customer's problems and demonstrating the ways in which these problems can be solved.

Problem analysis in turn requires a systematic approach, based on a logical series of questions. The first questions should be so-called *Situation* questions, designed to isolate the prospect's present buying habits. A business traveller might, for example, be asked about the airlines they choose, the routes on which they fly, how often and in which class of service. All of these would be examples of Situation questioning. Next, *Problem* questioning will be needed. These are the questions which are designed to make the prospect think of any areas where the present situation is unsatisfactory. The salesperson might ask about the prospect's experience of the punctuality record of one of the airlines they are choosing, if there is a suspicion that this airline is performing poorly. Hopefully, the prospect will admit that they have been the victim of a number of flight delays. If they do, it will be time to move on to *Implication* questions. These build the significance of the problem in the prospect's mind. In the case of delayed flights, there is an almost limitless number of Implications. These can include cases where the prospect arrived late for an important meeting, or where they had to travel the previous evening – with extra costs in accommodation and time away from office or family – in order to be sure that they arrived at a morning meeting on time. Finally, there will be the requirement to ask so-called *Need/Payoff* questions.[15] These put into the prospect's mind the idea that there might be a solution to their problem. Again, using the delayed flight example, this would be the point at which the salesperson would describe the – hopefully much better – punctuality performance of the airline they are representing.

Once proper questioning about needs has been undertaken, it will be safe to proceed to the point where the salesperson can move from the task of developing interest into that of converting interest into the *Desire* to make the purchase. This will involve presenting the solution to the customer's problem, and then moving on to the benefits of adopting the solution using a 'This Means That …' statement.

Promoting Desire may also involve the handling of Objections. The prospect may, for example, say that they do not believe the salesperson's claims, or that they regard the suggested solution as being too expensive.

Whatever the Objection, it must be handled professionally. The salesperson must ask as many questions as they need to do in order to understand the exact nature of the Objection. They must then make the Objection as specific as they can. It is not possible, for example, to manage an Objection well if the prospect merely says "X is a bad airline" or they don't fly X because the carrier is 'always late' Questioning should establish exactly what experiences have led to the view that the airline is a

---

[15] The SPIN cycle is fully described by its inventor, Neil Rackham in 'SPIN Selling' Gower Press 1995.

poor one, or that its punctuality performance is disappointing. Once this has been done, counterbalancing points can be given which address the precise concerns. These can often take the form of statements as to why the situation has improved since the unsatisfactory incidents took place.

The last stage of the AIDA model follows on from the nurturing of Desire. It is that of *Action*. Despite the importance of the earlier stages of the sale, nothing concrete has been achieved until the prospect has been persuaded to buy the product or service on offer. Salespeople must have the courage to risk rejection and ask for the deal, once the signs are there that the earlier stages of the sale have been completed successfully. These signs can be identified from the body language of the prospect, or by the fact that they start using so-called Verbal Buying Signals – for example, asking about the details of a deal rather than discussing whether the deal should be concluded or not.

In applying the general AIDA model to the specifics of the airline industry, two features stand out. Firstly, airline sales executives do not sell a tangible product in the way that, say, a second-hand car dealer does. Rather, for the greater part of the time, their task is to sell a long-term relationship with customers such as travel agents or corporate travel buyers. Therefore, the signing of an initial deal is always the beginning of the task of building a relationship, rather than the end of a process. Also, airline salespeople generally become involved in long sales campaigns. They can rarely expect to close a deal after merely one visit to the prospect. They therefore need skills in the managing of sales campaigns and in measuring progress through a campaign. This will involve the question of reaching the right decision-makers, something which was discussed in Section 2:2:3.

10:2 Sales Planning

10:2:1 The Sales Budget

Given the challenging and complex nature of the sales task in the airline industry, sound planning will be essential if it is to be accomplished successfully.

Such planning will need to take place at different levels. An overall sales and marketing plan will be needed for the airline as a whole, and preparing this will be the responsibility of the Executive Vice-president for Marketing working with the other senior managers of the company. Amongst the crucial issues that this will settle is the total budget that will be available to underwrite the sales effort.

At a lower level, comparable sales and marketing plans will be needed for each sales region in the airline's network. These will, amongst other things, decide how the overall sales budget should be allocated between the regions, and how each region will spend the available funds. The latter will require decisions on the so-called 'Communications Mix', the ways in which the different forms of marketing communication are brought together to make up, hopefully, an integrated and successful policy.

Any form of budget-setting is likely to involve a difficult and contentious internal debate. Such debate, though, is likely to be especially intense when it involves decisions about the money to be spent on the sales and marketing effort. No-one, presumably, would dispute the point that some cash will be needed to support sales and marketing. The problem is that measuring the return obtained on such spending is notoriously difficult. It also does not produce a tangible result in the way that spending the same money on a fixed asset such an aircraft would. It is therefore important that sales and marketing managers should be able to make the case for the money they need in a persuasive and credible way.

Traditionally, one can find three ways in which this case has been made. Two of these are simple and straightforward, but unfortunately wrong. The third is much more difficult, but is the one most likely to lead to a positive outcome.

Of the incorrect methods, it still happens that budget requests are made using the so-called Percentage of Revenue method. This is where the request is made for a promotional budget based on a fixed percentage of the revenue which the sales and marketing team have achieved in the last year or which they will be expected to produce in the next one.

This concept certainly has the merit of speed and simplicity, but it is fundamentally incorrect. It ties spending to the prevailing market conditions. If the market is buoyant, revenue will rise naturally and promotional spending with it. If market conditions deteriorate, there is a risk that revenues will fall and that promotional spending will therefore follow. The worst possible situation could then result, with a downward spiral of falling revenue leading to a smaller promotional budget which will in turn cause a further loss of revenue.

The promotional budget should actually follow exactly the opposite pattern to the one which will result from the Percentage of Revenue concept. When the market is growing strongly, an airline operating in that market will be able to increase its own revenue in line with the market for only a small promotional spend. When the overall market is stagnant or declining, success for the individual firm can only come by it increasing its share of the market. Growth through increasing market share is notoriously difficult, and will only come about through a determined, and costly, marketing communications effort.

The second common way for a promotional budget to be settled is for it to be based on what was agreed for the previous year with an adjustment for inflation. Whilst such an approach may be inevitable in the real world of corporate politics, it results in the promotional budget being at roughly the same level year after year without the necessary questions ever being asked as to whether it is correctly pitched or not.

This last point leads us on to the correct way to set a promotional budget, which is known as the Task-Based Method. Under this, the budget is set by first asking and then answering a series of questions about the money which will be needed if the target revenue and profit for the year is to be achieved. Whilst there can be no precise answer to these questions, the fact that they are asked at all means that a sound approach to sales budgeting is more likely.

Of these questions, the first has already been mentioned, but its influence on decision-making should be the reverse of that implied by the Percentage of Revenue concept. If a market is stagnant or declining this is an indicator that higher promotional spending will be needed.

It will also be necessary to take account of the spending of the airline's competitors. Whilst in principle it may not be necessary to exactly match the budget of a high-spending rival, there will at least need to be a reasonable relationship with the expenditure of others. If there isn't, the airline's efforts will simply be swamped.

The problem, of course, in the airline industry is that airlines have to compete both in their home market, where they should be dominant, and at the other end of the routes they fly, where the home airline is likely to be in a similarly strong position. Therefore, it is often the case that in overseas markets even airlines with a large promotional spend are being heavily out-spent. They therefore have a particular need to ensure that every dollar they have is made to work as hard as possible.

Besides the question of the promotional spending of competitors, the number and quality of these competitors will be of obvious importance. A carrier fortunate to have only a small number of poor quality competitors in a particular market should not spend a great deal on persuading people to fly with it who will do so anyway. Instead, the money should be used in other, difficult markets or kept for the time when conditions become more challenging.

The nature of the marketing task in any particular year will also need to be considered. It may be a year in which new routes are to be launched, or when a major product upgrade is to take place. If it is, substantial extra cash will be needed to ensure that these new developments are explained and promoted to actual and potential customers.

A further, important question will be that of brand positioning. As was discussed in Section 8:3, airlines sometimes attempt a fundamental repositioning of their brand. As we saw then, a case in point was the Canadian carrier Wardair which attempted – unsuccessfully – to change from being a leisure travel airline to one with a substantial presence in the business travel market. Something as ambitious as this will only stand any chance of being successful if it is underwritten by a substantial promotional budget.

Other airlines may not be attempting a major brand repositioning. They do, though, need to strengthen their brand. They may, for example, have carried out attitude studies which show that the airline is perceived in a poor light by potential customers in terms of such crucial issues as punctuality and customer service. If they have, some honest assessment of the situation will be required. It could be that these attitudes are a legacy of a time when the carrier thoroughly deserved a poor reputation, with today's situation much better. If they are, then investment in marketing communications will be justified because this can be used to persuade customers to give the airline another chance and to experience today's improved product standards. If, on the other hand, today's standards are as bad as ever, it is a delusion to think that marketing communications expenditure can rescue the situation. It will probably make things worse. There will be a temptation to embark on a communications campaign aimed at getting people to try the airline again. When they do, and find that things are the same, they will feel betrayed and tricked by the messages that have been put out to them. In such a situation, any available funds should be spent on addressing the product and service weaknesses which are at the heart of its problems, with investment in marketing communications a much lower priority. Whatever is spent should be focussed on making non-controversial, factual claims about such aspects as network and flight timings, rather than on the making of false claims about an improving product.

A final and inevitable factor will be the cost of the different forms of marketing communication. Generally, media buying costs have risen in recent years. In the future they may fall as the advent of, in particular, digital television increases competition in attracting advertising and promotional spend. The problem then will be that the fragmentation of the different media will make it harder and harder to reach a target audience effectively – indeed this is already the case. Overall, it is likely that the cost of marketing communications will rise at least as fast as the rate of inflation, and any bid for a promotional budget should reflect this.

10:2:2 The 'Communications Mix' [16]

Once a budget has been obtained, the airline marketing manager's task is to decide how to spend the budget in the most effective way. In doing so, they have a clear problem: the number of ways in which money can be spent is now a bewildering one. Choosing between them will therefore require a great deal of thought and analysis. It is possible to spend money on sponsorships, database marketing, media relations, trade entertaining, on various forms of advertising (including through the Internet) and through personal selling through investment in a field sales team.

Each of these will have different advantages and disadvantages. Our next task is to discuss them in turn, and also to consider the ways in which each technique should be used to ensure that it provides the best value-for-money. Once we have done so, it will become clearer as to how the different methods can be combined into an optimum Communications Mix.

10:3 Marketing Communication Techniques

10:3:1 Sponsorship Policy

The term 'Sponsorship' is used to describe a situation whereby a firm has its name associated with an event, a team or a competitor, in exchange for money.

In recent years, sponsorships have become increasingly important in marketing communication generally. They have certainly done so in the airline industry. It is not difficult to see why. A successful sponsorship can result in a firm's name becoming widely known, very quickly. This can be especially valuable for a new airline, or for an established operator opening a new route into a market area where it has had no previous presence. Sponsorships can also help in building and reinforcing brand values. They can provide useful opportunities for corporate hospitality and trade entertaining. They can sometimes produce directly increments of new business, especially if an airline is nominated as the 'Official Carrier' for an event, as part of a deal to sponsor it. Lastly, they address problems associated with the fragmentation of media advertising opportunities which multi-channel broadcasting has caused.

Despite these advantages, the question of sponsorship remains a

---

[16] For more detailed coverage see P R Smith, J Taylor, "Marketing Communications: An Integrated Approach", Third Edition, Kogan Page 2003 and C.Fill 'Marketing Communications' 4th Edn 2005 Prentice Hall

controversial one. It is notoriously difficult to measure and quantify the benefits obtained from sponsorships, and the suspicion will therefore always remain that a great deal of the resources put into them are wasted. This is an especially serious point because airlines everywhere find that they are inundated with sponsorship requests. Many carriers are identified as national representatives, and many people in the countries where they are based see sponsorship activities as the airline's patriotic duty. Also, there is a perception that air tickets are available to airlines free-of-charge, and that giving away tickets in a barter deal associated with a sponsorship costs them nothing. The problem here is that when a carrier agrees to a sponsorship in return for free tickets, they have fewer seats left to sell to revenue passengers. They must accept that there will be a significant cost associated with a free ticket, if this results in a potential revenue passenger being denied a seat on the flight of their choice, and such tickets must therefore be seen as a form of currency. Only if such tickets are truly offered on a subject-to-load basis can they be seen as having a negligible cost.

There are a number of rules which must be followed to ensure a successful use of sponsorship. Crucial amongst these is that the airline must decide what are the values which underlie its brand, and must only undertake sponsorships which reinforce them.

For all airlines, the cornerstone of their brand is safety. The sponsorship rule which flows from this is absolutely clear. No airline should have anything to do with any event which is dangerous. The risks of a catastrophic accident giving as association between the airline's name and danger and death is simply not worth taking. It is remarkable how many airlines have ignored this fundamental rule in recent years with, for example both Air Canada and Qantas sponsoring Formula One motor racing and Emirates having its name associated with power-boating.

For many airlines, a reputation for quality is also crucial to their brand development. They should not, therefore, sponsor downmarket events with a poor public image. They have to be very careful, too, to be perceived as a 'Winner'. This will help them in turn to penetrate the business travel market where people who are themselves successful will want to be seen to be travelling with the airline which is a market leader. It might be thought that the best way to be seen as a winner would be to get involved in sports sponsorship and to pick competitors and teams that do well – ideally to pick those that win the events in question. Whilst this is undoubtedly true in principle, it is also extremely risky. It may not matter a great deal if the selected teams or competitors do not win, but still perform well. It will certainly matter if they are humiliated. A more cautious, but much safer option is therefore to sponsor an entire event, rather than one of the individuals or teams in that event, and this is normally the policy which should be adopted.

A final, but important value underlying all airline brands is that of caring. Carriers should not get involved in any activities which have an adverse effect on the environment. They should at the same time be especially attracted by activities which are associated with charities and other good causes.

Once a decision has been made in principle as to the activities with which the airlines wishes to be associated, steps must be taken to ensure that the maximum value-for-money is obtained from them. Here, it is first of all important that the airline should if possible be the sole sponsor – certainly no other airlines should be involved. Too many sponsors can result in the identity of each individual firm being lost. Also, the event should be one where substantial media exposure can be guaranteed, exposure in which the sponsor's name will feature prominently.

In terms of assessing whether or not a sponsorship provides value-for-money, its likely full costs should be should be quantified. This costing must include items such as any client hospitality provided, and any promotional back-up offered through special giveaways etc. Then, at least for a major sponsorship, research should be commissioned, related to its objectives. If the principal objective is to raise awareness, the research task will be an easy one. A study will be needed in the relevant market area of awareness levels before and after the sponsorship, with, hopefully, a significant positive change being the result. Where the objective is to improve the image and perception of the airline, the required research will be more complex and will almost certainly involve a quantitative study, and also some qualitative, focus group-based, research.

10:3:2 Database Marketing [17]

Like sponsorship, Database Marketing has been increasing quickly in importance in airline marketing communication. In Section 9:3, we discussed the role of Frequent Flyer Programmes in enabling airlines to produce effective databases. Today, storing and processing database information is cheaper than it has ever been. At the same time, carriers are seeking to make better contact with their retail customers as a component of their strategy to secure greater control of their distribution channels and they have seen database marketing as a way of doing so. The subject

---

[17] For further discussion of the principles of database marketing see G M McCorkell, "Direct and Database Marketing", Kogan Page 1997 and D Bird "Commonsense Director Marketing" 4th Edition, Kogan Page 2000.

remains, though, controversial and in this section we have to look at both the advantages and disadvantages which Database Marketing brings, and the decisions which will have to be made to ensure that it brings the best possible results.

With advantages, beyond question the main one is that, if it is properly applied, database marketing will allow for finer market segmentations and better targeting of marketing messages, in a way that media advertising, for example, cannot. We have now moved away from a proposition that airlines' markets can be divided into just 'business' and 'leisure' travellers. In business travel, customers can be divided up by the routes they fly and the class of service which they (or their employer) choose. A tactical advertisement announcing, say, an increase in frequency on a particular route will be seen by many people who never fly that route. One which describes a re-launch of Business Class will be seen by many people – and may irritate them – who are forced to travel in Economy and who will merely learn what they are missing. Database marketing should avoid this problem.

In leisure air travel, there is an increasing need to recognise discreet market segments, especially amongst discerning, up-market travellers. People vary, for example, in their stage-of-life and personal circumstances. Travel needs will also be distinctly different for families with young children compared with couples or singles. Preference may vary according to age. Also, hobbies and interests form an increasingly useful basis for market segmentation. People who travel, for example, for winter sports, golf, fishing etc all form distinct and potentially valuable market segments.

Database Marketing allows for fine segmentations, and permits messages to be prepared and communicated which demonstrate an airline's ability to meet a precise set of needs. Traditional media advertising cannot offer the same opportunities.

Other features of Database Marketing are that it permits tactical messages to be communicated quickly, and only to those people that the airline wishes to tell. Buying advertising space may involve delay if the space has to be booked in advance. It will also mean that offers of, say, discounted fares become generally known, rather than knowledge of them being confined to those people whom it is in the airline's interest to approach.

Despite these very significant advantages, the use of database marketing in the airline industry remains controversial. If the selected medium for using a database is the telephone, many people still regard an unsolicited telephone call as an invasion of their privacy. The same may apply to a mailshot, fax or Email, albeit to a somewhat lesser degree. With these latter media, though, the problem is one of over-use. The modern executive's in-tray or in-box is awash with database marketing communications. Many of these will be ignored and thrown straight into the waste paper bin or deleted. Only the most professional of messages will be seen and acted upon.

A further, important point with Database Marketing is that it must be viewed as an expensive form of marketing communication. The costs of a database marketing campaign might at first appear to be small in comparison with one based on, say, media advertising. The relevant cost, though, is not the total cost but a unit cost measure expressed in Cost-per-Thousand terms. Using such measures, database marketing can be a high-cost solution.

Putting all these points together, the conclusion is clear. Database marketing campaigns must be executed with the utmost professionalism. If they aren't, the only result will be a costly waste of time and money.

To achieve such professionalism, there are a number of rules which must be followed:

Responsibilities and Timescales
Successful Database Marketing requires a proper definition of objectives and a sound action plan is which is properly formulated and communicated. This should be made the responsibility of one individual.

"Integration"
Database Marketing should never be implemented on its own, without proper consideration being given to its integration into the firm's wider marketing communication activities. At a narrow level, this may mean a simple, but very necessary co-ordination between the breaking of a media advertising campaign, and the sending out of a mailshot based on it. More broadly, though, it will be necessary to ensure that no contradictory messages are sent out. An airline seeking to position itself as a premium brand, aiming mainly at the business air traveller, should not put out advertising targeted at that market segment whilst at the same time sending out mailing material of poor quality emphasising the wide availability of cheap fares.

Databases
Sound information in a convenient-to-use form is absolutely essential for successful Database Marketing. A great deal of attention may be devoted to the production of attractive mailing material, but if this material is then sent to the wrong people, a campaign based on it has no chance of success. Indeed, poor material sent to exactly the right people will achieve more.

In some senses, database management is now less of a problem that it once was, because computing power and the relevant software is now cheap and widely understood. However, problems associated with obtaining the necessary data and processing it are increasing through time rather than easing.

In searching out database information, some fundamental divisions of the data can be made. Firstly, it will be necessary to obtain *demographic* details about the target audience for a campaign. This will obviously include names, addresses and titles. It is important that names should be correctly spelt and titles accurate. If a job title is to be used, this should reflect a person's status with the organisation they work for.

A further requirement with demographic data is that it should be de-duplicated. It might be thought that duplicates in a database are a minor problem, resulting in a small increase in mailing costs as the same communication is sent to one recipient twice. Duplicates are much more serious than this, because they give the impression that the company sending out the mailing is incompetent and inefficient. Few people will buy from a firm when this is their perception of it. Fortunately, modern database management software generally includes a de-duplication package and the use of this can eliminate many of the problems.

In seeking out demographic information, by far the best sources are those based on situations where people volunteer to be included in a database. Besides addressing to a large degree invasion of privacy issues, cases where people offer their names voluntarily are generally much easier to deal with under the terms of the relevant data protection laws in different countries.

Of potential sources of database information, attention has already been drawn in Section 9:3 to the value of a Frequent Flyer Programme. People can be asked when joining a programme to provide all necessary information about themselves. They will then keep this information up-to-date for all the time that they are a programme member, because they will be anxious to ensure that their mileage statements and free tickets are sent to the right address.

Another possible source of database information is to invite people to join a travel club. As we have already seen, the leisure travel market is changing, with significant numbers of people now searching for individually-tailored holidays, often centred around their hobbies and interests. They are also prepared to spend regularly and heavily to obtain these holidays. This development gives a classic opportunity for database marketing, and it may well be worthwhile to form a club which will enable database information to be collected and regular communication to be maintained with members.

A final opportunity to obtain database information which people have volunteered comes with the question of low fares offers. Many airlines invite people to volunteer their Email addresses. Once they have done so, they are regularly sent information about flights where there are substantial numbers of empty seats and where the airline is able to offer them particularly attractive low prices.

Despite the attractions of databases for which people have volunteered, it will often be necessary to go beyond them. In particular, "volunteer" databases can only include people who currently fly with the airline concerned, or who at least are reasonably well-disposed towards it. They do not give opportunities for increasing market share by enabling people to be reached who are currently flying with other carriers.

Where the aim is to reach a competitor's customers, it will generally be necessary to buy in lists. Today, these lists are often based on geographical principles, with addresses being obtained from the Electoral Register and classified according to the neighbourhoods in which people live. The proposition is that people who live near to one another will have income levels and spending patterns that are to a significant degree similar. The problem with these lists is that they go out-of-date very quickly. The Electoral Register is only up-dated once a year, and by the time the information is in a form ready to be used in database marketing campaigns it may no longer be accurate enough.

Much the same applies to magazine circulation lists and trade directories as sources of database information. In principle, these can be useful in business-travel orientated campaigns. Databases founded on them may, though, go out-of-date quickly, particularly those derived from lists for free-circulation trade papers.

Once the necessary demographic data has been obtained, this must then be combined with the relevant activity data. Airlines need to know where people fly, in what class of service and how often. They need also to be able to capture this data, and marry it to the demographic information they are carrying in their databases. Only then can they produce effectively-targeted marketing campaigns.

A final requirement in database management is that the database should be properly integrated with an airline's Customer Relations activities. We have already seen in section 9:2:3 that someone who complains, with a justified grievance, provides carriers with an important opportunity. If the complaint is dealt with well, it can result in a strengthening, rather than a weakening of the relationship between that person and the airline. Having said this, it will be particularly annoying if someone complains, for example, about a delayed flight and then receives a mailshot shortly afterwards in which the airline boasts of its fine punctuality performance. They should not do so, if there is a proper integration between the marketing and customer relations databases. Indeed, if there is, this may result in an important opportunity because someone who complains will also at the same time be providing information about themselves. If their complaint is handled sympathetically, they will then be well-disposed towards the airline in question and may respond to future database marketing messages. Therefore, those who complain and express satisfaction at the way in which their complaint has been dealt with should be added to the airline's marketing database.

Copywriting[18]

The subject of copywriting for Database Marketing remains extremely controversial. What is certainly true is that the investment made in building and maintaining a database can be leveraged substantially if is used well through the production of good material.

With decisions about copywriting, the first requirement is clearly that a statement should be made as to the objectives which a particular campaign should meet. These objectives can vary substantially. It may be that the intention is simply to give information to an airline's existing customers on a particular route about, say, a change in flight timings. Another possible objective is that the campaign should encourage these existing customers to fly more through, for example, the offer of bonus Frequent Flyer miles or a move to a higher status in the airline's loyalty programme. A third, and much the most challenging, possible objective is that the campaign should be targeted at people who are currently flying with other airlines, with the objective being to change their choice-of-carrier decision.

Alongside decisions about objectives, a choice will have to be made about the medium to be employed. A first possibility is that the database will be used for a telemarketing campaign, in which case the copywriter's task will be to help to prepare the script which those working the telephones will use. This will have the benefit of immediate impact, but as previously mentioned may be resented by those who are called. Secondly, the mail may be used. This will allow for the preparation of attractive mailing material but, as we have already seen, this material may be put into the waste paper bin without even being opened. Email provides a different choice, but it may be difficult to obtain a suitable database of Email addresses and emails are easily deleted without being read. Spam filters will also stop the delivery of a proportion of messages.

For the remainder of this section, we will mainly assume that the mail

---

[18]   Copywriting in database marketing is further analysed in J. Watson. "Successful Creativity in Direct Marketing". Institute of Direct Marketing. 1993.

is the selected medium, as this is the one which provides especial challenges in copywriting.

With decisions made about objectives and medium, the copywriting process can begin. It should follow a series of easy-to-state, but difficult to apply, principles. The first of these follows the AIDA model already mentioned in Section 10:1:1. All material should aim to catch people's attention through a bold headline promising them a worthwhile benefit . It should interest them in the proposition to be made through showing an understanding of their problems. A solution should be presented in a persuasive and credible way, with every effort being made to anticipate possible objections and to deal with these. Finally, a course of action should be proposed, with clear information being presented as to how to follow this.

In using the AIDA model, there is a never-ending debate over the length of copy that should be employed. It is certainly the case that people are becoming busier and busier, and that their willingness to read long copy is lessening all the time. Because of this, communications which are designed simply to impart information should certainly be kept short and to-the-point. It is less clear, though, as to whether or not a 'short-is-best' conclusion will always be appropriate where the objective of a campaign is to radically change people's buying behaviour.

Here, it should be born in mind that any database, no matter how well prepared, will consist of two groups of people. The first are those who should not, in fact, be on it at all because they have no interest in the propositions being made and will never buy the products or services in question. In history, there has been no example of a perfectly-targeted database. The second group of people are those who do potentially have such an interest.

In copywriting for Database Marketing, no time should be spent worrying over the fact that mailing material has not been read by people who will never buy the product anyway. The tragedy of the campaign will be if people with a genuine potential interest cannot be persuaded to act upon this and buy the product.

For these people, it is unlikely that a major change in their buying behaviour will be achieved by short copy. They have to be thoroughly convinced that the firm seeking their business has an understanding of their problems, and that it can solve these problems better than the existing firms from which they are currently buying. It is most unlikely that they will be so convinced by a few words.

If long copy needs to be employed – and there will be cases where it is essential – the style adopted can go a long way to ensuring that resistance to reading it is overcome. Short sentences and paragraphs will be needed, broken up by frequent sub-headings. It will also be necessary to talk in plain, rather than flowery, language. "Correctly co-ordinated schedule" may put people off reading further whereas "right timings" will not.

A particularly useful tactic may be to employ a P.S. at the end of a letter. If this is well written, it can deal with any dissonance people may feel about carrying out the actions proposed in the main body of the letter. It may also be the first thing that they see when looking at a letter and may persuade them to go back and read the earlier body-copy.

In terms of the style and quality of the material to be sent out, this should reflect the objectives of the campaign. An airline re-launching its Business Class service and seeking to persuade potential passengers that the new product is of the highest possible quality, will be unlikely to do so by the use of cheap and shoddy mailing material. On the other hand, a mailing may have the purely tactical purpose of informing customers about a forthcoming fares increase. If it has, it would be a mistake to dress up such a mailing with extravagant expenditure on high quality production.

A final, very important rule with copywriting is that, wherever possible, it should be made interactive. Effective campaigns are generally based on encouraging potential customers to respond to an attractive offer. This might be in order to obtain a free giveaway or to participate in a prize draw for free tickets or bonus Frequent Flyer miles. Making an offer may overcome people's dislike of the 'invasion of privacy' aspect of database marketing. It may also be a means of obtaining from them further, useful, database information about their travel patterns and service preferences.

"Gatekeeping"

Today, in most countries, the post is reasonably reliable and the services which back up fax and Email mostly very efficient. It is therefore possible to ensure that a database marketing message reaches the home or the office of the target recipient. This, though, is the beginning and not the end of the task, because it will be an altogether bigger challenge to ensure that a marketing message is read and acted upon. Many people will simply throw away what they perceive to be 'Junk Mail' into the waste paper basket without even bothering to open it, whilst in the office situation, a secretary may be told to throw away any direct mail items without even putting them into their boss's in-tray. There is an active debate in the literature on direct mail as to how it is possible to ensure that an envelope will be opened and the contents read.

In addressing the problem, there are two possible approaches. One is to employ subterfuge. In extreme form, this consists of writing 'Private and Confidential' on the outside of an envelope. This should at least ensure that the envelope is placed in the relevant in-tray. A similar approach, though less extreme, is to make a direct mailshot look exactly like an ordinary business letter. This at least ensures that the letter will be opened as the receiver will hope that there will be an important business communication inside or, better still, a cheque.

As a general rule, deceit can be rejected as a way of getting envelopes opened. It is true that both these methods will succeed in a narrow sense, but they will fail to assist in getting the recipient to act on what they find inside the envelope once they have opened it. They will realise that they have been tricked – the so-called "Betrayal Factor" – and because they have been, they are unlikely to respond in a positive way. Similar issues arise with the question of giving emails a 'clever' title in the hope that this means that they will be opened rather than deleted.

The second approach to addressing Gatekeeping problems is much to be preferred. This consists of putting a message on the outside of the envelope saying to the recipient that there is a very good reason for them to open it and, if they do, they will be pleased with the offer contained inside. Preparing such a message should be easy. After all, if there is nothing inside the envelope which will make someone pleased they have opened it, why is it being sent in the first place ?

10:3:3 Media Relations

It is impossible to over-estimate the importance of a sound approach to Media Relations in airline marketing communication. Air transport is regarded as immensely newsworthy by editors of newspapers, magazines and television and radio programmes. Because of this, an airline which fails to cultivate strong Media Relations can suffer a great deal of bad publicity when things go wrong. One which does will not only head off this kind of trouble. It will also be well-placed to obtain favourable coverage when positive things happen such as new route introductions or product and brand re-launches.

Sound media relationships require in turn a systematic approach to achieve them. Every effort must be made to foster the goodwill of journalists through trade entertainment and the offer of free travel on the airline's network. At the same time, helpful background information must be produced. This will include well-written press material, containing quotes from the airline's most senior management.

Poor Media Relations will result from any attempt to treat journalists with contempt – a sometimes-understandable emotion which must be firmly resisted. Cover-ups should also be avoided. If, for example, an airline has an emergency landing of one of its aircraft, nothing will be achieved by denying that such an incident has occurred. Instead, emphasis should be placed on the skill with which the airline's staff handled the situation, and the fact that the carrier has been able to maintain its strong safety record.

10:3:4 The Field Sales Team

Of all aspects of airline selling and sales planning, none generates greater controversy than the question of the management of the airline field sales team. Disagreements occur over the role that field sales executives should play and the recruitment and motivation policies which should be employed. The purpose of this section is to address these issues.

The Role

Until relatively recently, the role of an airline field sales executive was a straightforward one. The fact that competition in the industry was highly regulated meant that the pace of change was slow. Regulation also meant that all airlines charged the same fares. There was therefore no need for sales executives to seek out customers and negotiate deals with them. Instead, the job was essentially a flag-waving one, with a heavy emphasis on trade entertainment and hospitality and – in many markets – on the consumption of large quantities of alcohol.

Today, the situation could not be more different. As deregulation has come about, so the pace of change in the industry has accelerated. In turn, sales executives now have to accept the challenge of keeping their knowledge up-to-date in a rapidly-changing marketplace. They also have to collect – and communicate to those who need to know – market intelligence data about the activities of competitors. Crucially, they have to negotiate deals with the business houses and travel agencies for which they are responsible. As was discussed in Section 2:2:4, the nature of marketing to the business air traveller has changed fundamentally over the last ten years. Instead of the 'Customer' being business travellers themselves, increasingly firms have sought to use their bargaining power to negotiate deals with airlines whereby discounts were demanded in return for loyalty. Negotiation of these deals is today a normal part of the work of the airline field sales executive. Likewise, today travel agents remain important customers of airlines. Because of the urgent need for cost control, many airlines are requiring their field sales executives to retain the support of agents whilst ensuring that commissions are reduced or eliminated. The field sales executive will be expected to negotiate deals with them, and to monitor their performance, in the most difficult of circumstances.

Besides important market intelligence and sales negotiation roles, the airline field sales executive is today expected to carry out an important customer relations role. One of the challenges of their job is that they are not selling a tangible product. Rather, they have to sell a long-term relationship with a relatively small number of demanding clients. They can only do so if they work hard to support their clients in the jobs that they in turn have to do. Today, the supply of information is not usually the problem, in that modern Global Distribution Systems such as Galileo, SABRE and Amadeus make available almost limitless quantities of information about schedules and fares as do airline websites and the sites of on-line travel agents and search engines. Rather, the challenge is to use this information in a creative and imaginative way to build sales, and the sales executive must be prepared to work with their travel agency accounts in particular to ensure that this is done.

Recruitment Criteria

It is clear from the above that the airline sales executive is now required to do a professional selling job. The question of recruiting the right person is a crucial one which all airline sales managers will have to address from time-to-time.

There are, of course, a number of basic requirements. The person selected must be articulate and persuasive, something which can be tested at an interview. A person who cannot convince an interviewing panel that the firm should take them on is unlikely to be able to persuade a travel agency to increase its sale of the airline's tickets. They should also be of a clean and tidy appearance, as scruffiness will be taken by clients as a sign of a cheapskate company. A current clean driving licence will also be needed.

A much more contentious question is the previous experience that should be required. Carriers have a number of possible recruitment sources for their field sales executives. They can aim to hire people with a proven selling track record, even it this has been obtained from outside the aviation industry. They can simply approach experienced airline sales executives who are currently working for other airlines. They can recruit from the travel agency industry or from those who work in corporate travel departments. Lastly, they can transfer people who already work for them, but in non-sales jobs.

Hiring people from other industries is an especially interesting option. It can certainly be argued that true salespeople are born and not made, and that the great sales success stories have often been achieved by insecure people who are driven to sell as they seek reassurance that they are likeable. In that sense, someone who has a proven selling track record is saying a great deal about themselves, despite their lack of airline industry experience. Even here, it can certainly be argued that, generally, airlines are likely to be better at training people in airline industry familiarisation rather than in the skills of selling.

Despite this, the issue is not a clear-cut one. The problem is that, for reasons which will be discussed in the next section, airlines do not generally reward their sales people on a basic-plus-commission principle. Instead, a reasonable salary is paid, together with perhaps a relatively small bonus if the annual target is reached. This therefore begs the question as to why someone who has achieved success in commission-based selling should want to come and work for an airline, where they certainly will not starve but neither will they have an opportunity to achieve very high earnings. The answer often is that they are burnt out and are looking for an easier life with a steady monthly salary. If they are, they should be rejected out-of-hand.

Hiring – or rather, poaching – fully trained and experienced sales executives from other airlines might seem in many ways to be the ideal solution. These people will have industry knowledge and – hopefully – proven selling skills. They will also have established industry contacts and perhaps will bring some useful inside information about a competitor.

In many situations, airline will have little choice but to use this recruitment source as they will not have the training budget available to spend on appropriate staff development. This will be especially the case for small airlines, or at the minor stations of larger carriers. The dangers of poaching, should, though, be emphasised. Someone who brings market intelligence with them may be disloyal enough to move in a year or two's time, giving away in turn the trade secrets of the airline they have joined. Also, people who move from one airline to another in quick succession begin to lack credibility with their trade contacts, especially if the different carriers they work for are also competitors.

The travel agency industry may give some attractive recruitment opportunities. People with work experience as travel agents should have a good understanding of the travel business. They will also have seen airline sales executives at work, and will know of examples of the job being done badly.

With a final possible recruitment source, the airline's own staff should be looked at seriously. There will almost certainly be people who are doing other customer contact jobs who have the qualities which will be needed to do well as a field sales executive. They will already have a knowledge of the airline, and can be expected to bring a greater degree of loyalty and commitment compared with those brought in from outside.

The ideal age for an airline sales executive is a final, interesting recruitment issue. The person hired has the difficult task of ensuring that they get on well with the young people who generally make up the clerks who work in travel agencies, whilst at the same time being able to present themselves as credible company negotiators with senior management both in travel agents and business houses. Because of the negotiation role, there is probably a minimum age of early to middle twenties – few people will warm to the idea of being asked to complete a deal with a child. At the same time, an older person applying for a job as a junior sales executive should be viewed carefully. They may have many qualities which will make them exactly right for the job, but one's concern would be that they lack ambition and are simply looking for an easy ride towards a well-deserved retirement.

Motivation of Airline Field Sales Executives

This is a very difficult question. In many industries money is used as the prime motivator for a sales team. Members of the team are paid a small retainer, and then a substantial commission on everything they sell. Generally, airlines have found a basic-plus-commission reward structure difficult to devise and implement. Airline salespeople are not selling a specific product to a clearly identifiable customer in the way that, say, someone selling double-glazing is. Rather their task is to build a long-term relationship with a group of clients, and, in the case of relationships with travel agents, to encourage the agent to sell rather than doing the selling themselves. Also, there are complications in deciding who has been responsible for a sale being achieved. A common situation is for a business house to use a travel agent, but for different members of the airline sales team to be responsible for the relationship with the business house and the travel agent. If this is the case, both will claim any commission that might be available. The person responsible of the business house will argue that they have done all the persuading, with the travel agent being simply presented with a fait accompli with regard to choice-of-airline decisions. The person calling on the travel agent is unlikely to see things in the same way.

The difficulties associated with commission-based reward structures mean that few airlines are able to use them. Instead, salespeople are generally paid a reasonable salary, with a relatively small bonus on offer if they reach their annual sales target. In turn, because of this, a wide range of policies will be necessary to ensure the a high level of motivation in the members of the sales team, because the cutting-edge that commissions might provide will not be available to the sales manager.

Of these motivation methods, the annual salary on offer will be an obvious starting point. Here, it is important that the salary should be comparable to that paid to salespeople working for rival airlines. It is very de-motivating to realise that others are being paid more for doing exactly the same job. The annual bonus should also be a worthwhile one, with the salesperson involved in the setting of the targets which must be achieved in order to earn it.

Training will be an important part of the motivation process. The point was made in the last section that airline salespeople are now expected to take on a challenging, professional selling role. They cannot do so successfully unless are equipped with the necessary knowledge and skills. Training must therefore encompass both product knowledge and selling skills, and it must be on a continuous basis given the pace of change which is now characteristic of the industry.

Career progression and advancement will also be an important factor in maintaining the interest and commitment of the most capable people. Providing a clear way ahead may be difficult or impossible for a small airline, or at an outstation of a major carrier. In other situations though, members of the team must feel that if they perform well the necessary training and development policies are in place to allow them to advance to sales management positions.

Questions of expenses and corporate hospitality are often a festering sore in many sales teams. What is important is that salespeople should be able to give their clients a comparable level of hospitality to that on offer from their competitors. It is de-motivating if only the basics can be given when rivals can offer generous treatment.

A very important general heading with sales force motivation is that of the tools to do the job. If a firm has high expectations, it should be prepared equally to invest heavily in resources. For airline salespeople, these resources will include a modern, reliable car and a management information system which allows them to be fully up-to-date both with what is going on within the airline and what business is being obtained from the accounts for which they are responsible. A final requirement is for there to be an adequate level of office back-up and support, with meeting rooms available when necessary.

The last, but perhaps the most contentious question in a motivation policy is the part to be played by fear. It is most certainly true that an element of fear must always be present. If the members of a sales team know that however poorly they perform and however lazy they are they will always have a job, it will be almost certainly impossible to obtain high levels of performance from them. At the same time, though, the role of fear should not be overdone, and it should not be seen as a substitute for other motivational methods. It may from time-to-time be necessary to fire people for laziness or dishonesty, but dismissing people for incompetence raises questions about who is incompetent and who therefore should be fired. A person who is dismissed because they cannot do the job may have been wrong for that job in the first place. In that case they should not have been hired and the incompetent person is the one who did the hiring. A second, still worse possibility is that they did have the potential to make a success of the difficult job of being an airline sales executive, but the manager responsible for them could not provide an environment in which they could give of their best. The necessary skills and qualities are relatively rare, and for an airline to lose someone with potential in these circumstances should be seen as a case of criminal negligence. It is their manager, and not them, who should be fired.

10:4 Airline Advertising

Advertising is, of course, no more than another marketing communication method available to airlines. It is, though, so important, and so controversial, that it needs a special section of its own. The purpose of this part of the book is to look at what advertising can and cannot do for airlines, and to discuss the decisions which have to be made in preparing and implementing an advertising policy.

10:4:1 The Functions of Advertising

No advertising campaign will be successful unless clear objectives are set for it, and the performance of the campaign monitored against these objectives. In turn, it is necessary to decide what advertising can and cannot do, so that any objectives which are set are achievable ones.

Clearly, advertising can be expected to promote corporate image and corporate brand values. It will also play a role in building sub-brands such as those which airlines have built around cabin classes or service concepts. With shorter-term objectives, advertising can be used to provide tactical information about service changes such as the introduction of a new route or a new type of aircraft. It can also sell special offers such as those associated with discount fares or bonus Frequent Flyer miles.

More controversially, airlines may see advertising as a way of influencing policy-makers and opinion formers so that their policy objectives are achieved. No carrier can operate independently of the political process. They may rely on this process for favourable treatment with regard, for example, to the award of international route rights. Increasingly, too, they are having to lobby over environmental questions of noise and pollution in order to ensure that limitations on their freedom-of-action are kept to a minimum. Advertising may be able to play a subtle but useful role in positioning an airline as a good corporate citizen.

A final function of advertising which some would claim and many dispute is that advertising can help in a staff motivation policy. Motivating customer contact staff to give outstanding service is a notoriously difficult task, especially in large mature airlines. The fact that staff members see their airline advertising in newspapers or on the television may help them to feel part of a team. If in these advertisements they see role models providing warm and friendly service to customers, this may in turn subtly affect their behaviour when dealing with customers in real life. Unfortunately, this theory only works in situations where motivation is already high and service standards already good. Where morale is poor, using advertising as a form of brainwashing will only make matters worse, with the added problem that the airline's customers will see claims being made in the advertising which their experience of the product will not match. This will add significantly to their anger and disenchantment.

10:4:2 Advertising Decisions

Setting the Brief

All good advertising campaigns start with a clear decision about what the campaign should achieve. This in turn can only be decided in the context of an overall marketing communications policy, with a proper integration of any advertising which is undertaken with other forms of communication such as sponsorships or Database Marketing.

The brief itself should be as detailed as possible, and should include a statement of the objectives that a campaign should meet and the criteria which will be employed to decide whether it has succeeded or failed. It is also important that the brief should be agreed and signed by the airline's most senior management at the earliest possible stage. It is a peculiar, but vitally important feature of advertising that everyone regards themselves as an expert about it, especially CEO's. In practice, no campaign will be implemented without the Chief Executive's approval, and it is always a costly disappointment if a great deal of work is done, only for the resulting advertising to be vetoed shortly before it is launched. Such occurrences can never be prevented entirely, but their frequency can be minimised by ensuring that the Chief Executive at least agrees with the brief before work begins.

Agency Selection

Choosing an advertising agency is a very important decision, where mistakes will prove very costly.

As a first point, advertising should be recognised as a professional discipline where outside help from a specialist agency will be needed.

Some low fares airlines have in recent years attempted to produce their own advertising as a cost-saving measure, but the results have generally looked very amateurish. Also, even for cost-saving, the policy is of doubtful value, because agencies will be paid commission by the media where they buy advertising, whereas firms booking their advertising space themselves generally will not be.

Once it has been decided that an agency will be appointed, the question arises as to which one to choose. The good news here is that in the advertising industry, airline accounts are perceived as very attractive ones. Besides being seen as fun to work on, they give an agency a great deal of prestige. Therefore, when it becomes known that an airline is seeking to appoint an agency, or to replace one they already have, there will be no shortage of firms willing to pitch for the account.

For many international airlines, a crucial question will be whether or not the agency can give a true global coverage. It is important that, in particular, brand-building advertising should be consistent across all markets. It may therefore be better to choose an agency with a large number of offices in different countries. This will, though, restrict choice to the comparatively small number of agencies which can credibly claim a global presence. If a smaller agency is selected, then it will have to be one which has well-established links with other agencies located in the overseas markets which the airline serves.

When choosing an agency, an overwhelming emphasis should be placed on its record of being able to produce original, imaginative and exciting work. Still, far too much airline advertising is hackneyed and stereotyped. It consists of pictures of blissfully happy passengers being served wonderful food by beautiful girls. If an agency's initial proposals include any variations around this tired theme, they should be shown the door with the utmost speed.

Once those agencies with the necessary creative skills have been isolated, other issues may come into play. There may be an attraction is the idea of appointing an agency which can supply a wide variety of services under one roof. These may include a media planning and media buying unit – most agencies would expect to provide this service. It may also be helpful if the agency can provide direct mail and sales promotion expertise and – increasingly important today – a unit able to deal with issues associated the airline's Internet presence.

Today, the fashion is rather away from this 'one-stop-shop' principle. An agency may be strong on one area and weak in others, and it may be better for clients to put together their own group of experts by calling in people from smaller, specialist agencies. This will, though, impose a major management task as the proper integration of the different forms of marketing communication will be a vital requirement. It would be a serious mistake if, for example, the firm's advertising was putting out different messages compared with its direct mail material.

One final point is that the appointment of an advertising agency should be seen as a strategic, long-term decision. Some firms may feel that it is a smart move to change their agency very frequently, because this keeps their current agency on its toes and also allows them to benefit from a flow of new ideas every time a new agency is appointed. This view is a mistake. Besides being very costly – substantial fees will be charged by each new agency to finance their initial work on the account – frequent changes of agency are unlikely to result in consistent and successful advertising. It will take time for the agency to fully understand their client's business and for the necessary personal relationships to be established. Also, as we saw in Section 8:2:1, the essence of brand-building is that the brand values which should underlie a firm's advertising must remain consistent on a long-term basis. Whilst a determined client might ensure such consistency when working with a succession of agencies, achieving it will be much easier if agreement can be reached with one agency at an early stage as to what these brand values are, with the same agency charged with communicating them over a long period of time.

Media Buying

Once an agency has been selected, there are then a large number of decisions which will be made using the agency's professional advice. It is important, though, that the airline should maintain an independence of thought, otherwise it risks merely becoming a slave to the agency's whims.

Media buying choices will decide where the airline's advertising will be seen, by whom, at what cost, and in what form advertising messages can be communicated. In making them, it will always be necessary to decide first on how best to spend the available budget. No airline will have the money to spend limitless amounts on advertising. Also, for carriers away from their home base, they will always be wrestling with the problem that locally-based airlines will be able to outspend them, often by a factor of several times. Their task will therefore be to make an impact against a competitor with far greater resources – always advertising's most difficult challenge.

In attempting to achieve this impact there are two possible approaches. Firstly, advertising expenditure may be spread evenly throughout the year. This ought to ensure that the airline will not be forgotten, but the difficulty will be in making a worthwhile impact. Secondly, advertising may be put out in short, concentrated bursts in the hope that, if it is memorable enough, this will carry the airline through the times when, because of budget limitations, it is doing no advertising at all. Of these two possibilities, the second is to be very much preferred. In today's world, it is hard enough to get noticed, given the proliferation of different advertising media and the way in which people are becoming increasingly bombarded with advertising messages. Making a strong investment, even if it has to be over a short time, is the best way of ensuring that you are.

Media buying choices will, of course, be decided by the objectives of a campaign, in terms of both its target audience and whether or not the campaign has a strategic or merely a tactical objective. To reach the business air traveller, there are now a well-established number of possible media choices. These will include business-orientated newspapers such as the Wall Street Journal and the Financial Times, and news magazines such as Newsweek and The Economist. In terms of television advertising, then commercial breaks in the main evening news programmes and some sporting events may bring a suitable audience profile.

With leisure air travel, weekend newspapers will prove useful, as will specialist magazines such as those aimed at enthusiasts for particular sports. The Internet, too, provides an increasingly exciting medium as it allows a destination to be sold in an attractive and interesting way, alongside messages about the best way to reach the destination in terms of a choice-of-airline decision.

With questions of strategic campaigns, a long-term brand-building objective may well justify investment in the time and money to make TV commercials. These allow messages to be put across using sound and pictures in a way which print media cannot match. There may well, though, be a gap of months between an ad. being planned and it being ready to launch. This is often too long in the rapidly-changing world of today's deregulated aviation market. Newspaper advertisements, on the other hand, should be quick to produce and also usually can be placed at short notice with little or no advanced booking of space being required. They are often the most effective way of communicating messages about, say, a seat sale in a market which suddenly and unexpectedly turns down.

The cost of the different media will obviously be a crucial question when deciding between them. Here, it is important not to be misled by the up-front, invoiced costs. Rather, a Cost-per-Thousand (CPT) measure should be used. Thus, for example, the media buying costs of television advertising can appear very high. If, though, this expenditure allows a large audience to be reached in the right way at the right time, it can represent good value-for-money.

Creative Strategies
Successful creative strategies are, of course, at the heart of all worthwhile

advertising. One is often tempted by a rule which states "There is only one rule – there are no rules". There are certainly examples of airline campaigns which seem to fly in the face of all logic yet appear to have been very successful, and others which looked soundly-based at the outset which have proved to be disastrous. Such a conclusion, though, is not helpful. There have to be some basic guidelines, even if it will always be possible to quote exceptions to them.

For a start, all campaigns where the budget is sufficient should be research-based. Common sense, intuition and past experience are all important aspects in the evaluation of an agency's creative proposals. They cannot, though, always prevent mistakes being made. Advertising proposals should be researched through well-structured market studies using representative members of the campaign's target audience. Continuing research will also be needed as a campaign runs, research which should be related to its objectives and to measurement of the extent to which these objectives are being achieved.

Secondly, airlines should invest in decent quality-of-production of all their advertising, even if this means that within a given budget, less money will be available for media buying. All airlines have to base their appeal on the fundamental proposition that they are safe, whilst many are attempting to build brands which position them as quality up-market producers. Cheapskate advertising will soon be associated in passenger's minds with a poor quality company. If there isn't the money available for reasonable production quality, it is better to do nothing.

As a further proposition, all airline advertising should be fundamentally honest. "If you cannot say it honestly, shut up and talk about something you can say honestly" is a sound dictum. Passengers – particularly regular business travellers – are not misled or fooled by false claims in airline advertising. Rather, they are angered and alienated by them. Besides the problems the offending airline may run into with the bodies that regulate advertising content, it will also increase many times over the anger of those caught up in its service failings. People take a long time to forgive a firm if they feel that they have been tricked into buying its product through deceit.

In deciding on the creative content of their advertising, airlines and their advertising agencies are usually faced with a difficult dilemma. Should they aim to include many arguments in an ad. as to why the airline should be chosen, or should they merely try to say one thing in a persuasive and convincing way ?

The proposition in favour of including many arguments is, at first sight, easy to make. If an ad. succeeds in capturing somebody's attention, a prime selling opportunity is being lost unless a substantial number of arguments are put forward to persuade them to buy. The risk is, though, that no message is communicated effectively, in the enthusiasm to put across a great many. A better approach is to try to say one thing, using individual arguments to support a single proposition in a memorable way. If this is done well (in the case of, say, a television commercial), only a relatively short one will be needed. Further commercials can then be made within a given budget, to make up an overall campaign in which all the required messages can be communicated.

The balance between long-term, corporate brand-building advertising and short-term tactical campaigns poses a significant, and increasing dilemma, in the airline industry. Deregulation, where it has occurred, has lead to instability, where tactical messages have often been needed to communicate changes in prices or product to customers. At the same time, airline sales managers have come under increasing pressure to achieve their end-of-year sales targets and they often worry that they will be fired if they fail to do so. They will always therefore be lobbying that a high proportion of advertising spend should be directed towards the tactical campaigns that they hope will help them. It is a great mistake, though, to merely consider tactical questions when setting advertising objectives. Section 8:2:2 looked at the importance of brands and showed how quickly a brand can die unless constant attention is given to maintaining and strengthening it. A significant amount of advertising expenditure must therefore be directed at the brand, and great care must be taken to ensure that frequent tactical messages – which are inevitable today – do not undermine fundamental brand values.

A final question with creative strategies is the difficult one of the balance between local and global advertising approaches. Perhaps more than in any other industry, airline brands need to be global, and it will be a problem if people travel around the world and see the airline they are flying with putting forward totally contradictory messages in different markets. This might lead to a conclusion that all advertising should be controlled centrally, with creative work carried out by one agency in the airline's home country. This will also allow the advertising production budget to be spent in a concentrated way, with, in particular, quality work being done on expensive television commercials. The problem is, of course, that there are substantial market-by-market and culture-by-culture differences in what is acceptable and persuasive and what is not.

In a difficult area, the best approach is probably to appoint a lead agency, with overall responsibility for brand positioning and brand values in the airline's most important home-base market, and to in turn appoint sub-agencies in the airline's overseas markets. These agencies should then be given clear, but limited opportunities to adapt or change centrally-produced material in order to make it suitable for local markets.

Monitoring Success/Advertising Life Cycles

It is essential that thorough procedures are in place to decide whether or not an advertising campaign is meeting its objectives. No matter how well initial research is done, disasters do occur, and without a formal monitoring process, the fact that a campaign is failing may not be picked up. Even successful campaigns, though, eventually run out-of-steam because of Product Life Cycle effects. They then need to be replaced with new approaches. Deciding on the moment to do this will be difficult. Those with the task of doing so need to be helped by having available quantitative data from a monitoring programme.

The monitoring methods which should be used will vary with a campaign's objectives. The easiest case will be with advertising designed to make people respond to an offer. For example, an advertisement may offer a 'golden hello' of free miles in the airline's Frequent Flyer Programme for those applying to join the programme before a deadline date. If it also contains a cut-out coupon or special Freephone number, it will be possible to precisely measure the response, or the lack of it.

Other advertising will have a longer-term, more strategic objective. The airline may, for example, have gone through a difficult period with failing product standards. Its advertising might then be designed to persuade people that things are now improving and that the time has come to try the airline once again. If it is, a significant boost to bookings once the campaign has begun would be taken as an encouraging sign. Also, it might be possible to test people's attitude towards the airline by talking with members of its sales team who regularly meet travel agents and corporate customers.

For advertising with a brand-building objective, precise measurement of the results is notoriously difficult. It will be necessary to invest in initial market research designed to define levels of awareness of potential customers and the attitudes they adopt towards the airline. As the campaign is implemented and develops, more will have to be invested to repeat this research, and also to ask people if they remember seeing the airline's advertising and, if they do, what they recall about it. Successful campaigns will show a growing awareness, a positive move in attitudes and a high level of recall of the content of the advertising.

10:4:3 What are the Features of 'Good' Airline Advertising?

Of course, good research data will be particularly valuable in deciding whether advertising is working or whether it isn't. There will be many occasions, though, when such data is simply not available. This will especially be the case when Area Sales Managers have to decide whether or not centrally-produced advertising will be valuable in the market areas for which they are responsible. In such situations, a checklist will at least result in the right questions being asked prior to a decision being made.

The basis of such a checklist will be a judgement as to whether or not the ad. is likely to attract and hold attention. If it will, it must also be professionally produced, with no accusations being possible that it is a cheapskate effort. It must certainly be credible, as damage will result if it is not. It must also be persuasive, showing an understanding of the customer's True Needs, and demonstrating the ways in which the airline can meet these needs. The degree to which the ad. is likely to persuade will be increased if it can demonstrate that the airline can credibly offer a Unique Selling Proposition to the customer. (For example, "First Flight of the Day" or "Only Airline Flying the A380"). Finally, it will be necessary to study the ad. very carefully to make sure that it is compatible with the airline's long term development of its brand values.

10:5 Selling in the Air Freight Market

With air freight consistently growing faster than the passenger side of the business, the question of effective marketing communication with its freight customers is one of growing important to many airlines. Some of the issues are the same as on the passenger side and some are unique to air freight.

10:5:1 The Sales Task in the Air Freight Market

One of the major differences between air freight and air passenger marketing is the degree of existing market penetration. It is true that on the passenger side, airlines face competition on short-haul routes from buses, private cars and especially from rail services. On medium and long-haul routes, though, their penetration is almost total. Virtually everyone who travels now flies, with surface transport restricted to the specialist market for cruising (even here, airlines often benefit by flying people to their port of embarkation).

With freight, things could not be more different. Surface transport provides formidable competition on all routes, either in the form of trucking and roll-on/roll-off ferries (in short-haul markets) or deep-sea container services on long-haul routes. This competition is especially difficult for airlines to deal with because it is almost always based on the proposition of cheaper freight rates than those which are available from air transport.

Given this competitive scene, the most straightforward selling task is that based on the need to secure a high share of the existing air freight market. Here, airlines mainly aim their efforts at the air freight forwarding industry. Still, a very high proportion of this traditional market (over 90% in many cases) passes through the hands of freight forwarders. Also, because much of the traffic consists of smaller consignments which are consolidated into larger consignments by forwarders, they, rather than the shippers who provide the original shipments, have the dominant role in deciding which airlines will be used. Marketing efforts, therefore, need to be concentrated on the senior management teams of large forwarding firms in pursuit of long-term relationships and also on the clerks in these firms who are responsible for routeing and carrier-choice decisions for individual consignments.

A much more difficult, but more exciting, opportunity comes with the task of converting existing surface transport traffic flows into air freight. Air freight's market penetration when calculated on a weight basis is still very low. On most routes, still only 2 or 3% of the goods that move do so by air. The remaining traffic is transported by much cheaper surface modes. This is not to suggest, of course, that all such traffic is potentially available to airlines – much of it is too low in value for air freight to make any sense. It is still true, though, that if air freight could double its market penetration from 2% to 4%, this would in turn double the size of the air freight market.

In carrying out this market development work, those airlines that attempt it have to use a fundamentally different approach. These is little point in approaching the forwarding industry. Most major forwarding firms have a substantial presence in both air and surface traffic. Therefore, they are unlikely to see a worthwhile incentive to convert surface traffic into air freight, as this will often merely be moving traffic from one part of their business to another. Instead, approaches have to be made to the firms which are the originators of the traffic. These approaches have to be at a high level of management. The task of making the case for air freight is a challenging one. It involves arguing that there are tradeoffs to be made between the higher transport costs (brought about by the fact that air freight's rates are generally more expensive), and the savings that can be made in packaging, insurance, stockholding and warehousing costs. These tradeoffs can generally be made only by senior managers with a wide span of responsibility over all the relevant areas.

There is one final area of air freight marketing which is potentially the most interesting of all, because air freight gives opportunities for firms to do things which they simply cannot do if they employ slower surface transport. This is the most obvious in the case of perishable goods, which, if surface modes are used, can only be sold in local markets. These in turn will often be saturated with the product in question, with only low prices therefore on offer. Use of air freight allows them to be flown to much more distant markets where prices will be much higher and profits potentially greater.

Even for non-perishable goods, air freight may give firms the chance to open new markets. Use of air freight allows firms to begin to sell in overseas markets with the minimum of delay once they have made a decision to enter. They can do so without a large and inflexible investment in overseas warehouses. This is because the speed of air freight allows stock to be held in a single centralised warehouse and then to be shipped to customers once orders have been placed. In a very true sense, air freight allows marketing to be carried out on a global basis.

Because of the new opportunities which it gives, the most promising kind of air freight marketing consists of generating entirely new traffic flows by persuading firms to take advantage of them. This approach is in principle an especially appealing one because the resulting traffic will not be vulnerable to poaching by surface transport operators. It will, though, place high demands on an airline's field sales team, because it will require them to perform a consulting role with a firm's senior managers.

10:5:2 *Marketing Communication Methods*

For all the different tasks in the air freight market, personal selling by a team of freight sales executives is generally very important, and more so than is the case in the passenger business.

This is especially the case for the many airlines which restrict their ambition to competing for their share of the existing air freight market. To do so, they will need a sales team which calls regularly on the major forwarding firms, both at their head offices and at regional branch offices. They will need in turn to offer generous corporate hospitality, as well as opportunities for key decision-makers to travel on overseas familiarisation trips. With advertising and promotion, most airlines see a role for some advertising, usually placed in the trade magazines which circulate amongst the forwarding community. This advertising usually merely describes the benefits of using one airline rather than another, with a dull and repetitious emphasis on the quality of ground handling.

For the more challenging tasks of converting surface traffic into air freight and of building entirely new flows of air freight business, a personal selling approach will again be needed. It will, though, be of a very different kind. Airline salespeople will have to aim to make contact with high level managers, and be prepared to run a sales campaign which may take months or years to bring to fruition. During this time, they will have to carry out extensive studies to prove that airfreight can be a cost-effective way forward. Such studies will need to be backed up by advertising messages, with these placed in locations such as the Financial Times and Wall Street Journal which are read by senior management.

SUCCESSFUL AIRLINES ......

✈ Acknowledge that selling and sales management makes up a crucial, final stage in the marketing process.

✈ Define and distribute a sales budget using a Task-based method, rather than simplistic arguments based on a percentage of revenue philosophy.

✈ Make analytical decisions about a Communications Mix, so that the different methods of marketing communication are combined together in an optimum way.

✈ Spend money on each communication technique in a rigorously planned and strategic way.

11 The Future of Airline Marketing

This Sixth Edition of "Airline Marketing and Management" has been prepared against a backdrop of what is still an industry facing rapid change and continuing financial problems. Two years of terrorism and war fears which began on September 11 2001 had a very serious and continuing effect on demand, an effect which, in an unstable world, may recur at any time. We have also seen that in aviation it is a dangerous statement to say that, "Things can't possibly get any worse". People were indeed saying this in 2003, when things did get worse with a rapid increase in the price of aviation fuel which has continued up to the present time.

Given the extent of the gloom which still prevails, it is difficult, but very important, to keep a sense of perspective. The industry has endured turbulent times before – admittedly at a reduced scale compared with today – and has come through them. Travel still has a great hold on many members of the world's population, and rapid economic growth in China and India is seeing the emergence of very large new markets Also, despite all the problems, some airlines are continuing to be very successful, as new business models emerge which seem capable of dealing with today's situation. More widely, a healthier and better industry may be the result of today's difficulties. In many ways, traffic growth has acted as a drug providing a fix which has allowed the industry to survive despite poor standards of management.

So what does the future hold over, say, the next ten years? Airlines will certainly have a substantial demand for their product, though in this writer's opinion at least, it will be a long time before we see a return to the inflated levels of demand growth seen in the boom years of the late 1990s. A substantial, though declining, proportion of this demand will be in the business travel sector. This sector will be very different from the one to which airlines have become accustomed, in that it will be much more price-sensitive and volatile. Leisure traffic will make up an even greater proportion of demand than at present, and it will be even lower-yielding than it is today. Only airlines with the keenest levels of operating costs will be able to carry it profitably. One bright spot will be continuing growth of the air freight market, the one market which airlines have which is not vulnerable to wars and the threat of terrorist attack. The problem for traditional airlines will be that most of this traffic will be carried by the small number of giant global Integrators rather than by them.

The marketing environment of the airline industry will certainly remain volatile and difficult. The established trends towards deregulation and liberalisation will continue, and, at least towards the end of a ten-year timescale, may encompass the long-overdue changes in ownership and control rules which will allow aviation to finally take its place amongst other global industries. Airport slot allocation will almost certainly come to be based on market principles, though the question of who should keep the proceeds from slot sales will always be a difficult one. Environmental issues will become even more important, and carriers will face justified limits on their growth and freedom of action unless they can demonstrate that they are taking al possible steps to minimise the environmental impact of their activities, even if these steps involve substantial costs.

As we have seen, only a supreme optimist would now suggest that airlines won't have to deal with the consequences of an unstable world political scene, and the ups and downs of a volatile world economy. They will have to address social change, with the ageing of the population and the changing nature of the world of work likely to have a particularly significant impact.

Technology will also affect airlines. In particular, ways of using electronic forms of communication to reduce the amount of business travel an executive has to undertake will continue to develop, and will significantly worsen airline's vulnerability to downswing periods. Also, new aircraft technology will give important opportunities which must be embraced.

Environmental questions will result in continuing – probably worsening – problems in expanding infrastructure capacity alongside demand. Taxation on airlines will also increase as governments follow a "polluter pays" policy.

In response to this difficult industry environment, the question of airline strategies will see revolutionary change. Around the world, we will see short-haul and medium-haul routes transformed by the principles currently being employed by the so-called "Cost Leader" airlines. The successful carriers will be well-managed "Cost Leader" players, and those threatened Differentiation airlines which are able to re-model their ways of working to get within striking distance of the cost levels of the Cost Leaders. Those that fail to do so will disappear as significant competitors in these markets. On long-haul routes, there will be less radical change, and the better-managed of today's Differentiation airlines have a good chance of survival and prosperity.

Given these strategic changes, the airline product scene will also see a considerable transformation. First Class service will have disappeared on all but a small number of routes, even in long-haul markets. Its replacement will be enhanced Business Class products, and perhaps, to a small degree, dedicated Business-Class-only products using 737BBJ and A319CJ aircraft. On short-haul routes, in contrast, there seems to be little hope that Business Class will survive at all. Instead, the emphasis will be on value-for-money offerings on single class aircraft. Everywhere, there will be an increase in point-to-point services and a decreased emphasis on hubbing, though A380 and 747-8 aircraft will find employment on the densest routes.

With pricing policy, the future is unlikely to see greater stability in airline pricing structures. The continuation of the well-established deregulation process and growing airline skills in storing, manipulating and communicating fares data, are likely to lead to instability, as airlines battle to match prices to the price elasticities of the different sub-segments of the market and to fill in the trough and even out the peaks in demand. Again this will place an absolute premium on speedy decision-making. Pressures will also increase for a simplification of airline pricing policies, to reduced overheads costs and to ease the selling task.

The area of distribution policy will see some of the greatest changes in the future. Over the next ten years, there will be a further fall in the proportion of tickets sold by travel agents, from the present industry average of around 70% to 50% or even less. This change will be brought about by an emphasis on electronic means for airlines to deal directly with their customers, and will bring about both a valuable further reduction in commission costs and a necessary increase in airlines' ability to control their distribution channels effectively. It will not, though, be an easy change to manage, because of the adverse reaction of traditional travel agents to it and because of the setting up of increasingly powerful on-line travels agencies. The entry of very powerful search engines into travel retailing may turn out to be a particularly worrying development.

In terms of those Differentiation airlines that are successful, one of the most important characteristics will be that they are successful in identifying their most important customers, and establishing a warm, deep and long-term relationship with them. In doing so, they will still make use of Frequent Flyer Programmes, though, in a saturated marketplace, the role of FFPs will be more to provide a source of data for airlines so that they can target individuals with attractive offers, rather than them being the broad-brush incentive programmes they have tended to be in the past.

With the question of marketing communication, brand building and brand maintenance will become crucial. The airline business has been slower to adopt these concepts than many Fast-Moving Consumer Goods firms. The reason is probably that up until now there has had to be a great focus on operational questions such as those associated with safety and punctuality. In the future, though the ability to build and maintain strong brands will be a necessary requirement for success. If it is, it will require marketing communication spending which is substantial, well-thought out and seen in a strategic, long-term way rather than as a tactical exercise which can be reduced or ditched as soon as times become difficult.

All in all, the future will be an exciting and challenging one. Working in the airline industry will be stressful – dealing with an accelerating pace of change always is – but it will provide tremendous opportunities for those privileged to make their living from this still dynamic and fascinating industry.

Glossary of Aviation Terms

Accidental No-Show
A passenger who fully intends to use a booking they hold, but who is prevented from doing so by unavoidable circumstances e.g. road congestion.

Air Operator's Certificate
A certificate, issued in the UK by the *Civil Aviation Authority*, by which an airline's safety standards are controlled. Withdrawal of its AOC would ground an airline.

Air Services Agreements (sometimes "Bi-lateral Agreements")
Treaties between governments which set out the rules under which international *Scheduled Services* will be operated. The international network of air Services Agreements was negotiated following the failure of the *Chicago Convention* of 1944 to agree on a multi-lateral basis for post-war aviation.

Airport Co-ordination Ltd
The company responsible for Slot allocation at the UK's congested airports. To ensure neutrality, thirteen airlines now have a shareholding in ACL.

Anti-Trust Immunity
In the USA, the Anti-Trust laws are those which forbid collusion between supposed competitors, and impose draconian penalties on firms which are guilty of violations of them.

For strategic alliances between US and European airlines to work effectively, immunity from the Anti-Trust laws is essential. The US government has used such immunity as a bargaining chip in its quest to conclude *Open Skies Agreements* with individual European governments.

Apparent Need
Factors claimed by Customers to govern their choice-of-airline decisions.

Association of European Airlines
The trade association of Europe's schedules airlines, based in Brussels.

Available Seat-Kilometre (ASK)
An output measure in air transport, defined as one seat available for sale flown over one kilometre.

Available Tonne-Kilometre (ATC)
An output measure in air transport, defined as a tonne of uplift capability flown over one kilometre.

Bermuda Agreement
The name given to the Air Services Agreement between the UK and the USA first negotiated in 1946, it has always been a restrictive agreement and was made even more so when re-negotiated at Britain's insistence in 1977. The US government regards the Bermuda Agreement as anti-competitive and is seeking to have it replaced by a so-called *Open Skies* agreement.

Cabotage
Has two meanings:

    1. An air service between a mother country and one of its colonies e.g. UK – Bermuda. As empires have been broken up, so the number of routes in this category has declined into insignificance.

    2. Domestic rights in a foreign country. Still firmly resisted by almost all countries, except those in the European Union. The USA is notably opposed to Cabotage despite its ostensible "Open Skies" approach.

Capacity
Many Air Services Agreements limit the commercial freedom of the airlines receiving *Designation* to mount the capacity of their choice on a route. Often, a 50/50 split of capacity between the airlines of the two countries, is required with capacity normally defined in terms of number of flights.

Capital Lease
Alternative name for finance lease.

Charter Service
An anachronistic description of an air service which is not operated according to a published timetable and where the seats are not on retail sale to the public because they can only be bought through a wholesaler.

    The distinction between *scheduled* and Charter services has now been abolished with the European Union but is still significant in some long-haul markets.

Chicago Convention
An international meeting held in 1944 with the aim of agreeing on the post-war basis on which international air services would take place. Though Chicago saw substantial achievement in technical fields, it failed in its primary aim of achieving a consensus on economic aspects. There was a fundamental disagreement between the free market philosophies of the USA and the remaining governments which were represented, who all favoured tight regulation.

Civil Aviation Authority
A government quango, responsible for a number of functions in the UK

aviation industry including safety, air traffic control and the regulation of air travel organisers through the ATOL system. It also in some cases regulates airport landing fees.

In terms of economic regulation the CAA decides which airlines will receive route licences where the relevant Air Services Agreement limits the number of airlines which can receive Designation.

Clearing House

A bank run by IATA to assist airlines in making interline payments to other carriers.

Code-Sharing

The process whereby an airline uses the two letter code of another carrier to identify its flights. Began as a result of passengers' preference for *on-line* rather than *interline* connections. Now often used by carriers to form co-operative, rather than competitive relationships with other airlines.

Consumer

The person who actually boards an aircraft. May, or may not, also be a *Customer*.

Controllable Cost

Cost with the control of airline management e.g. labour, commissions.

Cross-Elasticity of Demand

Relationship between the demand for a product, and the price or quality of competing products. In airline economics, a relevant cross-elasticity on short-haul routes is that with surface transport.

Customer

The person who makes decisions on such aspects as choice of transport mode, choice-of-airline and class of service. May, or may not, also be a *Consumer*.

Damp Lease

The lease of an aircraft together with qualified flight crew but no cabin crew.

Deliberate No-Show

Someone who deliberately does not turn up for a flight on which they hold a reservation. A common reason is that the person concerned has made multiple bookings for their return journey.

Demand

The number of people coming forward to fly. Is not an absolute number, but rather a relationship with the price of air travel.

Demand Factor

The average number of passengers who wish to book on a particular flight. Of little use for planning purposes because of variations around the average.

Department of Transport
Is the Department of the UK government responsible for aviation matters. In particular, carries out the negotiation of *Air Services Agreements*.

Department of Transportation
The Department of the US government responsible for economic aspects of the American airline industry.

Departmental Costs
Cost classification whereby costs are divided according to the department responsible for them e.g. Flight Operations, Maintenance and Engineering.

Deregulation
A process whereby traditional controls over entry, capacity and pricing are removed. Even in a so-called "deregulated" market airlines will still be subject to regulation of their safety standards, and to the controls associated with questions of collusion, anti-competitive behaviour and mergers and take-overs.

Derived Demand
A product which is not consumed for its own sake, but rather to give access to something else. Almost all air travel is a derived demand.

Designation
Under the terms of an *Air Services Agreement*, the number of airlines from each country which can fly on the routes between the two countries signing the agreement. Many ASAs are still *single designation*, though some allow for *dual designation* (e.g. UK - Japan). A small number permit *multiple designation* (e.g. UK - South Africa).

When more airlines wish to fly a route than can do so under the terms of an ASA, someone has to decide which will, and which will not, operate. In the UK this function is carried out by the Civil Aviation Authority, though conceivably in the future it may be taken over by the European Commission on a EU-wide basis.

Differential Pricing
A pricing philosophy whereby prices are varied to reflect different demand elasticities between different market segments.

Direct Operating Costs (DOCs)
Airline costs which are aircraft-related e.g. fuel and oil, landing fees. Of most relevance to airline fleet planning decisions.

Direct Subsidy
A payment to an airline by the government which owns it. Will appear on the revenue side of the profit-and-loss account.

Dry Lease
The lease of an airframe only. Normally only of interest to airlines already operating the aircraft in question.

Economies of Scale

Unit cost advantages enjoyed by large scale producers. Generally held to be small in air transport, though they are perhaps now increasing.

Economies of Scope

Advantages of marketing muscle-power available to large producers. In air transport, an effective frequent flyer programme is an example.

Federal Aviation Administration

The department of the US government responsible for safety and technical aspects of the American airline industry, and for air traffic control.

Fieldlength/Range Diagram

The relationship between available fieldlength, aircraft take-off performance and the trade-off between payload and fuel (range).

Fifty Per Cent Rule

The rule, operating with the European Union which states that 50% of so-called "new" slots must be given to *New Entrant* airlines rather than being awarded to incumbents. A "new" slot is defined as one which becomes available through an increase in the airport's capacity, or because another airline has given it up.

There is general agreement that the Fifty Per Cent Rule has done little to enhance competition, because it has resulted in valuable slots often being awarded to very weak airlines. There are proposals to change it but after a lengthy consultation period still nothing has been agreed.

Finance Lease

A lease for the full operating life of an aircraft. Lessee may have an interest in aircraft residual value. Must appear on balance sheet. Mainly undertaken for tax reasons.

Fixed Costs

Costs which do not vary with output e.g. aircraft ownership.

Fleet Age Profile

Relative ages of the aircraft in an airline's fleet.

Fleet Commonality

A situation where an airline has only a small number of aircraft types in its fleet. Benefits come through in such areas as pilot training and spares inventories, but may mean that some potential routes cannot be flown, or are operated with the wrong type of aircraft.

"Fly America"

A policy of the US government whereby all air transportation paid for by the US government has to be undertaken by US airlines. Has been used by some European governments to question the true nature of American "Open Skies" credentials.

Fortress Hub

A situation where in a deregulated market, an airline seeks to control competition by achieving a high degree of dominance at a particular airport.

Freedoms of the Air

A description of the operating rights of designated airlines under the terms of an Air Services Agreement.

There are six relevant freedoms:

1st	The right to overfly a country's airspace without landing
2nd	The right to land in a foreign country for non-traffic purposes such as refuelling
3rd	The right to set down commercial traffic carried from an airline's home country to a foreign country.
4th	The right to bring back commercial traffic from a foreign country to an airline's home country.
5th	The right for an airline to fly commercial traffic between two foreign countries on a flight originating in its home country.
6th	Arguably, the 6th Freedom is not a "Right" comparable to those contained in Nos 1-5. It refers to airline's using their home base as a hub or stopping point in order to fly passengers and freight between two foreign countries. In practice it is a combination of two sets of Third and Fourth Freedom rights.

See also *Cabotage*

Gateways

Under the terms of an Air Services Agreement, the points in each country which can be served in each country by the airline receiving *Designation*. Details of Gateways are usually set out in a confidential *Memorandum of Understanding* rather than in the Agreement itself.

Grandfather Rights

The principle by which an airline, once granted an airport *Slot*, will keep it in perpetuity providing it is used with sufficient regularity.

Grandfather Rights are being increasingly criticised as a way in which the Slot allocation system is biased in favour of long-established incumbents at the expense of new entrants. Incumbents, though, defend it as a necessary basis for planning and investment.

Within the European Union, the principle of Grandfather Rights has been modified by the so-called *"Fifty Per Cent Rule"*.

Income-Elasticity of Demand

Relationship between changes in income, and the demand for a product. In developed countries, air travel demand is highly income-elastic (ie. it is a desirable luxury which people purchase in larger quantities if their disposable income increases).

Gross Yield

Yield before the payment of commission

Indirect Operating Costs (IOCs)
Costs which are airline, rather than aircraft related e.g. Reservations. Of no relevance to airline fleet planning.

Indirect Subsidy
A situation where airline costs are reduced by favourable treatment by a government. e.g. government loan guarantee reduces borrowing costs.

Input Costs
Airline cost classification method whereby costs are divided up according to the input they are used to purchase e.g. labour, fuel etc.

Interline Connection
A connection whereby the inbound flight to a hub and the outbound flight from it are with different airlines. Passenger dislike of interline connections was the driving force behind the growth of *code-sharing*.

International Air Transport Association (IATA)
The trade association of most of the world's international airlines.

IATA has a number of important functions, including those of the settlement of inter-airline accounts through the Clearing House, and providing a forum within which airlines can co-ordinate their schedules planning.

Historically, IATA's most controversial function has been concerned with so-called *Tariff Co-ordination*. Air Services Agreements were generally written in terms which exclude price competition between airlines. IATA provided the forum within its Traffic Conferences whereby airlines met together to agree on fares and cargo rages. Today, Tariff Co-ordination activities continue but they are mainly only concerned with full, interlinable fares. Mostly, airlines introduce cheaper promotional fares outside of the IATA framework.

International Civil Aviation Organization (ICAO)
ICAO is the specialist body of the United Nations dealing with aviation. Its most important functions concern the setting of technical standards through the so-called Annexes to the Chicago Convention.

Market Segmentation
The process whereby a market is divided up as a prelude to a product/price/promotion decision.

"Marketing Myopia"
A situation where a firm takes too narrow a view when answering the question "What business are we in?"

Memorandum of Understanding
Supposedly, all Air Services Agreements are public documents. However, there are often confidential Memoranda of Understanding which set out the true restrictions on competition which the Agreement encompasses.

Net Yield
Yield after the payment of standard commissions.

Net Net Yield
Yield after the payment of both standard and override commissions.

New Entrant
Under the *Slot Allocation* rules, defined as an airline with four or fewer services per day at the airport in question.

No-Show
A passenger who holds a booking on a flight and who fails to turn up to use it. Can be divided into *accidental* and *deliberate*.

Non-Scheduled Service
An alternative name for a Charter service.

Notice of Termination
All *Air Services Agreements* contain a one year Notice of Termination clause which allows a government to require an Agreement to be renegotiated if it is regarded as no longer being appropriate.

On-Line Connection
A connection whereby both the in-bound flight to a hub and the outbound flight from it are with the same airline. *Code Sharing* is sometimes used to give the impression that a connection is on-line when in fact it is *interline*.

Open Skies Agreement
A form of Air Services Agreement promoted by the USA in which the restrictive conditions of traditional ASAs are replaced by Freedom in terms of entry, capacity and pricing.

The USA's promotion of competitive ASAs does not stretch as far as agreeing to *Cabotage*, nor to the abolition of the controversial *Fly America* policy.

Open Skies Agreements have now been signed between the USA and many European governments, but the validity of these is now being challenged by the European Commission which argues that they run counter to the principles which underlie the *Single Aviation Market*.

Operating Lease
A lease for less than the full operating life of an aircraft, with the lessee having no interest in the aircraft residual value. Does not have to appear on balance sheet.

Operating Licence
The basis of airline regulation with the *Single Aviation Market* of the European Union. In order to obtain an Operating Licence an airline must qualify for an Air Operator's Certificate regarding its safety standards, and must comply with rules about its financial fitness.

Once it has an Operating Licence, an airline can fly anywhere in the EU, with no artificial distinction between *Scheduled and Charter* services.

The only constraint on this freedom of entry is the very important one of airport *Slots*.

Operating Permit

The question of which airlines will exercise the *Traffic Rights* set out in an *Air Services Agreement* will be decided by the government of the home country. However, once Designation has been obtained, the airline in question will still have to obtain an Operating Permit from the government of the country at the other end of the route. Such a Permit can only be refused on grounds of safety, or if the airline in question does not conform to the relevant *Ownership Rules*.

Orient Airlines Association

The trade association of Far East airlines, based in Manila.

Output-related Costs

A cost classification method which relates airline costs to the decisions airline managers must make. Can be divided into:

- seat-related e.g. meals, drinks, airport passenger charges
- flight-related e.g. fuel and oil, landing fees
- route-related e.g. route-related advertising
- airline-related e.g. reservations system.

Ownership

The question of airline ownership and control is still an extremely contentious one. All *Air Services Agreements* are written in terms which state that the Traffic Rights defined by the Agreement can only be exercised by nationals of the countries signing the agreement.

Passenger Load Factor

A measure of the relationship between output produced and output sold. It is calculated by dividing an airline's *Revenue Passenger Kilometres* by its *Available Passenger Kilometres*.

Payload-Range Diagram

For a given aircraft type, a diagram describing the trade-off between payload and fuel (range).

Peaking

Changing levels of demand through time. As all air transport output is instantly perishable at the time of production, a very important question is when demand arises, not just its quantity.

Price-Elasticity of Demand

The relationship between changes in price and changes in the quality bought. In air travel, business demand tends to be relatively price-inelastic, and leisure air travel highly elastic (i.e. a small change in price will have a disproportionate effect on the quantity bought).

Prorating
The process by which fares are divided up between the airline who fly a passenger on different sectors of a multi-sector journey. Airlines use the IATA *Clearing House* as the mechanism to make and receive the necessary payments.

Public Service Routes
The small number of routes with the European Union to which the principles of freedom of entry implicit in the *Single Aviation Market* do not apply. They are routes to isolated communities where there is a social service requirement for air services to be maintained. A monopoly can be granted to an airline for a period of time on such a route to enable it to become established.

Revenue Dilution
A situation where a customer pays a lower price than that which they are prepared to pay. In a *Differential* pricing system a combination of fare conditions and capacity controls are used in order to minimise dilution.

Revenue Management
A process by which an airline decides which seats are to be sold at which prices and in which currencies.

Revenue Passenger-Kilometre (RPK)
An output measure in air transport, defined as a filled seat flown over one kilometre.

Revenue Tonne-Kilometre (RTK)
An output measure in air transport, defined as a tonne of payload flown over one kilometre. The payload can either consist of freight, or passengers and their bags converted into weight.

Scheduled Service
A now-anachronistic description of a service which will be operated on a year-round basis, irrespective of short-run variations in demand, and with seats on retail sale to the public. The opposite of *"Non-scheduled"* or *"Charter"* services.
The distinction is still significant in some long-haul markets where scheduled services are regulated through the system of *Bi-lateral Agreements*, whereas charter services are the exclusive responsibility of the government of the destination country.

Scheduling Committee
The Committee responsible for overseeing the *Slot Allocation* process at congested airports. Membership of the Committee is open to all airlines serving the airport in question, provoking the criticism that the system is biased against new entrants.

Seat Accessibility
The probability of a *customer* being able to obtain a seat near to the

departure time of a flight. Should be divided into "high" and "low" rather than "good" or "bad".

Single Aviation Market

The term used to describe the present, largely deregulated, regime for aviation within the European Union. In a progressive process of reform, the old, restrictive system based on Air Services Agreements has been replaced by one based on freedom of market entry and access, the abolition of controls on capacity and the virtual, but not complete, deregulation of pricing.

Slot

The right granted to an airline to use an airport for either a landing or a takeoff at a particular time.

As the airline industry has grown and the provision of aviation infrastructure has failed to keep place with this growth, so the question of slot allocation has become steadily more contentious.

The allocation of slots at a congested airport is carried out by an appointed *Slot Co-ordinator*, using principles based on the concept of *Grandfather Rights*. With the European Union, these principles have been supplemented by the so-called *"Fifty Per Cent Rule"*.

Slot Allocation

The process by which it is decided which airlines should use which slots at a congested airport. It is the responsibility of the appointed *Slot Co-ordinator*.

Slot Co-ordinator

The person appointed by an airport *Scheduling Committee* to oversee the allocation of airport *Slots*. At many airports, the Slot Co-ordinator is still an employee of the largest airline using the airport. As airport congestion has increased, this has increasingly been seen as unsatisfactory and the attempt has been made at some airports to introduce a greater degree of transparency and neutrality into the slot allocation process. At congested UK airports the Slot Co-ordinator is now an employee of *Airport Co-ordination Ltd.*

Spill

Customers who request a seat on a particular flight but cannot be accommodated because the flight is full.

Start-Up Economics

The economics of new airlines. New carriers often have cost advantages over longer-established rivals, suggesting few benefits for airlines from *economies of scale* or learning curve effects.

Status Goods

Those goods where if the price increased, the quantity bought also increases. In airline economics, the First Class seat may be a Status Good.

Tariff Co-ordination
A function of the International Air Transport Association, whereby IATA arrange Traffic Conferences with which airlines can meet to discuss fares and cargo rates.

Traffic Rights
A description, within an *Air Services Agreement*, of the rights that can be exercised by the airlines designated by each country. See *Freedoms of the Air*.

True Need
Factors which actually govern customers' buying decisions, as opposed to *Apparent Needs*. Can include such human failings as greed, laziness and the desire for recognition/status.

Uncontrollable Cost
Cost largely outside the control of airline management e.g. Air Traffic Control charges.

Uniform Pricing
A pricing policy whereby all customer are charged the same, as opposed to the varied price levels of *Differential* pricing.

Unit Costs
Costs incurred per unit of output (e.g. cents per RPK).

Variable Costs
Cost which varies with output e.g. fuel & oil.

Weight Load Factor
A measure of the relationship between output produced and output sold. Is calculated by dividing an airline's *Revenue Tonne Kilometres* by its *Available Tonne-Kilometres*.

Wet Lease
A lease of an aircraft to include trained flight and cabin crew opposite of *dry lease*.

Yield
Revenue earned per unit of output (e.g. cents per RPK). Can be divided into *gross*, *net* and *net net* yields.

Glossary of Marketing Terms

ACORN
A classification of residential neighbourhoods. Social grading using district of residence. This and other similar classification methods are becoming more important now in airline direct and relationship marketing.
Action
Fourth stage of a sale. Involves *closing* the deal.
Advertising Agency
Specialist firm providing advertising services. Agencies are rewarded by the fees they charge to clients, and the commission paid to them by advertising media.
Advertising life cycle
Cyclical increase, followed by decline, in the impact of advertising. Life cycles can vary from days up to many years.
Advocate
A term in Relationship Marketing whereby a customer not only buys a *firms's* product, but actively recommends that others should do so.
AIDA
Stages of a sale, divided into *attention, interest, desire* and *action*.
Apparent need
The needs which those taking part in the work of a *Decision-Making Unit* will admit to, and will claim form the basis for their opinions.
Assumptive close
Closing technique whereby the sales executive assumes that the order has been given by, for example, starting to fill in an order form.
Attention
The first stage of a sale.
Attitude
Predisposition on the part of a customer to behave in a particular way.
Boston Box
Framework for decision-making with respect to a firm's *Product Portfolio*, based on the two variables of growth in the total market and the share of the market held by the firm's own product.

Brand
Product where customers perceive significant differences between the offerings of competing suppliers. These differences can be either "tangible" or "psychological".

Brand equity
The price premium obtainable from a strong brand, in comparison with prices paid for a commodity product.

Brand mapping
Graphical representation of the position of different brands.

Brand positioning
The values that position a brand from other, competing brands.

Brand stretching
Extending a brand's scope by using it to market another product.

Brief
Instructions given to advertising agency by client.

Buyer
Representative of purchasing department in industrial buying. *True need* will be to obtain a good deal from the seller, in order to justify existence.

Cash Cow
Situation in the *Boston Box* where a firm's product has a high share of the total market, but where total demand is no longer growing strongly. Competitive pressures should therefore slacken, allowing good profits to be made. However, the "cash cow" may not remain profitable for long.

Closing
The point at which the sales executive attempts to complete a sale.

Commodity
Products where customers perceive no difference between the offerings of competing suppliers.

Communications Mix
Mix of spending on different methods of communicating with customers.

Competitive advantage
Factor which will enable a firm to outperform its competitors.

Consumer
Person who actually experiences the product.

Consumer Marketing
Marketing targeted at the individual or the family unit.

Creative strategy
Interpretation of *brief* by advertising agency.

Customer
Decision-maker with regard to choice of supplier and type of purchase.

Database
The use of a database in direct marketing.

Database Marketing
Information about customers and potential customers held on computer. Must include information about purchasing history.

Decider
Final decision-maker in model of industrial buying behaviour.

Decision-Making Unit
Process whereby a firm makes industrial buying decisions. Often includes the elements of *deciders, users, influencers, gatekeepers* and *buyers*. Those taking part in a DMU will have both *apparent* and *true* needs.

Decline
Final phase of *Product Life Cycle*, characterised by declining sales. Its onset is a sign that the product should be withdrawn and resources devoted to new products where demand is growing.

Demographics
Characteristics of a *market segment* in terms of age, sex, income levels etc.

Derived demand
Demand which does not arise for its own sake, but as a result of another demand. (Almost all air travel is a derived demand).

Desire
Third stage of a sale. The "desire" phase will also require answers to any objections which the prospect may raise.

Destroyer
A term in *relationship marketing* whereby a person not only does not buy from a firm, but actively tries to persuade others not to do so as well.

Differential Pricing
Situation where prices are varied according to customers willingness/ability to pay.

Direct mail
Direct marketing using the mail or fax. Now characterised by rapidly-growing consumer resistance, and increasing legal constraints.

Direct marketing
Marketing by direct contact between supplier and retail customer.

Direct representation
Communicating with customers through a field sales force.

Display advertising
Advertising material for the *point-of-sale*.

Dissonance
Feelings of concern experienced by buyer once sale has been concluded.

Distribution channel
Channels through which suppliers make the link between themselves and the final customer.

Diversionary marketing
Marketing aimed to increase share of existing demand (opposite of *generative marketing*).

Dog
Boston Box situation where a firm's product has only a low share of a stagnant or declining market. The investment message is "give up".

"Do nothing case"
Analysis of possible future position of a firm, if its present strategies are continued unaltered.

Dual-positive suggestion
Closing technique whereby the prospect is offered two positive alternatives from which to choose.

Early adopters
Customers who follow *Innovators* in purchasing a new product. Their coming into the market corresponds with the *growth* phase of the *Product Life Cycle*.

Early majority
Customers who follow *Early adopters* in purchasing a product. Their coming into the market corresponds with the part of the *Maturity* phase of the *Product Life Cycle*.

Explicit need
Need which customers express for themselves. Much more powerful in major sales than the alternative of an *implied need*.

FMCG
Fast-moving consumer goods.

Frill
Minor aspect of product detail, easily matched by competitors.

Gatekeeper
Player in model of industrial buying behaviour. Controls access into the firm's *Decision-Making Unit (DMU)*. Tactics to deal with gatekeepers include "kill", "by-pass", "frighten" and "convert".

Generative marketing
Marketing aimed at growth through increasing the size of the total market for a good or service. Of vital importance in air freight market.

Goal statement
Broad, usually qualitative statement of the nature of firm's business.

Growth phase
The second stage of the *Product Life Cycle*. It will be characterised by rapidly rising sales. However, this increase in sales will attract the attention of competitors who will begin to develop their own rival products.

Implication
Consequence for a firm of a problem. One of the central skills required in

industrial marketing is the ability to build the implications of a problem being experienced by the customer.

Implied need

Statement by customer of problem. Sales executive must convert the implied need into an *explicit* need.

Income elasticity

Relationship between changes in demand and changes in customers' disposable income. Can be subdivided into:

Income Elastic Demand: Change in demand more than the change in income.

Income Inelastic Demand: Change in demand less than the change in income.

Industrial marketing

Firm-to-firm marketing.

Influencer

Contributor to a *Decision-Making Unit (DMU)*, who will not actually use the product or service once it has been bought, but whose opinions will still influence the final decision of the *DMU*.

Innovators

The first consumers to adopt a new innovation. Their willingness to do so reflects a combination of psychological need and financial resources. Only a small proportion of consumers come into this category. Their coming into the market corresponds with the *Introductory phase* of the *Product Life Cycle*.

Intention

Statement of how a customer's behaviour might change in the future, if the supplier changes his product specification and/or price.

Interest

Arousing interest constitutes the second stage of a sale.

Internal marketing

The process of selling the concept of marketing to different departments within a firm.

Introductory phase

First stage of the *Product Life Cycle*. It will be characterised by low sales and low or non-existent profits.

Laggards

The last customers to come into the market for a product. They correspond to the *decline* phase of the *Product Life Cycle*.

Late majority

Customers who follow the *Early Majority* in buying a product. Their coming into the market corresponds with the later part of the *Maturity* phase of the *Product Life Cycle*.

Lifestyle
Market segmentation based on the values and aspirations that individuals hold.

Lifetime value
The purchases made by a customer over the whole period during which they buy from a particular supplier.

Likert scale
Method of measuring attitudes in consumer surveys. Runs from "Agree strongly" to "Disagree strongly".

Loyalty marketing
Marketing based on giving rewards to customers who are regular purchasers. Likely to be especially valuable in industries where *switching costs* are low.

Marketing Mix
Marketing process expressed as four "P"s - product, price, promotion and place. Other "P"s such as "politics" now often included.

Marketing myopia
The mistake of taking too narrow a view when answering the question "What business are we in?"

Market segment
Group of customers who have sufficient in common to form the basis for a product/price/promotion combination.

Maturity phase
The third stage of the *Product Life Cycle*. Growth in sales will slow and then stop, due to market saturation and increasing competition. A product *relaunch* may be necessary.

Media advertising
Advertising by purchasing space or time from media suppliers.

Media buying
Purchasing of advertising space.

Media relations
Communication with customers by obtaining beneficial publicity through communications media.

Need
A customer requirement which it is essential that suppliers should meet. Can be divided into *apparent* and *true*, *implied* and *explicit* needs.

NPD
New Product Development.

Objection
Point raised by prospect against making a purchase. Must be answered at the *Desire* stage of the *AIDA* model.

Objective
Specific, quantified statement of the progress which a firm intends to make over time.

OTV
Opportunity-to-view. Quantitative measure to guide the amount of *media-buying* necessary to ensure that advertising has the desired impact.

Pareto's Rule
Generally applicable rule stating that 80% of profits are derived from 20% of customers.

"Percentage of Revenue"
Method of setting promotional budget. It is quite wrong, as it ties promotional spending to market conditions.

PESTE
Method of establishing a *scenario* using the five headings of Political, Economic, Social, Technological and Environmental.

Planning horizon
Period of years ahead for which strategic plans are formulated.

Planning system
Framework within which strategic plans are formulated. Describes, too, participants in the planning process.

Point-of-sale
Point of contact between supplier and customer.

Position Audit
Framework for analysing a firm's present position using the four headings of *strengths*, *weaknesses*, *opportunities* and *threats*. Also known as *SWOT* analysis.

Pricing elasticity
Relationship between changes in price and changes in demand. Can be subdivided into:

Price Elastic Demand = change in price produces a greater change in demand.

Price Inelastic Demand = change in demand is less than the change in price.

Problem child
Alternative name for *wildcat* in the *Boston Box*.

Product Life Cycle
Model exploring the relationship between demand for a product and time. Its message is that product development is a never-ending process for the successful firm.

Product Portfolio
Range of products being offered by a particular firm.

Promotional budget
Amount of money available in a given time period for communication with customers.

Psychographics
A description/summary of *attitudes* in a *market segment*.

Quality Gap
A concept in *Relationship Marketing* to describe a situation where a customer's experience of quality is above or below their expectation.

Random sample
Sample where all members of a target population have an equal chance of inclusion.

Relationship marketing
A marketing philosophy whereby a firm gives equal or greater emphasis to the maintenance and strengthening of the relationship with its existing customers as it does to the necessary search for new customers.

Relaunch
Initiative undertaken during the *maturity* phase of the *Product Life Cycle*. Can take the form of product enhancement, price cuts, increased promotional spending, or a combination of all three.

Resistors
Consumers who can never be persuaded to come into the market for a particular product.

Sales promotion
Attempt to increase sales through running competitions and similar activities.

Scenario
An analysis of the most likely future situation facing a firm. Is often prepared using the technique of **PEST** analysis.

Semantic Differential Scale
Method of measuring attitudes in consumer surveys.

Sensitivity Analysis
Testing of the resilience of a strategic plan by reworking it using different, pessimistic, assumptions.

Social grading
Classification of households according to head-of-household's occupation.

Sponsorship
Communicating with customers by having the firm's name associated with a particular individual, team or event. May be a cost-effective way of building awareness and image, but poor method of closing business.

Star
Situation in the *Boston Box* where a firm's product has a high share of a rapidly growing market. High share should enable some profits to be made

but the growth in the total market will result in heavy competition. High investment to protect the dominant position will therefore be necessary.

Status goods

Goods where an increase in price is associated with an increase in demand.

Switching Costs

The costs of changing from one supplier to another. Where switching costs are low, there is likely to be a need for *loyalty marketing*.

SWOT Analysis

Alternative for *Position Audit* (qv).

Synergy

Situation where a firm producing two or more products together can obtain lower costs than firms producing each product separately.

Task based method

Correct method of fixing promotional budget, based on the question "what do we need to spend?"

Test Marketing

Marketing initiative taken on an experimental basis over only a small part of the market area it is hoped eventually to penetrate.

Tracking

Monitoring the success of advertising through the progress of a campaign.

Tradeoff

Situation where additional costs are incurred in one area of marketing, in order to secure more than compensating benefits in another.

Trial close

The sales executive testing to see whether the prospect is willing to buy, without seeking a "yes" or "no" answer.

Uniform pricing

Situation where all customers are charged the same, irrespective of their willingness/ability to pay.

User

In *Decision-Making Unit*, person who will actually use the product. Will want to gain maximum utility from product and to protect status. May be less concerned about price.

USP

Unique selling proposition. Statement of where a product is uniquely different from its rivals.

Want

Customer requirement which may be important, but not essential, for suppliers to meet. Can be divided into "tangible" and "psychological."

Wear-out

Cyclical decline in the impact of advertising towards the end of the Advertising Life Cycle.

Wildcat
Boston Box situation where a firm's product has a low share of a rapidly growing market. The investment message is to spend money to improve position in the expectation that profits will come in the longer term. Also known as *Problem Child.*

Index

AAdvantage 149
Abuse of a Dominant Position 254
Accidental no-shows 170
Advanced Purchase Fares 195
Advanced Turbo-Prop (ATP) 143, 155
Advertising 279-287
Advertising Life Cycles 286
Advocate Relationship 242, 243-244
Aer Lingus 125, 160
Ageing population 65-66
Agency Selection 280-282
Airbus 115, 121, 160, 163, 178
Airbus A318
Airbus A319 94, 132
Airbus A320 123, 148, 149, 160, 173
Airbus A330 32, 39, 133, 165, 173, 177
Airbus A340 32, 163, 165, 173, 177
Airbus A350 32
Airbus A380 84, 106, 161, 165, 177, 178
AIDA Model 257-258, 271
Aircraft utilisation 38-39, 101
Air Asia 91
Air Berlin 222
Air Canada 59, 101, 115, 126, 160, 264
Air Europe 238
Air France 56, 59, 61, 64, 110, 132, 143, 180, 225, 232
Air Freight Forwarders 21, 22, 86, 92, 223-225, 288
Air Mauritius 133

Air New Zealand 59
Air Services Agreements 53-54, 138, 162, 183
Air Seychelles 133
Air Traffic Control 61, 62, 84
Airline Deregulation Act 52
Airport Co-ordination Ltd 62
Airport service 172-173
Aldi 88, 89
Alitalia 61
Alliances 110-117
'All Business Class' 66, 130-133, 233
Al-Qaeda 50-51
Amadeus 84, 116, 219, 275
American Airlines 109, 110, 116, 117, 126, 131, 149, 165, 216, 217, 218, 219, 223, 249
'Ancillary Revenues' 97
Ansett Airlines 52
Ansoff Matrix 156-158, 180
Anti-Trust Immunity 110
Apollo 217
"Apparent" Needs 11-12, 30, 233
Asda/Walmart 209, 230
Atlasair 86, 178
ATR 72 155
Australian Airlines 52
Austrian Airlines 234

Barriers to Entry 78-81
Belly–hold capacity 45-47
"Betrayal Factor" 273
BMI Baby 101
BMW 228, 237
Body Shop 229

Boeing 83, 105, 121, 144, 160, 164, 178
Boeing 707 177
Boeing 717 144
Boeing 737 94, 123, 132, 148-149, 160, 173
Boeing 747 84, 164, 165
Boeing 747F 176
Boeing 757 131, 160, 176
Boeing 767 164, 173
Boeing 777-300ER 32, 164, 173
Boeing 777-200LR 32, 163
Boeing 787 32, 166
Bombardier Dash 8 155, 173
Boston Box 151-156, 180
Boston Consulting Group 152
Brand 209, 226-241
Brand positioning 232-236, 261
Brand stretching 229, 238-239
Branson, Sir Richard
British Aerospace 143
British Airways 24, 56, 59, 64, 66, 77, 101, 109, 110, 117, 118, 125, 131, 132, 133, 143, 144, 161, 169, 180, 201, 217, 231, 232, 249
British Caledonian 138
British Midland Airways 94, 96
"Bucket Shop" 20, 82
Bulk Unitization Programme 204
Business Class 10, 31, 33, 66, 70, 77, 91, 99, 118, 123, 144, 159-160, 161, 174, 182, 186-187, 214, 228, 250, 252, 266
Buyers 14

"Cabotage" 53, 78
Carbon Trading 74
Cash Cows 154-155
Cathay Pacific 110, 117
"Cattle Truck Handling" 95
CDG Airport 95

Cendant Corporation 219
Channel Tunnel 155
Chapter 11 Bankruptcy 60, 126, 199
Charleroi Airport 104
Charter Airlines 38, 101, 133-135, 188, 208
Chartered Institute of Marketing 1
Chicago Convention 53
Civil Aeronautics Board 52
Climate Change 73-74
Club World 231
CN Touristic 134
Coach Class 65
Code-sharing 108, 111-112, 128
Combi aircraft 178-179
Commissions 81, 92, 125, 147, 206
Commodity 209, 226-227, 240
Communications Mix 260, 263, 290
Concorde 132, 143, 232
Connexion-by-Boeing 144
Consolidation 21
Consolidators 19, 20
Consumer 9
Consumer Marketing 2, 48
Continental Airlines 109, 110, 172
"Controllable" costs 201
Copywriting 270-272
Corporate Business Traveller 24, 28, 37
Corporate Travel Manager 150
Cost-per-Thousand (CPT) 283
"Cost Leader" airlines 18, 32, 87-88, 89-105, 114, 122, 124-125, 127, 134, 154, 158, 217, 221, 292
Creative strategies 283-286
Cross-border Ticketing 98

Customer 8-11, 19, 20-22, 23-25, 48, 81
Customer relations 175, 244, 246-248

Dallas Love Field Airport 94
"Dash-for-Cash" 198-199
Database Marketing 265-273
Deciders 12
Decision Making Unit (DMU)
Decline Phase 147-148
Deep Vein Thrombosis (DVT) 39, 103
Deliberate No-shows 170
Delta Air Lines 60, 101, 109, 110, 117, 126, 193, 214, 219, 232, 249, 252
Delta Express 101
Demographics 35-37
Denied Boarding Compensation 172
Department of Transportation 99
Deregulation 28, 51-56, 140, 182-183, 208
Design density 176
Destroyer relationship 242
DFW Airport 94
DHL 93, 204
Differential Pricing 186-194, 205
Differentiation 87-90, 105-110, 114, 158, 293
Directional imbalances 40
"Disintermediation" 86-87
Disney 19 , 228
Diversification 137-138
Dogs 155-156
"Do-Nothing Case" 157
Dusseldorf Airport 132

"Earn-and-Burn" rights 112, 249
Easyjet 28, 53, 85, 91, 94, 95, 99, 221, 222
Economic Market Investor Principle 60
Economic Perishability 43-44
Economies of Scale 79-80, 85, 111, 147, 189
Economies of Scope 111
Embraer 123, 168
Emergency Traffic 42-43, 44
Emirates 106, 111, 172
Engine Alliance 153
Environmental taxation 72
Eos Air 131, 232
Eupo-Air 82
European Commission 104
European Court 54
European Low Fares Airline Association 105
European Parliament 104
Excel Airways 134
Expedia 216
Eva Airways 24

Fairlines 130
Federal Aviation Act 52
Federal Express 55, 93, 129-130, 157, 204
Field sales team 274-279
First Class 9, 10, 33, 65, 66, 70, 118, 159-160, 161, 174, 182, 186-187, 214, 250, 252
"First Mover Advantage" 106
"Five Forces" 76-87
Fleet commonality 93
Focus strategies 89-90, 129-135
Fokker 154, 238
Ford 218
Four Corners Travel 144
"Four Ps" 2-3
Franchising 239-240

Frequency 11, 30, 31, 42, 233
Frequent Flyer Programmes 3,
    11, 18, 30, 33, 35, 83, 108,
    113, 122, 128, 131, 149-150,
    239, 241, 248-256, 265, 268,
    293
Freight-of-all Kinds(FAK)pricing
    204
Freighter aircraft 42-44

Galileo International 84, 116,
    219, 275
Gatekeeping 12-13, 272-273
Gatwick Airport 95, 124
General Cargo Rates 203
General Electric 153, 154
General Electric Capital Aviation
    Services (GECAS) 207
GF-X 224
Global Distribution Systems
    (GDSs) 56, 71, 99, 101, 108,
    112, 116, 125, 184 , 217-233,
    239, 275
Global warming 72
Go 125
Gol 91
Google 210, 223
Grandfather Rights 62-63, 78,
    122, 124, 138, 162, 169
Growth Phase 146

Hapag-Lloyd Express 134
Heathrow Airport 62, 124, 169
Hub-and-Spoke 57, 163-164

IATA 28, 105, 114, 183, 200,
    203
Iberia 56, 125
IKEA 88
ILFC 207
Imitative buying 143

Independent business traveller
    24, 28, 68, 91-92
Industrial buying behaviour 12-
    15
Industrial Marketing 2
In-flight service 31-34, 173-174
In-flight surveys 27, 175
Influencers 15
Innovators 150
Insurance costs 45
Integration 267
Integrated carriers 21, 83, 223
International Standards
    Organisation (ISO) 176
Internet 71, 82, 91, 125, 134,
    214-217
Islip Airport 94

Jetblue Airways 94, 95, 193, 222
Jetstar 101
Jetstream 61 155
JFK Airport 94, 95
Joint purchasing
"Just-in-Time" 45-47
"Jugular Marketing" 128

KLM 56, 109, 110, 160
Korean Air 58

Laggards 150-151
Laker Airways 232
LaGuardia Airport 94
Landing Fees 94-95, 101
Lauda Air 234
Learning curves 80, 146, 147
"Legacy" airlines 1, 58, 101,
    106, 117-129, 190, 191, 192,
    193, 194
Lifetime Value 241
Logistics 7-8, 22, 46
"Lost-in-the-Middle" 87, 89, 135

Low Cost Carriers 1, 132, 170, 191
Lufthansa 59, 64, 115, 128, 132, 133, 144 , 157, 160, 249, 255

McDonalds 228
McDonnel-Douglas 160
Malaysia Airlines 59
Market segmentation 22-27, 40-42, 48
Marketing – definition 1
Marketing emergency 42
Marketing Mix 2, 147
"Marketing Myopia" 7, 48
Marks and Spencer 89, 90
Marlboro 230, 236
Maturity phase 146-147
Maximum stay conditions 195
Maxjet Airways 130-132
MD-11 176, 177
MD-80 160
Media buying 282-283
Media relations 273
Mercedes 228
Metroair 101
MGM Grand Air 130
Microsoft 92, 216
Midway Airport 94
Minimum Charge 190
Minimum stay conditions 194
"Miles-and-More" 132
Monarch Airlines 134
My Travel Lite 134

Newark Airport 94
Northwest Airlines 60, 109, 110, 160, 219

OAG 28
Qantas 59
O'Hare Airport 94
Olympic Airways 61

OneWorld 110, 111
On-line connections 108
"Open Skies" agreements 54, 110
Operating emergency 42
Orbitz 216
Overbooking 170-172
Oversegmentation
Operating Lease 141
Opodo 216
Orly Airport 62, 95

Packaging costs 45
Panalpina 87
Pan American 237, 249, 252
Passenger Rights 104-105
Percentage-of-Revenue Method 260
PESTE Analysis 4, 49-50
Physical perishability 43
Porter, Michael 76 , 82, 104, 105
Porter's Five Forces 74-83
Point-of-sale service 168
Power of Customers 78-81
Power of Suppliers 81-83
Pratt and Whitney 153, 154
"Preferential" fares 197
Premium Economy 10, 131
"Premium Traffic" 65, 66, 118
"Presenteeism" 69
Privatair 132
Privatisation 58-60
Product Life Cycle 36, 43-44, 103, 142-151, 180, 255, 286
Psychographics 35-37
Punctuality 29, 34, 166-167, 175, 233, 235

Qantas 264
Quality control 174-177, 245, 246
"QC" (Quick-Change) aircraft 178-179

Rackham, Neil 258
Relationship Marketing 35, 68, 241-256
Reservations 160-161
Retailers 207
"Retreat-to-core" 123-124
Revenue Dilution 196
Revenue Management 4, 98, 120, 121, 169, 184-186, 191-192, 199-200, 205
Rogers E.M. 139
Rolex 228
Roll-on/Roll-off 41
Rolls-Royce 89, 153, 154
Routine perishable traffic 43-44
Routine Non-perishable Traffic 44-48
Ryanair 28, 53, 91, 94, 95, 99, 103, 104, 119, 125, 221, 222

Saab 2000 143
Sabena 61, 117
SABRE 84, 116, 217, 219, 223, 275
Safety stock 46, 47
SAGA 67
Sainsbury's 209, 230
Sales budget 245-248
SARS 117
SAS 101
Schedules planning 154-158
Schiphol Airport 95
Scope Clauses 128
Seat pitch 101, 133-134, 159, 186-187
'Seventh Freedom' 55
Selling 5
Shipping Manager 22
Shuttle 169-170, 237
Shuttle-by-United 101
Singapore Airlines 106, 117, 166

Single Aviation Market 53, 60, 77, 91, 183
Skyteam 110, 111, 232
Skytrain 232
Slot Allocation 61-64, 79, 153, 292
"Slot Co-ordinator" 62
Smith, Fred 157
Snowflake 101, 232
Song 101, 232
Southwest Airlines 28, 90, 94, 95, 96, 99, 100-101, 119, 138, 221, 222, 233
South African Airways 125
Specialisation 137-138
Specific Commodity Rates 203-204
Spey Engine 154
SPIN Cycle 258-259
Sponsorship 233, 235, 263-265
Standby fares 170, 196-197
Stars 153-154
Star Alliance 110, 111, 115, 232, 255
Start-up Economics 80
"State Aid" 60, 104, 135
Status goods 145
Stansted Airport 132
Strasbourg Airport 104
Substitution 77-78
"Sum-of-sector-fares"
Superprofits 57, 208-211, 229, 230
Swiss International Airlines 132
Swissair 117, 160
Switching costs 81-82, 83

Tango 101
Tariff Co-ordination 114, 183
Task-based Method 261, 290
Tay Engine 154
Terrorism 50-51

Tesco 90, 209, 230
Thai International 174
Ticket flexibility 29
"Ticketless Travel" 169
TNT 93, 204
"Tourism Saturation" 75
Trade cycle 64-66, 118, 121,
    201, 253210, 234, 239
Traffic Rights 138, 153
Trailfinders 82
Transatlantic Common Aviation
    Area (TCAA)
Trans-Australia Airlines 52
Transfer connection
Travel agents 17-18, 85, 91, 208,
    210, 211-217, 221-222, 231,
    276, 293
Travelodge 88
Travelocity 216
Treaty of Rome 55, 199
True needs 11-12, 16, 30, 232
TUI 134
TWA 219, 249

Uncontrollable costs 201
Uniform Pricing 186-194, 205
Unique Selling Proposition
    (USP) 273
Unit Load Devices (ULDs) 86,
    180, 204
United Airlines 60, 65, 101, 109,
    114, 126, 131, 249, 255

Upper Class 231
UPS 55, 93, 129-139, 204
US Airways 101, 109, 126, 169
Users 14

"Value Added" focussing
Valujet 103
Van Cleef and Arpel 228
VARIG 58
Videoconferencing 7,70-71, 77`
Virgin Atlantic Airways 10, 111,
    131, 172, 231, 238
Virgin America 238
Virgin Blue 53, 91, 238
Visiting-Friends-and-Relatives
    (VFR) 25

Wardair 238, 239
Warehousing costs 288
"War-on-Terror" 50, 117, 123
Westjet 91
Wet leasing 86, 178
Wholesalers 207
Wildcats 152-153
"World Offers" 234
Worldspan 84, 219
World Traveller Plus 161

Yield Improvement Programme
    (YIP) 200-201

Zip 101

LEARNING RESOURCES CENTRES